IRISH WOMEN'S SPEECHES

Irish Women's Speeches

Voices that Rocked the System

BY

SONJA TIERNAN

UNIVERSITY COLLEGE DUBLIN PRESS

PREAS CHOLÁISTE OLLSCOILE
BHAILE ÁTHA CLIATH
2021

First published 2021
by University College Dublin Press
UCD Humanities Institute
Belfield
Dublin 4
Ireland

www.ucdpress.ie

ISBN 978-1-910820-90-2 pb

Cataloguing in Publication data available from the British Library

*The right of Sonja Tiernan to be identified as the
author of this work has been asserted by her*

Typeset in Scotland in Plantin and Fournier by Ryan Shiels
Text design by Lyn Davies
Printed on acid-free paper by SprintPrint, Hume Centre,
Park West, Dublin 12, Ireland

Contents

And she did not know that she carried armour

Kate O'Brien

For my parents, Marie and Chris Tiernan

List of Illustrations

1. The latest kind of "Boy"-Cotting. *Weekly Freeman*, 5 March 1881 Depicting the campaign by Anna Parnell and the women of the Ladies Land League. Courtesy of the National Library of Ireland.
2. The Sweating Crusade, *New Zealand Observer and Free Lance*, 25 June 1892. A woman knight, thought to represent Harriet Morison, lances the sweating monster. Courtesy of the Alexander Turnbull Library, New Zealand.
3. Kate Sheppard Memorial, Christchurch, New Zealand. Left to right: Meri Te Tai Mangakāhia, Amey Daldy, Kate Sheppard, Ada Wells, Harriet Morison, Helen Nicol. Photograph by Charlotte Hall Tiernan.
4. Countess Markievicz. Photograph taken months before she gave her speech to the Students' National Literary Society. Courtesy of the National Library of Ireland.
5. Peace meeting at Mansion House, Dublin, July 1921. Left to right: Kathleen Clarke, Countess Markievicz, Kathleen O'Callaghan and Margaret Pearse. Photo by W. D. Hogan, 1921. Courtesy of the National Library of Ireland.
6. The King & Queen at a House Party in Mount Stewart, 1903. Lady Londonderry second on left, beside King Edward VII. Courtesy of the National Portrait Gallery, London.
7. Margaret Hinchey leading a demonstration on behalf of the Women's Trade Union League, New York, February 1914, the day after her meeting with President Woodrow Wilson. Courtesy of the Library of Congress.
8. Margaret Hinchey addressing a group of striking carmen in Union Square, New York, October 1916. Courtesy of the Library of Congress.
9. Cumann na mBan protest outside Mountjoy Prison during the Irish War of Independence, 23 July 1921. Courtesy of the National Library of Ireland.
10. Eva Gore-Booth pictured in front of her sister, Countess Markievicz, at a public reception following Markievicz's release from prison, Dublin, June 1917. Courtesy of the Irish Capuchin Provincial Archives.

11. Hanna Sheehy Skeffington with her son, Owen, New York, 1918. Courtesy of the Library of Congress.
12. Mary MacSwiney, Hotel St. Regis, New York, December 1920. Left to right: Anna Ryan, Harry Boland, Mary MacSwiney, Muriel MacSwiney and James O'Mara. Courtesy of the National Library of Ireland.
13. Jennie Wyse Power, circa 1880s. Creative Commons Universal Public Domain.
14. Standing Committee 14th Sinn Féin Ard Fheis, Dublin, 21 February 1922. From left to right back row: Sean Milroy, Walter Leonard Cole, Henry O'Hanrahan, Pádraig O'Keeffe, Kevin O'Sheil, Jennie Wyse Power, George Augustine Lyons, Darrell Figgis, Seán Mac Caoilte, George Murnaghan, Austin Stack, Thomas Dillon, Kathleen Clarke, Éamonn Duggan, Kathleen Lynn, Arthur Griffith, Éamon De Valera, Michael Collins, Harry Boland, Hanna Sheehy Skeffington. Courtesy of the National Library of Ireland.
15. Irish Women Workers' Union members on the steps of Liberty Hall, circa 1914. Delia Larkin seated centre. Courtesy of the National Library of Ireland on The Commons.
16. Frances Condell with President John F. Kennedy at Greenpark Racecourse, Limerick, 29 June 1963. Courtesy of Glucksman Library, University of Limerick.
17. Bernadette Devlin's European election poster, 1979. Courtesy of Irish Election Literature.
18. Bernadette Devlin mural by the Bogside Artists on Rossville Street, Derry. Photograph by Kenneth Allen. Creative Commons Attribution-ShareAlike 2.0 license.
19. Peace Jam's 10th anniversary Nobel Peace Prize winners. Left to Right: Desmond Tutu, the 14th Dalai Lama Tenzin Gayatso, Betty Williams, Jody Williams, Rigoberta Menchú Tum, Adolfo Perez Esquivel, Shirin Ebadi, and Mairead Corrigan Maguire, 15 September 2006. Photograph by Ivan Suvanjieff, GNU Free Documentation License.
20. Siobhán McKenna, New York, 8 January 1959. Photograph by Talbot NY, Creative Commons.
21. Nan Joyce election leaflet for Dublin South-West constituency, November 1982. Courtesy of Irish Election Literature.
22. *The Alice Glenn Report*, Jan/Feb 1987. Courtesy of Irish Election Literature.
23. Inez McCormack (left) with Margaret Ward at the first Reclaim the Night protest in Belfast, November 1987. Courtesy of Margaret Ward.

Acknowledgements

Researching and writing this book has been immensely rewarding, mainly due to the inspiring people that have supported the process through advice and permission to include texts and images.

I am indebted to those who granted me permission to reproduce extracts from their speeches. While organisations are noted in related notes, I would like to thank those individuals who I contacted directly requesting permission to reproduce their words. With many thanks to Mamo McDonald and to Jade Pepper of the Irish Countrywomen's Association for organising contact. Mamo's passing in June 2021 will continue to be mourned by many people across Ireland. Her speech included among these pages, provides a vivid reminder of Mamo's astute and effervescent campaign for social reform. With many thanks to Nora Owen for her permission and to Cliona Doyle of Fine Gael for organising contact. To Bríd Rodgers and to Ann McDonagh of the SDLP for arranging permission. Monica McWilliams for permission to include extracts from her speech and for taking the time to offer valued insights. Adi Roche for her encouragement and support and to Norrie McGregor of Chernobyl Children International for arranging related material. Saffa Musleh for permission to include her speech and for her thoughtful engagement with me on this topic. To Mary McAleese for her gracious and encouraging response. Elizabeth Coppin for permission to reproduce her speech and image, and for her heartening emails about the book. Also to Maeve O'Rourke for arranging contact with Elizabeth. This generosity is greatly appreciated. It is an honour to include these speeches and I hope that I have done the orators justice.

This book owes much to the works of other historians and academics, especially those who read and advised on various aspects. To Margaret Ward who has been an exceptional source of advice throughout much of this process and has made perceptive recommendations and provided material including Inez McCormack's original speech. Margaret's work has been a huge inspiration for my own research, as can be seen by the many references to her publications cited in this volume. Barbara Brookes, who I have been most fortunate to work with in New Zealand, for taking time to read and comment on Harriet Morison's section and for the many discussions about this publication. Any errors or misinterpretations remain my own.

I am grateful to have received support and financial aid for research through the Moore Institute Visiting Fellowship at NUI Galway. Many thanks to John Cunningham for his sponsorship of my application and to Sarah Anne-Buckley and Barry Houlihan for their support during my time in Galway and beyond. The Keough-Naughton Library Research Award afforded me time at the University of Notre Dame where I was offered immense support. I am grateful to all of the Irish studies faculty there but especially to Bríona Nic Dhiarmada for her hospitality, friendship and engaging conversations which helped shape my initial research and for her advice to include Alice Glenn. Aedin Clements for her support in accessing material both in the Irish Studies collection at Notre Dame and remotely during a challenging time of Covid-19 restrictions. Beth Bland who, as always, ensured that my time at Notre Dame was productive and enjoyable.

Publication of this book would not be possible without the dedication and hard work of others. Emer Lyons painstakingly transcribed speeches from original texts and recordings, much more than could be included in the final cut. Many thanks to Lisa Marr for her attention to detail and efficiency when proof reading and compiling the bibliography and index. Lisa's work has been invaluable and ensured the timely completion of this volume. To Jennifer Redmond and Margaret Ward for their keen and encouraging feedback to my original publication proposal. Noelle Moran, who is undoubtedly the most supportive and efficient editor I have worked with. It has been a pleasure to work with you and all the UCD Press team including Conor Graham, Cormac Kinsella, Gemma Kent, Nigel Carré and Ryan Shiels.

I am forever grateful for the encouragement of friends to publish this book especially; Jennifer Glansford, David Greene, Denise Broe, Annemarie Kelly, Denise Casey, Simon Markey, Joy McDonnell and Siobhán Breathnach. Colleagues both past and present for their unwavering support, most especially Liam McIlvanney who has listened, on an almost daily basis, to this book develop, and his positive outlook has helped me stay focussed. It is wonderful to enjoy such collegiality. To previous colleagues, especially John Appleby and Trish Ferguson, who I initially discussed the idea of a book on Irish women's speeches with and who both encouraged me to pursue it.

My final thanks are to my family for their endless support and encouragement. To my parents, Chris and Marie Tiernan, for teaching me the importance of women speaking out and offering their insights on many of the women included here. To my brother Barry Tiernan for being a considerable support for our family throughout an unprecedented time, I cannot ever thank him enough. My mother in-law, Bernie Hall, whose encouragement is much appreciated. Finally, I am indebted to my wife, Charlotte Hall Tiernan, for her advice, understanding and being a wonderful sounding board, without Charlotte this book would have taken twice as long to write.

SONJA TIERNAN
November 2021

Foreword

'Men don't like sopranos' former Leader of the Labour party, Joan Burton, said to me once. In those four words she captured a whole wall of male prejudice that still faces women from the moment they open their mouths in public. *Their voices are too high, too whiny.* And, if they speak louder to overcome male heckling: *Their voices are too shrill.*

I come from the generation of women who were catcalled whenever they dared to stand up and speak. In my time at UCD in the 60s, most women who spoke at the Literary and Historical Society were tolerated if they were the daughters or sisters or girlfriends of well-known men or if they were very pretty. Without either of these passports, they were shouted down. And being pretty carried its own problems, even for women lecturers. Nuala O'Faolain, then lecturing in English in UCD, almost caused a riot when she appeared on the dais wearing what was normal then for every young woman from Berlin to San Francisco: dark tights and a mini skirt. Most women lecturers were careful to dress like secular nuns. That way they didn't upset the boys.

Indeed, it was often from behind the disguise of a nun's garb that women wielded authority and influence. By hiding under long black robes and veils everything that made them attractive as females – hair, female curves, legs – they were allowed to wield authority as matrons of large hospitals or headmistresses of schools or superiors of religious orders. They developed demure voices stripped of emotion or local accent and as such they were allowed to express opinions but not in a way that challenged the male hierarchy, either religious or political.

The assumption was that women didn't need to be heard. After all, didn't they have fathers, and husbands and brothers to speak for them? High Court Justice Tom O'Higgins said as much in 1973. Here's what happened. When housing activist Máirín de Burca was charged with obstruction after a housing protest at Leinster House, she realised she would be judged by an all-male property-owning jury. So on the basis that one should be judged by one's peers, she took a constitutional case challenging the Irish system of all male juries (which Senator Jenny Wyse Power had railed against in 1927 in a speech included here). Dismissing de Burca's case Mr O'Higgins said he must assume 'that the members of an all-male jury will not disregard their oaths simply because the defendant is a woman.' Happily, the Supreme Court thought differently.

As a young reporter on the *Nationalist and Leinster Times* in the 60s and early 70s, I can count on one hand the women I heard speak in public. Almost all would have been on local authorities. One was Nancy Moore, a Newbridge councillor on Kildare County Council. Nancy was an Independent, as were many women politicians in those days. The lowly status they were given in political parties meant they fared better as lone wolves. On my rounds collecting news in County Kildare for the *Nationalist and Leinster Times*, I would always call last to Nancy. We'd go to the hotel next door for a gin and tonic and then she'd give me a political read on local affairs that has rarely been bettered in 50 years in political journalism.

Still, it was only when Mary Robinson won the Presidency in 1990, that it became normal that a woman would speak for Ireland. Like many Irish households during that election, ours had witnessed lots of arguments as to the merits of Mary Robinson, Austin Currie, and Brian Lenihan. I voted early and met my husband later in the day. 'All right, all right,' he said, 'I voted for her. Are you happy now?' 'What's equally important, are you happy?' I asked. He was and never had any reason to change his mind. It's important that Mná na hÉireann elected Mary Robinson. What's just as important, it wasn't just Mná na hÉireann who elected Mary Robinson.

So it's from that agonisingly slow progression to two women Presidents, a number of female party leaders and a gradual increase in the number of women politicians, academics, business leaders, that we now look back at those brave and independent-minded women who spoke out in the past.

What makes this book so rich is not only the wide range of speeches but the history and context in which each is carefully placed. Everyone will have their favourites but one of mine is the speech made by the poet, feminist and social reformer, Eva Gore-Booth in May 1916 to the London Society, entitled 'Dublin in the Aftermath of the 1916 Rising'. Having first read in London that her sister, Constance Markievicz, had been killed in the Rising, Eva was relieved to find she was alive, and made her way to Dublin to visit her sister in Mountjoy Jail. Her account of that journey and of the bewildered state of people in the city after the 1916 executions, is surely one of the most vivid descriptions of that time and was one of the first accounts of it given to an English audience. There's little rhetoric here. We're conscious more of Eva's concern for her sister; for the family of the murdered Francis Sheehy Skeffington who had fought for women's rights as Eva and her sister had; for the family of executed 1916 leader and colleague of Markievicz in Stephen's Green, Michael Mallin. We're made conscious too of her desperate attempts to have revoked the death sentence imposed on Roger Casement in London. The British public saw the Rising as a treacherous blow when Britain was fighting the World War I, and Eva's speech was an attempt to change that attitude. Delivered only weeks after the Rising, it has an astonishing freshness and immediacy about it, all the more so because Eva's views are so modern, so far ahead of her time. As is so often the case with women speakers, she saw the price that families paid for war and political upheaval, the misery inflicted on mothers and children.

It often took courage for women to speak out, moral and physical courage. Look what it cost Margaret Hinchey, an Irish immigrant laundry worker whose speech to the Equal Suffrage League in New York is quoted here. Margaret spoke out for women's worker's rights and votes for women in America in the early 1900s and found herself blacklisted by every factory in New York. Extraordinary as it may seem, the peace women of the mid 1970s in Northern Ireland, Mairead Corrigan and Betty Williams, were under constant threat for speaking out for peace in Northern Ireland. They were even guarded by Norwegian police when accepting the Nobel Prize for Peace in Oslo in 1977. It is telling that asking for peace should be regarded in some quarters as such a threat.

It takes particular courage to speak out when discrimination and a lack of education makes you less confident. Traveller activist, Nan Joyce, kept it short and simple when she addressed a seminar run by the Third World Agency, Trócaire, in Galway in 1983. Trócaire is a Catholic agency. So Nan went straight to the point. Trócaire, she said, directed its efforts at those in the third world suffering from poverty and discrimination. How could they call themselves Christians if they ignored the Third World conditions and social discrimination suffered by travellers in Ireland? Nan's speech grabbed the headlines. She was giving a voice to those who were never heard in public forums. The need to hear that voice was brought home to me in an online discussion I took part in recently about the problems of getting older. After we'd complained about becoming tired and ill and pushed to the sidelines, the writer and Traveller activist, Rosaleen McDonagh, spoke up. Travellers, she said, didn't have those problems because so many of them don't live much past 60.

Didn't we know this? Well, if we did, maybe we had forgotten it and what Rosaleen had done was to widen our view, to make us appreciate that living to be old was a privilege. We needed to hear her, speaking for her community, to educate us to that fact.

The voices that have been silent are the ones we must hear. When the women quoted here broke their silence, they expanded our view of what it is to be human because they represent half the race. We may not always agree with them but without them we'll have only half the story.

OLIVIA O'LEARY
November 2021

Introduction

The story of Ireland is best told through the voices of its women. Women have been at the centre of every stage of Ireland's evolution from a colonised island to an advanced independent country in the twenty-first century. Through their speeches, Irish women have inspired change, altered laws and instilled hope. Women's speeches have helped shape modern Ireland and aided the development of societies globally. Through women's words, it is possible to track a comprehensive history of Ireland and trace the depth of Irish influence abroad. *Irish Women's Speeches* showcases 33 inspiring speeches by women of Ireland from the nineteenth century to the present.

There has long been recognition of the power of speeches in the course of modern Irish history. Over the last two centuries, audiences have witnessed great Irish speeches made from diverse platforms, such as courtroom docks and during graveside eulogies. The record of speeches can thus provide an alternative history. Numerous volumes of Irish speeches have previously been published. Volumes compiled in the nineteenth century often praised the skill of speechmakers with grandiose titles.[1] Volumes published in the twentieth century often focused on the fight for Irish independence.[2] One common aspect of these publications is that they contain only speeches by men. In this way, men were positioned as the predominant thinkers, the reformers, the politicians, and, ultimately, the people who mattered in Irish history.

In the twenty-first century, volumes of speeches include Irish women, but often the female voice appears tagged on. The most thorough of such volumes is undoubtedly *Great Irish Speeches* by Richard Aldous.[3] Only five speeches in this volume are by women, equating to a mere ten per cent of those chosen to reflect what Aldous describes as 'the speeches that changed Ireland'.[4] Yet women's speeches provide a different perspective when examining how and why Ireland has changed over the last two centuries. The political and social struggles experienced by Irish men since the nineteenth century were experienced by Irish women too.

Women were particularly vocal on issues relating to the Irish land war, the struggle for independence, the plight of trade unionism, and in demands for peace. In their speeches, Irish women assessed these situations from a different perspective, often considering the implications for the most vulnerable in society. Irish women fought against deeper injustices brought about by inequalities specific to gender. Women were excluded from full citizenship when they were denied the right to vote or to stand for government, restricted from serving on juries, discriminated against in the workplace, and excluded from equal access to education. Many women were victims of gender-related brutality, including domestic violence and being incarcerated in religious-run institutions. Women spoke out on these issues even when positioning themselves in vulnerable or dangerous situations.

It is fair to say that records of speeches made by Irish women are more challenging to source than those made by their fellow countrymen. There are numerous reasons why speeches by women seem almost obscured. If a woman had the opportunity and the inclination to speak publicly, it is less likely that her speech would have been recorded for posterity. There are many examples of women's voices being purposely supressed. Lucy Fitzgerald, the sister of United Irishman Lord Edward Fitzgerald, addressed a heartfelt plea to Irishmen to continue the fight for Irish freedom, a fight that her brother had died for. The text of her address was supressed by her stepfather, William Ogilvie.[5]

The fact that women in Ireland were banned from standing for general election prior to the twentieth century excluded female speakers from these official records. When women gained formal access to the political structure, female voices often remained absent from the political record in Ireland. In notable debates in the Houses of the Oireachtas related directly to women's interests, such as women on juries in 1924 and the introduction of the Mother and Child Scheme in 1951, the issues were debated entirely by male politicians. Although female politicians were at times present in such debates, issues were often corralled to include only male speakers.

Irish Women's Speeches showcases 33 speeches from over the course of the last 140 years. The earliest speech included was given in 1881 by Anna Parnell on the plight of evicted tenants and the land war then ongoing in Ireland. The most recent speech is by Catherine Connolly, given in January 2021 during the Dáil statements on the release of the Report of the Commission of Investigation into Mother and Baby Homes. A concerted effort has been made to include a speech from each decade of the twentieth and twenty-first centuries, tracking the social and political developments during this time. There may appear to be an overrepresentation of speeches in certain decades, but this is reflective of events during those dates. Five speeches in this volume were delivered during the 1910s, for example. This decade was particularly turbulent globally: it was the height of suffragette activity in

2

many countries, which was closely followed by World War One. In Ireland, the fight for independence was intense during this decade. The number of speeches selected from the 1980s and 1990s reflects the political climate in Ireland at that time, including highly emotive referenda on issues relating to abortion and divorce as well as the signing of the Good Friday Agreement.

The speeches that follow were delivered to a wide range of audiences and from a vast array of podiums. Due to Ireland's unique political situation, speeches from political stages include addresses to both Houses of the Oireachtas, at the Parliament of Northern Ireland, and at the British Houses of Parliament.[6] It is significant that one-third of the speeches presented in this volume were delivered outside of the island of Ireland. Of the 12 speeches delivered abroad, two are addresses to the United Nations. Siobhán McKenna, who is best remembered as an actress, was a determined human rights activist. McKenna gave an impassioned speech to the UN demanding the repeal of the apartheid system in South Africa. More recently, Adi Roche's address to the UN General Assembly on the Chernobyl disaster resulted in the UN declaring an annual International Chernobyl Disaster Remembrance Day. Such prestigious forums testify to the high regard in which Irish female activists and orators are held. Further evidence of this high regard was seen when Betty Williams and Mairead Corrigan were awarded the Nobel Peace Prize for 1976. Williams delivered the acceptance speech in Oslo City Hall, Norway, while under the protection of Norwegian police due to threats on the two women's lives.

Irish women also travelled to gain international support for Irish causes, as evident from the speech by Anna Parnell in 1881 in Glasgow City Hall on behalf of the Irish National Land League. Hanna Sheehy Skeffington gave no fewer than 250 public talks during her tour of America in 1918. Contributions to social reform are evidenced through the speeches of Irish emigrants abroad. Harriet Morison's speech reveals her vast contributions, which helped establish New Zealand as the first true democratic country. Morison's speeches advanced the votes for women campaign, which convinced the New Zealand government to extend the vote to women in 1893. There is now a statue honouring Ulster-born Morison in Christchurch, New Zealand.

Records of speeches have been discovered through various sources. Many of the orators featured in this volume did not keep written records, and in such instances, there are no archival collections on which to depend. In some situations, it is possible to track speeches through newspaper accounts. Such is the case with Margaret Hinchey, an Irish immigrant working in the laundries of New York city at the turn of the twentieth century. Journalists viewed Hinchey as an anomaly and someone who could provide them with attention-grabbing headlines. Hinchey's speeches were not recorded for posterity, rather journalists noted her every word because her activities could sell newspapers, leaving historians with a vital record. In contrast,

3

Hanna Sheehy Skeffington's speech at Madison Square Garden was recorded by a secret service agent, tasked with reporting on her activities as she was deemed a risk to the British war effort.

Locating an agreed upon text of a speech is often problematic. Indeed, one of the most celebrated speeches in Irish history – Robert Emmet's speech before his sentence of execution – has several conflicting accounts.[7] Often speeches were simply not recorded, either by an audience member or by the speaker. A prime example of that here is the speech by Nan Joyce, a dominant voice for Traveller rights in Ireland. Joyce did not leave an archive of papers behind. She was a regular public speaker and recognised as an inspirational orator. Her speech to a Trócaire seminar in Galway was powerful and has been included in this volume through piecing together various newspaper accounts. When speeches have been recorded and successfully sourced, there may be further limitations on publication due to copyright. The speeches contained in *Irish Women's Speeches* are either out of copyright or available through re-use of public sector information, or relevant individuals and organisations have granted permission for publication.

The range of topics addressed by the orators in this volume is breath-taking, identifying the impressive contributions that Irish women have made and continue to make towards the development of societies globally. Labour activism is a recurring theme throughout this volume. Some speeches relate to the rights of workers, such as that of Saidie Patterson, addressing a gathering to justify a large-scale textile strike in Belfast, and Helen Chenevix's presidential address to the Irish Trade Union Congress. However, the issue of labour is one that is addressed in many other speeches. Labour rights was a key reason for demanding votes for women, as argued by Harriet Morison and Margaret Hinchey. Other speeches point to a lack of gender equality in specific employment sectors; Mamo McDonald highlighted the disadvantaged position of women in agriculture.

Equality issues related to gender, class, race and religion across the broad spectrum of politics, business and personal rights are evident throughout. Jennie Wyse Power's speech in Seanad Éireann identified how women were being denied rights as full citizens of the Irish Free State. Mary McAleese makes a fervent call for gender equality in the Catholic Church. Other speeches attend to the mistreatment of women at the hands of the Catholic Church, such as Elizabeth Coppin's speech detailing her incarceration in state-endorsed religious institutions. Saffa Musleh's speech shows the pertinent need to redefine the outdated perception of how an Irish person looks. Issues of ethnicity are also explored in Nan Joyce's formidable speech exploring racism and discrimination experienced by Irish Travellers.

Speeches relating to Irish nationality show the fiercely opposing views of the women of Ireland. In 1909 Constance Markievicz delivered her now famous speech imploring the young women of Ireland to join the fight for

Irish independence. Two years later, Theresa, Marchioness of Londonderry delivered a speech that led to the most successful mobilisation of unionist women against the Home Rule bill, in an attempt to keep Ireland within the realm of the British Empire. Markievicz and Londonderry were born in England. Both women had deep connections with Ireland, and their dedication to the country ensures their inclusion here. The title of this book refers to Irish women and includes women who were born in Ireland but also those who have a deep association with the country. Such is also the case with Mary MacSwiney, who was born in London but moved to Ireland at the age of six. MacSwiney viewed herself as Irish, and, indeed, her rejection of any association with England is perhaps evident in her endorsement of the IRA's bombing campaign in England in 1938.

The long and complex campaign for civil rights justice and to establish political stability in Northern Ireland, after the onset of the Troubles, is expressed through the speeches of women across five decades, from the 1960s until 2010. Speeches relating to politics and human rights in Northern Ireland include those given by Bernadette Devlin in her role as an MP in the House of Commons; Betty Williams, co-founder of the Peace People; Inez McCormack, a trade unionist and human rights activist; Bríd Rodgers, a founder member of the Social Democratic and Labour Party; and Monica McWilliams, co-founder, and leader of the Northern Ireland Women's Coalition party. Through these particular speeches, it is possible to trace the key roles that women played on the journey from violence to achieving peace in Northern Ireland.

The complexity of Irish feminism is most apparent in the topics addressed. Speeches relating to the divorce and abortion referendums most clearly reflect how feminists could take opposing sides in the interests of women. In 1986 Alice Glenn TD presented a strong argument against the introduction of divorce, arguing that women would suffer financially and emotionally if divorce was legalised in Ireland. Yet, at the same time, Mary Robinson was campaigning for the introduction of divorce from a feminist perspective. In the wake of the repeal of the Eighth Amendment to the Constitution in 2018, it is interesting to read the speech by Nuala Fennell, a steadfast feminist activist. Fennell, then Minister of State for Women's Affairs and Family Law, delivered a powerful speech in Dáil Éireann in favour of introducing that Amendment in 1983, which effectively prohibited abortion in Ireland. In 2018, when the Amendment was finally overturned, Clare Daly described the same Amendment as 'A ball and chain that dogged us all our adult lives' in her speech to the Dáil.

Each of the speeches that follow has been carefully selected because it has mobilised strong support for a cause, changed public opinion or led to a change of law. The selection is not representative of every issue raised by Irish women in a public forum during the time period. The text of each speech has not been altered from the original. In some instances, paragraphing has been included for ease of reading; speeches in original newspaper reports or in parliamentary debates are often recorded without any paragraph structure. Most speeches are not recorded here in full as many of the original speeches are lengthy. MacSwiney's speech to Dáil Éireann was only one of her speeches delivered during the treaty debates, and the selected speech included in this volume lasted for two hours and forty minutes. MacSwiney's contribution on that day totals just under 15,000 words, and it would not be feasible to include all her comments here. Therefore, the most significant extracts from the speeches have been recorded. Many of the speeches, including MacSwiney's, can be read in full in their original source and some may be viewed online; where possible this is cited in related sections.

A detailed introduction precedes each speech, illuminating the context in which the speech occurred and assessing the impact the speech made or the consequences for the speaker. Each introductory section explores the background of the orator and those connected with them. This aspect is particularly useful when tracing networks of related people and organisations. For example, in Catherine Connolly's speech, on the publication of the Mother and Baby Homes report, she mentions the 'painstaking work' of Catherine Corless. Therefore, the introductory section provides a background of Corless, who first exposed the horrendous abuses at the Tuam Mother and Baby Home.

Many of the female speakers included in this volume were supported in their cause by networks of other women and their inclusion is of equal importance. This is particularly evident in Monica McWilliams' speech relating to the peace negotiations that led to the Good Friday Agreement. The introductory section notes other significant women including May Blood, Bronagh Hinds, Pearl Sagar and Jane Morrice, founder members of the Northern Ireland Women's Coalition (NIWC). The NIWC ensured that human rights, equality and inclusion shaped the Good Friday Agreement. Each of these women are deserving of a dedicated section and difficult decisions were made in the interest of covering a broad spectrum of topics and time periods. Each introductory section also showcases the pioneering work of feminist scholars, which has been employed in the research on that theme. The reference notes in each section provide an insight into the vast and impressive work that has been done by past and present scholars of women in modern Ireland.

Irish Women's Speeches: Voices that Rocked the System is a record of Irish women whose words continue to shake people out of apathy and enthuse new generations. It is a record of women who, as Mary Robinson noted in her presidential acceptance speech, 'instead of rocking the cradle, rocked the system'.[8]

ONE

Anna Parnell

1852–1911

Speech on behalf of the Ladies' Land League
City Hall, Glasgow, Scotland

19 AUGUST 1881

'The landlords will be beaten with a vengeance.'

At a packed reception in Glasgow City Hall, Anna Parnell delivered a provoking and entertaining speech that roused her audience in support of the land war in Ireland. Parnell proved to be an engaging and inspiring speaker, often scattering witty comments amidst difficult subject matter, as can be seen in her speech in this section. This speech was part of her Scottish tour that month. Glasgow was a significant site to gather support for the Irish cause with a population of 70,000 Irish immigrants, the largest Irish community in Scotland at that time.[1] Parnell's speeches attracted the attention of journalists, especially in Ireland, Britain, and America. Journalists often recorded her entire speeches and the reaction of audiences in great detail. Her speeches exhibited her keen awareness of current politics, at a time when women were entirely excluded from formal politics in Britain and Ireland.

The land war in Ireland emerged alongside a wave of famine that revisited Ireland in 1879 due to an accumulation of bad harvests and economic depression. The famine never reached the deadly proportions of the Great Irish Famine of the 1840s due in part to the formation of organised support networks for tenant protection. At this time only three per cent of Irish farmers owned their land, with the remainder renting from landlords who often controlled large estates overseeing hundreds of tenant farmers.[2] Tenants unable to pay their rents because of failed harvests faced eviction, destitution and possible starvation. The young radical nationalist Michael Davitt helped found the National Land League of Mayo at Castlebar on 16 August 1879 with the manifesto 'the land of Ireland belongs to the people of Ireland.'[3] Davitt's own family had been evicted from their land in Mayo when he was only four years of age. He encouraged Charles Stewart Parnell to launch the Irish National Land League in Dublin on 21 October 1879. Charles was elected president and was the only Protestant member of the executive, with Davitt taking position as secretary. The league campaigned aggressively for rent reductions and tenant protection from evictions through the three fs: fair rent, free sale and fixity of tenure.

Charles was first elected as an MP for Meath in 1875, after which his sister Anna became intensely interested in politics. From 1877 Anna began attending House of Commons sessions, where, to observe proceedings, she was confined to the ladies' cage, a system that kept women away from the main political domain. She published a series of articles in the American journal the *Celtic Monthly*, aptly titled 'How do they do in the house of commons: Notes from the ladies' cage.'[4] When the Land League was first established, Anna was in New Jersey visiting her mother and her sisters, including Fanny. Anna and Fanny established a Famine Relief Committee in America to support those affected in Ireland. The sisters moved to New York and devoted themselves to this cause, inspiring Fanny to establish a Ladies' Land League (LLL) in New York. The organisation of women across America grew quickly, seeing the formation of 25 branches of the LLL comprising 5,000 members.[5]

Davitt visited America often during this time, seeking financial and political support for the work of the Land League. During these visits Davitt worked closely with Anna, whose organisational skills greatly impressed him. On 2 November 1879, leading members of the Land League, including Davitt, addressed a crowd of over 8,000 people on part of the Gore-Booth estate, at Gurteen in County Sligo, warning local tenants 'of impending famine and dire misfortune before us'.[6] Davitt and two other members of the Land League, James Daly and James Boyce Killeen, were arrested under a charge of using seditious language and imprisoned in Sligo. The case was eventually dropped, and the three men were released without charge.[7]

With the male leaders of the league under increased threat of imprisonment, Davitt proposed that a women's branch of the Land League be formed in Ireland. Anna was summoned back to Dublin. She was elected as the organising secretary of the Ladies' Land League at a meeting in Dublin on 27 January 1881. Anna insisted that 'an address be issued to women in Ireland and overseas explaining the objects of their organisation'.[8] She also stipulated that an annual subscription, not less than five shillings, be paid by members. Anna immediately began a speaking tour of Ireland encouraging tenants to challenge excessive rents.

The first open air meeting of the LLL was held on 14 February 1881 in Claremorris, county Mayo. Anna Parnell was the main speaker and instantly earned the respect of her audience. Her speech was declared as an 'undoubted success' in the *Freeman's Journal* the following day. Taking a high-profile public platform was a new direction for politically conscious women in Ireland; a fact that Parnell was most aware of. Historian Margaret Ward highlights that 'from her earliest speeches she [Anna] made it plain that she expected men to respect the women's organisation.'[9] This was, as Ward observes, 'crucial both ensuring that women heard what she was saying and in building their confidence as political actors'.[10]

Anna's leadership of the Ladies' Land League was highly effective, and she inspired women across Ireland to directly challenge the landlord-tenant system by disputing unreasonable rents and opposing evictions. Members of the LLL supported tenants by attending evictions and recording details on specifically designed eviction forms.[11] Members of the league also supported evicted tenants practically with food and shelter where possible. An overall register was compiled that became known as the Book of Kells which included a record of every estate across the island of Ireland, the number of tenants on the estate, how much rent was paid, the official valuation of the land and detailed information on landlords, including an assessment of their character.[12] Anna and other members of the league actively engaged in a propaganda campaign, writing to newspapers in Ireland and abroad with details of evictions. Anna's speeches often included extensive portrayals of such evictions and descriptions of tenants subjected to violence at the hands of the Royal Irish Constabulary (RIC), as can be seen in her speech at Glasgow.

Anna actively sought members from outside of the island of Ireland, and branches of the LLL were formed in Australia, New Zealand, Britain, America and Canada. She regularly travelled abroad on speaking engagements, especially to cities with large populations of Irish emigrants such as Liverpool and Manchester. Many of these emigrants had left Ireland due to the Great Famine of the 1840s, and she found such audiences receptive to her message. As Ward observes, Parnell faced condemnation from some quarters due to her sex. She and the Ladies' Land League were subject to attack from religious leaders. The Archbishop of Dublin, Dr Edward McCabe, compiled a pastoral letter on 12 March 1881 that was read at every mass in Dublin that week.[13] In it, McCabe attacked members of the LLL for defying the true virtues and responsibilities of womanhood, announcing that the daughters of our Catholic people are called forth, under the flimsy pretext of charity, to take their stand in the noisy arena of public life. They are asked to forget the modesty of their sex and the high dignity of their womanhood by leaders who seem utterly reckless of consequences.[14]

The attack by the Archbishop generated a huge debate on the subject in the highest of forums, including in the House of Commons. Alexander Martin Sullivan, who had succeeded Charles Stewart Parnell as MP for Meath, publicly denounced McCabe's attack. Sullivan's wife Frances (née Donovan) was chair of the London branch of the LLL.

Parnell's tour of Scotland was well received; she spent the month of August 1881 touring villages, towns and cities there promoting the work of the league and gaining support for tenant rights in Ireland. She was accompanied to her talk in Glasgow by John Redmond, a home rule politician who worked alongside her brother Charles and had recently been elected as MP to New Ross in county Wexford.[15] In her speech Parnell attacked the basis of the Land Law (Ireland) bill that had been introduced by William Gladstone, then Prime Minister of Britain.[16] Gladstone had returned as Prime Minister in the 1880 general election, in the midst of the then raging land war in Ireland. In an attempt to resolve the conflict, Gladstone re-examined the Land Act that had been in place since 1870. Gladstone's new act was first introduced in April 1881, and after much debate in the House of Commons, it received royal assent on 22 August, just three days after Anna's speech in Glasgow. Gladstone attempted to realign rents through court arbitrations, a system that Anna pointed out was biased towards landlords. The act was orchestrated to help quash the work of the Land League and indeed resulted in wealthier landlords leaving the league to apply for a rent re-evaluation through the court system.

Much of Parnell's speech centred on the Mitchelstown evictions as an example of the persecuted position of tenant farmers. The Mitchelstown evictions had by then reached alarming proportions. Anna, Lady Kingston owned the large estate at Mitchelstown in county Cork. The tenants in this area depended on butter production for their income and were gravely affected when butter prices plummeted in 1878 and 1879.[17] With the support of the Land League, tenants in Mitchelstown sought a ten per cent reduction in their rents that was refused by Lady Kingston. By December 1880, in line with Land League principles, a large representation of tenants marched to Mitchelstown Castle and offered what they considered a fair rent to Lady Kingston. When this offer was rejected, the tenants withheld rent and used what little income they had to pay for food and supplies in their local village. This event sparked an intense dispute that would continue over the coming years. By June 1881, it was reported that seven hundred soldiers and three hundred police camped outside Mitchelstown Castle under the command of General Thomas Steele. The gathering of one thousand men protected the landlord and oversaw a number of evictions over the next month, during which time Anna Parnell arrived at the town. Her brother Charles addressed the Mitchelstown evictions in the House of Commons, noting specifically how his sister was affected.[18]

Through her speeches Anna inspired an organised political movement of women and oversaw the establishment of five hundred branches of the LLL. When the male organisation was supressed in October 1881 and the leaders imprisoned, the LLL acted as the sole organisation campaigning against a system that prioritised landlords' incomes above tenants' rights. Ward testifies that Anna was 'highly critical of a situation – illustrated by the slogan "Rent at the Point of a Bayonet" – that saw landlords receiving their rent while the league incurred legal costs. Anna condemned the policy as a 'Great Sham', and attempted to encourage a genuine resistance to landlordism.'[19] The LLL was proclaimed illegal in December 1881, but Anna continued to hold mass meetings in pursuit of her cause.

A treaty was finally reached with the leaders of the Irish National Land League in May 1882. Charles and the other male leaders were released from prison, and the Land Act was amended. However, a hostile rift emerged when the male leaders expected the LLL to continue as a 'charitable agency only'.[20] In the midst of hostile arguments, Fanny Parnell died unexpectedly on 20 July, possibly from rheumatic fever.[21] A request to bury her remains in Ireland was refused by her brother Charles, and within days, on 2 August 1882, the LLL was disbanded. Anna never spoke to her brother Charles again. She moved to England and settled in Devon under the assumed name of Cerisa Palmer. In 1907 Anna wrote a detailed account of the Land League and of the women's vital contribution to the movement, which she fittingly titled *The Tale of a Great Sham*. The fate of this manuscript and the almost erasure of the LLL from the records of Irish history over the following decades is a testament to how Irish women's contributions were undervalued and often ignored in political histories. Anna died at the age of 59, while swimming at the Tunnels Bathing Beaches in Ilfracombe, Devon, on 20 September 1911. An inquest returned 'a verdict of accidental death by drowning'.[22] No relatives attended Anna's funeral.[23]

The Tale of a Great Sham remained unpublished until 1986, when Dana Hearne happened upon the memoir while researching for a project on Charles Stewart Parnell in the archives of the National Library of Ireland in Dublin.[24] Hearne recounts that Anna found it difficult to source a publisher for her memoir, which is extraordinary since this was 'particularly at a time when C. S. Parnell's glorious memory was vivid in the Irish mind'.[25] Indeed, a grand statue of Charles Stewart Parnell adorns the main thoroughfare in

Dublin city on O'Connell Street at the entrance to a square named in his honour. The 19-metre-high structure was unveiled on 1 October 1911.[26] Hearne worked tirelessly to have the entire text of the manuscript published, first by Arlen House in 1986 and more recently in 2020 by University College Dublin Press. This important contribution by Hearne has gone some way to recovering Anna Parnell and the Ladies' Land League to a position of importance in Irish historical discourse.

There are no statues honouring Anna Parnell, and it transpired that her final resting place had been neglected for some years. In 2013 Lucy Keaveney, co-founder of the Countess Markievicz School, visited Anna's grave in north Devon with her husband, John. The couple were dismayed that it took them some time to identify Anna's grave, which was overgrown with weeds. Keaveney later met with then Minister for Arts, Heritage and Culture, Jimmy Deenihan, and this 'led to a government-funded restoration of Anna Parnell's grave in Devon'.[27] Keaveney later initiated discussions with Brendan Teeling, Dublin deputy city librarian and representatives of Dublin City Council regarding a possible memorial for Anna. On 20 September 2021, a memorial plaque to Anna Parnell was unveiled by Dublin Lord Mayor Alison Gilliland at the AIB bank premises on O'Connell Street, the original offices where the Ladies Land League operated from. The date was chosen to commemorate Anna's death on that day 110 years previously. Anna Parnell's speeches remain as a testament to her driven commitment to establishing a more equitable Irish society.

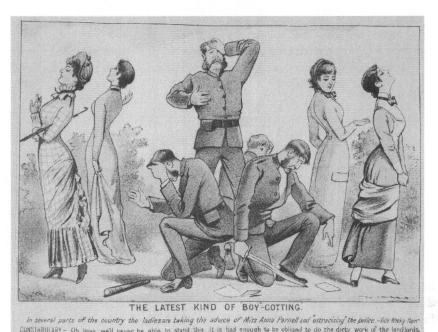

THE LATEST KIND OF BOY-COTTING.

In several parts of the country the ladies are taking the advice of Miss Anna Parnell and "ostracising" the police.—Vide Weekly Paper

CONSTABULARY— Oh, boys, we'll never be able to stand this. It is bad enough to be obliged to do the dirty work of the landlords, but this bates. We have nothing for it but to resign."

1. The latest kind of 'Boy'- Cotting. *Weekly Freeman*, 5 March 1881. Depicting the campaign by Anna Parnell and the women of the Ladies Land League. Courtesy of the National Library of Ireland.

'I said a few words, and although few they seem to have made up in quality for what they wanted in quantity.[28] I said that "Mr Gladstone— (hisses)—was a hypocritical, bloodthirsty miscreant, who is having the Irish people murdered at home to gratify his own vanity." (Loud cheers.) ... Mr Gladstone has brought in and passed what he called, and what the English and Scotch people, and probably the Welsh also, if we knew what they were talking about, would call a beneficent healing measure for Ireland. (Laughter.) ...

The Land Bill is a long and complicated measure, but I think the kernel of it is this. There are three Commissioners who have the power of fixing the rents in Ireland on the application of landlord or tenant. These Commissioners are all landlords' men more or less—(hear, hear)—and it is quite certain that they will only reduce rents, if they reduce them at all, to what they believe the tenant would pay if there were no Land Court at all. (Cheers.) ... [Mr Gladstone] knows that while the Irish tenants have the Land League at their backs they will not be in any hurry running to the three landlords who constitute the Land Court. He therefore must try to crush the Land League, to crush the Irish tenants, and to force them as the only resource to see what his Land Court will do for them.

I have seen with my own eyes the means he takes in Ireland to force the tenants into the arms of the Land Court. On the 8th of last month I was in Cork, and I there heard that there were to be evictions carried out on the property of Lady Kingston at Mitchelsto[w]n, and I went to see how these things were done. (Cheers.) The first object that met my eyes was a very large army. There were red coats, green coats, foot soldiers, and horse soldiers. (Laughter.) . . . I did not know at first what all the army was for, but I afterwards found out that it was to protect the Sheriff against me—(laughter) . . .

I may say that all that I did was to advise the tenants not to pay rent. . . . On the third day the resident magistrate thought he had had enough of that kind of thing. It was too slow for him. (Laughter.) So the police were ordered to draw their batons, and the soldiers to canter along the road terrifying and scaring out of their wits unfortunate poor old men and women who were not quick enough to get out of their way. Then the bailiffs began to smash the furniture. I don't know whether you know the orthodox way to remove a man's furniture in Ireland when he is being evicted. It is to take a crowbar and to smash the article until it is reduced to such proportions that it can be thrown out of the window, to save the trouble of carrying it downstairs. (Hisses.) . . .

The fourth day, these proceedings had their natural effect. The people threw stones at the policemen. They would hardly have been human if they had not been provoked to do something of the kind. I was not there on the fourth day, but having read in the newspapers that things were getting pretty lively I returned on the eighth day. We were stopped. . . .

I suppose they stopped us to prevent us hurting the Sheriff. (Laughter.) We did not care to stop there all day looking at the soldiers. They were not amusing. (Laughter.) So we turned into a field, intending to get on the highway again. But four policemen came down the field and intercepted us. They told us, with their batons drawn, that we were not to attempt to cross the hedge into a field nearer the Sheriff. . . .

There was a hay field near in which a man named O'Keefe was making his hay. He was one of Lady Kingston's tenants who had renegaded and paid his rent. (Hisses.) He thought that by making our acquaintance he might be able to rehabilitate himself in the public esteem, for if a man pays his rent, making no resistance, he is more or less boycotted. (Laughter.) He called on us to come into his field;

but I knew better than accept the invitation. He then began to walk towards us.

I don't suppose he wanted to fight the four policemen. I imagined that he wanted to be introduced to me. (Laughter.) But the four policemen thought he was a crowd obstructing and intimidating the Sheriff, and they shouted to him, "Get out of that with you"—that was to say, out [of] his own field. Not content with that, they jumped over the hedge, rushed on him, and beat him with all their might. He stood his ground bravely, and walked slowly backwards, the three young fellows beating him with their batons; and when they had got him to the other side of the field one of these gave him a crack on the head which just missed fracturing his skull (that was what the doctor said) and then left him. The four policemen then returned and gave us information that if we went into that field we should get the same. ("Shame.") . . .

And now I just wish you to remember how all these things are done. It is to terrify the Irish people to give up the means by which they have hitherto succeeded in reducing their rents. . . . I hope the tenants on Lady Kingston's estate have inaugurated a new era. Eight of those tenants who could have paid have suffered themselves to be evicted, and I see that they intend to remain out. By giving up their houses they have set an example which I hope in six months will be universal all over Ireland. (Applause.) Then the people will be under no necessity of accepting the Land Bill; the landlords will be beaten with a vengeance. I would therefore ask you to see that the tenants on Lady Kingston's estate who remain out and those who follow their example incur no unnecessary loss or suffering. (Applause.) . . . Do you back them up, give them your money, and encourage them; don't give them up till the very last moment. (Cries of "Never" and loud cheers.)'[29]

TWO

Harriet Morison

1862–1925

Speech on women's suffrage in New Zealand
Dunedin City Hall

12 APRIL 1892

'The mind is the standard by which humanity must be gauged, not the garments worn.'

At a large gathering in Dunedin on 12 April 1892, Harriet Morison gave an inspiring speech in support of women's suffrage.[1] The meeting attracted an audience of 1,200 people and established Dunedin as the centre of the New Zealand suffrage movement. Dunedin was then the largest and most industrialised city in New Zealand; it had a large Irish population of whom the majority were women.[2] Morison herself was an emigrant from Ulster.[3] More than 40 women and a number of men occupied the stage that evening, many delivering speeches, but it was Morison's speech that attracted the most attention. Her speech was printed in its entirety by many journalists, and large sections were quoted in a number of newspapers.[4] Ultimately, Morison's speech helped New Zealand become the first self-governing country in the world to grant women the right to vote in general elections. Thus, New Zealand became the first true democracy.

By the 1890s the suffrage movement in New Zealand was gaining traction. Historian Barbara Brookes affirms that '[John Stuart] Mill's 1869 *The Subjection of Women* had done much to persuade a number of men in the New Zealand Parliament of the unjust denial of women's political rights.'[5] Such thinking inspired many leading politicians in New Zealand to take direct action to secure votes for women. In August 1878 Robert Stout, then Attorney General and Minister of Lands and Immigration, introduced an Electoral bill in which he proposed extending voting eligibility to female ratepayers. Stout's proposal was overthrown, but the move inspired the government's Qualification of Electors bill the following year, which recommended extending the vote to female property owners, a proposal that was only narrowly defeated.

In 1879 universal suffrage was granted to all men over 21 years of age in New Zealand, removing all property qualification. The introduction of universal suffrage undoubtedly inspired more women to seek political franchise. The women's suffrage movement quickly emerged outside of the parliamentary circle, initially encouraged by female temperance advocates. The Women's Christian Temperance Union (WCTU) was introduced to New Zealand by Mary Leavitt, an American envoy who arrived in the country in January 1885. Brookes describes how the movement was based on the ideal 'that Christian women had a duty to rid the world of the threat that alcohol posed to homes and families'.[6] The onset of the gold rush in New Zealand from 1861 attracted an influx of European settlers, Pākehā, who brought with them a drinking culture connected with male violence and lawlessness. The escalation of drink-related social problems had negative repercussions for the indigenous Māori population. Leavitt strongly encouraged women in New Zealand to become politically active in order to impress social reform, and 'the temperance crusade was broad enough to unite some Māori and Pākehā women.'[7]

Kate Sheppard, now recognised as the predominant suffragist in New Zealand, became a founding member of the New Zealand Women's Christian Temperance Union. By February 1886, 15 branches of the WCTU had been established across New Zealand. At their first annual convention, the WCTU committed to work for women's suffrage, and signed petitions were sent to members of the House of Representatives in 1886 and 1887. Such campaigning inspired Sir Julius Vogel, then Colonial Treasurer, to introduce the 1887 Women's Suffrage bill. Although the bill was supported by a majority, it was withdrawn at the committee stage. The following year, the WCTU published a leaflet itemising *Ten Reasons Why the Women of New Zealand Should Vote* which they again distributed to every member of the House of Representatives.[8]

In the midst of this growing momentum for women's suffrage, a new union was founded, the Dunedin Tailoresses' Union (DTU), which would greatly impact on the cause of votes for women. The union was established in July 1889, becoming the first women's trade union in New Zealand. The DTU was founded to protect tailoresses from exploitation in the wake of revelations about their 'sweated labour' in the latter part of 1888 and early 1889. Rutherford Waddell, an Irish man and a presbyterian minister, brought national attention to the deplorable conditions for workers in clothing factories and home-workers in Dunedin. Waddell's sermons inspired the *Otago Daily Times* to conduct an investigation into this sweated labour. In 1891 the DTU confined its membership to women workers, and Harriet Morison was appointed vice-president. Morison was also a member of the WCTU, and she brought a new vibrancy to the trade union. Melanie Nolan and Penelope Harper attest that 'Morison understood the importance of public relations, and actively fostered links between women wage-earners, the community, and the media.'[9]

2. The Sweating Crusade, *New Zealand Observer and Free Lance*, 25 June 1892. A woman knight, thought to represent Harriet Morison, lances the sweating monster. Courtesy of the Alexander Turnbull Library, New Zealand.

Under Morison's feminist leadership, the DTU campaigned vigorously to improve the wages and working conditions of women, first in Dunedin and later Morison acted as organiser for branches in Auckland, Wellington and Christchurch. Morison was forthright in asserting that women's working conditions could only be improved by giving women a say in the political running of their country. Eighteen-ninety-one was a key year for Morison to take up her new position; the previous year a Women's Franchise bill was presented to parliament by Sir John Hall, then a leading parliamentary advocate of female suffrage. The bill was defeated, as Brookes notes, 'in part because opponents still believed there was no strong evidence that women wanted it'.[10]

Now was the time to prove to male politicians that the majority of women in New Zealand did want political franchise. Just five weeks after Hall's bill was defeated, the WCTU began organising a national petition for women's suffrage. The task could only be completed with the help of dedicated collectors, who would canvas their local areas and collect signatures. Morison enlisted the support of the Federated Tailoresses' Union, which by then had an impressive membership of nearly 2,000 women.[11] On 14 August 1891, eight petitions, signed by 9,685 women, demanding votes for women were sent to the government. Brookes describes how Hall 'dramatically unrolled the seventy-four yards of petition before the House'.[12] Hall's Female Suffrage bill was eventually defeated, this time by the Legislative Council.[13] However, the petition generated much debate in public forums across New Zealand. The *Evening Star* newspaper published a full 'resume of the voting powers of women in different parts of the world', noting particularly that the United States has made 'great progress' in this area and, indeed, women in Wyoming then voted 'on all questions on the same terms as men'.[14] The article correctly foretold, somewhat forlornly, that the bill in New Zealand was sure to be voted down by a 'small majority'.

Morison was all the more determined in her cause for women's suffrage, and by 1892 she dedicated much of her time to addressing public gatherings on this topic. The speech in this section was given at the largest of such gatherings. Marion Hatton, also a secretary of the Tailoresses' Union and a member of the WCTU, presided and opened the meeting with a short address. Morison then put forward the resolution that 'the time has arrived when the Parliamentary franchise should be conferred on the women of New Zealand, not as a privilege, but as a right.'[15] Morison proceeded with a clear argument as to why this right should be afforded to women. She attacked each argument put forward by opponents to women's suffrage in a measured and often humorous style, highlighting the ridiculous basis of such claims. The journalist for the *Poverty Bay Herald* recorded the audience's reaction, including points of laughter. At the conclusion of Morison's speech, a Miss Cannon seconded the motion, after which Robert Stout, by then a prominent politician in New Zealand having served as Premier in two governments, took the stage. Stout declared his absolute commitment to the cause of women's suffrage, concluding that 'if the franchise were extended tomorrow this colony would have no cause to regret it; but, on the contrary, such an extension was desirable if we were to progress as a good people, and ever to become a great nation.'[16]

The meeting was an overwhelming success and convinced Morison to establish an organisation dedicated solely to campaigning for women's suffrage. Along with Marion Hatton and Helen Nicol, Morison co-founded the first Women's Franchise League in New Zealand. The first branch was based in Dunedin. Like her co-founders, Nicol was a staunch supporter of the temperance movement. It may well have been a difficult decision for the three women to set aside their personal crusade for temperance and focus solely on suffrage. This was, however, a strategic move, as noted by historian Dorothy Page: 'they would remove the question of temperance entirely from the debate, with the dual aim of deflecting the jibes of their pro-alcohol opponents and attracting non-temperance women to their cause.'[17] Indeed, the league enticed more women to the cause, whatever their views on Christianity or temperance.

The first meeting of the Dunedin Women's Franchise League was held just 16 days after Morison's speech. One hundred and fifty women gathered at the Choral Hall in Dunedin on 28 April 1892. The inaugural meeting was a great success, with 50 women joining the league and a full committee elected. Hatton was elected as president along with Lady Anna Stout.[18] Morison was elected as a vice-president, and Nicol took the position of secretary.[19] The Women's Franchise League spread swiftly across New Zealand throughout the following months. A general election was due the following year, and the league stepped up their activities with members holding public gatherings in towns and cities advocating for women's votes. One final petition was planned, and this time the results greatly exceeded all those previously gathered.

Thirteen petitions carried the signatures of 31,872 women who demanded the right to vote in the upcoming general election. Richard Seddon, Premier of New Zealand, introduced a women's suffrage clause in the 1893 Electoral bill. The bill successfully passed through the Legislative Council on 8 September. On 19 September 1893, the governor, Lord Glasgow, signed the Electoral Act into law, ensuring that women would be included on the electoral register for the upcoming election on 28 November.[20] This was an extraordinary success for the Women's Franchise League and the WCTU. Although women in a number of other territories had gained the right to vote, New Zealand was the first to extend this right across an entire country on an equal basis with men.[21] The 1893 Women's Suffrage Petition remains on permanent display at the Archives of New Zealand in Wellington. It is fitting that the suffrage petition is included as one of the three constitutional documents that shaped Aotearoa New Zealand along with The Declaration of the Independence of New Zealand (He Whakaputanga o te Rangatiratanga o Nu Tireni) and The Treaty of Waitangi (Te Tiriti o Waitangi).[22] The fact that the majority of women in South Dunedin, 57 per cent, signed the suffrage petition, as opposed to the national average of 25 per cent, is a testament to the dedicated work of the Dunedin suffragists.[23]

Morison died on 19 August 1925 at the age of 63 at her home in Auckland. Her passing did not gain vast media attention. Announcing her death, the *Auckland Star* incorrectly stated that she was born in Scotland and paid brief attention to her trade union organising on behalf of women.[24] The *Evening Star* and the *Stratford Evening Post* wrote briefly of her trade union work and her position as an officer in the Labour Department in charge of the women's employment bureau in Auckland, a position Morison held from 1908 to 1921.[25] There was no mention of Morison's tireless work on behalf of women's suffrage, nor were there any obituaries carried in local Dunedin newspapers.

In the centenary year of women's suffrage, Morison was given her rightful place among six women represented in the Kate Sheppard Memorial in Christchurch. The monument was unveiled by Governor General, Dame Catherine Tizard on 19 September 1993. Sheppard is positioned as the central life-size figure, and the other women represented are Te Tai Mangakāhia, the first woman to address Te Paremata (the Māori parliament); Amey Daldy, president of the Women's Franchise League in Auckland; Ada Wells, organiser of the Christchurch suffrage movement and the first woman elected to the Christchurch City Council; and Helen Nicol. Morison's speech remains as testimony to the impressive feminist legacy she left behind.

3. Kate Sheppard Memorial, Christchurch, New Zealand. Left to right: Meri Te Tai Mangakāhia, Amey Daldy, Kate Sheppard, Ada Wells, Harriet Morison, Helen Nicol. Photograph by Charlotte Hall Tiernan.

'I submit that all thoughtful and intelligent women desire this right; and if a few thoughtless and frivolous women say they do not wish it, is that any reason why those who do want it should be deprived of it?

Women compose nearly one-half of the adult population, and they have to obey the laws the same as men, and should have a voice in the framing of the laws they are called upon to obey. Women have to pay taxes the same as men, and taxation without representation is tyranny and an utter violation of the spirit of freedom, so characteristic a spirit in the present age.

It is urged by the opponents of this righteous measure that women's sphere is her home. I with all my heart believe that women's highest and holiest duties lie first in her home—but from her home to the world. Let me ask, however, can all women be offered a home? No, I contend they cannot. Women are compelled to go into the battle of life to earn their daily bread. The laws of competition and the factory system compel women to leave their homes and face life's battle, and I think women as wage-earners have a right to a voice in those laws that control this competition, and they cannot have a voice, or be properly represented, unless they have the ballot in their own hands. (Applause.)

It is again said that it will destroy the harmony of the domestic circle to introduce politics therein. Why should it be so? What is there in politics that this should be the case[?] If there is anything in politics that will have the effect of setting the wife against her husband, the sister against her sister, surely the same causes are at work to set the father against the son, and the brother against brother. (Applause.) Yet we do not hear of very serious strife arising because men related by the nearest ties of kinship differ in their political views. . . . Do wives and their husbands at present agree in their opinions upon everything outside of politics[?]—(Laughter and applause.) . . .

It has been said it will destroy woman's influence in her home, but let me ask you, friends, does it destroy woman's charms because she has mastered intricate subjects, and passed with honor examinations at the universities, and has attained the right to append to her name the letters B.A. or M.A.[?] Does that lessen her charms? Nay, I affirm it rather increases her attractions in the eyes of all good and true men.

. . . What is there about politics of a degrading nature? Are politics so bad that women would be demoralised by coming in contract [sic] with them? If so, then man is responsible for their condition—(loud applause)—and perhaps the best argument to meet that objection would be to extend the franchise to women, and I will undertake to say that the political atmosphere will be purified. . . . (Loud and continued applause.)

Then it is urged by our opponents that to grant the franchise to women would be to give a dual vote to some men. Thus, a man with a wife and two adult daughters will, according to our opponents, for all practical purposes, have four votes. That contention, however, is not correct. It assumes that the man has all the brains, while his wife and daughters have none. (Laughter and applause.) The supporters of the women's franchise, however, contend that the franchise should be extended to the man's wife and daughters because they are gifted with sufficient intelligence to use it for the welfare of the race.

Again, it has been urged that because they cannot take part in active warfare or defend the country they shall not vote. . . . The contention is that because women are physically weaker than men, and unable to fight, they shall not vote. Assuming this to be so, logically the same argument must be applied to all weak and delicate men, and also to men after they have attained that age which unfits them for warfare. . . . Because men can fight they must rule! Women's lives may be sacrificed as a result of rash men's notions of national honor, or because of some trumpery commercial dispute; but they must suffer death, and often worse than death, because they cannot fight. Perhaps there would have been fewer fights had women's calm counsels been listened to in the past. . . . But I deny that woman has no patriotism. History bristles with instances of her self-sacrificing devotion to her country and people. What of Joan of Arc, and the Florence Nightingales who have gone out to the battle field, and amid shot and shell have nursed the wounded and dying[?] . . .

Another argument raised by our opponents is, they do not wish to be brought under what they very vulgarly term petticoat government. Well, I am astonished that Britons can be found in this the nineteenth century to raise such an objection. Have they not been under petticoat government for the last fifty years and over? (Loud applause.) Has the British nation lost anything by Queen Victoria being at the head of affairs instead of a king in this the nineteenth century? (Applause and laughter.) . . . But were the autocratic powers she was possessed of abused, or, if abused, whether more so than in the case with, say, Charles I.? But if Governments are to be tested by the garments worn, I would honestly like to know what difference there is between petticoat government and pantaloon government. I contend that the mind is the standard by which humanity must be gauged, not the garments worn.

Woman is denied the franchise because her intellect is said to be lower than man's. Is this so? Do our girls in the primary schools not pass the standards as readily and at the same age as the boys? Is not the record in the sphere of higher education in proportion to their numbers quite as good as that of boys? . . . (Loud and continued applause).[26]

THREE

Countess Constance Markievicz
1868–1927

Address to the Students' National Literary Society
25 Rutland Square, Dublin

28 MARCH 1909

'Arm yourselves with weapons to fight your nation's cause.'

At first glance, Countess Markievicz appears an unlikely advocate of Irish independence. She was born into a prestigious Anglo-Irish family, the Gore-Booths of Lissadell, who were among the largest landowners in the West of Ireland. Markievicz rejected her aristocratic background and became a significant voice for Irish nationalism and social reform. She is one of the few women to reach iconic status in the history of the fight for Irish freedom. Markievicz converted to the cause of Irish nationalism in 1908 and that year joined two of the most prolific nationalist organisations: Sinn Féin, the republican political party, and Inghinidhe na hÉireann (Daughters of Ireland), the nationalist women's organisation.[1] The following year Markievicz delivered the speech in this section calling on Irish women to take active roles in the political affairs of the nation. Markievicz was a passionate and inspiring orator, although she was later to become what Senia Pašeta describes as 'an aggressive and flamboyant speaker who enjoyed wearing military uniforms and carrying weapons'.[2]

Her speech to the Students' National Literary Society was one of her earliest on the topic of Irish nationalism, and it remains one of her most renowned. The society was a centre for radical thought and debate in early twentieth-century Dublin, surpassing literary themes to include topics on the rights of workers and the treatment of Irish political prisoners.[3] Markievicz's speech was unique: a female orator encouraging women to

Photo] [Lafayette

COUNTESS MARKIEVICZ.

4. Countess Markievicz. Photograph taken months before she gave her speech to the Students' National Literary Society. Courtesy of the National Library of Ireland.

become politically active at a time when Irish society was overwhelmingly regulated by men.[4] The venue in which Markievicz spoke was a significant site; 25 Rutland Square was then the base of the Gaelic League (Conradh na Gaeilge).[5] The house was later to be the meeting place of the Supreme Council of the Irish Republican Brotherhood on 9 September 1914, where they undertook to organise a rising against British rule in Ireland.[6] More significantly, in terms of female activism, the building would also become the headquarters of Cumann na mBan (The Women's Council).[7] Rutland Square was officially renamed Parnell Square in 1933, in honour of the nationalist politician Charles Stewart Parnell, who often stayed on the Square.

Markievicz's speech was reported in newspapers across Ireland under various attention-provoking titles.[8] The complete text was later printed as a pamphlet by Inghinidhe na hÉireann.[9] On the title page, Markievicz's chosen name in the organisation, 'Macha', is printed. Members of Inghinidhe na hÉireann elected to call themselves after a heroine of ancient Ireland. Markievicz chose her name in honour of Macha, the sovereignty goddess of Irish mythology. Her address to the Students' National Literary Society marks a clear point in her life from when she dedicated herself to the cause of Irish independence. The text provides an insight into her primary objectives. It also signals a clear commitment to seeking full equality for women in a proposed new Irish state; this feminist aspect of Markievicz's politics is often overlooked by historians, who focus predominantly on her military activities.

Her speech opens with a brief outline of the history of Irish female political activity. Markievicz points to the work of stalwart activists such as Anna and Fanny Parnell who founded the Ladies' Land League. While the league is acknowledged as the first political association of Irish women, by the time of Markievicz's speech the work of the Parnell sisters was vastly disregarded.[10] The next female-led political organisation in Ireland was Inghinidhe na hÉireann, founded by Maud Gonne in 1900.[11] Hanna Sheehy Skeffington explained that Gonne formed the organisation because she 'found that all the male groups, even the cultural ones, of the early Irish Renaissance movement were automatically closed to women'.[12] In her speech, Markievicz particularly praises Gonne's opposition to the visit of Edward VII to Dublin in the summer of 1903. The protests by Inghinidhe culminated in the 'battle of Coulson Avenue', where, as Margaret O'Callaghan and Caoimhe Nic Dháibhéid describe, 'in mourning the death of Pope Leo XIII Maud flew a series of black petticoats from her home in defiance of the festive atmosphere of official Dublin.'[13] Markievicz provides advice for the young women of Ireland to continue this work by engaging in and supporting the nationalist struggle while keeping women's emancipation to the forefront. This advice included encouraging women to buy Irish goods and to support Irish education but also to take up arms to fight for Ireland, if necessary. It is now apparent that the advice Markievicz gave to the young women of Ireland was the direction that she herself was committed to follow.

Markievicz concludes her speech by calling on the women of Ireland to bring forth a Joan of Arc to free the nation. A national heroine of France, Joan of Arc led the French in liberating the city of Orléans in 1429 and was finally captured by the English enemy forces. She was sentenced to death and burned at the stake in 1431. She became an important figure of inspiration to the suffrage movement. Markievicz dressed as Joan of Arc for a suffrage pageant in 1914.[14] Markievicz was later referred to as Ireland's Joan of Arc by many people including Hanna Sheehy Skeffington.[15]

When Markievicz delivered her speech to the student society, women under British rule had little equality with their male counterparts. Arguably at the core of this inequity was the fact that women had no voting rights in general elections, nor were they eligible to stand for election in Britain or Ireland. This situation ensured that the government of the day was an entirely male body, placed there by an exclusively male electorate. The previous year, Sheehy Skeffington and Margaret Cousins established the first militant suffrage organisation in Ireland, the Irish Women's Franchise League. The activities of the Irish suffragette organisation began with a low-key approach. In the British general elections of January and December 1910, the Irish Parliamentary Party (IPP) held the balance of power and formed a government with the Liberal Party under Prime Minister Henry Asquith. The main objective of the IPP was to achieve home rule for Ireland.

Irish suffragettes demanded that female suffrage be included in the terms of any home rule bill sought. The home rule issue caused a divide between nationalist and unionist women in Ireland, a point that Markievicz spells out in her speech. This split would intensify over the following years in the run-up to the introduction of a third Home Rule bill in 1912.[16] The IPP refused to include suffrage for women in their aims, and like many nationalist women, Markievicz sought support elsewhere. The main orchestrators of the Easter Rising, an armed rebellion against British rule in Ireland, promised gender equality in an independent Ireland. The subjection of women became a vital concern to those who signed the Proclamation announcing an Irish Republic. James Connolly, Markievicz's close ally, wrote that the 're-establishment of the Irish State' is useless unless it embodies the 'emancipation of womanhood'.[17] The Proclamation, first read by Patrick Pearse outside the General Post Office on Easter Monday in 1916, was distinctly addressed to Irishmen and Irishwomen as equal citizens, vowing that a future 'permanent National Government... would be elected by the suffrages of all her men and women'.[18]

Numerous women, including Markievicz, took active roles to fight for the ideals expressed in the Proclamation during the rising. Many women fought under the auspices of the Irish Citizen Army and supported the insurrection through the Irish women's paramilitary organisation Cumann na mBan.[19] Markievicz took up arms and was second-in-command of a group of combatants first in St Stephen's Green and later in the Royal College of Surgeons. Six days after the rebellion began, the leaders surrendered to protect civilian life. A total of 16 men were executed by British forces following the rising. Markievicz was sentenced to death, but this was later commuted to life imprisonment. Approximately 1,800 people were imprisoned, including 77 women.[20] Those imprisoned were released gradually over the following months. Markievicz was one of the final prisoners to be released in June 1917. However, she would spend numerous periods incarcerated over the following years. In April 1918 Markievicz was arrested and imprisoned in Holloway as a participant in a supposed plot with Germany. In this instance Markievicz was not charged with anything as there was no evidence to support this claim.

While Markievicz was in prison, the Representation of the People Act 1918 was passed. The act vastly reformed the British electoral system by removing property qualifications for men and granting women over thirty years of age, with certain restrictions, a vote at general elections. These two reform measures greatly increased the size of the Irish electorate. A further act, the Parliament (Qualification of Women) Act 1918, enabled women to stand for election. Seventeen female candidates stood in the British general election in 1918, including the pioneer English suffragette Christabel Pankhurst. Markievicz stood as a Sinn Féin candidate and was the only woman to be elected. She was returned as an MP for St Patrick's Division of Dublin, making her the first woman ever elected to the British House of Commons. In line with Sinn Féin policy, Markievicz rejected her seat; as politicians of constituencies based on the island of Ireland, Sinn Féin members refused to sit in a government based in England.

The elected members of Sinn Féin formed the first Dáil Éireann, government of Ireland, in 1919. When she was released from prison, Markievicz returned to Ireland and to her first sitting at the Dáil. She was later nominated as Minister for Labour, becoming the first female cabinet minister in Ireland. In the local elections the next year, 43 women were returned. In the general election of 1921, a total of six women were elected as TDs, including Markievicz. The other women elected were Kathleen Clarke, Ada English, Mary MacSwiney, Kathleen O'Callaghan and Margaret Pearse. This and the promise of equal voting rights was surely what Markievicz and the leaders of the Easter Rising had envisioned. However, this is the point where the promise of gender equality in an independent Ireland started to unravel. Those men who signed the Proclamation had all been executed following the rising. The future of the Irish Free State was in the hands of others. The Anglo-Irish Treaty, first established in December 1921 in an attempt to end the Irish War of Independence, would grant dominion-like status to a Free State Ireland but contained an article for the north of Ireland to opt out. This was neither full independence nor unity for Ireland. All six female TDs opposed the treaty as did Cumann na mBan.

As an opponent of the treaty, Markievicz lost her seat in the June 1922 general election.[21] A civil war erupted between the pro-treaty and anti-treaty sides. Markievicz spent much of the civil war on the run or in prison. She became a founding member of the Fianna Fáil party upon its establishment in 1926. She was elected as a Fianna Fáil candidate for Dublin South in the 1927 election. Markievicz died five weeks later, at the age of 59. When she died in a public ward of Sir Patrick Dun's hospital, her legacy quickly began to unfold. Due to ongoing hostilities with the Free State government, Markievicz was denied a state funeral. Five days before her death, Kevin O'Higgins, then Minister for Justice, was assassinated by anti-treaty supporters. O'Higgins received a state funeral, and his body lay in state at the Mansion House. In contrast, Markievicz's body lay in the Pillar Room of the Rotunda hospital, near to where she had given her speech to the Students' National Literary Society.

Markievicz proved to have earned the respect of the people of Dublin, who lined the streets in their thousands to honour her funeral cortege. It reportedly took three hours to process her coffin the relatively short distance to Glasnevin cemetery, where one hundred-armed Free State soldiers stood guard to ensure that there would be no volleys fired by anti-treaty supporters over her grave. Her burial was delayed, supposedly because the grave diggers did not work on a Sunday but possibly in an attempt by the Free State to reduce the numbers in attendance. She was buried the next morning amid an even greater number of Free State forces.

An attempt to honour Markievicz was made in 1932, when a bust of her was unveiled in St Stephen's Green, where she initially fought during the rising. Such tributes escalated over the following decades, and Markievicz has reached iconic status in Irish history. A number of statues in her honour exist in Dublin, most notably in the grounds of the Irish parliamentary building, Leinster House. There is also an impressive statue designed by John Coll located in Rathcormack in Sligo, the county of Markievicz's childhood home. The nearby Gaelic Athletic Association stadium in Sligo is named Markievicz Park, and a number of local streets and buildings in Sligo and in Dublin carry Markievicz's name. While accounts of Markievicz's activities are recorded in many historical publications, her own words and this speech in particular remain the most significant record of her personal commitment to secure Irish independence and gender equality.

5. Peace meeting at Mansion House, Dublin, July 1921. Left to right: Kathleen Clarke, Countess Markievicz, Kathleen O'Callaghan and Margaret Pearse. Photo by W. D. Hogan, 1921. Courtesy of the National Library of Ireland.

'I take it as a great compliment that so many of you, the rising young women of Ireland, who are distinguishing yourselves every day and coming more and more to the front, should give me this opportunity. We older people look to you with great hopes and a great confidence that in your gradual emancipation you are bringing fresh ideas, fresh energies, and above all a great genius for sacrifice into the life of the nation.

In Ireland the women seem to have taken less part in public life, and to have had less share in the struggle for liberty, than in other nations. . . . Now, I am not going to discuss the subtle psychological question of why it was that so few women in Ireland have been prominent in the national struggle, or try to discover how they lost in the dark ages of persecution the magnificent legacy of Maeve, Fheas, Macha and their other great fighting ancestors. True, several women distinguished themselves on the battle fields of '98, and we have the women of the *Nation* newspaper, of the Ladies' Land League, also in our own day the few women who have worked their hardest in the Sinn Féin movement and in the Gaelic League, and we have the woman who won a battle for Ireland, by preventing a wobbly Corporation from presenting King Edward of England with a loyal address. But for the most part our women, though sincere, steadfast Nationalists at heart, have been content to remain quietly at home, and leave all the fighting and the striving to the men.

Lately things seem to be changing . . . so now again, a strong tide of liberty seems to be coming towards us, swelling and growing and carrying before it all the outposts that hold women enslaved and bearing them triumphantly into the life of the nation to which they belong.

We are in a very difficult position here, as so many Unionist women would fain have us work together with them for the emancipation of their sex and votes – obviously to send a member to Westminster. But I would ask every Nationalist woman to pause before she joined a Suffrage Society or Franchise League that did not include in their Programme the Freedom of their Nation. "A Free Ireland with No Sex Disabilities in her Constitution" should be the motto of all Nationalist Women. And a grand motto it is. . . .

Now, here is a chance for our women. Let them remind their men, that their first duty is to examine any legislation proposed not from a party point of view, not from the point of view of a sex, a trade or a class, but simply and only from the standpoint of their Nation. Let them learn to be statesmen and not merely politicians. Let them consider how their action with regard to it may help or hinder their national struggle for independence and nothing else, and then let them act accordingly.

Fix your mind on the ideal of Ireland free, with her women enjoying the full rights of citizenship in their own nation, and no one will be able to side-track you, and so make use of you to use up the energies of the nation in obtaining all sorts of concessions – concessions too, that for the most part were coming in the natural course of evolution, and were perhaps just hastened a few years by the fierce agitations to obtain them. . . .

If the women of Ireland would organise the movement for buying Irish goods more, they might do a great deal to help their country. If they would make it the fashion to dress in Irish clothes, feed on Irish food – in fact, in this as in everything, LIVE REALLY IRISH LIVES, they would be doing something great, and don't let our clever Irish colleens rest content with doing this individually, but let them go out and speak publicly about it, form leagues, of which "No English goods" is the war-cry. . . .

I daresay you will think this all very obvious and very dull, but Patriotism and Nationalism and all great things are made up of much that is obvious and dull, and much that in the beginning is small, but that will be found to lead out into fields that are broader and full of interest. You will go out into the world and get elected onto as many public bodies as possible, and by degrees through your exertions no public institution – whether hospital, workhouse, asylum or any other, and no private house – but will be supporting the industries of your country . . .

To sum up in a few words what I want the Young Ireland women to remember from me. Regard yourselves as Irish, believe in yourselves as Irish, as units of a nation distinct from England, your Conqueror, and as determined to maintain your distinctiveness and gain your deliverance. Arm yourselves with weapons to fight your nation's cause. Arm your souls with noble and free ideas. Arm your minds with the histories and memories of your country and her martyrs, her language, and a knowledge of her arts, and her industries. And if in your day the call should come for your body to arm, do not shirk that either.

May this aspiration towards life and freedom among the women of Ireland bring forth a Joan of Arc to free our nation!'[22]

FOUR

Theresa Londonderry
1856–1919

Speech at the formation of the Ulster Women's Unionist
Council YMCA, Wellington Place, Belfast

23 JANUARY 1911

'Ulster will not let herself be cut adrift.'

The Irish home rule crisis of the early twentieth century brought the organising of unionist opposition to a considerable new height, including the formation of the largest women's political organisation on the island of Ireland at that time. The establishment of the Ulster Women's Unionist Council (UWUC) on 23 January 1911 was undoubtedly one of the most momentous events in the history of female political activism in Ireland.[1] Within just over a year of its formation, membership of the council had grown to an estimated number of between 115,000 and 200,000 women.[2] The UWUC, initially established as a support organisation for the male only Ulster Unionist Council (UUC), played a fundamental role in the movement to oppose home rule for Ireland.

The foundation of the UWUC was certainly not the beginning of unionist women's political organisation on this issue, but it was the most effective development. The unionist and suffragist Isabella Tod founded a Belfast branch of the Women's Liberal Federation to oppose the first Home Rule bill of 1886.[3] Among much female organising against the second Home Rule bill in 1893, a petition was signed by 20,000 women and presented to parliament.[4] This monster petition was organised by Theresa, 6th Marchioness of Londonderry, who became the most significant force behind the UWUC, and her speech in this section was inspirational for unionist women in Ulster.[5]

The call for home rule, seeking self-government for Ireland within the British Empire, first entered serious political debate in 1870 with the formation of the Home Government Association by Donegal barrister and later MP Isaac Butt. The Irish question entered a new realm when then British Prime Minister William Gladstone proposed the first Home Rule bill. That first bill was rejected by parliament in 1886, and a second bill was defeated in 1893 by the House of Lords. The Home Government Association evolved into the Irish Parliamentary Party (IPP), an official parliamentary party comprised of Irish MPs seeking home rule as their main objective. The movement gained momentum among Irish nationalists into the twentieth century with John Redmond as leader of the IPP. Unionist women retaliated in 1907, forming an organisation against home rule in North Tyrone, and two years later the women of Derry followed suit, forming the Women's Registration Association.[6]

In the 1910 British general election, the IPP held the balance of power, a fact about which Lady Londonderry was particularly concerned. Redmond now held a powerful position in the House of Commons with 70 elected MPs. The introduction of a third Home Rule bill then seemed imminent. While women remained excluded from voting in British general elections, unionist women sought another outlet to voice their opposition and vigorously campaign against home rule. There was a well-grounded belief that a government based in Dublin would govern in the interests of the Catholic majority on the island, which led unionists, especially Ulster protestants, to fear what they considered 'Rome rule'.[7]

Lady Londonderry was, as Rachel E. Finley-Bowman has termed, an 'ideal unionist' to take up the cause of opposition.[8] Londonderry was the daughter of a British Conservative MP, Charles John Chetwynd-Talbot, and she claimed to have held an interest in politics from the age of ten.[9] Her gender excluded her from either standing or voting in general elections, however her marriage to Lord Charles Castlereagh in 1875 provided her with access to the political sphere and allowed her to engage directly on the Irish question. When Castlereagh succeeded as the sixth Marquess of Londonderry in 1884 and to a peerage in the House of Lords, Lady Londonderry excelled in her role as Marquess. She joined numerous civic societies, including the Primrose League's Women's Grand Council in support of conservative politics. Londonderry's husband served as Lord Lieutenant of Ireland from 1886–9, during which time the first Home Rule bill was defeated and she became even more committed to the cause of sustaining Ireland's position within the British Empire. At the family's Ulster estate, Mount Stewart in county Down, Lady Londonderry hosted the highest-ranking politicians and royalty, from whom she sought support for her cause. A photograph taken in 1903 shows one such gathering: it includes King Edward VII, Queen

Alexandra, and Princess Victoria alongside Lord and Lady Londonderry.[10]

The UWUC was founded at a crucial time in the home rule debate; by then Ireland was entering a time of crisis with a staunch divide between nationalists and unionists on the issue. Londonderry was key to the council's formation and was elected as the first vice-president. In advance of the meeting on 23 January 1911, to formally constitute the council, a circular was issued advertising the meeting which stated that all discussion will be restricted to the subject of the union. This was a clear declaration that the anti-home rule movement must be placed above all other political issues, including the fight for women's suffrage. By 1911 the suffragette campaign had escalated across Ireland and Britain. Londonderry, a vehement anti-suffragist, ensured that the question of votes for women was a forbidden topic at any UWUC forum.

Londonderry chaired the well-attended meeting in a room at the YMCA building in Belfast city and delivered the speech in this section, titled 'The fight against home rule'. The meeting gathered wide media attention. The *Belfast News-Letter* was forthright in its endorsement of Londonderry, noting in its edition the next day that under her inspiring lead, the UWUC 'will prove a valuable weapon in the fight against Home Rule'.[11] It was, however, Londonderry's speech that gathered the most media attention, being reported in newspapers across Ireland and the United Kingdom. The *Belfast News-Letter* was also full of praise, describing her speech as a:

> model of destructive criticism against the Nationalist demand, and an eloquent plea for the maintenance of the Union in the interests of Great Britain as well as Ireland. . . . Lady Londonderry exposed the fraudulent character of the Home Rule agitation.[12]

The London-based *Globe* observed that 'not many ladies take so energetic a part in politics as Lady Londonderry.'[13] Reports in newspapers in the south of Ireland, including the national newspaper the *Irish Independent* and the *Dublin Daily Express*, quoted extracts from Londonderry's speech without comment.[14] Londonderry's speech not only inspired women at the meeting to join the UWUC, but the positive media attention ensured that women further afield were encouraged to join the anti-home rule campaign.

As Finley-Bowman notes, although the UWUC 'pledged to fill its membership with both "the peeress and peasant," the support of women like Theresa Londonderry, meaning wives of Ulster Unionist Peers and Ulster Unionist Members of Parliament, was pursued more urgently.'[15] By securing members with influence, membership of the council grew rapidly, as did their funds. The council was formed as a permanent association, with an office in Belfast at Donegal East Square overseeing the work of local branches throughout Ulster. A constitution was drawn up, clearly stating the sole aim of the organisation:

> to secure the maintenance in its integrity of the Legislative Union between Great Britain and Ireland, and for this purpose to resist all proposals . . . which have for their object the establishment of any form of an Irish Parliament . . . all other questions . . . shall be subordinated to the single issue of the maintenance of the Legislative Union.[16]

Minutes were recorded at each meeting; these highlight how the sole aim of the council was repeatedly stressed, including a pledge taken by members to restrict their discussions to anti-home rule. Londonderry later explained the reasoning behind the establishment of the UWUC:

> To express the feelings of the people of Ulster, who have fought with every means in their power to remain associated with England. . . . We banded ourselves together to see how we might best organise ourselves to impress our fellow-countrymen in England with the fact that Ulster will not consent to the tearing asunder of this country.[17]

This need to educate people as to the threat of home rule for Ireland was fundamental to the work of the council. Members spread this unionist message across Ireland, England and Scotland by speaking at meetings, distributing information pamphlets and organising intimate drawing-room gatherings.

When the Parliament Act passed in August 1911, the anti-home rule campaign became all the more crucial. The act reduced the power of the House of Lords by removing the veto over public bills with a power of delay. While the second Home Rule bill had been rejected in this way, the House of Lords would now be limited in its power. Londonderry protested that this 'deprived the Unionists of their greatest bulwark against Home Rule'.[18] Londonderry would see her concerns realised on 11 April 1912, when the Liberal Prime Minister, Henry Asquith, introduced the third Home Rule bill to parliament. While the bill was facing lengthy debate through the House of Commons, male unionist organisers Edward Carson, leader of the Irish Unionist Party, and James Craig, MP for East Down, sought a suitable way to retaliate. Carson and Craig were by then involved with organising volunteers to resist the Home Rule bill by military force if required.[19] Carson and Craig resolved to create a pledge for the men of Ulster to sign, formalising their commitment to resist home rule. The Ulster Solemn League and Covenant was drawn up based on the style of the Scottish National Covenant of 1638.[20] The 28 September 1912 was designated as Ulster Day when unionist men were asked to pledge to 'use all means which may be found necessary to defeat the present conspiracy to set up a Home Rule Parliament in Ireland'.[21] Carson believed that as women were excluded from voting in general elections, they should not be entitled to sign the Covenant.[22]

While such unionist activity was firmly embedded within the male realm, the UWUC organised a separate covenant for the women of Ulster to sign, the Women's Declaration. The UWUC organised signing centres across each constituency and implored women to come out and sign on Ulster Day. The declaration took a more passive approach than the sentiments expressed in the male covenant, yet it stated clearly the unionist women's dedication to anti-home rule:

> We, whose names are underwritten, women of Ulster, and loyal subjects of our gracious King, being firmly persuaded that Home Rule would be disastrous to our Country, desire to associate ourselves with the men of Ulster in their uncompromising opposition to the Home Rule Bill now before our Parliament, whereby it is proposed to drive Ulster out of her cherished place in the Constitution of the United Kingdom, and to place her under the domination and control of a Parliament of Ireland. Praying that from this calamity God will save Ireland, we hereto subscribe our names.[23]

An impressive number of women signed the declaration, in total 234,046 female signatures were recorded, of which 228,991 were based in Ulster, outnumbering male signatures taken in Ulster by over ten thousand.[24] Such affirmation ensured that Lady Londonderry and the UWUC gained respect from the leaders of the UUC, especially Carson.

The third Home Rule bill was carried over to the House of Lords in January 1913, where it was duly voted down. Without the power to veto, the defeat in the House of Lords simply meant that the bill now faced a two-year wait to pass into legislation. Londonderry was nominated as president of the UWUC in April 1913 when Mary Anna, Duchess of Abercorn stepped down following her husband's death. In reality, Londonderry had already been assuming the role of president before formally accepting the position. Londonderry continued leading a highly active anti-home rule campaign but now also directed the UWUC to support the Ulster Volunteer Force (UVF), a paramilitary force formed in January of that year. The council established a fund to provide for any volunteer who suffered disability in the course of protecting Ulster and to provide for their families in case of any loss of life. Additionally, the women of the UWUC formed an Ambulance and Nursing Corps and gathered necessary medical supplies. This was in preparation for a civil war with nationalists in the south of Ireland. The third Home Rule bill was finally passed as the Government of Ireland Act in May 1914, providing for home rule for the 32 counties of Ireland. When Britain declared war in August 1914, the enactment of the bill was postponed.

Londonderry continued to serve as president of the UWUC until 1919. On 28 January 1919, she addressed the UWUC annual meeting, announcing her retirement:

> The Ulster Women's Unionist Council was formed in 1911 to help the Men's Unionist Council to preserve the Union between England and Ireland, which was settled by Act of Parliament in 1800, (the then Lord Castlereagh being Chief Secretary for Ireland) and to express the feelings of the people of Ulster, who have fought with every means in their power to remain associated with England in a legislative union. I may say with truth that there never was a prouder moment in my life than that which I was elected President of such an influential body. I believe at the time, we were the largest number of women to band ourselves together for political work.[25]

Londonderry died on 15 March 1919, within just months of her resignation. The Government of Ireland Act, which became law on 23 December 1920, established provisions for two devolved parliaments; one based in Dublin governing 26 counties of Southern Ireland, and the second based in Belfast to govern Northern Ireland, comprising six counties of Ulster.

The UWUC was established with a single objective of defeating home rule for Ireland; the eventual partition of the country saw this aim defeated. However, six counties of Ulster did remain under British rule, and the council continued to support unionism in Northern Ireland. Following the partial enfranchisement of women in 1918, the UWUC no longer received support from male unionist leaders such as Edward Carson, who did not want to encourage women standing for election. Lady Londonderry's greatest legacy is the establishment of a viable and successful female unionist movement that continued to support female unionist political action in Ulster. Diane Urquhart notes that, 'perhaps most interestingly, the council also developed a female slant to unionists' anti-home rule agenda appealing to women's maternal and protective sensibilities with the claim that the security of their homes and well-being of their children would be endangered by home rule.'[26] Lady Londonderry's speech provides an insight into this interesting development.

6. The King & Queen at a House Party in Mount Stewart, 1903. Lady Londonderry second on left, beside King Edward VII. Courtesy of the National Portrait Gallery, London.

'It gives me great pleasure at this momentous time at a meeting comprised of Ulster women all banded together to confer and endeavour to see and know how best we may organise ourselves to impress our fellow countrymen in England with the fact that Ulster will not consent to the tearing asunder of this country from the predominant partner – England.

This is all the more necessary as we feel the question of home rule was not fairly put before the electors by the Government. First, we must realise that since 1895, when the battle of the Union was last fought, a great many changes have taken place. A new generation has arisen who thought till a few months ago, and still think judging from their attitude during [the] last general election, that the battle was over for all time. The English people have not seemingly noticed that Mr. Redmond and the Nationalist members have been fighting and manoeuvring to get an English Government entirely dependent on their votes, and they have succeeded in so doing. . . .

English people forget that Ireland manages her own local affairs in exactly the same way as England and Scotland do, by means of county councils. England and Ireland are now brought so close together by means of telephones, telegrams, and quick transit that distance is absolutely annihilated, and to think of separating politically two islands in such close proximity is absolutely beyond comprehension. Another point that we should endeavour to bring before the English people is this, that the Nationalist party have never acknowledged the King's Government in Ireland, nor the heads of that Government. The Nationalist party is essentially disloyal; none of the usual loyal toasts are ever drunk and the National Anthem is never sung at their gatherings, though they affect to have a great personal loyalty, in words, for the occupant of the Throne. It should also be remembered that every law-abiding citizen in Ireland is free and enjoys the same privileges as any one of his Majesty's subjects throughout the British Empire. . . .

Mr. Redmond and his friends have appealed the Irish-American extremists, who have subscribed the money which Mr. Redmond has had for this election. Though the savings banks of Ireland, as shown by statistics, are full of money, it was necessary for him to go to America to get funds for the last election. If Ireland really desires an independent Parliament, why does she not find the money herself? Mr. Redmond, speaking at Waterford in 1909 said, "first Home Rule – a subordinate Parliament: after that anything you like will be possible." That is substantially and truly the whole philosophy of the combination as between the Redmondite "constitutional" movement for Home Rule and the Irish-American movement, for snapping the last links that bind Ireland to England . . .

It seems inconceivable that so violent a change should be forced on loyal citizens in Ireland when half the electorate of Great Britain is against it, when Ireland is at last on the way to solve her problems in a peaceful way and simply because the balance of power happens for the moment to be in the hands of the politicians who have been the bane of the country.

. . . How constantly during last few months has the South African Union Federation been thrown in our teeth by Radical members and the Redmondites as an example of what Ireland would be under Home Rule?[27] But the facts of the case are entirely different. Every colony connected with the British Empire governs herself and is self-supporting. England does not finance them as she does Ireland. Everything goes to show that since Ireland has been united to England she has prospered in every way. "Union is strength" and is it likely that we in Ulster would give our consent to tearing England and Ireland asunder!

. . . I earnestly trust that this great and important meeting will be but the beginning of real and solid work and a thorough organising of the women of Ulster, and I earnestly appeal to the Loyalist women all over Ireland to do the same as we are going do – to begin work at once, to canvass voters, to trace removals, and to endeavour to bring every single voter to the poll during elections, so that every seat in Ulster shall be won for the Union. It has been well said that every election is now not won by speeches and meetings, but on the doorstep, by the distribution of literature and by personally canvassing the people. We must impress upon England and Scotland the fact that Ulster will not let herself be cut adrift. . . .

I feel certain that the women of Ulster will be in no way behind the men in striving for so noble a cause. The whole aim and object the Unionist party, and for which was formed, is to preserve the legislative Union between England and Ireland, and to consolidate the Empire.'[28]

FIVE

Margaret Hinchey
1870–1944

Speech to the Equal Suffrage League
Hotel Astor, New York

4 FEBRUARY 1914

'They say the Irish women don't want to vote.'

On 3 March 1913 Inez Milholland, a labour lawyer and a noted public speaker, donned a white cape and rode a white horse down Pennsylvania Avenue in Washington DC, leading a suffrage procession of two dozen floats and thousands of women.[1] The women's suffrage campaign in America was by then at its peak, and this spectacle was held the day before Woodrow Wilson's inauguration as 28th President of the United States of America. Wilson was not a supporter of votes for women, and this demonstration signalled that campaigners intended to pursue a dedicated course of action to change his mind. Margaret Hinchey, described by the *New York Times* as 'the Irish vote getter', became central to Wilson's eventual conversion to the cause of women's suffrage.[2] Hinchey, an Irish immigrant laundry worker, was among a group of women chosen to address Wilson on 2 February 1914 at the White House. The speech in this section was given by her to members of the Equal Suffrage League on her return to New York and highlights the importance of a franchise for working immigrant women.

Hinchey was born on 10 December 1870 in Limerick to Thomas Hinchey and his wife Mary (née Maloney.)[3] Details about her early life are sketchy at best. Hinchey emigrated to America sometime around 1897 and lived in New York until her death. By 1914 Hinchey had become an effective and highly respected public speaker, which led to the remarkable meeting between an immigrant laundry worker and the President of the United

7. Margaret Hinchey leading a demonstration on behalf of the Women's Trade Union League, New York, February 1914, the day after her meeting with President Woodrow Wilson. Courtesy of the Library of Congress.

States. The suffrage movement in America was originally led by white middle-class women who pursued equality with their male counterparts. Hinchey played a valuable role in securing votes for female immigrant workers to improve their deplorable and often dangerous working conditions. On 22 March 1911 Hinchey co-founded, along with four others, the Wage Earners' League for Woman Suffrage (WELWS), organised for and by factory workers.[4] One of the co-founders, Leonora O'Reilly the daughter of Irish immigrants, was elected president and became a close personal ally of Hinchey's. Days after the WELWS was formed, New York witnessed the greatest industrial tragedy in its history to date.

On Saturday afternoon, 25 March 1911, a fire broke out on the eighth floor of the ten-storey Asch building in Manhattan. The top three floors of the building housed the Triangle Shirtwaist Factory, with 600, mainly young female, immigrant workers crammed inside. The owners of the factory, Isaac Harris and Max Blanck, favoured locking exit doors during work hours to prevent workers from stealing material.[5] Locked doors on the premises that day ensured that the workers were trapped inside while the fire spread from the eighth floor upwards. Sixty-two women jumped out of ninth floor windows to their death while horrified New Yorkers looked on powerless. The ladders of the fire brigades would not reach beyond the sixth floor of the building. One hundred and forty-six people died in the fire, the oldest of whom was only 43 and the youngest among the dead were 14 years of age.[6]

Harris and Blanck were charged with manslaughter but were acquitted of any wrongdoing on 27 December 1911 by an all-male jury.

WELWS called for the empowerment of working immigrant women within the suffrage movement, citing the tragedy of the Triangle Shirtwaist Factory as a result of oppressive and dangerous working conditions. In order to give voice to female workers, Hinchey and her co-founders insisted that only working women could be 'full voting members of the organisation'.[7] Hinchey later joined the Women's Trade Union League (WTUL), and in January 1912, she helped organise a major laundry workers strike, resigning her position as forewoman of the laundry in which she worked. Through her numerous labour campaigns, Hinchey was eventually blacklisted from employment in the factories of New York. In October 1913, O'Reilly arranged employment for Hinchey as a paid organiser for the Woman Suffrage Party (WSP) based in New York city. This organisation was founded by Carrie Chapman Catt, then leader of the National American Women's Suffrage Association (NAWSA). Catt argued that women's suffrage could only be achieved nationally by first winning a vote on the issue in New York State. The WSP was formed to generate a grassroots demand for this change, and Hinchey excelled in her role as a public speaker for it.[8]

When the annual convention of the National American Suffrage Association met in Washington DC, Hinchey was invited to address the audience at the Columbia Theatre.[9] Speeches that day were also given by Jane Addams and State Senator Helen Ring Robinson; both women were from privileged white American backgrounds.[10] The gathered audience were not accustomed to hearing working immigrant women address them, but Hinchey's speech made a lasting impression.[11] Hinchey began her speech by describing the plight of female laundry workers in New York city who work 'seventeen and eighteen hours a day, standing over heavy machines for $3 and $3.50 a week'. Hinchey stressed that if these workers strike to seek higher pay or better conditions, they 'are clubbed by the police and by thugs hired by our employers, and in the courts our word is not taken and we are sent to prison'. She recounted a report by an agent of the Child Labor Society who investigated the tenements in New York's Greenwich Village, then home to a large immigrant population.[12] The agent 'found mothers with their small children sitting and standing around them. . . . They were working by a kerosene lamp and breathing its odor and they were all making artificial forget-me-nots. It takes 1,620 pieces of material to make a gross of forget-me-nots and the profit is only a few cents.'

Hinchey's speech gained public accolade. Not surprisingly, Hinchey was one of 35 women chosen to appeal directly to President Wilson for women's suffrage on 2 February 1914 at the White House. There is no transcript of what was said at the meeting that day, but two days later Hinchey recounted her experience in a speech to the New York Equal Suffrage League. She described the president's seemingly embarrassed reaction when she implored him to grant women the vote. Wilson bowed his head and attempted to avoid answering her, but she continued candidly saying, 'President, we women are able to take care of ourselves; that's why we want the vote. Why, when the men of Limerick were fighting the English, the women of Limerick were fighting too, and gave the Redcoats a bitter pill to swallow.'[13] Hinchey's speech in this section is taken from her address to the Equal Suffrage League. Her speech was printed in the *New York Times*, which reported how a 'laundry worker makes effective speech'.[14]

Hinchey began working at a young age, and it is unlikely that she received much formal education; letters remaining from her to Leonora O'Reilly show evidence of poor educational standards.[15] Due most likely to her lack of writing skills, Hinchey did not leave an archive of her papers or transcripts of her speeches, thus newspaper accounts are the most detailed record left to researchers. Hinchey's direct approach and engaging manner during her speech to the Equal Suffrage League gained her more attention from journalists. Hinchey also impressed Jeannette Rankin, Montana's most iconic suffragist. Rankin invited Hinchey to Montana, where she campaigned among working-class men with huge success. The *Daily Missoulian* newspaper described her as a remarkable orator, who made audiences 'laugh and weep, but applaud little because they fear to lose a word of her powerful appeal on behalf of women'.[16] Hinchey played a central role in securing votes for women in Montana. A referendum on the issue was called on 3 November 1914 at which 53 per cent of the men voted in favour of extending the vote to women. Montana became the tenth state in America to grant women suffrage, although this did not include Native American women.[17]

Hinchey returned to New York triumphant. She continued her work on behalf of the Woman Suffrage Party, focusing her efforts on Irish male voters.[18] A proposed referendum for suffrage in New York passed approval through state legislatures and would take place on 2 November 1915. In June of that year, Hinchey took to the trenches for the cause, climbing down to Irish labourers excavating for an extension to the subway line. Hinchey led a band of women carrying green banners with 'Votes for Women' emblazoned on them in Gaelic lettering.[19] She sought out voters in Catholic clubs and Irish societies across the city. Journalists from the *New York Times* accompanied Hinchey throughout much of her canvassing, describing how 'her face gets her into the men's meetings and her tongue keeps her there.'[20] Once she enters the room, the journalists admire how 'she has hardly opened her mouth before they are all shouting for "votes for women."' She teamed up with Margaret Foley, a Boston-born daughter of Irish immigrants, who was a paid organiser of the Massachusetts Woman Suffrage Association.[21] Newspapers reported 'Maggie and Maggie to shake for votes for women', extolling how the women injected 'Irish vim into the campaign'.[22] The referendum, held on 2 November 1915, was a huge disappointment for suffragists across the United States. On the question of a women's suffrage amendment to the New York Constitution, a total of 1,304,340 men voted, and the amendment was defeated by 194,984 votes.

Hinchey continued to collaborate with other Irish women campaigners in America. On 5 October 1916, she shared a stage with the renowned Irish labour activist, Mother Jones. Mary Harris Jones, originally from Cork, moved to North America as a child. She became known as Mother Jones when she began her long campaign for workers' rights in America. Jones' husband and four children died of yellow fever and she relocated to Chicago in 1867. Jones opened a seamstress shop which was destroyed in the Chicago fire of 1871, after which she became progressively more involved with socialist and labour causes. Jones was arrested on numerous occasions for purportedly enticing workers to strike in demand for better wages and employment conditions. She was described as 'the most dangerous woman in the country [America]' by a West Virginian prosecution attorney, during her trial for organising a meeting with striking miners in 1902.[23] She co-founded the Industrial Workers of the World, 'a radical labour union committed to the organisation of unskilled workers'.[24] Jones had a reputation as an inspiring orator and many volumes have been published that include her galvanising speeches.

Hinchey accompanied Jones to a meeting at Mozart Hall in New York to address wives of striking carmen, reports of numbers in attendance vary between 200 and 500 women. Jones reportedly urged the women to riot by declaring, 'You, the wives of the strikers, ought to be out raising hell. This is the fighting age. Put on your fighting clothes'.[25] As the women in attendance began to get boisterous, Hinchey took to the stage and appealed for calm. However, a small number of women left the hall and attacked one of the cars of the New York Railways Company and arrests followed. Hinchey was interviewed by a female journalist, Blanche Brace, who attended the meeting. Brace asked Hinchey if they had planned this riotous behaviour when organising the meeting. Hinchey's response showed how her protesting style differed immensely from that adopted by Jones. Hinchey replied she did not have anything to do with the demonstration and 'that every laundry-worker in New York would scorch Mayor Mitchell's shirts as often as he sent them to the laundry, just by way of a "sympathetic strike."'[26]

Hinchey concentrated her efforts once again on the suffrage campaign. A second referendum on women's voting rights was held in New York on 6 November 1917. In the run-up to the referendum, Hinchey stepped up her speaking engagements, and this time she went further by writing to Irish American newspapers. In a letter to the editor of the *Gaelic American*, the paper owned by Irish nationalist and exile John Devoy, Hinchey called on 'Irishmen true to their race and to themselves to champion woman suffrage'.[27] The letter written on 17 October was printed just days before the referendum. In it she reminded Irishmen that their fellow countrymen had fought and died for the independence of all Irish people during the Easter Rising, noting how 'a year ago in Ireland the new Constitution drawn up by Connolly, McDermott and other Irish patriots contained a clause that granted the ballot to Irish women.'

The amendment was carried by 54 per cent in favour, and the women of New York were granted full voting rights three years before the Nineteenth Amendment extended voting rights to women across the United States.[28] President Wilson altered his stance on the issue, and on 30 September 1918 he addressed senate imploring senators to extend voting rights to women, nationally.[29] Hinchey was a victim of her own success: when the referendum was passed in New York, she lost her job with the Woman Suffrage Party. Hinchey was forced to return to work in the laundries of New York.[30] She wrote to O'Reilly about the distress of her situation: 'I lost my bread and also lost the light when I lost my work – now I have to work long hours in darkness and take my rest in a cellar.'[31] She was by now critical of the WSP, seeing 'it is not a League for the working women only a political organisation.' Hinchey later secured a job with better working conditions as a subway guard. In 1919 a welfare bill was passed in New York to supposedly protect the conditions of working women. The bill banned women from working more than eight hours a day and restricted those hours to fall between 6 a.m. and 10 p.m. Hinchey lost her job because her work required more flexibility.

Hinchey returned to lobbying government for the rights of women workers. She secured a job as an elevator operator and told a journalist that 'I am working an eight-hour day now, but there is no law compelling my employer to keep within a fixed time limit.'[32] In 1920 she joined the National Woman's Party (NWP), which began campaigning for the Equal Rights Amendment to the Constitution. The proposed amendment would guarantee equality for all citizens, regardless of sex. Hinchey rose to the rank of secretary of the New York branch of the NWP, and in that role she met with yet another president of the United States.[33] In January 1926 Hinchey addressed President Calvin Coolidge, exclaiming that 'the people who are working for the welfare laws do not know what they do to working women. We ask for the Equal Rights Amendment to the Constitution to prevent the adoption of protective laws which only cost us our good jobs to give us others more poorly paid.'[34] Due to Hinchey's engaging oratory style, she appeared regularly in the pages of newspapers from 1911 until 1926. It is possible to trace Hinchey's life through these newspaper accounts; unfortunately she disappears from public notice after this time.

Hinchey was a progressive political activist; in 2021, women across America continue to campaign for the introduction of this Amendment to the Constitution to be ratified in every American state. Hinchey died in New York city in February 1944. No obituary was published to honour Maggie Hinchey, yet her remarkable life led her to meet with two presidents of the United States. Her speech provides a rare glimpse into the politics of this often-overlooked Irish female activist.

8. Margaret Hinchey addressing a group of striking carmen in Union Square, New York, October 1916. Courtesy of the Library of Congress.

'You ladies might think I had the nerve to go down to see the President. . . . You might think when I said I was a laundry woman that the President would get together his dirty collars and cuffs to give me, but he did nothing of the kind. He didn't give us the vote, but I think the 500 working women made a fine impression. I have great faith in the President. There were only 35 of us went in, but when he heard that the others were outside he wanted them all to come in and he had a warm, hearty handshake for every working woman.

When he listened to me he bowed his head and said yes, he knew. "I am in an embarrassing position," he said, "my party"—

We don't want him to get away from his party. We could help every true Dimicrat [sic] . . . if the women voted. I'm not a bit discouraged, but we've got to push every man of them to the very pin of his collar. No one has a right to go up to Albany and make a pill for me to swallow whether I want to or not.[35]

And I can't see for the love of me why the antis follow the suffragists to the White House.[36] That isn't the home.

And they say the Irish women don't want to vote. I'll go down to Washington and I'll tell them that the Irish do want the vote. I told an Irish woman that I met at a ball—I went to see the President, but

I went to a ball, too—that they said we didn't want the vote. "They have a nerve to say the Irish women don't want the vote," she said. "There's a society for every County in Ireland and not an anti will get into one of them. We'll have a procession march up Fifth Avenue with green banners with 'Erin go Bragh' and 'Votes for Women' on them," she said.[37]

We working women kept our noses to the grindstone and we never read the papers, but when some of you ladies began to work for the vote we saw that there might be something in it. There are different religions, but there is one God and He is constantly driving one thing into our hearts and consciences and that's justice. And all kinds of people say that the working woman doesn't want the vote. Maybe I'm speaking too broad, but you'll excuse me, I'm Irish.

I could tell you some things about the work of the women in the laundries that would put the hair of your head standing. . . . The engineers got a raise of $2 the other day. They have a strong union and votes back of it. They did not have to strike. You never hear of the "Big Six" striking, but when the shirt waist girls strike they are arrested for asking other girls not to take their positions.[38] We went to Mayor McClellan at that time saying we represented 30,000 women.[39]

"Thirty thousand women are nothing to me," he answered. Would he have said that of 30,000 voters? . . . All I ask of the women is to think. . . . If there was only one woman in the United States she should have the vote.'[40]

SIX

Agnes O'Farrelly – Úna Ní Fhaircheallaigh
1874–1951

Inaugural address at first meeting of Cumann na mBan
Wynns Hotel, Dublin

2 APRIL 1914

'Each cartridge will be a watchdog to fight the sanctity of the hearth.'

One hundred women met in a room of a Dublin city centre hotel at 4 p.m. on Thursday, 2 April 1914 to establish a nationalist organisation seeking liberty for Ireland. Cumann na mBan (Irish Women's Council) was formally established that day and a constitution adopted at Wynne's Hotel.[1] By October of that year, 60 branches had been established across the country with many local branches boasting membership of at least 100 women. At the end of that year, Cumann na mBan held a national convention, and the membership and configuration of the organisation continued to grow. The women of Cumann na mBan would play an active role in gaining Irish independence from British rule and in the major events before, during and after the foundation of the Irish Free State. However, the foundation of the organisation caused much controversy within the Irish feminist community at the time, mainly due to the speech in this section by Agnes O'Farrelly.

The formation of Cumann na mBan was connected with the foundation of the male nationalist paramilitary organisation the Irish Volunteers a few months earlier.[2] It was deemed necessary by Irish nationalists to form an organisation in response to the activities of the Ulster Volunteer Force (UVF). While the UVF was a male-centred paramilitary organisation with the purpose of opposing home rule for Ireland, unionist women played a pivotal role in that campaign.[3] The force of female political activity was

51

somewhat undervalued by the organisers of the Irish Volunteers. Eoin MacNeill oversaw the first recruitment meeting of the Irish Volunteers in the Rotunda Rink in Dublin. That meeting was attended by 7,000 people including a number of women, who were seated on 'a gallery specially set apart for them'.[4] The physical separation of the women at that meeting positioned them as observers of the male activity taking place. As historian Margaret Ward aptly comments, 'this exclusion appears even more insulting when one remembers that at that time a number of Irish suffragists were serving jail sentences because of their militant campaign for the vote.'[5] Ignoring the fact that so many Irish women were now politically active, there was little mention of women's roles in the fight to support home rule at that first meeting.

The manifesto of the Irish Volunteers, promulgated at the Rotunda meeting, embodied this male-centred approach by particularly specifying that 'their ranks are open to all able-bodied Irishmen.'[6] The only mention of the role of women in the manifesto was at a support level, noting that 'there will be work for women to do, and there are signs that the women of Ireland, true to their record, are especially enthusiastic for the success of the Irish Volunteers.'[7] There was a general welcome for the formation of the Irish Volunteers from a range of nationalist quarters. The *Sinn Féin Weekly* newspaper announced how the Irish Volunteers 'inaugurated itself with enthusiasm . . . so far as public feeling is concerned, it is strongly with the movement.'[8]

MacNeill, vice-president of the Gaelic League and a Professor of Early Irish History at University College Dublin (UCD), had been invited to lead the organising of the Irish Volunteers. His close friend Agnes O'Farrelly played a central role in the Gaelic League and was a lecturer in modern Irish, also at UCD. In 1902 O'Farrelly founded the Irish Association of Women Graduates and Candidate Graduates along with Mary Hayden, who became the first professor of modern history at UCD. Through this association, O'Farrelly campaigned for gender equality for women seeking education and for employment terms within academia. It is not surprising that O'Farrelly took a deep interest in the formation and development of the Irish Volunteers. Her support of the organisation and her own traditional views ensured that she was the ideal woman to preside over the inaugural meeting of a female auxiliary to the volunteers. Her speech in this section forms the initial basis on which the female nationalist organisation first operated.

From the outset it was clear that O'Farrelly was interested in attracting a particular type of woman into the new organisation. Ward observes that the meeting time of 4 p.m. on a Thursday afternoon was 'hardly convenient for working women'.[9] Indeed the timing ensured that the wives and daughters of Irish Volunteer members would attend, women who did not necessarily need to work in paid employment. O'Farrelly's speech at the inaugural meeting also established that members of Cumann na mBan would play a support role to the male organisation. Her speech was published in the pages of the *Irish Volunteer*, a paper printed to transmit orders and report on the activities of the volunteers. The placement of O'Farrelly's speech, under the heading 'Woman's work: In the national cause', on the same page as a poem by Francis Phillips highlighted the subordinate position of the women's organisation.[10] Phillips' poem, 'Cheer for the volunteer', idealised the masculinity of the Irish Volunteers from the opening verse:[11]

> Erin's pulse is beating still,
> Erin's soul has caught the thrill,
> Manly sons our ranks will fill,
> Manly hearts to lead 'em.

After her speech, O'Farrelly directed the adoption of the Cumann na mBan constitution, which set out four distinct objects:[12]

> To advance the cause of Irish liberty.
> To organise Irishwomen in furtherance of this object.
> To assist in arming and equipping a body of Irishmen for the defence of Ireland.
> To form a fund for these purposes to be called 'The defence of Ireland fund.'[13]

A provisional committee was formed, and it was decided that 'women of Irish birth or descent alone are eligible for membership.'[14] Mary Colum and Louise Gavan Duffy were appointed as joint secretaries. The activities of the members were laid out to include scouting during periods of enemy activity, despatch carrying, propaganda, removal and care of arms and ammunition, assisting in the escape of prisoners, collecting funds, and commandeering supplies. Such activities by Cumann members would prove to be of prime importance during the Easter Rising of 1916 and the War of Independence (1919–21).

Branches of Cumann na mBan were quickly established after that inaugural meeting. At a meeting two weeks later on 17 April at the Lord Mayor's residence, the Mansion House, the central branch and the Inghinidhe na hÉireann branches were formed.[15] Cumann na mBan continued to attract more members, and further branches were established throughout the country. However, the initial establishment of the organisation continued to cause much dispute. O'Farrelly's inaugural speech drew so much attention that other speakers on that day were greatly overshadowed, including even the flamboyant Countess Markievicz.[16] O'Farrelly's speech generated backlash from feminist activists, predominantly members of the

Irish Women's Franchise League. The dispute played out in the pages of national newspapers, consuming the time of the cumann working committee.

In an attempt to promote the work of Cumann na mBan, a large gathering was staged in the Mansion House on 2 May. Prominent female speakers took to the stage, including the historian and nationalist Alice Stopford Green who became a central organiser for arming the Irish Volunteers.[17] The event was disrupted by those expressing criticism of the organisation; these protests were led by Hanna Sheehy Skeffington. O'Farrelly asserted in a letter to the editor of the *Irish Independent* that 'Mrs. Sheehy Skeffington was not invited to speak, nor did she receive permission to do so. Neither is she a member of Cumann na mBan.'[18] She dismissed Sheehy Skeffington's claims that the organisation placed women in a subordinate position by asserting that the aim of 'the Irishwomen's Council is the demand for nationhood first and reforms within the nation after'.[19] A letter from Sheehy Skeffington duly appeared in the pages of the same paper the following day, with a scathing assessment that 'Any society which proposes to act merely as an "animated collecting box" for men cannot have the sympathy of any self-respecting woman.'[20] Sheehy Skeffington contrasted the foundation of the nationalist female organisation to that of the women's unionist group by noting:

> I venture to remind these women that the Ulster Unionist Women's Council acted on a different basis and that Sir Edward Carson had promised them in reward for their services a place in his Provisional Government; and I suggested that the Irishwomen's Council might see it on a footing of equality with men, and given a share in the Executive and in the Council of the men's organisation.[21]

The secretaries, Colum and Gavan Duffy, responded to the paper with indignation, stating that Cumann na mBan was 'in no sense a ladies' auxiliary society. It has its own committee, its own Constitution, and its own objects.'[22] The secretaries failed to mention the auxiliary roles of objects three and four: to assist with the work of volunteers and to fund their activities. Instead, the women focused on the first two objects, which they claimed were the 'most important'. As their ultimate proof, the women noted that many of the Cumann na mBan members were 'keen suffragists'. In later life Gavan Duffy admitted that she 'did not think her [O'Farrelly's] ideas advanced enough'.[23]

The onset of World War One caused a split in the Irish Volunteers that had deep implications for Cumann na mBan. John Redmond, the leader of the Irish Parliamentary Party, supported the British war effort. At a landmark speech to Irish Volunteers at Woodenbridge in county Wicklow, Redmond appealed to the volunteers to join the British army. Redmond's tactic was that by supporting the war effort, Ireland would be granted home rule. Eoin

MacNeill and many other Irish Volunteer leaders refused to support this call and insisted that the volunteers continue with their campaign to seek independence for Ireland. The volunteers split, with the vast majority supporting Redmond. The Irish Women's Franchise League demanded that Cumann na mBan declare their position. Redmond had made his position clear about not including suffrage for women in the Home Rule bill and therefore got no support from those quarters. Cumann na mBan held a meeting at their central branch on 6 October 1914 to discuss their way forward. A manifesto was drawn up, on which members voted. Members who disagreed with the new manifesto resigned, including the constitutional nationalist Bridget Dudley Edwards. The secretary of the central branch, Elizabeth Somers, issued a statement in the *Irish Volunteer*:[24]

> We feel bound to make the pronouncement that to urge or encourage Irish Volunteers in the British Army cannot, under any circumstances, be regarded as consistent with the work we have set ourselves to do. At this time when powerful influences are at work to confuse and obscure the national issue, and when Ireland needs all her sons, we call on Irishmen to remain in their own country and join the Army of the Irish Volunteers—the Army which was founded to gain Ireland's right and guard these rights when gained.[25]

The move to reject Redmond caused O'Farrelly to formally split from Cumann na mBan. This was a new beginning for the organisation as members sought to move forwards without the influence of O'Farrelly's traditional approach.

By the start of 1915, the face of Cumann na mBan began to change when Florence McCarthy was appointed as an organiser. McCarthy travelled the country on a recruiting drive, and branches were duly opened in towns and villages nationally. Ward notes that by the end of that year, 'Cumann na mBan had come a long way from the original image of a group of rather genteel women, earnestly collecting for the national cause. A militaristic fervour was sweeping through the organisation.'[26] Members wore a uniform, and branches were sectioned into squads with concentrated aims with a squad commander and section leaders. Some branches initiated rifle practice, with the Belfast members becoming the most proficient shots.[27] In August 1915 the fenian Jeremiah O'Donovan Rossa's remains were brought back from New York for burial at Glasnevin cemetery in Dublin. The funeral was a massive display of nationalism organised with the support of Cumann na mBan and the Irish Volunteers. An estimated 20,000 people took part in the funeral procession from Dublin's city centre to the graveyard. Uniformed members of Cumann na mBan were a prominent feature and led to a visible display of female paramilitary nationalism. The organisation had by then spread to cities outside of the island of Ireland, especially in areas with large Irish communities.

Testimony to the strength of the Cumann na mBan organisation abroad, Margaret Skinnider, a member of the Glasgow Cumann na mBan branch, became an expert shot and acted as a sniper during the Easter Rising, serving as a member of the Irish Citizen Army. Three Dublin branches were active during the rising, and Countess Markievicz was by then its president. Sixty Cumann na mBan members played key roles during the rising, although none played an active fighting role. Only women associated with the Irish Citizen Army, including Markievicz and Skinnider, took up arms during the rebellion. Cumann na mBan members engaged in crucial activities carrying despatches, nursing, and cooking in the midst of heavy fighting on the streets of Dublin.

After her split from Cumann na mBan, O'Farrelly remained active in nationalist circles. She launched an unsuccessful campaign for the reprieve of Roger Casement's death sentence in 1916 and later joined a committee of women to negotiate for peace and avoid a civil war in 1922. O'Farrelly stood unsuccessfully as an independent candidate in the general elections of 1923 and June 1927 for the NUI (National University of Ireland) constituency. She committed much of her time to expanding the use of Gaelic language and was a founding member of the Ulster College of Irish based in Donegal, where she also had a house in which she regularly entertained. She was appointed as professor of modern Irish at UCD in 1932, a position she held until her retirement in 1947.

In 1937, when the draft Constitution of Ireland was released, O'Farrelly along with other prominent feminists, including Sheehy Skeffington, campaigned to remove articles discriminating against women. O'Farrelly wrote poetry, prose and a novel, publishing in Irish and in English. Among her publications are *The Reign of Humbug* (1900), *Leabhar an Athar Eoghan* (1903), *Filidheacht Seghâin Uí Neachtâin* (1911), a novel *Grádh agus crádh* (1901), and poetic works *Out of the Depths* (1921) and *Áille an Domhain* (1927). O'Farrelly did not marry and lived at 38 Brighton Road, Rathgar in Dublin. She died on 5 November 1951. There is an oil painting of her by the esteemed Irish artist Seán Keating in the Royal Hibernian Academy Dublin.

On 3 April 2014, a plaque was unveiled by Jimmy Deenihan, Minister for Arts, Heritage and the Gaeltacht, to commemorate the centenary of the founding of Cumann na mBan. The plaque, on the site at Wynn's Hotel, notes that the inaugural meeting was presided over by Agnes O'Farrelly, who gave the inaugural address. The text of her speech remains as a reminder of the complex position of women's participation in the Irish nationalist movement.

9. Cumann na mBan protest outside Mountjoy Prison during the Irish War of Independence, 23 July 1921. Courtesy of the National Library of Ireland.

'We have called this meeting of Irishwomen to meet the present national crisis, and to take measures for the liberty of the nation. We have here women of various opinions in national life, but they are ready, we believe, to merge their divergent views in face of the common danger. . . .

We may be told that it is not the business of women to interfere. Is anyone so stupid as not to see that the liberty or the enslavement of the nation affects every home and every individual, man and woman and child in the country?

Are the women to stand idly by whilst the dearest and most sacred things in life are at stake? Is the independence of the men of Ireland of no consequence to those who share their hearths and homes? If it is not our business then, in the name of Heaven, whose business is it?

Is not the liberty of the children of Ireland, the life-blood of the nation, at stake? Is not our own liberty – the liberty of the women of Ireland – wrapped up with the common liberty of the nation? Is not the interest of the men of this country our interest? With them we stand or fall. . . .

Recent events following rapidly on each other show us clearly that the time has come for Irishwomen to back up by every legitimate means the efforts of their countrymen. . . .

We have, therefore, come here today to declare for the integrity of the nation, and for its inalienable right to self-government. We have come here to pledge ourselves to advance in every way in our power the liberty of Ireland. We offer our homage to the integrity and patriotism of the men who have given up the best years of their life to the fight initiated by Moore and Butt and Parnell; we offer our homage to the men who on Irish soil are forming the nucleus of a great Volunteer force for purposes of national defence and to back up and add the crowning triumph to the work of our representatives. . . . What can we women do to help, or must we allow our liberties and our future to be bartered to the Imperial interests of the moment? Our Provisional Committee in framing the rules of the Cumann na mBan or Irishwomen's Council, have outlined a scheme of work the details of which can be elaborated by the various branches of the organisation which, we have no doubt, will be at once formed throughout the country. Indeed in many centres the women are clamouring to be allowed to take a share in the long-drawn out struggle for liberty and nationhood. The hearts of the women are in the work. They only want to be organised. Wherever the men of Ireland are fighting for liberty they will not hesitate to help them. From the very nature of things the role of the women will be different from that of the men, and rightly so. It is not ours to undertake physically and directly the defence of the nation except in a last extremity and in the direct stress of war; yet, if such call were to come, I have no hesitation in saying that the spirit which animated the women of Limerick when they took the place of the men in the undefended breach is as much alive in Ireland to-day as it was two hundred years ago. Our first duty is to give our allegiance and support to the men who are fighting the cause of Ireland, whether in the British House of Commons or at home here in Ireland organizing National Volunteer corps. . . . We have considered ways and means to that end, and our Provisional Committee have come to the conclusion that our first and immediate duty is to help toward the National Volunteer movement in our midst. We see plainly that an untrained and unarmed people are but a weak and defenceless mob, and it is due to our national self-respect to organise and equip those Volunteer companies which have arisen almost spontaneously as the outward and visible expression of a long dormant idea. . . . Let this be distinctly understood. We shall do ourselves the honour of helping to arm and equip our National Volunteers. Each rifle we put in their hands will represent to us a bolt fastened behind the door of some Irish home to keep out the hostile stranger. Each cartridge will be a watchdog to fight the sanctity of the hearth. We shall start first-aid classes, and later on, if necessary, ambulance corps. Our constitution which will be formally placed before you embodies that idea and makes clear that the interests and the liberty of the nation we love and reverence will come first with us in this organisation.'[28]

SEVEN

Eva Gore-Booth
1870–1926

Dublin in the aftermath of the Easter Rising
The London Society

MAY 1916

'For one glorious week, Ireland had been free.'

On Sunday, 30 April 1916, at her home in London, Eva Gore-Booth read
a newspaper article that announced that her sister Countess Markievicz
had been killed in Dublin.[1] The article described the horrors of the Easter
Rising, a rebellion to overthrow British rule and establish an independent
Ireland. The account included details of her sister's body being found in St
Stephen's Green in the centre of Dublin city. After a traumatic search for
more information, Gore-Booth confirmed that her sister had not been killed
but had played a leading role in the fighting and was now imprisoned by the
British authorities.

In the immediate aftermath of the rising, information was slow to pass
from Ireland to England, resulting in sensationalist articles such as the
Lloyd's Weekly Newspaper account that Gore-Booth had read. The lines of
communication had been severed by Irish republicans who controlled the
General Post Office (GPO), and telegraph poles had been badly damaged
during fighting. Ireland was placed under martial law, and all travel in to
or out of the country was heavily restricted. Within a few days Gore-Booth
managed to receive special permission to enter Ireland to visit her sister in
prison. She travelled by ship from Holyhead to Dublin with her partner
Esther Roper. Gore-Booth was by then a successful author and a prominent
campaigner for social reform in England. The events that followed over the
coming days inspired her to write an eyewitness account that she presented

to the London Society on her return to England. The speech in this section provides one of the first accounts of Dublin in the aftermath of the Rising given to an English audience.

The Easter Rising occurred in the midst of World War One. Nationalist leaders, including Patrick Pearse, viewed the war as an ideal opportunity to strike a blow for Irish freedom, evoking Daniel O'Connell's declaration that England's difficulty is Ireland's opportunity.[2] The British public were horrified that Irish people would plan a rebellion at a time when tens of thousands of British men were being killed in the war against Germany and her allies. Gore-Booth's speech was, above all, an attempt to educate people in England about why Irish people had taken violent action against British forces. This objective is particularly evident when Gore-Booth concludes the piece with a story of her return journey from Dublin to London. After disembarking at Holyhead port in Wales, Gore-Booth caught a train to London; a woman travelling in the same carriage talked loudly about the rebellion and declared the Irish to be ungrateful and cowardly. This story was recounted by Gore-Booth as a typical example of how people in England misunderstood the Irish pursuit of liberty and freedom.

On Easter Monday, 24 April 1916, a group of Irish nationalists launched a strike for freedom from British oppression. Patrick Pearse stood at the front steps of the GPO on Sackville Street, now O'Connell Street, in the centre of Dublin city and announced the Republic of Ireland, Poblacht na hÉireann. Pearse read a proclamation that had been signed by him and the other members of the provisional government of Ireland: Thomas Clarke, Seán MacDiarmada, James Connolly, Thomas MacDonagh, Éamonn Ceannt and Joseph Plunkett. The flag of the republic was raised and so began an armed rebellion. The main fighting forces were the Irish Volunteers and the Irish Citizen Army, with Cumann na mBan directly active.

Markievicz was centrally engaged in the rebellion and took up arms as an Irish Citizen Army commandant; she was second-in-command to Michael Mallin, based initially in Stephen's Green. Within hours British snipers took up position in buildings overlooking the green, and troops on the roof of the Shelbourne Hotel directed machine gun fire into the park. It was impossible for the rebels to maintain their position. On Tuesday, Mallin, Markievicz and their troops relocated to the enclosed premises of the College of Surgeons nearby. Within days Dublin city was in ruins, and numerous unarmed civilians, as well as many nationalist fighters and British soldiers, were killed or wounded. Over 16,000 British soldiers were now in position fighting against the Irish insurgents. Machine guns placed at Trinity College blasted Sackville Street, and a British patrol vessel, the *Helga*, shelled buildings from the River Liffey. Under heavy fire Irish insurgents retreated from the GPO. The provisional government agreed to surrender on Saturday, 29 April. At

12.45 p.m. Cumann na mBan member Nurse Elizabeth O'Farrell was sent to inform General Lowe that Pearse would negotiate a surrender. Pearse later surrendered unconditionally, 'in order to prevent the further slaughter of Dublin citizens'.[3]

Gore-Booth arrived in Dublin amid stories of British military atrocities. During the days after the rebellion, bodies were discovered buried in cellars and yards of buildings in the North King Street area of the city. It transpired that at least 14 innocent civilians had been dragged from their homes and shot, supposedly by South Staffordshire Regiment soldiers.[4] Gore-Booth's speech begins with an emotional description of sailing into Dublin Bay, but she quickly changes to an account of how Ireland has been subjected to military oppression at the hands of British forces for generations.

Gore-Booth was in Dublin when the worst of the reprisals began. General John Maxwell, appointed as Commander-in-Chief of Ireland, immediately began exacting what he considered to be justice. He organised closed court-martials for all the leaders of the Rising and those presumed to be leaders. Unlike civil trials, court-martials did not include a jury or allow legal counsel, and sentencing could be more severe. In these trials the sentence for many was death. The executions began swiftly, when Pearse, Clarke and MacDonagh were shot on Wednesday, 3 May, only three days after the fighting had stopped. All of these executions took place by firing squad in Kilmainham Gaol in Dublin city. Gore-Booth focuses much attention on the cruelty of the executions both for those executed and the men who were ordered to kill them.

Markievicz was being held at Kilmainham Gaol when many of her friends were executed. She was court-martialled on 4 May under a charge that she 'did take part in an armed rebellion and in the waging of war against His Majesty the King, such act being of such a nature as to be calculated to be prejudicial to the Defence of the Realm and being done with the intention and for the purpose of assisting the enemy'.[5] Markievicz pleaded not guilty to the charge but guilty of attempting to 'cause disaffection among the civilian population of His Majesty'.[6] Under order of the convening officer, Maxwell, and the court-martial president, Brig-General C. J. Blackader, Markievicz was sentenced to death by firing squad. Gore-Booth instantly appealed this sentence. Two days later she learnt from Prime Minister Asquith's secretary that Markievicz's sentence was commuted to penal servitude for life. Gore-Booth would spend many of her remaining years vigorously campaigning against capital punishment in England.

The details mentioned by Gore-Booth in her speech inspired her into action in support of those affected by the rising. She called to Markievicz's home at Surrey House in the Dublin suburb of Rathmines, which had been seized by the British military and ransacked. The soldiers had crushed every one of Markievicz's lantern slides, ripped her clothes and dug up the garden. While Gore-Booth and Roper surveyed the house, a large crowd gathered outside. The resemblance between the sisters was so striking that local people mistook Gore-Booth for Markievicz, whom they thought had escaped from prison and returned home. The fact that Gore-Booth could easily be mistaken for her rebel sister caused serious concern that she would be shot in error. Gore-Booth was not deterred.

Gore-Booth had lost many friends through the events of the rebellion, including Francis Sheehy Skeffington, whom she refers to as 'Skeffy' in her speech. While he supported the cause of Irish freedom, Sheehy Skeffington did not take up arms in the military uprising as he was a devoted pacifist. He was arrested during the rebellion and brought to Portobello Barracks, where he was searched and questioned further. Without any explanation the captain of the guard, J. C. Bowen-Colthurst, brought Sheehy Skeffington and two other unarmed civilian men into the yard of the barracks. On his order all three men were illegally shot dead by a firing squad.[7] Once Gore-Booth learnt about the death of Sheehy Skeffington, she wrote to his wife Hanna, 'I am so appalled and miserable about Sheehy Skeffington. Your suffering is too dreadful. The story is shocking and horrifying.'[8]

Gore-Booth visited Hanna Sheehy Skeffington at her home, 11 Grosvenor Place, near Markievicz's house. When Gore-Booth arrived, she was horrified to see the recently widowed woman and her young son sitting in the front room of a dishevelled house with broken windows. Shortly after Sheehy Skeffington was killed, Bowen-Colthurst had arrived at Grosvenor Place with a company of soldiers seeking evidence to justify the shooting. Gore-Booth later wrote of the horror, noting how Bowen-Colthurst 'raided his victim's house, fired a volley into the window and kept the seven-year-old boy and his mother under arrest while he searched and [ran]sacked the house'.[9] Gore-Booth felt a special affinity with the murdered man, whom, like James Connolly, she described as 'an enthusiast on the subject of the freedom of women'.[10] After listening to Hanna Sheehy Skeffington that day, Gore-Booth rationalised why 'Skeffy' had been shot: 'militarism had struck down its worst enemy – unarmed yet insurgent Idealism.'[11]

Gore-Booth was also concerned by the fate of Michael Mallin's family; he had been executed four days before her prison visit. Markievicz mentioned this as the case of her dead colleague's wife. Mallin and his wife, Agnes, had a young family: three sons and one daughter. Agnes was pregnant at the time of Mallin's execution, and she went into hiding with her children. Gore-Booth was able to track the whereabouts of Agnes, and she provided her with financial aid and introduced her to a local Inchicore priest, Fr Ryan, who agreed to help protect the Mallin family. Agnes gave birth to a baby girl, Mary Constance, four months after her husband was executed.

In her speech, Gore-Booth makes mention of Roger Casement, who had been arrested before the Easter Rising began. He was captured on Banna Strand, on the coast of county Kerry, where he landed from a German U-boat. The submarine was meant to rendezvous with the *Aud*, a German ship captained by Karl Spindler that was carrying a shipment of guns to arm the Irish Volunteers.[12] Casement was treated differently to the other leaders of the Rising as he had previously been employed by the British Foreign Service. In 1911 Casement had been knighted for his humanitarian work in the Congo and Brazil. Through his investigations he exposed how the owners of rubber plantations were exploiting indigenous locals through a system akin to slavery. Casement was sentenced to death in a public trial at the Old Bailey for his part in the Rising, a trial that Gore-Booth attended to offer him support. She became a central figure in the campaign for the reprieve of Casement's death sentence.

Gore-Booth launched a high-profile international campaign for his reprieve, claiming that Casement was attempting to stop the rebellion and therefore his charge of high treason and this death sentence should be dropped. She persistently lobbied the highest-ranking politicians, including Prime Minister Asquith; the Foreign Secretary, Sir Edward Grey; Liberal peer Lord James Bryce; the director of the war trade department, Lord Alfred Emmott; and the Home Secretary, Herbert Samuel. An enquiry was launched based on Gore-Booth's claims. A confidential report held in the British parliamentary papers confirms that the information sent by Gore-Booth – including statements from witnesses, her letter of testimony and her own account of Casement's circumstances – was circulated to members of the British Cabinet as late as 21 July 1916.[13] Ultimately, she was unsuccessful, and Casement was executed on 3 August at Pentonville Prison.

Her devotion to Casement and to Sheehy Skeffington continued long after their deaths. In 1918 Gore-Booth published a volume of poetry, *Broken Glory*, which is dedicated to the memory of 3 August 1916, the date of Casement's execution.[14] The volume comprises 27 poems that focus on the atrocities of the Easter Rising and the Great War. Her poem 'Government' equates the killing of Christ with the execution of Casement: 'Jesus Christ a thousand years ago . . . And Roger Casement, just the other day.'[15] Similar religious imagery is evident in her poem 'Francis Sheehy Skeffington; Dublin, April 26, 1916', comparing Sheehy Skeffington with Jesus, 'who in the Olive Garden agonized'.[16] This small volume is packed with strong political sentiments and includes a set of poems dedicated to Markievicz in prison.[17]

Although mainly remembered as a poet and a suffragist, through her experiences of the Easter Rising, Gore-Booth became a tireless campaigner for Irish independence and human rights. She actively supported contentious objectors to war, through the work of the No Conscription Fellowship.

She contributed to the successful overturning of a law to extend military conscription to Ireland in 1918 through an intense media campaign, and she continued to advocate for the rights of political prisoners.

Gore-Booth died of colon cancer on 30 June 1926 at her home in Hampstead with Esther by her bedside. A stained-glass window was designed in 1928 incorporating an image of Gore-Booth with an extract from one of her poems underneath. The window was installed in the Round House in Ancoats, Manchester, where she taught poetry classes as part of the University Settlement project to educate local factory women. In 1986 the building was demolished, and the current whereabouts of the stained-glass window is unknown. There are no other memorials to Eva Gore-Booth. Esther Roper dedicated the remaining years of her life to publishing Gore-Booth's final works and editing a complete edition of her poetry. When Esther died in 1938, she was buried with Eva in a single plot at St John's churchyard in Hampstead. Gore-Booth's speech provides vital insights into the plight of Irish people during tumultuous years and is a powerful reminder of her tireless work to reconcile these injustices.

RETURN OF I.R.A. PRISONERS, JUNE, 1917.
COUNTESS MARKIEVICZ ARRIVES AT LIBERTY HALL, DUBLIN.

10. Eva Gore-Booth pictured in front of her sister, Countess Markievicz, at a public reception following Markievicz's release from prison, Dublin, June 1917. Courtesy of the Irish Capuchin Provincial Archives.

'As the *Leinster* steamed into Dublin Bay on that May morning of 1916 the world seemed transfigured with beauty and delight. . . . Yet, as the syren suddenly shrieked out its harsh warning, the sight of a great mass of khaki-clad soldiers crowding round the gangway shook the glamour of the scene and brought queer memories of past generations.

. . . An endless procession of soldiers, with every kind of weapon, always on the same errand, always going, as they are going now, to conquer and hold down Ireland.

. . . Ten minutes after that the world turned black, as I read the words that shrieked in huge letters from every hoarding in the town: "Execution of James Connolly." "James Connolly shot this morning."
. . .

Afterwards, the story went round that one of those told to shoot him was a miner, one who had personal cause of gratitude to him.[18] But he did not know who it was he was going to shoot. Anyway, he stood there with the rest, submissively waiting for the word of command. So would any other soldier, the very man who joked about executions would have done it. Without anger or hate or any conscious cruelty, but simply because he was told to. So insidious a thing is that vile creeping obedience that deprives man of his sense of right and wrong, his very soul and will and mind. . . .

And my thoughts rushed back to that dreadful Sunday in London when I had read in *Lloyd's Weekly News* a circumstantial account of the finding of my sister's dead body in Stephen's Green, and of the terrible days that followed, when I had almost wished the discredited story had been true, so much worse does it seem to the human mind to be executed coldly and deliberately at a certain hour by the clock than to be killed in the hurry and excitement of battle. Perhaps this is because such a death is so wholly unnatural. . . .

But the worst had not happened. My sister, condemned to death for her part in the Rebellion, had been reprieved.

And now I was on my way to visit her in prison. . . .

The Dublin streets were terrible. They had a sort of muddled desperate look, rather like but infinitely more tragic than the look one used to see in London on an air-raid night, just after the warning was given. As if everybody, even the very houses, were crouching down, hiding from something. . . .

The Mountjoy porter looked at our permits, and presently the big iron gate was unlocked and we crossed the yard into that inner building which is the prison itself. As I walked through the long corridor, my mind was obsessed by one horrible thought: "They have shot all her friends; James Connolly and Eamon Ceannt only that day: did she know? should I have to tell her?" Afterwards I knew that this was a quite unnecessary anxiety. She knew everything. The shots that killed Padraic Pearse and the others she had listened to morning after morning in her cell at Kilmainham.

Suddenly there was her face behind a sort of cage: it was cut into sections by the cross-bars. But one could half see, half guess how calm and smiling she was.

She talked very fast, and was full of all sorts of commissions she wanted carried out, asked a great many questions and seemed only really puzzled by one thing: "Why on earth did they shoot Skeffy?" she said. "After all, he wasn't in it. He didn't even believe in fighting. What did it mean?"

At the time I could not answer her: afterwards I found out. . . .

There was much to hear: her adventures in the Rebellion, details of her court-martial, her anxiety for the wife of a dead colleague who was ill, in hiding and without money. Many and very insufficient directions as to how to find her. About her own treatment the prisoner had not much to say. She was a "convict" and a "lifer" and that was all about it. And anyway, it was splendidly worth while.

For one glorious week, Ireland had been free . . . and then back she went to stories of that wonderful time, of the night-scouting and the trench in Stephen's Green and the machine-gun on the Shelbourne and how they were forced to retreat into the College of Surgeons. And how they could have held out for days, and the shock and grief of the order to surrender on that Sunday morning when I had run up and down London trying to find out if she was really dead. And she told of the executed colleague who had marched with her down Thomas Street where Emmet had been hung a hundred years ago, for the same cause, by the same power. . . .

Roger Casement had been taken from Arbour Hill Barracks to the Tower. There was a feeling of strain and embarrassment everywhere. People broke down and wept for very little, even in the streets. Dazed and miserable, with the sound of the bombs still in their ears, they were beginning to collect in groups and tell one another stories of individual sufferings, injustices and atrocities. . . .

On the way back to London about a week later, travelling up from Holyhead, was a woman in the carriage with us who talked about the Rebellion. "Dreadful people the Irish," she was saying, "so cowardly too, and ungrateful, to stab us in the back like that, after all we've done for them!"[19]

EIGHT

Hanna Sheehy Skeffington
1877–1946

Speech on anti-conscription in Ireland
Madison Square Garden, New York City

4 MAY 1918

'I for one will lose no sleep at any time over the extinction of the British Empire.'

Hanna Sheehy Skeffington travelled to America in December 1916, in the wake of the Easter Rising and the murder of her husband Francis (Frank). At that time an estimated 20 million people in America were Irish by descent, and Irish America played an influential role during the campaign for Irish independence. During her 18-month stay, Sheehy Skeffington addressed more than 250 meetings of interested groups and spoke at political rallies. Before she returned to Ireland, she delivered the speech in this section to an audience at Madison Square Garden. The venue was a massive indoor arena in Manhattan that hosted large-scale public events. A secret service agent, tasked with reporting on her activities, duly recorded every word that Sheehy Skeffington said, a fact of which she was most aware and commented on in her speech. The agent also reported the reaction of her audience, unwittingly showcasing her flair for rousing public speeches. As Sheehy Skeffington's biographer Margaret Ward observes, 'her oratory and ability to stir her audience are vividly demonstrated in the report.'[1]

The actions of British authorities during and after the Easter Rising were causing a reverse effect to that intended. While the authorities intended to suppress the Irish nationalist movement, the executed leaders became martyrs for their cause, and many people at home and abroad now sympathised with the plight of Irish nationalism. Political instability in Ireland was growing. It seemed imperative to alert Irish America to the current crisis in Ireland.

John Byrne, a friend of Frank's now living in America, appealed to Sheehy Skeffington to 'put her case before the American people'.[2] She resolved to take up this challenge and arranged to smuggle documents pertaining to British atrocities, including the murder of her husband, with her into America. Her primary goal was to appeal for American recognition of an Irish republic by highlighting the injustices that Irish people faced under British rule.

Sheehy Skeffington was being closely monitored by British intelligence in Ireland. The process of getting to America would be a long and complicated ordeal, complete with disguises and assumed identities – a plan that Ward notes 'might appear more appropriate in the pages of a spy novel'.[3] Hanna managed to get a ferry from Belfast to Scotland, where she adopted a new identity for her and her son, Owen. In Scotland, she was aided by Margaret Skinnider, who had returned to her home in Glasgow to recover from injuries she sustained fighting in the rising.[4] Hanna returned briefly to Dublin and continued preparations for her travel to America and to arrange speaking engagements while there. When the timing was right, she returned to Glasgow, where she assumed again her false identity of Mrs Gribbin, the name of a Scottish woman who had emigrated to America. She was reunited with Owen, who was given the new identity of Eugene Gribbin. Together they sailed to America, arriving in New York in December 1916 where they were joined by Skinnider.

Sheehy Skeffington had not evaded the long arm of British intelligence, who, on discovering her travel arrangements, demanded that American authorities detain her on arrival and deport her and Owen back to Ireland. Hanna and Owen successfully disembarked without the attention of law enforcement. However, Hanna was accused by British authorities of breaking the Defence of the Realm Act, a law that enforced strict codes of censorship on activities thought to unsettle the British war effort. She would now face a precarious situation when she elected to return to Ireland, a fact which she also focused on in her speech.

By 1918 Sheehy Skeffington was a well-seasoned political campaigner. Along with Margaret Cousins she had established the Irish Women's Franchise League in 1908, the first militant suffrage organisation in Ireland. She campaigned vigorously for votes for women, a cause for which she had been arrested and imprisoned on many occasions. Now she focussed her attention to the cause of Irish independence and seeking justice for her husband. This speech was the final one given during her American tour and focuses on the issues surrounding her husband's murder by a British officer and on a cause that Frank had fought for, namely, anti-conscription.

The recruitment of Irish men into the British armed forces was keenly encouraged by John Redmond who pledged to support the British war effort and appealed to the men of the Irish Volunteers to enlist.[5] Frank Sheehy

Skeffington instantly began organising anti-military meetings in Dublin, attesting that Redmond simply 'sold Irish people to the British army for nothing'.[6] Frank conducted anti-recruitment meetings on a regular basis at Beresford Place in Dublin. At one such meeting on 23 May 1915, he declared that 'The only power that has ever done us any harm is England; the only power that is doing us any harm now is England.'[7] An undercover Royal Irish Constable (RIC), Patrick McCarthy, attended the meeting and made a complete report of Skeffington's speech to British military intelligence. Skeffington was arrested under the Defence of the Realm Act. His speech was deemed to cause 'disaffection and to prejudice recruiting'.[8] He was sentenced to six months imprisonment with hard labour and bail of £50.

On his release from prison, Frank travelled to New York, where he stepped up his campaign against Ireland's inclusion in the Imperial war effort. He made speeches and wrote several articles for American newspapers vilifying Redmond's decision. By October 1915 headlines in the *New York Times* declared that 'Redmond committed his country to the war for nothing.'[9] It seemed only fitting that now Hanna would follow up on this cause in New York.

Frank did not take up arms in the Rising as he was a devoted pacifist; instead he attempted to keep order in Dublin city by preventing the looting of shops during the fighting. Together Frank and Hanna formed a citizens' militia, enlisting the help of many priests and other civilians. On Tuesday, 25 April 1916, Frank called a public meeting in the head office of the Irish Women's Franchise League at Westmorland Chambers, in the shadow of the fighting. On his way home that evening, Frank was arrested and questioned; he was unarmed and did not resist. Members of the RIC had been closely monitoring him since he began his anti-recruitment activities. This time no charge was placed against him, but he was taken to Portobello Barracks where he was searched and questioned further. The following morning, without any explanation, the captain of the guard, J. C. Bowen-Colthurst, brought Frank and two other civilian men into the yard of the barracks. On his order all three men were shot dead by a firing squad. Neither of the other two men – Thomas Dickson, editor of a loyalist paper the *Eye-Opener*, and Patrick McIntyre, editor of the anti-Larkin paper the *Searchlight* – had any connection with the Rising.

Hanna published and circulated a detailed statement describing her husband's unlawful execution and the harassment experienced by her and her family. This statement was the first step in seeking a full enquiry into his murder. Eva Gore-Booth described how Hanna 'pursued her relentless and irresistible way, disentangling the motives and circumstances of the murder, and bringing it home to the responsible authorities'.[10] Sheehy Skeffington lobbied the Prime Minister's office seeking justice. Eventually, the British Prime Minister, Henry Asquith, was compelled to grant an official enquiry into Frank's death.[11] In August 1916, Bowen-Colthurst was tried by court martial, found guilty of murder, and declared insane.[12] He was sent to Broadmoor Criminal Asylum but later discharged, and it was rumoured that he retired from service receiving half-pay.[13] This was certainly not the justice that Sheehy Skeffington sought.

Weeks before Sheehy Skeffington delivered her speech at Madison Square Garden, the home rule debate and the cause of conscription reached a crisis situation in Ireland. The Irish Convention, a panel of Irish representatives established by then Prime Minister Lloyd George reached their decision on the appropriate action to establish home rule for Ireland. In March 1918 the convention recommended the enactment of the Irish Home Rule bill under the condition that conscription would be extended to Ireland. On 16 April 1918 the extension of the Military Service bill, enforcing conscription in Ireland, was announced. This new legislation would ensure that all Irish men between the ages of 18 and 50 years of age would be conscripted to join the British army. On 18 March a meeting was held in the Lord Mayor of Dublin's residence at the Mansion House. The Lord Mayor, Lawrence O'Neill, hosted the meeting which saw the formation of the Irish Anti-Conscription Committee. The committee developed an anti-conscription pledge, denying 'the right of the British government to enforce compulsory service in this country, we pledge ourselves solemnly to one another to resist conscription by the most effective means at our disposal'.[14] As noted by Hanna in her speech, this pledge was based on one that Frank had previously established.

By the end of April, British intelligence in Ireland claimed to have uncovered a Sinn Féin plot with Germany. By 18 May, 73 members of the organisation, including Countess Markievicz, had been imprisoned. It was now imperative to gain American support against the conscription of Irish men into the British army, a task with which Sheehy Skeffington fully engaged. A full outline of the proceedings of the anti-conscription conference in the Mansion House was compiled by Éamon de Valera and addressed to Woodrow Wilson, then president of America. Lord Mayor O'Neill arranged to personally meet with Wilson and give him the documents, which were later published as a pamphlet.[15]

Sheehy Skeffington's speech was a vital part of the Irish strategy, given at a significant time in the campaign. She concluded by stating that 'if conscription is defeated in Ireland, it will be defeated by the spirit of Sinn Féin.' Her audience is reported as cheering wildly and waving rebel flags and hats at this final remark. Despite British insistence, forced conscription of Irish men into the British army was never introduced. Irish women would prove to be the main instigators behind the successful rejection of this legal extension.[16]

Sheehy Skeffington and her son departed for Ireland on 27 June 1918; American authorities cleared them to travel home. Hanna was, however, subjected to a strip search before boarding the ship. She arrived back in Dublin as a dedicated nationalist and supporter of Sinn Féin. Sheehy Skeffington is undoubtedly one of the most significant feminist activists of twentieth-century Ireland. Her radical feminist activism spanned five decades. She made significant contributions to the causes of nationalism and pacifism and the formation of the Irish Free State and she engaged with political affairs in Europe and America. Her American tour established her place in Irish nationalist politics. One month after Hanna Sheehy Skeffington died, the fifth edition of her lecture 'British militarism as I have known it' appeared in print.[17] This was the first lecture given by Sheehy Skeffington on her tour of America, to a packed audience at the illustrious Carnegie Hall on 6 January 1917. Four earlier editions had sold out. Sheehy Skeffington had written a new foreword to the publication in the weeks before she died, asserting her commitment to the fight against British imperialism.

Right up to the point that death took her, Hanna was politically active and, as the title of Ward's biography attests, 'fearless'. She continued to write letters and articles in support of numerous causes. During the strike by national school teachers in 1946, she reminded readers of the *Irish Press* of the gender inequalities that teachers faced, noting how women teachers make up 65 per cent of the teacher union members, yet they are denied 'equal pay for equal work while requiring the same educational training. Indeed, in many cases laying on the women extra burdens.'[18] This letter was to be her last to the newspaper. Sheehy Skeffington died following a heart attack on 20 April 1946. She is now buried bedside Frank in Glasnevin Cemetery in Dublin.[19]

President Michael D. Higgins unveiled a memorial plaque commemorating Sheehy Skeffington's campaign for female suffrage on 13 June 2018, as part of the centenary celebrations of votes for women. The plaque on Ship Street, beside the entrance to Dublin Castle, is at the site where Sheehy Skeffington and members of the Irish Women's Franchise League broke windows as part of a suffragette protest, for which the women served one month in prison. Her place in Irish history has been established through years of research and many publications written by historian Margaret Ward. Hanna Sheehy Skeffington's speeches remain as testimony of her formidable character.

11. Hanna Sheehy Skeffington with her son, Owen, New York, 1918. Courtesy of the Library of Congress.

'Mr Chairman, ladies and gentlemen, at this late hour I am not going to keep you by making a speech. I feel that I have spoken so often already in this country that I would now prefer to leave it and go home to help keep Ireland free from conscription and safe for democracy (*applause*). This was to have been my last meeting in New York but the British Government has decided otherwise. I learned last week

74

in California that my passport to Ireland has been withdrawn. I think I know the reason for that, as you know, Mr Preston, the Federal Attorney in San Francisco, was very anxious to lock me up in Angel Island (*hisses*). Mr Preston, however, did not succeed and it seemed to me that England would like Uncle Sam to lock me up, and therefore she has refused a passport, but I have confidence that Uncle Sam will not lock me up (*applause*). And it seems to me that if it is to be decided in this country that it is treason to the United States to talk against conscription in Ireland, then I think the best place for any self-respecting man or woman is prison (*wild applause*). And my friends, if enough of you, as apparently you do, agree with that sentiment, there will not be prisons big enough to hold us Irish in this country (*applause*). The ground has been amply and ably covered by the other speakers. I am not going to weary you now by going over reasons against conscription. People have said to me "But the British Empire may depend upon Irish conscription." Now, I say deliberately this, – and I hope the Secret Service men are listening to me and have their pencils sharp (*wild applause*). I say, if the continuance of the British Empire depends upon the life of a single Irish conscript, then I say, let the British Empire be wiped out (*wild applause*). And I for one, and there are a good many others who think like me; they may be aliens, but they are friendly aliens. I for one will lose no sleep at any time over the extinction of the British Empire (*wild applause*). . . .

I am interested particularly in the anti-conscription movement in Ireland because it was my husband Francis Sheehy Skeffington who first advised that pledge which has since been administered generally throughout Ireland. I heard him at many meetings in Dublin administering that pledge to thousands of Irish men, and it was on account [of] administering that pledge that he was done to death at the bidding of the Liberal Government (*hisses*). And I heard these men swear with uplifted hands in P., as he administered the oath "If England should conscript us, we swear we will not go" (*applause*). [A]nd that is the spirit that is winning today. We Irish were never more attacked and maligned than we are at present; but, for my part, I am proud of Ireland today (*applause*). She is standing practically alone in her fight, and she is the only country in the world today that says that she will choose her quarrel and know what she is dying for if she is to die.

You need not worry about the psychology of the Irish people. Everyone knows that the Irish love a fight; but everybody who respects the Irish race know that we like to choose our fight (*applause*). We are not going at this hour. Who will dare to blame us or to deride us?

75

We are not going to be driven to that slaughter-pen in Flanders at the bidding of a government that is dripping red with the blood of our best countrymen (*applause*)....

I remember a story of a woman in Ireland which reminds me of the Irish question today. The Irish question has now become, as Mr Lloyd George confesses, an international one, and we thank God for that, because there is not a nation in the world, with the exception of Great Britain, that would not willingly see Ireland free. This old woman in Ireland had an important law suit on, and she engaged no lawyer; and after a time when her friends came to her and said "You are very foolish; why do you not engage counsel?" And she said "No! I will not engage counsel; I do not need them." And her friend said "Why?" And she smiled knowingly, and she said "I have got a few friends on the jury." No, we feel exactly like that in Ireland today. We feel if our case comes up before an international tribunal of nations, we are all right; we need no one to plead for us; we have got a few good friends on the jury.'[20]

NINE

Mary MacSwiney
1872–1942

Speech at Dáil debates on the Anglo-Irish Treaty
Earlsfort Terrace, Dublin

21 DECEMBER 1921

'Nobody will tell me that I am not an Irish Republican.'

On 21 December 1921 Mary MacSwiney, TD for Cork city, rose to address Dáil Éireann, delivering a momentous speech.[1] For two hours and forty minutes, MacSwiney outlined her objections to the Anglo-Irish Treaty with clarity and passion. Ronan McGreevy, journalist and author, describes these debates as 'the most extraordinary in Irish parliamentary history, suffused with a passion which is hard to understand, knowing what we know now, by people who had endured danger, jail and bereavement.'[2] MacSwiney's speech showcases the key role played by women in the earliest stages of governing a new Irish state. MacSwiney's contributions also provide a lens through which we can better understand how women became vastly excluded from official political discourse in the foundation years of the Irish Free State.

MacSwiney was one of the first women elected to serve in either an Irish or British government. The Parliament (Qualification of Women) Act 1918 enabled women to stand for election for the first time in British general elections.[3] A further act, the Representation of the People Act, was passed that year reforming the British electoral system by removing property qualifications for men and granting women over thirty years of age, with certain restrictions, a vote at general elections. These measures vastly increased the size of the Irish electorate. In Ireland the Sinn Féin Party, founded by Arthur Griffith in 1905, was victorious at the election. The Irish Parliamentary

Party, now under the leadership of John Dillon since Redmond's death earlier that year, was almost wiped out at the polls. Sinn Féin secured 73 seats out of a possible 135 in the election. Countess Markievicz was returned as an MP for St Patrick's Division of Dublin and thus became the first woman ever to be elected to the British House of Commons.

The elected members of Sinn Féin formed the first Dáil Éireann, government of Ireland, in 1919. The first Dáil met in January 1919, and on the same day two Royal Irish Constabulary (RIC) members were shot and killed by members of the Irish Volunteer forces, who became known thereafter as the Irish Republican Army (IRA). This confrontation is now generally accepted as marking the beginning of the Irish War of Independence, a bitter conflict between Irish republican and British forces. An auxiliary force of RIC men was quickly recruited by British authorities. The force became known as the Black and Tans due to their semi-military style uniforms of khaki trousers and dark green tunics. The new force, of mainly English recruits, quickly gained a terrifying reputation because of their brutality and indiscriminate shootings.

Violence escalated over the following year. On 20 March 1920, Tómas MacCurtain, lord mayor of Cork, was brutally assassinated by RIC members at his home in front of his wife and his son. Mary MacSwiney's brother Terence succeeded MacCurtain as lord mayor. Terence played a leading role in the organisation of the Irish Volunteers in Cork and as an elected Sinn Féin candidate stood in the first Dáil.[4] On 12 August 1920, Terence was arrested while chairing a Sinn Féin court in Cork and sentenced to two years in prison. He was sent to Brixton prison, where he maintained a hunger strike. Mary, along with her sister Annie and Terence's wife, Muriel, staged a vigil outside of the prison which drew international media attention. Terence's hunger strike lasted for 74 days before he succumbed to death on 25 October. His plight and the attention mustered by the women outside the prison led to extensive support for him across Ireland and internationally, especially in America and more surprisingly across Britain. That same month, the British Prime Minister, Lloyd George, implemented the Restoration of Order in Ireland Act, which gave British police and military forces extra powers on the island of Ireland.

Prior to her brother's death, Mary MacSwiney was an active political campaigner. She co-founded the Munster Women's Franchise League in 1911, along with the now celebrated authors Violet Martin and Edith Somerville, who wrote collaboratively under the name Sommerville and Ross. When the Irish Volunteer movement was expanding, MacSwiney moved her attention from suffrage to nationalism, establishing a Cork branch of Cumann na mBan. She was active in the republican movement before the Easter Rising. During Easter week 1916, she was arrested in front of the class that she taught at St Angela's Ursuline convent school. Her arrest, in her place of employment, led to her immediate dismissal from her teaching post. In the aftermath of the Rising, she dedicated much of her time to campaigning on behalf of those imprisoned for the cause. In 1917, MacSwiney was elected to the committee of Cumann na mBan and gained national notoriety. After Terence died, MacSwiney assumed many of her brother's political roles.

Following the path of Hanna Sheehy Skeffington, MacSwiney went to America, arriving in New York on 4 December 1920 along with Terence's widow, Muriel. The women were welcomed by huge crowds of Irish sympathisers and a band playing on the pier. For the next seven months, MacSwiney engaged in a public speaking tour of America, admonishing British rule in Ireland. At a large gathering in the Oddfellows Hall in New York on 10 December, MacSwiney claimed that by supporting Britain in the war effort, Americans had 'not made the world safe for democracy' but had 'only made it safe for the British for a short time'.[5] She gave evidence in Washington before the highly publicised American Commission on Conditions in Ireland. Jane Addams, the American suffragist and social reform activist served on the executive of the commission; she later became the first woman to receive the Nobel Peace Prize in 1931. Among MacSwiney's many witness contributions to the commission, she gave an account of how British authorities attempted to Anglicise Ireland by repressing the native Irish language. Her brother Peter J. MacSwiney then a citizen of New York, also gave evidence, as did Muriel.[6] The two women garnered much American support for the Irish cause. Muriel was awarded the Freedom of New York City in 1922, the first woman to receive such an honour.

Before she left Ireland, Mary MacSwiney, had witnessed devastation in her home county of Cork: the city centre had been destroyed by British forces who set fire to buildings in a reprisal for an IRA attack at Kilmichael. While she was on her speaking tour of America, approximately 1,000 people were killed in the fighting in Ireland. Cork suffered the worst of the violence with over half of the total deaths occurring there. MacSwiney returned home to Ireland for the general election of 24 May 1921. She was elected as TD for Cork city. Five other women were also elected to the second Dáil: Kathleen Clarke, Ada English, Kathleen O'Callaghan, Constance Markievicz, and Margaret Pearse. Four of the six female members of the Dáil were close relatives of men who had been killed in the fight for Irish independence. On 11 July, a truce was called between the IRA and British forces, and negotiations began to formalise a peace agreement. Within months of MacSwiney's election, the Anglo-Irish Treaty was established.

In early December 1921, Arthur Griffith, chair of the Irish treaty committee, and Michael Collins, then Minister of Finance and director of IRA intelligence, were tasked with leading the treaty negotiations in London.[7] Lloyd George gave the Irish delegates an ultimatum on 5 December to either accept the terms of the treaty or face the full wrath of war against British forces. The Irish delegates signed the treaty in the early hours of 6 December. The terms of the Anglo-Irish Treaty granted dominion-like status to a Free State Ireland and contained an article for the north of Ireland to opt out. This was neither full independence nor unity for Ireland. In addition, an article of the treaty stipulated that elected officials would be required to sign an oath of allegiance to the British crown in order to take their seat in an Irish parliament, which was seen as abhorrent to many republicans.

Although the British government had conceded many items, the treaty sparked bitter arguments among Sinn Féin members in the Dáil debates that followed from 14 December 1921 to 7 January 1922. The debates took place at University College Dublin premises on Earlsfort Terrace. All six female TDs vehemently opposed the treaty, as did members of Cumann na mBan. On 20 December, TD Kate O'Callaghan highlighted the importance of the female voices present in the Dáil chamber during these debates:

> The women of Ireland so far have not appeared much on the political stage. That does not mean that they have no deep convictions about Ireland's status and freedom. It was the mother of the Pearses who made them what they were. The sister of Terence MacSwiney influenced her brother, and is now carrying on his life's work. Deputy Mrs. Clarke, the widow of Tom Clarke, was bred in the Fenian household of her uncle, John Daly of Limerick. The women of An Dáil are women of character, and they will vote for principle, not for expediency.[8]

The Dáil treaty debates involved intense and emotional contributions from many TDs. MacSwiney's contributions were the most uncompromising expressions of Irish republicanism. Her speech on 17 December lasted for one hour. Her speech on 21 December, in this section, was the longest speech by any TD during these debates. During her speeches she endorsed IRA threats against TDs who supported the treaty and at one stage warned that even the very blades of grass stained with the blood of fallen republicans would rise up and continue to fight for Irish independence.

On the 7 January 1922, members of Dáil Éireann voted 64 to 57 to accept the Anglo-Irish Treaty. This was a landmark in modern Irish history which saw the establishment of the Irish Free State, which would become the Republic of Ireland in 1949. However, it was also a bitter loss as six counties in the north of Ireland – Antrim, Armagh, Derry, Down, Fermanagh, and Tyrone – would be excluded from the new Irish state and remained within the United Kingdom. This situation embittered MacSwiney and the other female TDs, especially those whose relatives had died fighting for Irish independence. After the vote was declared, MacSwiney delivered what was essentially the final contribution to the treaty debates. Her speech was scathing of those who had voted in support of the treaty, as she declared:

> I, for one, will have neither hand, act, nor part in helping the Irish Free State to carry this nation of ours, this glorious nation that has been betrayed here to-night, into the British Empire—either with or without your hands up. I maintain here now that this is the grossest act of betrayal that Ireland ever endured . . . This is a betrayal, a gross betrayal; and the fact is that it is only a small majority, and that majority is not united; half of them look for a gun and the other half are looking for the fleshpots of the Empire. I tell you here there can be no union between the representatives of the Irish Republic and the so-called Free State.[9]

The session concluded on a despondent note with de Valera describing, 'we have had a glorious record for four years; it has been four years of magnificent discipline in our nation. The world is looking at us now.'[10] It was reported in the Dáil records that de Valera then broke down and the meeting was adjourned.

The first general election of the Irish Free State was called in June 1922. The political landscape in Ireland was now greatly changed, and the election essentially became a vote in support or rejection of the treaty. In the run-up to the election, the promise to grant women equal voting rights with men was vehemently pursued in the Dáil by the female TDs.[11] This promise had been enshrined in the Proclamation of the Irish Republic signed by the leaders of the Easter Rising, declaring that representatives of an Irish government will be 'elected by the suffrages of all her men and women'.[12] A group of male TDs led by the main treaty delegates Collins and Griffith maintained that there was not enough time to update the electoral register, and therefore only women over 30 years of age received a vote in that election, while men over 21 were entitled to vote. It is more likely that the anti-treaty stance taken by so many Irish women was the cause of this exclusion. Collins and the pro-treaty side won the election. Only two female TDs were re-elected: MacSwiney and Kate O'Callaghan. As opponents of the treaty, both women refused to take their seats.

Ten days after the general election, a civil war between pro-treaty and anti-treaty forces erupted. MacSwiney actively supported the anti-treaty side but did not take up arms during the civil war. On two occasions, she was imprisoned for her protests, but she succeeded in forcing the government to release her. In November 1922 and again in April 1923, she followed her brother's path and went on hunger strike in prison; one hunger strike lasted for 24 days. MacSwiney was re-elected in August 1923 and continued with her stance against the treaty terms. The pro-treaty party, now organised as Cumann na nGaedheal, a predecessor of Fine Gael, won the election. Many more anti-treaty figures were imprisoned, and during a large-scale hunger strike in November 1923, three people died. The civil war finally ended, but the political divide would remain in the Irish political system for generations.

Éamon de Valera established Fianna Fáil, a new political party of anti-treaty politicians. Fianna Fáil won 44 seats in the general election of June 1927, and the elected TDs entered the Dáil after swearing the oath of allegiance. MacSwiney condemned de Valera for forsaking the ideal of republicanism. She lost her seat in that election and set about attempting to refresh the anti-treaty political movement. The Cumann na nGaedheal party remained in power until 1932, when Fianna Fáil assumed power through a general election.

In her final years, MacSwiney continued her anti-treaty campaign, never accepting the partition of Ireland or the position of the Irish Free State as a dominion of Britain. She supported the pursuit of independence through violent means, and in 1938 she endorsed the IRA's bombing campaign in England. In December 1938 MacSwiney was part of a group of TDs elected to the second Dáil who believed that as members of government before the signing of the Anglo-Irish Treaty, they remained the official Irish government. The group met with the IRA Army Council and signed authority of the Government of Dáil Éireann to the Army Council. This agreement provided the IRA with what they viewed as authority to act on behalf of the legitimate government of the Irish Republic.

MacSwiney suffered a heart attack the following year, and after a period of ill health, she died on 8 March 1942 in Cork, at the age of 69. The *Irish Press* newspaper reported that, 'Ireland has lost a gallant fighter for her cause.'[13] The *Belfast Newsletter* described her as an 'extremist Irish Republican' and pointed out that 'if she had been prepared to pledge allegiance to Mr. de Valera's Eire she would have been granted a substantial State pension' in her final years.[14]

As part of the decade of centenary commemorations in Ireland, 'Staging the Treaty', a re-enactment of the treaty debates, was scheduled to take place in the National Concert Hall at Earlsfort Terrace on 22 December 2021 and 7 January 2022. The event taking place over two ten-hour performances was planned to give audiences 'a sense of what it was like to be there'.[15] Speeches from the treaty debates were edited by poet Theo Dorgan, including MacSwiney's speeches, and directed by Louise Lowe. Dorgan noted that 'the contribution of women to the debate has to be seen in the context of their personal suffering. In MacSwiney's case she witnessed her brother, day after day, dying in Brixton Prison.'[16] MacSwiney's speech remains as a testament to her extreme republican views.

12. Mary MacSwiney, Hotel St. Regis, New York, December 1920. Left to right: Anna Ryan, Harry Boland, Mary MacSwiney, Muriel MacSwiney and James O'Mara. Courtesy of the National Library of Ireland.

'It is no use for you to look at your watches. Go out if you like, but this is probably the last time that I shall ever speak before you in public, in an assembly like this; certainly and most emphatically the last time until the Irish Republican Government comes back again with the full consent of the people, and I care not, and apologise not, if I take more of your time than you are willing to give. Those who want to hear the Treaty will stay and listen: those who are afraid of the Treaty can go out.

One thing more I want to say about that oath. I have said that I am ashamed of the arguments that have been brought about it. I am ashamed of the efforts that are being made on the other side of this assembly to show the people of this Dáil how they can drive, not one coach-and-four through it, but a coach-and-four through every line of it. That, I maintain, is not consistent with the honour of our people; it is not consistent with the attitude we have adopted towards the world and on which we have got the sympathy of the world. What use, you will tell me, is sympathy? It is this use, that it is the sympathy of the world and the judgment and conscience of the world that brought England to her knees in these negotiations. She has the military. I know that, but she cannot win this battle, for if she exterminates the men, the women will take their places, and, if she exterminates the women, the children are rising fast; and if she exterminates the men, women and children of this generation, the blades of grass, dyed with their blood, will rise, like the dragon's teeth of old, into armed men and the fight will begin in the next generation.

But I am concerned for the honour of my country before the world, and I tell the world that it is not the true voice of Ireland that has spoken so flippantly about oaths and their breaking. It is not the true voice of the people of Ireland that has spoken to you. Have no doubt about it whatever. This fight of ours has been essentially a spiritual fight; it has been a fight of right against wrong, a fight of a small people struggling for a spiritual ideal against a mighty rapacious and material Empire, and, as the things of the spirit have always prevailed, they prevail now.

Up to last December we had won the admiration of the world for our honour, and I tell the world that the honour of Ireland is still unsullied, and that Ireland will show it, and will show that Ireland means fidelity to the Republic and not the driving of a coach-and-four through the oath which she will never consent to allow her Ministers to take. This is a spiritual fight of ours, but though we are idealists standing for a spiritual principle, we are practical idealists, and it is your idealist that is the real practical man, not your opportunist; and watch the opportunists in every generation and you will see nothing but broken hopes behind them. It is those who stand for the spiritual and the ideal that stand true and unflinching, and it is those who will win—not those who can inflict most but those who can endure most will conquer.

The war of 1914 has left the world in a very different position from what the world was in before. . . . I stand here, and nobody will tell me that I am not an Irish Republican, but I can truthfully say, and I challenge any Member in this assembly to say otherwise, that in 1911 I did not believe that I would see an Irish Republic established in my generation. The war brought many changes; the war brought forth idealists and the self-determination of small nationalities. Their right to express their freedom in their own way was bandied about from one Government to another, and every Government in the world has been false to it but our own. Still, all the peoples of the world have not been false to it. The peoples of the world, including a growing number of the people of England, are true to that ideal; they want peace, and they know that peace can never be established except on the basis of truth and justice to all alike. Therefore our fight to-day has a chance of victory. You have told us it is between the acceptance of that document and war. If it were, with every sense of deep responsibility, I say then let us take war.

I am not speaking as a young, ardent enthusiast. I am speaking as a woman who has thought and studied much, who realises, as only a woman can, the evils of war and the sufferings of war. Deputy Milroy yesterday in a speech to which I shall not allude, for it made me ashamed to think the public was listening to it, acknowledged that the women are the greatest sufferers of the war. I would ask him, if it were a democratic proposition, to let the women of Ireland judge this, and I have no doubt what the issue would be.'[17]

TEN

Jennie Wyse Power
1858–1941

Speech on women on juries
Seanad Éireann, Leinster House, Dublin

30 MARCH 1927

'The civic spirit that is developing in women will be arrested.'

The Irish Free State was born on 6 December 1922. From the outset, there was a marked suppression of female voices in the newly established parliament. The almost exclusion of women in both houses of parliament was compounded by the fact that many female politicians adopted an anti-treaty stance. Jennie Wyse Power was the only leading member of Cumann na mBan to support the Anglo-Irish treaty, causing her to leave the organisation and join a newly formed women's association, Cumann na Saoirse (League of Freedom). Wyse Power would become a predominant voice on women's issues in the Seanad Éireann, the upper house of the Free State parliament. Her speech in this section provides a powerful example of her contributions to Seanad on behalf of women's equality.

Wyse Power was an executive member of Sinn Féin, serving as joint treasurer and sole treasurer at different times. She was elected as vice-president of the party in 1911. The Anglo-Irish treaty caused a bitter divide in Sinn Féin. The treaty led to a newly established Constitution of the Irish Free State, an article in the constitution determined that an oath must be taken by every member of the Oireachtas before taking their seat to, 'solemnly swear . . . that I will be faithful to H. M. King George V., his heirs and successors.'[1] Anti-treaty members of Sinn Féin refused to swear an allegiance to the British crown and therefore did not take their seats in government. During the civil war, Wyse Power, as joint treasurer of Sinn

Féin, 'froze the party's accounts, refusing republicans access to the money'.[2] The pro-treaty membership suffered losses in their leadership in 1922. Arthur Griffith, founder of Sinn Féin and then president of the Dáil, died suddenly of a cerebral haemorrhage on 12 August 1922.[3] Ten days after Griffith's death, Michael Collins was killed in an ambush in county Cork as part of the civil war conflict. Pro-treaty Sinn Féin leader William Cosgrave assumed the role as the first head of government of the Irish Free State. With Sinn Féin in disarray, Cosgrave formed a new political party, Cumann na nGaedheal (Party of the Irish). This party would remain dominant in Irish politics during the first decade from its inception. Wyse Power was appointed to the executive of Cumann na nGaedheal and was nominated to Seanad Éireann in 1922.

Wyse Power had a wealth of previous political experience: she played central roles in predominant Irish women's organisations for four decades before her election as a senator. Jane (Jennie) Wyse Power (née O'Toole) was born in Baltinglass, county Wicklow in 1858. She joined the Ladies' Land League in 1881 and took on the difficult and often dangerous task of league organiser in Wicklow and Carlow. She was a suffrage veteran and a close ally of Hanna Sheehy Skeffington. In 1883 she married John Wyse Power, a journalist and a founding member of the Gaelic Athletic Association (GAA); the couple had four children together. Wyse Power was

also a business woman and she opened a shop and restaurant called the Irish Farm and Produce Company on 21 Henry Street in Dublin city, where the family lived. The restaurant became a popular meeting place for Irish nationalists. In 1900 Wyse Power co-founded Inghinidhe na hÉireann and assumed the vice-presidency; later co-founding Cumann na mBan, she was elected as its president in 1915. She had served on the board of guardians of the North Dublin Poor Law Union (1903–12) and was elected to Dublin corporation in 1920.

Wyse Power served as a senator from 1922 to 1936. Her contributions to senate debates were passionate and measured. Not surprisingly, Wyse Power became a strong voice in defending female rights in this forum;

13. Jennie Wyse Power, circa 1880s. Creative Commons Universal Public Domain.

such contributions were all the more important as there was a distinct lack of such engagement on the floor of the Dáil.[4] Effectively, only one female TD served in the Dáil during the decade of Cumann na nGaedheal's power: Michael Collins' sister, Margaret Collins-O'Driscoll. She was loyal to the party and did not oppose its policies, which included the introduction of a series of laws restricting women's full public participation in the new state.

By 1925 Wyse Power became disheartened with Cumann na nGaedheal and resigned from the party. She kept her seat as an independent senator and made increasingly determined contributions to debates regarding women's status. That same year, Wyse Power presented a provoking objection to the Civil Service Regulation (Amendment) bill, a law that would preclude women from applying for Civil Service jobs. Her contribution in this instance helped defeat the bill in the Seanad, although this merely delayed its legal introduction until the following year.

In 1927 possibly the most controversial of the laws restricting women's full participation in the public affairs of the state, the Juries bill, came through the Seanad for debate. An earlier Juries bill introduced in 1924 included a clause for women to be automatically exempted from jury service on application. In 1927 Kevin O'Higgins, Cumann na nGaedheal member and Minister for Justice, claimed that 'a great majority' of eligible women had requested this exemption and that only ten per cent remained on the juries register because 'they had omitted, through thoughtlessness', to request an exemption.[5] These claims were presented without any evidence to support them or, indeed, without consideration of practicalities which may prevent women from serving.

O'Higgins now proposed a bill that would exclude women from serving on juries entirely. He maintained that it was not fitting for a woman to hear details of criminal activities, although women certainly heard such criminal details through other roles as witnesses or defendants at trials, and by 1927 there were female lawyers. During the committee stage discussion of the bill in the Dáil, O'Higgins stated a second reason for excluding women from jury service; put simply, a woman's place was in the home and not in public life. The Minister firmly asserted that 'it is the normal and natural function of women to have children.'[6] Through a staged process, including the Civil Service Regulation bill, the Cumann na nGaedheal government ensured that Irish women would find it difficult to follow a path outside of motherhood and life within the home.

While women's participation in formal politics was restrained, feminists organised through new and reformed networks in response to gender-biased legislation. In 1923, the Irish Women Citizens' Association (IWCA) was formed through a merging of the Irish Women's Suffrage and Local Government Association and the Irishwomen's Association of Citizenship. Wyse

Power became a member of the IWCA. The proposed Juries bill enthused a vibrant backlash from such feminist organisations. As evident from the newly adopted organisation name, members now focused their attention on gaining equal citizenship for women after achieving their original objective of equal suffrage. In order to appease the feminist backlash, Independent TD Sir James Craig proposed an amendment to the bill to include an option enabling eligible female ratepayers to volunteer for jury service. Craig held his seat for the Dublin University constituency and may well have been attempting to pacify members of the active Trinity College Dublin graduate women's association, a point alluded to by Wyse Power in her speech.

The Juries bill reached the floor of the Seanad for a second-stage debate on 30 March 1927. Wyse Power was the most vocal opponent to its introduction and the only woman to speak during that debate. In her speech in this section she was quick to point out that Craig's amendment was in fact a route to ensuring that women would be vastly excluded from serving on juries. This amendment allowed TDs to vote with a clear conscience, safe in the belief that they had not entirely excluded women from serving on a jury. However, Wyse Power acknowledged that, in fact, many women would not have the circumstances to allow them to volunteer for such a role.

The basis of Wyse Power's argument was strong and could not easily be disproved. She argued that women, like herself, had played an important role in establishing the Irish Free State and that through the Constitution of 1922, they were guaranteed equal citizenship with men. The Juries bill did in fact contravene the Irish Free State Constitution. Article 3 of the Constitution guaranteed 'without distinction of sex . . . the privileges and . . . the obligations of such citizenship rights to all citizens'.[7] Serving on a jury is defined in many countries as both a privilege and an obligation of citizenship. Excluding women from these basic aspects of citizenship would, as Wyse Power asserted, 'arrest the civic spirit' of Irish women.

Added to issues surrounding the citizenship status of women, as historian Caitriona Beaumont observes, 'the new legislation also affected the rights of women charged with criminal offences.'[8] Juries would be all-male, unless a woman applied for volunteer service, therefore 'young girls charged with infanticide and prostitution would be judged by twelve men who, it was claimed by women's groups, would have no empathy whatsoever with the accused.'[9] Since the publication of the report to establish the facts of state involvement with the Magdalene Laundries in 2013, it is evident that the court system, a predominantly male environment, contributed to the harrowing mistreatment of women and children.[10] The report found that girls and women were, at times, committed to Magdalene institutions from criminal courts. The Juries Act 1927 helped establish this gender-biased judicial system.

The Juries bill successfully passed through both houses of the Dáil and the Seanad on 18 May 1927 and was signed into law eight days later. Part two of the statute included a list of categories of 'persons exempted but entitled to serve on application'; the first category exempted simply stated, 'women'.[11] It was a bitter regression for the women of Ireland. Under British rule, Irish women had earned full and equal entitlement to serve on juries through legislation passed at Westminster in 1919. When the Irish Free State was established, the new government established a new judicial system through which women lost their automatic right to serve as jurors.

The introduction of this legislation was all the more surprising when considering that women had played a central role as judges in the Dáil or republican courts. The republican courts were established by the first Dáil as a system of national arbitration, sitting in local jurisdictions and parishes across the country. Cases were brought to the courts concerning a range of petty crimes and local disputes, while some courts specialised in land disputes. This was an endeavour, especially used during the War of Independence, to break away from the British legal system and administer law and order at a local level. The Dáil courts were presided over by women judges in many instances, including figures such as Hanna Sheehy Skeffington, and operated until 1924.

The constitutionality of the Juries bill was eventually successfully challenged and the law overturned but not until 1975.[12] The Supreme Court, on examining the legislation, 'declared the gender provision of the 1927 Act to be unconstitutional, holding that the model of jury trial contemplated by the present Constitution required that juries be drawn from panels that were broadly representative of society'.[13] The evidence presented to the Supreme Court highlighted the extreme gender bias of the Irish jury system. Over the previous ten years, only nine women had been eligible for jury service out of 700,000 people who had served. A Juries Act was passed in 1976 that included an obligation for all male and female citizens to serve on a jury if called.

Wyse Power held her position as a senator until 1936, representing the Fianna Fáil party in her final two years in this office. During that time, she remained outspoken on any legislation affecting women. She was a vocal opponent of the 1935 Condition of Employment bill which discriminated against female workers. The Seanad was dissolved under the Constitution (Amendment No. 24) Act in 1936 after the upper house delayed the enactment of constitutional changes put forward by the government. The Seanad voted against its own dissolution, but this was overruled by the Dáil. A new Seanad, in its present form, was created in 1937 under the newly designed Constitution of Ireland. Wyse Power did not seek reinstatement as a senator but retired in 1936.

Wyse Power died just over four years after her retirement from politics, on 5 January 1941. She died at her home, 15 Earlsfort Terrace in Dublin.[14] Her funeral mass was held at University Church on St Stephen's Green and she was buried at Glasnevin Cemetery on 7 January. The Lord Mayor of Dublin, Kathleen Clarke, who had served with Wyse Power on the Sinn Féin Standing Committee, proposed a vote of condolence at a meeting of Dublin Corporation on the day of the funeral. P. S. Doyle, Fine Gael TD and later Lord Mayor of Dublin, seconded the proposal. Doyle described how Wyse Power 'had taken a prominent part in every phase of the national movement.'[15] Wyse Power's obituary was carried in many Irish newspapers and the *Irish Press* announced starkly, 'Veteran Woman Nationalist Dead'.[16]

On 8 December 1991, a memorial plaque was erected in honour of Wyse Power by the West Wicklow Historical Society on the building where she was born, on Main Street in Baltinglass.[17] The plaque was erected in commemoration of the fiftieth anniversary of her death. Also in 1991, a plaque was installed at 21 Henry Street, at the site of Wyse Power's home and business. The plaque commemorates the signing of the 1916 proclamation which was signed at Wyse Power's restaurant before the Easter Rising. Jennie Wyse Power's speech is one of the few records of female contribution to parliamentary debate in the early establishment of the Irish Free State.

14. Standing Committee 14th Sinn Féin Ard Fheis, Dublin, 21 February 1922. From left to right back row: Sean Milroy, Walter Leonard Cole, Henry O'Hanrahan, Pádraig O'Keeffe, Kevin O'Sheil, Jennie Wyse Power, George Augustine Lyons, Darrell Figgis, Seán Mac Caoilte, George Murnaghan, Austin Stack, Thomas Dillon (faded), Kathleen Clarke, Éamonn Duggan, Kathleen Lynn, Arthur Griffith, Éamon De Valera, Michael Collins, Harry Boland, Hanna Sheehy Skeffington. Courtesy of the National Library of Ireland.

'There is little for me to say at this particular stage except to protest as strongly as I can, and my protest is entirely influenced by the fact that if this Bill becomes law the civic spirit that is developing in women will be arrested. In fact the suggestion that there shall be only male jurors in the future cuts at the very root of this development of the awakening of the civic spirit. We all know that in the past this spirit had been repressed and became stunted and did not grow. But by the happenings, political happenings if you like, during the last 50 years the men who led political movements and carried them in the main to success, utilised women in order to achieve their object. That utilisation of women helped in a great degree their civic spirit, and some of them, encouraged more or less by the way they have been thrust out, as it were, to do work that they never did before, came gradually into public life and have done social work which is generally regarded as successful. It is for that reason I deplore so much the Minister's attitude in this matter, not so much, perhaps, because we want to be on juries, or anything else, but because he is doing such an injustice to what is really a necessary asset to every State, the co-operation of its men and women.

92

The Minister by a bold stroke eliminated females from the panel. Sir James Craig—I am sure in a kindly spirit, I will not say anything else—put down in the Dáil an amendment giving women the right to ask for the privilege of being jurors. I give him all credit for his kindly spirit, but I think it would have been better, before he put down that amendment, if he had a little consultation with those who certainly knew better than he did that that amendment was entirely wrong, and that by it he was about to place a burden on women that perhaps he did not understand. Sir James Craig having been shown this side of the question, became very angry and threw up his hands in despair. He said: "Absolutely nothing will please you. I am like the old man and the ass."When he was angry, I am sorry to say, he made the statement I am about to read to you. He said: "That was not the reason why I put it forward. I said that between the ages of 20 and 40 the majority of women have a much more important duty to perform to the State than serving on juries, that their functions were motherhood and looking after their families, and they objected to these other women who have missed these functions and who wanted to drive to serve on juries those who have something else to do." Only that Sir James Craig was angry, and very angry, I do not think he would have made that statement.

None of the newspapers reported that, but the morning after the debate one of them set out to make a column of merriment of it for its readers. I commend the Deputy in his hour of need to the women voters of Trinity College. I think the Minister knew the material he had when he accepted this amendment. Naturally, Deputies were anxious to vote for anything rather than the total elimination of women. For proof of that I will read what one Deputy said: "This is the movement of a truculent minority, and this proposed amendment gives us a means out." The "means out" was a voluntary panel. The proposal was carried by 39 votes to 11. There were 50 votes in all. One wonders where were the other 50 Deputies. All who have thought out this question and who have given consideration to cases where women may be in the dock have come to the conclusion that it is right and proper that a proportion of women should be on juries in such cases. In the Dáil no consideration was given to that question. I think there is a general feeling in the country that in cases where women are concerned a proportion of the jury should consist of women. If consideration had been given to that point I do not think Deputy Sir James Craig's amendment, as embodied in the Minister's Bill, would be carried, because we know that out of that panel you will not get a sufficient number to serve on mixed juries.'[18]

ELEVEN

Dehra Parker
1882–1963

Address on equal franchise Parliament of Northern Ireland,
Presbyterian Church Assembly's College

15 NOVEMBER 1927

'The servant girls of Derry and Tyrone flocking behind him on the primrose path.'

On 15 November 1927, the only female MP in the Northern Ireland government took the parliamentary floor to address the question of extending votes to women on the same terms as men. On first consideration, this speech may appear to be a feminist call for gender equality. However, the content of Dehra Parker's speech provides an insight into more than just the gender imbalance in this newly formed government. Parker's speech exhibits a marked sectarian divide and power imbalance in the political structure that had existed from the establishment of the Northern Ireland government.

The Government of Ireland Act became law on 23 December 1920. While Ireland remained in the United Kingdom, this act, also known as the fourth Home Rule bill, established provisions for two devolved governments in Ireland. In the United Kingdom general elections of May 1921, candidates were elected for the separate Northern Ireland Parliament based in Belfast. The Parliament of Northern Ireland first met in the Presbyterian Church of Ireland College on Botanic Avenue in Belfast until construction of Parliament Buildings was completed in 1932 at the Stormont estate, where the Northern Ireland Assembly continues to sit since 1998.

Two women, Dehra Parker and Julie McMordie, were elected to the Northern Ireland House of Commons, and the first sitting was held on 7 June 1921. Parker stood for election as an Ulster Unionist Party candidate. When the Anglo-Irish Treaty was signed in 1921, the Parliament of Northern Ireland voted to exercise their right to opt out of the Irish Free State. This decision led to the formation of a boundary commission that reviewed the border between the then created Irish Free State and Northern Ireland. Due to the ongoing hostilities of the Irish Civil War, which included much sectarian violence in the north of Ireland, the commission could not begin its work until the end of 1924. The following year the border issue was finally decided.

The parliament of Northern Ireland comprised two chambers: a directly elected House of Commons of 52 members and an indirectly elected senate of 24 members. Senators were elected by members of the House of Commons along with a vote by the Mayor of Derry/Londonderry Corporation and a vote from the Lord Mayor of Belfast. The Ulster Unionist Party continually held a majority in both houses and thus legislated in favour of the unionist population of Northern Ireland. The British monarch was represented by a vice-regal governor, who delegated their executive powers to the government of Northern Ireland, which was headed by a Prime Minister of Northern Ireland. This devolved administration, within the United Kingdom, had self-government over much of the running of the new state, including law and order, agriculture, social services, local government representation, industry, education and internal trade.[1]

In the second general election of Northern Ireland in April 1925, the Ulster Unionist Party lost many seats but kept their majority; securing 32 seats, they took control under the leadership of James Craig, who continued as Prime Minister of Northern Ireland. Parker was elected as an MP for the county of Derry/Londonderry, the only woman to be returned in that election. The Nationalist Party, under the leadership of Joseph Devlin, secured ten seats and ended a period of abstentionism, taking their seats in the Northern Ireland parliament. As an opposition party the Irish nationalist MPs attempted to make changes to Northern Irish law, often unsuccessfully. One of the most debated areas for suggested change became equal voting rights for women.

The Irish Free State Constitution legislated for an equal franchise for men and women in 1922. The parliament of the United Kingdom was slower to introduce this equality measure. Only women over 30 years of age with certain property qualifications were then entitled to vote, while all male citizens over 21 were granted a vote at general elections. In November 1927, Joseph Devlin presented a private member's bill on the issue of representation of the people, seeking equal voting rights, to the Northern Ireland House of Commons. The move was quickly described as the 'Flapper Bill' by members of the house and the media.[2] The slang term *flapper* was applied derogatively, to denote a frivolous young woman who ignored conventional standards of behaviour. This bill was debated in the Northern Ireland

House of Commons over a number of days, in an overwhelmingly male environment with Parker being the only female present. As can be seen in her speech in this section, Parker often felt obliged to speak on government issues related to women, although she could not be described as a feminist.

This was the second reading of the bill, and from the outset of her speech, Parker focuses on the timing for introducing such a bill. According to Parker, this bill was a move by the Nationalist Party to establish the Northern Irish parliament as independent from the imperial government in Westminster. By entering this bill, Devlin may well have been attempting to outmanoeuvre the UK Parliament and identify the north of Ireland as independent thinking. By November 1927, work was already well under way on this issue in Westminster: the previous year an Equal Franchise Cabinet Committee had begun investigating the implications of granting an equal franchise. It seemed inevitable that this law would be passed through Westminster, a point alluded to at the conclusion of Parker's speech.

Parker became the longest serving female MP in the Northern Ireland House of Commons and later served as Minister of Health and Local Government from 1949 to 1957, becoming the first woman to serve in the Northern Ireland Cabinet. She was a regular contributor to parliamentary debates, exhibiting herself as a fluent orator with a dry wit. Parker's humour is directed at Devlin during this speech as she describes the 'servant girls of Derry and Tyrone' flocking around him in appreciation for providing them with an electoral vote. Specifically mentioning these two areas of Northern Ireland, which are recognised as having a majority Catholic population, is the first identifier of the sectarian divide in Parker's speech. She was an ardent and active unionist long before becoming an MP. Parker supported Lady Londonderry's campaign against home rule for Ireland and served as vice-chairman of the Ulster Women's Unionist Council from 1911 to 1930.[3] She supported the Ulster Volunteer Force by establishing a nursing unit during the home rule crisis between 1911 and 1914. During World War One, she was a staunch champion of the British war effort, for which she was bestowed with an Order of the British Empire in 1918.

James Craig recognised that Parker was an unfaltering defender of unionism as she always upheld the Ulster Unionist Party line. She was held in such high regard that she was selected to present the annual address at the commons following the king's speech in 1924. Parker was the first woman in Britain to be given such an honour at the opening of a parliamentary session. Many details in Parker's 1927 speech establish her support of unionism. Her reference to opening her first orange hall, a lodge of the Protestant fraternal order the Loyal Orange Institution, is welcomed by other unionist colleagues present.

While it is evident that Parker supports the move to grant women equal voting rights with men, she is clearly not a supporter of the bill being debated, possibly because it was presented by an Irish nationalist MP. The bill was defeated in the Northern Ireland parliament early in 1928. Shortly after this defeat, it was announced in the king's speech on 7 February 1928 that equal franchise would be made law in the following months. On 6 July 1928 the Representation of the People (Equal Franchise) Act was passed, finally granting women in the United Kingdom a vote in local and general elections on the same basis as men. The act was extended to cover Northern Ireland.

Parker's speeches in the Northern Irish parliament are clear examples of how the political institution facilitated unionist interests, upholding the link with the United Kingdom. Parker was the only female in the Northern Irish parliament from 1924 to 1929, and in that role she did not encourage women into politics or actively engage with issues of feminist interest. Although women had played a central role in unionist activity before the establishment of Northern Ireland, once established the parliament was controlled by male politicians. The position or, indeed, inclusion of female politicians in Northern Ireland did not improve greatly over the coming years. Yvonne Galligan has calculated that in elections 'between 1921 and 1969, women comprised 37 (4 per cent) of the 1008 candidates, of whom nine were returned as Stormont MPs'.[4] All of the elected females represented unionist interests; the voices of nationalist or Catholic women were excluded from mainstream politics, although nationalist women were extremely active establishing local social reform groups during this time.

When she entered parliament, Parker led a campaign against proportional representation (PR) as an electoral system. Galligan explains that 'mindful of the need to include minority communities in the governance process, the 1920 Act had provided for PR, in single transferable vote form (STV) and multi-member constituencies.'[5] In 1929, the system of PR was replaced with a first-past-the-post electoral system that benefitted unionist candidates. The dominance of unionist MPs in the Northern Irish government led to a deplorable situation for the Catholic community. Catholics were excluded from the main positions of power in key areas such as the police, judiciary and civil service. Unemployment rates among the Catholic population reached a crisis that had serious repercussions for voting rights. Only ratepayers were entitled to a vote in Northern Ireland local elections, and as the Catholic population was disadvantaged economically, they were less likely to be rate payers and to receive a vote.

Women played a central role in establishing a civil rights movement in Northern Ireland in the late 1960s onwards. In 1968 a violent sectarian conflict that became known as the Troubles began. Without a balance of representatives from nationalist and unionist communities or, indeed, female MPs in the parliament of Northern Ireland, the Troubles intensified. On 1 April 1972 the British Prime Minister, Edward Heath, suspended the parliament in Belfast and introduced direct rule from Westminster. William Whitelaw was appointed as Secretary of State for Northern Ireland. Political correspondent with the *Guardian* Ian Aitken announced that this move 'staggered Ulster Unionist MPs and many of their right-wing Conservative colleagues'.[6] Heath intended the suspension to last for one year; however, the Northern Ireland parliament was formally abolished in 1973. It was not until the Good Friday Agreement was signed in 1998 that a Northern Ireland assembly was established on the basis of a power-sharing agreement representing all sectors of the community. Parker's speech is testimony to the sectarian nature of Northern Ireland's government, controlled by unionist politicians, prior to this time.

'I am convinced that as the only woman Member in this House Hon. Members will have expected that I would have some words to say on a Measure of this character. (Hon. Members: Hear, hear.) Therefore, I rise reluctantly not to support the Second Reading of this Bill although I may state here and now that I am certainly agreed upon the principle of the Bill — not to support it but to express surprise that the Hon. Gentleman [Joseph Devlin] should have considered this an opportune time to introduce it . . .

I cannot help wondering in spite of what the Hon. Member has said . . . in fact he is always telling us he is very anxious — to show his independence and to cut us off from the apron strings that bind us to the Imperial Parliament. That was what he gave as his reason. I cannot quite believe that he was not actuated by other motives in the introduction of this Measure at this particular stage. I wonder if he had in mind the proverb about the early bird that always catches the worm. I also wonder whether he possibly had been indulging in visions of the future, whether he had visualised himself in the role of the Pied Piper of Hamelin, and whether he saw himself orating so passionately, as we well know in this House he can orate, pleading so persuasively as we know he can plead, with the servant girls of Derry and Tyrone flocking behind him on the primrose path. (Laughter.) That I must say flashed across my mind. I also thought that possibly he might see himself in the role of the great benefactor, crowned with laurels, by the youth and beauty of the Six Counties, going to be soon enfranchised, and that he would be crowned with laurels by them out of gratitude for the inestimable boon which he was about to confer. . . . I believe that every Member of this House, on both sides, is agreed that mentally there is equality of the sexes at the age of 21. I go still further, and I would say that in most cases woman matures earlier than man, and that whereas a boy of 18 or 19 years may still be a boy, a girl of 18 or 19 years is very often a woman. I do not believe that we could find anybody these days maintaining the positions that there was not equality of the sexes . . .

Personally, I would infinitely prefer to have seen universal franchise at the age of 25. That is my own point of view, because I do believe that very few men and women before they attain the age of 25 . . . take a very great interest in political work. I would like to tell Hon. Members a little story . . . which I think is an illustration of my argument, that up to 25 years, as a rule, both women and men are not so keenly interested in politics, and not perhaps so stable in their political views as they may be at a later stage. I am sure the Hon. Member will be interested to know that when I was very young

I was very ardently interested in Irish politics, in Irish poetry, in Irish literature and Irish history. . . . A little later on, when I became a little older, I was very much more interested, I candidly confess, in enjoying myself. I am afraid I did not give much time to political thought. . . . I was fully 25 years before I took any real intelligent interest in political discussions. I am going to say what the Hon. Gentleman (Mr. Devlin) will like. I was 27 years before I opened my first Orange Hall. (Hon. Members: Hear, hear.) Personally, I call that the dawn of common sense. I am sure Hon. Members opposite will rather call it the "rake's progress" or the "road to ruin". We will not quarrel on that subject. . . .

Youth is all very well, but youth — and there are considerable numbers of young people would be given the right to vote under a Bill of this nature — youth has illusions, youth has romance and youth has ideals. Thank God for that, because we could not do without them, but I do really think that I would prefer, as a nation, to be governed by realists and those who know Utopia is not within our reach and are not carried away by ideals and romance. That is why I would infinitely prefer to have seen universal franchise at 25. However, that I understand, is an impracticable proposition, and I will not dwell on it any longer. I do not want to say once more that, as far as equality of the sexes in franchise goes, I certainly consider that if the franchise is to be 21, it should also be 21 for women. As far as that goes I am in absolute agreement with the Hon. Gentleman's Measure. . . . Personally, I consider the Hon. Gentleman (Mr. Devlin) would be well advised to withdraw his Bill, as has been suggested by the Minister, and we could all vote with a clear conscience when the time comes next year or the year after.'[7]

TWELVE

Saidie Patterson
1904–85

Amalgamated Transport and General
Workers' Union strike speech
Belfast

JANUARY 1940

'We don't want anything we are not entitled to.'

Saidie Patterson, a working-class woman from North Belfast, led a trade union revolution in the 1940s that would restructure industrial relations. Patterson was a skilled orator and a strategic negotiator, striking better deals for workers, especially female workers, during a harsh economic era in Northern Ireland. Patterson was keenly aware of the dangerous environments that working-class women were forced to endure in return for low pay and unacceptable employment conditions. Patterson's mother was an out-worker for a local factory, a task that consumed much of her day in return for very low pay. When Patterson was 12 years old, her mother died during childbirth. This traumatic event caused Patterson to question, 'why was it that my mother had to be cared for by a kindly but untrained local "handy-woman," who was herself expecting a baby? And why was it that we weren't able to afford the 3s. 6d. for a doctor?'[1] Patterson resolved from an early age to work for better rights for working women.

Patterson began work as an assistant weaver at a young age in William Ewart & Son's mill on the Crumlin Road in Belfast. In the wake of World War One, the economic environment in Belfast was at an all-time low, and unemployment rates were high. The textile women workers were not unionised, mainly for fear of losing their jobs. The working conditions at Ewart's were deplorable: a flax dust coated the factory floor that, combined with damp linen and steam, produced during production, put workers at high risk of contracting tuberculosis. Conditions were often no better in other factories in Belfast at this time and so changing employer would make little difference, even if another job could be found. From her earliest years working on the factory floor, Patterson defended her female colleagues if they were mistreated by management. Although it would remain almost impossible to form an organised union for nearly two more decades, Patterson gained the respect and support of her colleagues in Ewart's.

The situation for workers did not improve throughout the following decade. In the winter of 1938, a survey of Belfast found that 36 per cent of families assessed were living in 'conditions classified as "absolute poverty"'.[2] That same year, Patterson first met Bob Getgood, then General Secretary of the Amalgamated Transport and General Workers' Union (ATGWU) and chair of the Northern Ireland Labour Party. With the threat of another war looming, availability of work began to steadily increase in Belfast. The city became a centre for aircraft industry and munition factories, with reinvigorated ship building works. With employment rates rising by 1939, trade unions stepped up their organisation and increased membership numbers. Ernest Bevin, then the most celebrated Labour politician and trade unionist in Britain, worked with Getgood to expand trade unions in Northern Ireland. Both men were well aware that in order to succeed they needed the support of the women workers, and they were equally committed to improving conditions for female as well as male workers. Getgood and Bevin approached Patterson to organise women workers. Patterson had the right attitude and dedication that the trade union leaders sought. In addition, as the largest linen producer in Europe, Ewart's was a significant employer of female workers and a key site through which the ATGWU could expand their organisation.

Patterson agreed to take on the role of secretary of the Textile Branch of the ATGWU on condition that Bevin and Getgood would call a strike should their demands not be met by Ewart's management. This was a turning point for trade relations in Northern Ireland. It was also a defining moment in Patterson's rise through the trade union movement and her campaign to improve employment rights for female workers. Patterson began organising evenings at her home to recruit female textile workers. By the end of 1939, the ATGWU was in a stronger position and presented management at Ewart's with a demand that 100 per cent of their workers must be members of the union. The ATGWU viewed the campaign to fully unionise Ewart's as key to expanding trade unions throughout the linen industry in Britain. Ewart's management formally responded to this demand with a statement:

The joining of a trade union is a matter entirely for each worker to decide, but the question of whether or not our works are to be what is termed a 'closed shop' is a matter for us to decide. We will not agree to the principle that we are only to engage such workers as a single or any trade union may decide.[3]

Furthermore, Ewart's indicated that this was a 'fundamental principle' of the linen industry on which they were not prepared to compromise. The ATGWU also refused to compromise, arguing that workers would only gain full recognition of their rights in this way. By now Patterson had amassed a large membership and had garnered a strong alliance between male and female workers in the linen industry, although women outnumbered the men greatly. Getgood pressed further with management, who again responded by claiming that it was ultimately against workers' rights to be forced into a chosen trade union, stating, 'We are aware that many individual workers either for reasons of conscience or for other personal reasons are unwilling to join any union, and we look upon it as the inalienable right of such individuals as free British subjects to make their own decisions on such matters.'[4]

Patterson prepared for action and organised an address to a group of Belfast citizens on the subject. Her speech in this section was given to a range of interested citizens, including business, clergy and university representatives. This was one of Patterson's first speeches on behalf of the trade union, and the current atmosphere generated immense pressure, yet she expressed a clear and determined message. Patterson hit at the core of inequality for women workers, describing them as the lowest paid and the hardest worked. She maintained the stance that the only way to improve working conditions was by the union representing 100 per cent of the workers at Ewart's. Evoking the unionist term 'No Surrender', Patterson cleverly inspired support from unionist quarters. However, she was firm in her resolution that this resistance should come from a united perspective, highlighting the ideal of a non-sectarian trade union movement. Patterson impressed her audience and garnered much support for the ATGWU that day.

After her speech, an ultimatum was given to Ewart's management that 100 per cent of their workers must be members of the ATGWU by Friday, 23 February 1940 or all union members would strike from Monday morning on 26 February. At the beginning of February, only 135 workers at Ewart's had failed to join the union. The threatened strike action was defended by many other unions, including the National Union of Printing, Bookbinding, and Paper Workers, who publicly pledged their support.[5] Such open support inspired many more Ewart's employees to join the union over the following days.

As the deadline approached, the likelihood of strike action seemed inevitable without full unionisation of the workforce. Two days before the strike date, Ewart's management announced that they had received a telegram from H. M. Ministry of Supply in London informing them 'that a labour dispute may interfere with urgent government contracts allocated to the firm'.[6] The company issued a damning statement to their workers, which was displayed throughout their factory site, announcing, 'Many of our employees have voluntarily joined the fighting forces. Many of you are engaged in producing cloth which is essential to the successful prosecution of the war. Are you prepared to stab our fighting men in the back by interrupting the flow of necessary equipment?'[7] This was an emotive attack during the early stages of World War Two, attempting to shame workers into remaining on the factory floor. Patterson retaliated in the most confident and uncompromising form, telling workers that although 'the employers have challenged our loyalty[, w]e know your loyalty too well to question it. Our fellow trade unionists have joined the fighting forces to give battle to those who destroy trade unions in Germany. . . . Don't permit anyone to destroy their unions, while they are away at the front.'[8]

By 22 February, only 26 workers remained outside the union. The *Belfast Telegraph* announced the impending strike under the heading '26 girls refuse to join the union.'[9] It was further reported that this group of female workers did not want to pay the union weekly contribution of 3d. The strike action began on 26 February as threatened. Patterson had guaranteed her female colleagues strike pay of 12 shillings a week, and they were fully supported by their male colleagues. Just under 2,000 workers initiated strike action at William Ewart & Son, which gained attention from linen firms across Europe. Bevin organised a meeting on the first day of the strike in the Wellington Hall of the Belfast YMCA. The hall was packed with attendees, and a host of male trade unionists, including Getgood, addressed the strikers, appealing for a calm and unwavering strike action. Patterson was the only woman to address the audience that day. Her address was simple and persuasive; calling on continued support for female workers, she began,

> Girls, many of you are already struggling to live on a pittance of less than a pound a week, and here I am asking you to come out on strike for twelve shillings a week strike pay. Well, it's like this – if we only manage to exist and no more on our present wage, have we the backbone to show the men that for a matter of principle we can do on even less for as long as it takes to see this thing through?[10]

The workers at Ewart's did show their backbone and remained on strike for seven weeks. During that time Patterson organised high-profile marches of female linen workers through the streets of Belfast. She took many stages and addressed numerous meetings, advocating for the rights of women workers in the linen industry. Journalists were keen to interview Patterson, and positive articles appeared in newspapers across Ireland and Britain. Such positive high-profile attention generated financial support for the cause from many quarters and enabled strike pay to be increased by four shillings to 16 shillings a week.

In the end, pressure due to the increasing loss of troops fighting at the front and the hardships endured at home during the war caused the ATGWU to broker a deal and return their members to work. However, the strike had changed the mentality of women workers at Ewart's, who now worked with the confidence that the mill could not operate without them. The women became committed members of the trade union and actively demanded better working conditions. By the end of 1940 a host of employment conditions had been introduced at Ewart's, including sickness benefit, holiday pay and legal aid schemes. The wages for workers at Ewart's increased by 15 per cent in that year, and the minimum wage for women workers was now guaranteed to be subject to regular review.

Patterson continued as a committed and successful trade unionist. Her work remained focused on the rights of female workers, which gradually began moving the trade union away from its traditional male-centred approach. In appreciation of Patterson's work, Queen Elizabeth II awarded her an MBE, an order of the British Empire award, in 1953. Patterson remained devoted to a non-sectarian approach in trade unionism, first expressed in her speech in this section. In 1962 the annual Labour Party's Women's Conference included representatives from Northern Ireland for the first time. Mrs. A. Ardis, the chair of the Northern Ireland Labour women's advisory committee, and Patterson, then secretary of the committee, attended. Patterson used the forum to press the issue of sectarianism in Northern Ireland. She informed delegates that, while the civil rights movement in America is concerned with a divide between black and white, the concern in Ireland is between orange and green.[11] Patterson worked tirelessly to bring Protestant and Catholic communities together, which was most apparent in her volunteer position on the Girls' Club Union, which brought girls from the Falls and Shankill Roads together. Patterson was an active member of the group for over 50 years.

As the Troubles in Northern Ireland escalated towards the end of the 1960s, Patterson dedicated much of her time to peace movements. Among her many peace activities, she became chair of Women Together, a progressive organisation of Protestant and Catholic women committed to peace in Northern Ireland. She received a number of awards for her peace work, including, at the age of 69, the World Methodist Peace Award.[12] She was the first ever recipient of this award in 1977; within hours of the award announcement, her grand-nephew, Robin Smyrl, was gunned down in county Tyrone in an IRA ambush as he drove to work. Smyrl was manager of the Northgate women's clothing factory and a part-time member of the Ulster Defence Regiment.[13] He was 25 years of age when he was killed. Patterson resolved to continue with her peace activism in her remaining years. Saidie Patterson died in 1985. In 2018, a blue plaque in her honour was placed at the Methodist Church on the Shankill Road, where she worshipped. The plaque was most fittingly unveiled on International Women's Day, 8 March.

'Workers do not make up their minds to go on strike unless something of very great importance is at stake. And the great importance of this strike is the right to have 100 per cent trade unionism.

Why do we want this? Because without this organisation we cannot hope to remedy the conditions under which we labour.

We, the women workers — the weavers and the winders — are probably the hardest worked and lowest paid section of industry inside the British Isles.

We have no machinery to regulate wages; no Trades' Boards to regulate or improve the conditions under which we work. Nothing exists in the way of protection, except our trade union — and that is why we want a strong 100 per cent trade union organisation, capable of demanding better conditions for the thousands of textile workers, instead of merely pleading for them.

We don't want anything we are not entitled to. We give the best years of our lives, month after month, year after year, to the production of linen. We think we are entitled to a little more than the bare necessities of life.

Neither are we fighting solely for ourselves — we are fighting for *all* the linen workers. For our success is their success; our defeat would be their defeat. But we are not going to be defeated, because we come of good fighting stock. We are Ulster workers and we say "No Surrender", but this time we are saying it with one voice and a united meaning.

It is rather strange that in all the appeals which have been made in the name of loyalty nobody has appealed to the loyalty of the employers. I wonder why.

To the men workers who have come out in sympathy with us, at a heavy financial loss, we want publicly to thank them for their support. To all the other I say, stand firm. Together, shoulder to shoulder, we will see this thing through.

And when we win — and we shall win — we will have laid the foundation upon which will be built a happier and a brighter life for all linen workers.

Thank you.'[14]

THIRTEEN

Helen Chenevix
1886–1963

Speech to the annual meeting of the Irish Trade Union Congress
Town Hall Killarney, Kerry

25 JULY 1951

'There is a long road to be travelled and it must be travelled.'

On Wednesday, 25 July 1951, Dublin woman Helen Chenevix addressed a gathering of 212 delegates of the Irish Trade Union Congress (ITUC) at their annual general meeting. Chenevix was by then a highly respected trade unionist and president of the ITUC, an organisation that represented the views of the main Irish trade unions. Her speaking style was later applauded by an *Irish Times* journalist, who noted how 'calm logic and courage pervaded all her arguments and she won the respect of employers, workers and Labour Court officials alike.'[1] Her presidential address received vast media attention and was reported in newspapers across the country.[2] This speech stood the test of time when in 1994 an extract was included in a centenary volume edited by Donal Nevin, former general secretary of the Irish Congress of Trade Unions.

In her speech, Chenevix assessed the current economic crisis which led to an increased number of labour strikes, warning that such action 'had become so cheapened by frequent use that sometimes a group of workers would resort to it for petty or sectional interests'.[3] Ultimately, she focused on gender and class inequalities which led to lower pay and unequal access to skilled employment. Chenevix was particularly scathing of the Irish government's lack of action in addressing inequalities in the structures of the Irish state.

Chenevix was a veteran labour activist, having come to trade unionism through the suffrage movement. She met Louie Bennett at a meeting of the Irish Women's Suffrage and Local Government Association; this was to be a life-changing event in both women's lives. The women established a lifelong partnership campaigning for women workers and social reform in Ireland. It is now generally accepted that Chenevix and Bennett were a couple; cultural historian Siobhán Kilfeather describes how they 'were part of an influential network of lesbians living in Dublin'.[4] That network included the republican and trade unionist Helena Molony and her partner, psychiatrist Dr Evelyn O'Brien. In 1911 Chenevix and Bennett founded the Irish Women's Suffrage Federation, an umbrella organisation coordinating the work of the many suffrage groups in Ireland. As noted by labour historian Frances Clarke, the federation was 'a politically independent, non-militant organisation[;] it linked a variety of suffrage societies throughout the country, and was subsequently instrumental in the formation of Dublin's Irish Women's Reform League and Belfast's Women's Suffrage Society'.[5]

Through her suffrage work, Chenevix became deeply aware of the particular injustices that working women experienced, and she became fully immersed in trade union activism through the Irish Women Workers' Union (IWWU). The women's union had been established in 1911 under general secretary Delia Larkin as a semi-independent branch of the Irish Transport and General Workers' Union (ITGWU) established by James Larkin in 1909. James Larkin was the first president of the IWWU, which became a central organisation during the 1913 Dublin lockout, a major industrial dispute affecting over 20,000 workers in Dublin. By 1916 the IWWU was in disorder. Following a clash with trade union and nationalist leader James Connolly along with a court case initiated by a former clerk against the union, Delia Larkin had returned to work in England in 1915.[6]

Chenevix and Bennett along with Molony and trade unionist Rosie Hackett set about reorganising the IWWU. Chenevix and Bennett success-fully moved to have the IWWU accepted as an independent union at the annual ITUC conference in 1917, and the women were elected as joint honorary secretaries the following year. Within just three years the women's union could boast a membership of 6,000. The now independent IWWU represented general and unskilled female workers, including laundry and factory workers but initially also nurses and midwives. Clarke notes that until Chenevix's retirement in 1957 'her work as an executive member of the IWWU occupied the greater part of her public life, though she received only a nominal payment.'[7]

Chenevix worked tirelessly not only to address gender inequalities in labour but also to eliminate class-based oppression. In 1949 her work was recognised when she was elected as vice-president of the ITUC. Founded in 1894 to act as a collective voice of organised Irish labour, the ITUC had many significant affiliated unions, including the ITGWU and the IWWU, and was a precursor to the current Irish Congress of Trade Unions. During the ITUC's 63-year existence, only three women served as presidents: Bennett was elected to this role twice, first in 1932 and again in 1948; Helena Molony was elected in 1937. In July 1950, at the ITUC's annual meeting in University College Galway, Chenevix was elected as president for a one-year term. Her term concluded at the annual congress in Killarney, at which she gave the speech in this section. Chenevix's speech displays her commitment to secure labour unity and her campaigns for reforms in education, health, and social policy.

In her speech, Chenevix refers to the International Labour Organisation (ILO) in Geneva. The ILO was formed in 1919 as part of the Treaty of Versailles at the end of World War One. The ILO was an important collaboration, initially between nine countries, to secure similarity of working conditions between member states and ultimately to avoid social injustice for workers.[8] Ireland automatically became a member of the ILO in 1923 when the Irish Free State joined the League of Nations. A general conference of the ILO met in Geneva on 6 June 1951, at which members accepted a recommendation to adopt 'the principle of equal remuneration for men and women workers for work of equal value'.[9] Chenevix drew attention to the government's failure to send either a woman or a representative from the ITUC to that meeting, highlighting the Irish government's slow approach to tackling the issue of equal pay.

Chenevix's focus on equal pay for work of equal value in such an arena, to a predominantly male audience, was a confrontational move. She was forthright in saying that the gender pay gap was not viewed as a concern by the 'male worker who is quite content to see the woman who works beside him drawing half or less than half his wage'.[10] Few female trade unionists at this time aligned themselves with the feminist movement; according to Chenevix, the feminist movement was led by female graduates who did not understand the issues facing working-class women. Historian Margaret Ayres found that from the 1920s the ITUC 'regularly passed motions in favour of equal pay but little action accompanied these claims'.[11] The 1950 annual report of the IWWU found that there was some success in challenging gender pay inequality but not enough, and therefore it became a key focus of Chenevix's speech. The ITUC was moved to action in 1959, when they established a Women's Advisory Committee to further women's interests. However, the Irish government would not take firm action on the issue of equal gender pay until the national wage agreements of the 1970s.

It is noteworthy that Chenevix addressed the recent move by the Irish Minister of Health, Dr Noel Browne, to introduce a mother and child scheme. Browne's proposal would improve health awareness and provide free medical care for mothers and for children under 16 years of age. The proposed bill had initially been put forward by the previous minister for health, Dr Jim Ryan, in 1947. The proposal came at a time when Ireland had the highest infantile death rate in Europe, and free medical services for mothers and children would certainly have reduced the deplorable death rate. There was negative reaction both from the medical profession concerned that their income from private patients would be reduced and also from religious sectors who advocated that the family should not be interfered with by state bodies. A general election was called in 1948 before any progress could be made on the bill.

When Browne took position as health minister, he reinstated the bill. The Catholic Archbishop of Dublin, John McQuaid, strongly objected to the proposal; in his statement on the issue, he maintained that 'the public authority, without qualification, is entirely and directly contrary to Catholic teaching on the rights of the family, the rights of the Church in education, the rights of the medical profession and of voluntary institutions.'[12] He claimed that only the Church, not the state or its institutions, should influence the family. Recognising the powerful position of the Catholic Church in Ireland, Taoiseach John A. Costello would not contradict their ruling. The Irish Housewives Association (IHA) was one of the few organisations to publicly support Browne. Chenevix was a prominent member of the IHA, and she regularly published articles in their magazine, *The Irish Housewife*.[13] The IHA demonstration at College Green in Dublin's city centre was perceived as anti-Catholic behaviour and drew condemnation from media sources. On Saturday, 12 April 1952, an article appeared in the *Roscommon Herald* entitled 'Dangerous trends in Ireland'; it effectively labelled the feminist group as communist. The article noted that the IHA 'had always been used as a medium of expression' by Marxists, communists, or fellow travellers.[14]

Browne had been forced to resign in April 1951 over the entire controversial episode. By the end of May, a general election was called, and a new Fianna Fáil-led government was in place by the time of Chenevix's speech; Ryan was once again appointed as Minister of Health. Negative backlash from the Church or the medical profession did not deter Chenevix from voicing her support of the proposed scheme and backing an ITUC request to Ryan demanding the introduction of 'a social welfare insurance scheme including a mother and child scheme'.[15] Copies of the request were distributed at the meeting after Chenevix's speech, as was Ryan's reply, which was recorded as follows:

> The Minister said in a letter that he would be glad to arrange for consultations after he had had an opportunity of considering various matters which were receiving attention in his department. He shared the view of the Congress Executive and was having the whole position in regard to the mother and child scheme re-examined.[16]

The proposed scheme would not automatically interest trade unionists, but Chenevix cleverly connects it with inadequate health insurance for workers, making the mother and child scheme a trade union issue.

Chenevix's awareness of class inequality impacting on labour issues is further evident in her focus on education. She campaigned vigorously for the school leaving age to be increased to 16, a point also addressed in her speech. This was an issue particularly class-related as parents with sufficient income could afford to keep their children in school longer in order to achieve the highest secondary level qualifications and to advance to further education. With the legal school leaving age requirement only 14 years of age, most children in Ireland were forced into early employment, having reached only a basic educational standard. In the years prior to this speech, Chenevix dedicated herself to campaigning on this issue. A School Attendance Act in 1926 required children to attend school only between the ages of six and 14. On examining the implications of such legislation, historian Diarmaid Ferriter noted that 'political lobbying about the need for children in rural areas to work on farms so as not to thwart cheap labour was reflected in the report of an interdepartmental government committee in 1935.'[17] Chenevix was afforded all the benefits of a solid education, having graduated from Trinity College Dublin with a BA in 1909; however, she was fully aware of the financial hardship that poorer families would incur and proposed that such families could be financially compensated by the government. Despite Chenevix's tireless campaign, the school leaving age was not increased until 1972 and then only to 15.

At the conclusion of the annual meeting, officers were elected for the following term, and Chenevix was elected to the National Executive Council of the ITUC. When Bennett retired in 1955, Chenevix was appointed as general secretary of the IWWU and adopted a different style of leadership stressing the value of 'collective contribution from members'.[18] She continued to serve on the national executive of the ITUC and to pursue equal access in education through a number of routes, including as a member of the ITUC education committee. Chenevix also continued to campaign for improved health for mothers and children as a councillor on Dublin corporation; she served on the child welfare committee and the committee for the National Maternity Hospital.

Chenevix remained a committed pacifist and maintained an association with global organisations, including the Fellowship of Reconciliation and the Women's International League for Peace and Freedom. She was a member of the Irish Pacifist Movement and occupied the vice-presidency for a time. Chenevix finally retired from the IWWU in 1957, at the age of 71, but she continued campaigning for peace and nuclear disarmament. She died at the age of 77 on 4 March 1963 and was buried three days later at Deansgrange

Cemetery, Blackrock, not far from where she was born. All major Irish newspapers carried her obituary, and many reported on her large funeral.[19] The funeral mass was conducted at Monkstown Parish Church and was a testament to the high regard in which she was held; the Archbishop of Dublin, Most Rev Dr G. O. Simms, paid tribute, noting that Chenevix's 'quiet resolution was evident throughout her life in her unhesitating support for great causes'.[20] When Louie Bennett had died in 1958, a plaque was placed on a bench in St Stephen's Green, Dublin, in her honour. After Chenevix's death, an inscription was added to the plaque, stating, 'Also of her life long friend and co-worker Helen Chenevix 1888–1963 who shared the same high ideals.' In Helen Chenevix's obituary, the *Irish Times* declared that 'she and Louie Bennett were two of the most remarkable Irish women of this century.'[21]

15. Irish Women Workers' Union members on the steps of Liberty Hall, circa 1914. Delia Larkin seated centre. Courtesy of the National Library of Ireland on The Commons.

'During the past two years the International Labour Organisation in Geneva have focused attention on the question of "equal pay for equal work" as between men and women. . . . This is a problem which bristles with difficulties and cannot be solved off hand either by the academic feminist who has never entered a factory or the male worker who is quite content to see the woman who works beside him drawing half or less than half his wage. One thing is clear. Whatever should be the basis of wage standards, it should not be the sex of the worker. If a man or a woman are doing the same type of work with equal skill and training, there is no justification for paying one of them less than the other. The whole question demands the serious consideration of both men and women workers, to both of whom the exploitation of women as cheap labour is disastrous.

The suggestion has been made that governments and public author-ities should set a headline in this matter. Last month the International Labour Conference adopted both a Convention and a Recommendation on the subject of equal pay and we hope very much that our Government will put them into force. But I think that they will need a good deal of pressure from the trade union movement to do so. . . .

In view of the importance and complexity of this subject it is to be regretted that the Government of the Republic did not see its way to send a woman to Geneva . . . when this question was under discussion, and that they adhered to their refusal to grant any representation to the Irish Trade Union Congress. . . .

In the matter of social legislation, the Republic still lags behind the North. Mr. Norton's Welfare Plan was never given the chance to come into operation, and Dr. Browne's Mother and Child Scheme was rejected with dramatic suddenness.

There is at the present moment a live interest in health connected with the controversies surrounding the Mother and Child Scheme, and in the North, the various problems arising out of the administration of the Health Scheme, still comparatively new. There is also a growing recognition of the fact that our National Health Insurance in the Republic is totally inadequate to tide any worker over an illness, a recognition exemplified in the fact that an increasing number of firms instituted sickness funds for their workers. Clearly now is the time to press forward, and keep pressing, in this matter of health services. A comprehensive and practical scheme for mothers, infants and school children would be a good beginning, but the adult worker and the aged need consideration also. . . .

It is in the field of education that the inequality between higher and lower income groups is most glaringly obvious. The rich man planning his children's education has a choice of good secondary schools with the university in the background, but with the man of small means it is far otherwise. For the great mass of our people the only education available is the primary school which the child leaves at fourteen or fifteen at most. If the child lives in a city he may very likely have been one of a class of sixty or seventy pupils, where teaching in the full sense is not possible; or, if he lives in the country, he may have had to attend school in a building no better than a tumble-down shack. How can we expect to have a mentally and physically healthy nation so long as the shadow of this disgrace remains on our national life?

There is a long road to be travelled and it must be travelled. The workers' organisations cannot afford to rest until the school-leaving age is raised to sixteen, with the necessary additional school buildings and additional teachers, with salaries befitting the importance of their work. We must also insist that special schools be provided for blind children, for crippled children, for deaf mutes, and for mental defectives. This is the bare minimum of the children's needs.'[22]

FOURTEEN

Frances Condell
1916–86

Speech to welcome President John F. Kennedy to Limerick
Greenpark Racecourse

29 JUNE 1963

'We, the women of Limerick and county, feel that we have a special claim on you.'

On 29 June 1962 Frances Condell became the first woman elected as mayor of Limerick in its 750-year history.[1] At the time of her election, much political discussion surrounded a prospective visit of the President of America, John Fitzgerald Kennedy, to Ireland.[2] Among her many attributes, Condell had a keen eye for Irish business development and international trade, traits evident in the speech by her in this section. Condell was undoubtedly mindful of the economic benefits that such a high-profile visit could yield for Ireland. This was to be the first state visit to the Republic of Ireland by a United States president. The Irish Embassy in Washington estimated that Kennedy's visit would produce publicity worth millions of pounds to the Irish economy. According to historian Ian McCabe, an audience of seventy million Americans would witness Kennedy's visit to his ancestral homeland through major networks, radio stations, and newspapers.[3] Condell set an optimistic goal of including a visit to Limerick in Kennedy's Irish itinerary.

Since 1945, Shannon airport, situated just over 20 kilometres from Limerick city, was the gateway between Europe and the Americas. A compulsory stopover at Shannon was a legal requirement for transatlantic flights until as recently as 2008.[4] Before being elected as mayor, Condell worked as a welfare officer for the Shannon Free Airport Development Company, assisting families, mainly from overseas, to settle into the area.

If Condell could promote Limerick as a location destination for American visitors, the county could be easily reached by incoming tourists, and the area would benefit immensely from income generated. Limerick was not originally considered as a location for Kennedy during his busy four-day itinerary in Ireland. The president was scheduled to fly to Dublin airport on the evening of 26 June 1963 as part of his European tour. While in the capital city he would address both Houses of the Oireachtas. To underline the importance of Kennedy's visit, a joint session of Dáil Éireann and Seanad Éireann was held on 28 June 1963, for the first time in the history of the Irish state. Fine Gael TD James Dillon later noted in the Dáil that this historic occasion was called for 'as a unique gesture of respect and admiration for the President'.[5] Other engagements during Kennedy's time in Dublin included his attendance at a reception hosted by President Éamon de Valera at Áras an Uachtaráin and a meeting with Taoiseach Seán Lemass at the American Embassy residence. The US president would also be awarded honorary degrees by the National University of Ireland and Trinity College Dublin.

As well as travelling to Dublin, Kennedy was scheduled to visit the counties of Cork, Galway and Wexford. Much attention was given to Kennedy's planned visit to Dunganstown in county Wexford. The president's paternal great grandfather, Patrick Kennedy, emigrated from Dunganstown in 1848 to escape the Great Famine. Less attention focused on the fact that Kennedy's maternal great grandfather, Thomas Fitzgerald, was born in Limerick in the town of Bruff. The Limerick connection on the Fitzgerald side of his family had deep significance for the president. At Kennedy's presidential inauguration ceremony on 20 January 1961, it was his mother's family bible that he placed his hand on to swear into office; the bible was originally owned by Thomas Fitzgerald.[6]

Conscious of such connections to Limerick, Condell contacted the then American Ambassador to Ireland, Matthew McCloskey, so often requesting a Limerick visit that he remarked, 'heaven protect me from a persistent woman'.[7] Condell was indeed persistent. After numerous letters and phone calls to Irish and American officials, she visited Dublin the month before Kennedy was due to arrive in Ireland. While there she met with Ambassador McCloskey and the Minister for External Affairs, Frank Aiken. Condell's sole purpose for her trip to Dublin was to discuss the possibility of awarding Kennedy the freedom of Limerick city at a public ceremony. The mayor was accompanied on her visits by Donogh O'Malley, then parliamentary secretary to the Minister of Finance, James Ryan. O'Malley had served as mayor of Limerick in 1961 but resigned his post to take up a government role. He was a strong and charismatic ally for Condell.[8]

One month before Kennedy was due to arrive in Ireland, Limerick still did not appear on the presidential schedule, a fact noted by a representative from the American Embassy in Dublin. When questioned on this by journalists from the *Limerick Leader*, the unnamed Embassy source said, 'Limerick people would no doubt visit Shannon which was not far from the city.'[9] Shannon may well be geographically nearby, but it is in the neighbouring county of Clare and Condell refused to accept anything less than a visit by Kennedy to Limerick county. Condell and O'Malley were undeterred in their aim. The pair were received on 23 May by President de Valera at Áras an Uachtaráin. After her meetings, Condell rang the *Limerick Leader* offices to inform newspaper staff that she was 'very pleased with these interviews, and most hopeful that the citizens of Limerick will be given the opportunity of seeing the president in person prior to his departure from Shannon'.[10]

Yet, over two weeks later, on 12 June, the *Limerick Leader* published a disappointing headline, 'Visit from U.S. President unlikely.' Condell remained persistent: she orchestrated a meeting with Pierre E. G. Salinger, the White House press secretary, when he arrived in Dublin and pleaded with him to arrange the visit.[11] In all, she visited ambassador McCloskey four times, wrote numerous letters, and phoned him requesting that he arrange for Kennedy to visit Limerick. In an interview conducted for the John F. Kennedy Presidential Library and Museum, Condell describes how this persistence paid off: 'So eventually he [McCloskey] rang me up one night about a quarter to one, at least, one morning . . . and he said, "You've got your wish, now will you get off my back?"'[12] This left Condell with just one week to find a venue and make all the necessary arrangements for a presidential visit.

It was agreed that Kennedy would visit Limerick on his return to Shannon airport before flying to England on 29 June for the remainder of his European tour. By this date, Condell would be in office exactly one year. A mayoral election was due before 29 June, but it was agreed by Limerick City Council to grant Condell an extended term of one week so that she could oversee the presidential reception, deliver the welcome speech and officiate Kennedy's freedom of Limerick city. Condell left no element of Kennedy's visit to chance. A site was decided upon within hours of the confirmed visit: Greenpark Racecourse, on the outskirts of Limerick city, would be the most suitable venue to accommodate a large audience and set up a required stage. Condell quickly made arrangements to prepare the venue. Two days before the president was due to arrive, 17 officials from the American Embassy in Dublin and from the Department of Foreign Affairs arrived at Greenpark to inspect the venue. The delegation was met by Condell, and they informed a journalist from the *Limerick Leader* that they were 'very pleased with the site'.[13]

Condell made a public call for all businesses in the Limerick city area to close between the hours of 12 noon and 3 p.m. on the day of Kennedy's visit, to ensure that locals could attend. She further requested that employers of any band members give those employees the day off so that they could participate in the musical welcome for the president.[14] On 28 June, Kennedy visited Cork city, and thousands of people lined the streets to get a glimpse of the president as he was driven through the city in an open-topped car. Condell was invited to attend the reception at Cork City Hall where the freedom of the city was conferred on Kennedy. While there, she had the opportunity of meeting the president for the first time. The Cork event had been scheduled well in advance, and City Hall was decorated with bunting and intricate floral arrangements. Condell seized an opportunity to ask the Lord Mayor of Cork, Seán Casey, if she could borrow the flowers for the next day. When Casey agreed, Condell quickly arranged the transfer of the floral displays by army drivers. Transport for the day of the presidential visit was arranged through the local undertaker, Frank Thompson, who provided a fleet of cars free of charge to ferry Condell and other Limerick dignitaries.

The gates to Greenpark opened at 9 a.m. on 29 June, while special Kennedy buses ferried people from Limerick city to the racecourse from the early hours. Representatives of the Kennedy ancestry had been invited and were among the 60,000 people who attended, with 500 gardai on duty.[15] On Kennedy's arrival at Greenpark Racecourse, Condell introduced the President to the all-male group of local dignitaries, including the Right Rev. Dr R. Wyse-Jackson, Church of Ireland bishop of Limerick; Most Rev. Henry Murphy, D.D., Catholic bishop of Limerick; Mr T. F. McDermott, city manager; and Mr T. M. O'Connor, county manager. Kennedy had been received by male dignitaries throughout his visit to Ireland up to that point. The fact that his wife, Jackie Kennedy, did not travel with him because she was heavily pregnant increased the male-centred approach of his Irish tour.[16] When Kennedy arrived in Dublin, he was met by a party of 50 male dignitaries. Jean Kennedy-Smith, later an American ambassador to Ireland, accompanied her brother and was the sole woman present. Condell was the only woman to organise a presidential visit to her city and to welcome President Kennedy during his visit to Ireland.

When Kennedy walked by the floral displays set up at Greenpark, including one arrangement of the American flag, he asked Condell, 'Haven't I seen this somewhere before?' Condell quickly replied, 'yes sir, we borrowed it. We knew you liked it so well.'[17] The *Limerick Chronicle* described the scene as 'one of the most colourful and spectacular of its kind ever seen in Limerick'.[18] Condell took the temporary stage at the racecourse and officially welcomed President Kennedy to Limerick. Her speech was a mix of good humour and diplomacy. She highlighted the past horrors of mass emigration from Irish shores which led to the deep-rooted connection between America and Ireland. A point made all the more poignant by the fact that the current

President of Ireland, de Valera, was born in New York to an Irish mother from county Limerick.[19] In her speech, Condell used these American bonds to call for further foreign investment in the area. Kennedy's visit to Limerick lasted less than half an hour, and in that time Condell presented a speech that earned her and Limerick national and international respect. While at Greenpark Racecourse, Kennedy was introduced to 60 of his Irish relations from the Fitzgerald clan, and Condell presented him with the freedom of the city.

Kennedy gave a short, casual and seemingly heartfelt response to the proceedings. He addressed his speech to his 'fellow citizens of Limerick', which received a huge cheer from those gathered, continuing, 'I want to express my thanks and also my admiration for the best speech that I've heard since I've come to Europe.' It was while in Limerick that Kennedy made one of the most astounding statements during his time in Ireland. The US President informed the people of Limerick, 'this is not the land of my birth, but it is the land for which I hold the greatest affection.'[20] After the festivities in Limerick, Kennedy travelled on to Shannon airport by helicopter for his final departure from the country of his ancestors. Condell was at Shannon to greet him, having been driven at speed by a Limerick-based garda car.

After his return to the United States, President Kennedy wrote to Ambassador McCloskey reiterating that Condell's speech was one of the finest that he heard during his tour of Europe.[21] Kennedy also wrote to Condell in the weeks after his visit. In a letter dated 22 July 1963, Kennedy thanked Condell for her gift of a Limerick lace tablecloth, saying, 'Mrs. Kennedy was simply delighted with this beautiful handiwork.'[22] He ended the letter in a charming and emotional manner, stating, 'I shall never forget the wonderful reception that greeted me in Ireland and I know that my visit there will remain one of my most treasured memories.'[23]

Kennedy did not live to return to Ireland; he was assassinated five months later. Condell received international attention for her speech at Greenpark Racecourse and entertained numerous high-profile invitations afterwards, through which she continually promoted Irish goods and industry. As a testament to her success, she was re-elected as mayor of Limerick again on 2 July 1963, days after President Kennedy's visit to the county. In June 1964 she attended the opening of the Court of Common Council, as the guest of the lord mayor of London. Condell was the first Irish mayor based outside of Dublin to be officially invited to the Mansion House in London. She dressed fully in Irish-made clothes for the event and presented dignitaries with Limerick hams. Condell continued to host high-profile visits of dignitaries to Limerick, including Kennedy's brother Senator Edward Kennedy; President Kaunda of Zambia; and 'Lady Bird' Johnson, wife of President Lyndon B. Johnson. After her term in office, Condell visited

America in 1966, promoting Ireland on radio and television programmes and meeting with Jackie Kennedy.[24]

Frances Condell suffered ill health from 1967 and withdrew from political life that year, having made a positive international impact in just a short time. Condell worked at various times throughout her career as a journalist and contributed poetry and prose regularly to the *Limerick Echo*, the *Church of Ireland Gazette*, *Woman's Way* and the *Irish Independent*.[25] Condell's health deteriorated, and she died in 1986, after what was described as a long illness, in the county she loved so dearly, Limerick.

16. Frances Condell with President John F. Kennedy at Greenpark Racecourse, Limerick, 29 June 1963. Courtesy of Glucksman Library, University of Limerick.

'In welcoming you here this afternoon on this racecourse, Mr President, I would like you to know, however, that we of Limerick have a lovely city of which we are very proud, steeped as it is in history and antiquity with its charter and first Mayor, reaching away back to the year 1197.

It was from our docks, Mr President, that many emigrant ships set sail for your shores and from which point of departure our people became yours. That time of great exodus is over, thank god, and I am sure you will agree with me that there are enough of us over there to keep you happy and to assure you of your faithful support at all times. The day has come when the point of departure and arrival has transferred itself from us, some 15 miles distant and in keeping with modern times, to an airport. . . .

Because of our proximity to the airport also we have the pleasure of welcoming each year many of your fellow countrymen and our returning emigrants. Now, with the setting up of the Industrial Estate at Shannon, in which five American firms have established themselves during the past couple of years, we have seen the introduction of a new type of American who is taking his place in our civic and social life, and who is bringing to our people the skills and techniques of industry.

We welcome you, Sir, on their behalf, as we welcome them on your behalf, and we trust that you will use your influence to send many more industrialists like them, not alone to Shannon but to our city of Limerick. I assure you that we shall be very pleased to see a concentration of American industry in Limerick. . . .[26]

While listening in awed admiration to your speeches in Germany on Wednesday last and later upon your arrival in Dublin, my mind was directed towards your three-fold headings, which you have given as reasons for your work and your visit to Europe.[27] As I listened to you, Mr President, I could not but interpret your reasoning to a modern idea based on the symbol of the shamrock and our Christian belief, that you, and your people with us, see three good reasons – for good living, for determined unity, and for working together towards world peace. Three good reasons sprigging from our common hereditary stem which inspire us towards your aims and the aims of all free people which we hope you will achieve, sir, as St Patrick did in the name of God.

You see, Mr President, we, the women of Limerick and county, feel that we have a special claim on you; we claim the Fitzgerald in you. May I repeat, we claim the Fitzgerald in you, sir, and we are extremely proud of that heritage. Over there, you see a large number of your relatives and connections, who have come to greet you from the distaff side. These good people have come to show our Limerick claim on you, and by their presence, they prove that the Fitzgeralds are proud of their own role and her dynamic father Honey Fitz, your reputable and colourful and most successful grandfather.[28] But in talking so much of the Fitzgeralds and the Kennedys, we must not forget one, another woman who is dear to our hearts, your lovely wife Jaqueline. We shall be pleased if you will take back with you over the Atlantic warmest greetings, Irish prayers and thoughts, from the mothers of Limerick city and county, to her whose gracious motherhood and wifely devotion and help to you has endeared her to us all.'[29]

FIFTEEN

Bernadette Devlin

B. 1947

Maiden speech at the House of Commons
Westminster, London

22 APRIL 1969

'We, the people of Ulster, are no longer to be fooled.'

On 22 April 1969, a day before her twenty-second birthday, Bernadette Devlin rose to give her maiden address in the House of Commons at Westminster.[1] At the age of just 21, Devlin was the youngest Member of Parliament (MP) in over 200 years and, as of 2021, the youngest woman ever to be elected to that position. Devlin gave this speech within an hour of taking her seat in parliament. Her address was uncompromising and direct, admonishing unionist politics in Northern Ireland and attacking the Westminster parliament for their lack of control. The following day, newspapers across Ireland, Britain and further afield were awash with reports of her speech, with many publishing the complete version. The *Irish Examiner* newspaper proclaimed that Devlin 'held an intense House spellbound with a vibrant, passionate speech'.[2] The *Strabane Chronicle* declared that she had taken 'London by storm', describing her speech as 'flawlessly delivered[;] it was an exposition of the case for social justice such as few experienced public men could have attempted.'[3]

Devlin, from a working-class Catholic family in Cookstown, a small town in county Tyrone, was elected as an independent Unity candidate for Mid-Ulster. She was a charismatic young socialist leader who would bring the civil rights movement in Northern Ireland on to an international stage.

Like many Catholic families in Northern Ireland as this time, Devlin's family was poor. After her father died, when she was only nine years of age, the family faced more hardship and became dependent on social welfare. Devlin credits her economically deprived background with instilling her with strong socialist beliefs. She was particularly aware of Irish history from an early age and describes how, as children, she along with her brother and four sisters 'developed an unconscious political consciousness from listening to the story of our country'.[4] Devlin's political consciousness was to develop when she became a student at Queen's University, Belfast, in 1965. She initially enrolled for an Honours Celtic degree but became disillusioned by the Gaelic Society, which she described as 'a small, inward looking group', and transferred to a degree in psychology.[5] She became intensely committed to helping improve the lives of people in Northern Ireland. Two years into her degree studies, Devlin's mother died at the young age of 47. Devlin continued with her studies while commuting between Cookstown and Belfast to help care for her younger siblings.

Devlin became involved with the Northern Ireland Civil Rights Association (NICRA), which was founded in 1967 to highlight injustices in Northern Ireland. Inspired by the civil rights movement in America, NICRA initiated a series of peaceful protest marches the following year. Devlin and her younger brother took part in the first civil rights march in Northern Ireland in August 1968, marching from Coalisland to Dungannon. When the group arrived at Dungannon, they were greeted by a police cordon outside of the town centre. Police officers corralled the marchers into the Catholic area of Dungannon, which caused Devlin to contemplate how the divide in Northern Ireland was intensified by the urban division into Catholic and Protestant ghettos. Devlin participated in the march out of a commitment to highlight the then deplorable housing and employment crisis in Northern Ireland. However, the civil rights march had been turned into a sectarian issue, partly caused by the police action.

With a fresh perspective, Devlin attended a march in Derry on 5 October 1968 arranged by the Derry Housing Action Committee (DHAC) with the support of NICRA. The DHAC was established in February that year at Magee College, to protest against housing conditions. This group was to become a pivotal organisation in the civil rights movement in Northern Ireland. For the first time, Devlin heard Eamonn McCann, one of the lead organisers, speak, and she was impressed by his ability to turn 'a mob into a non-violent force'.[6] As McCann addressed the crowd, the police charged from either side and beat people off the street with truncheons. The scene quickly turned even more violent as police launched water cannons at the crowd and onlookers alike. The violence at the peaceful civil rights march in

Derry attracted global media attention. The 5 October 1968 is now generally referred to as the day the Troubles began in Northern Ireland. Devlin maintained that in fact 'the Unionist government did the civil rights movement a favour. They gave it life in one day.'[7]

Days after the march, Devlin returned to Queen's University for the start of the new term and realised that the events in Derry had enraged many other students there. A protest march was organised on 9 October, when 2,000 students planned to march on City Hall in protest at the police brutality in Derry. When the protesters arrived at their meeting place in Shaftesbury Square, they were met by Ian Paisley with 1,000 of his supporters. Paisley, a militant Protestant leader and moderator of the Free Presbyterian Church, founded by him in 1951, was a powerful adversary. Paisley blended religious language with politics in his campaign to strengthen Protestant identity in Northern Ireland using anti-Catholic rhetoric.[8] Paisley and his followers were determined to suppress the student protest.

Devlin and her fellow students engaged in a peaceful march towards City Hall, although they were rerouted by the police to avoid a confrontation with Paisley and his supporters, who had by then gathered at their destination. Those involved in the march resolved to form their own organisation, and that evening the People's Democracy was established. Devlin played a central role in the group and was elected as one of ten organising members, known as the Faceless Committee.[9] The main aims of the non-political organisation were agreed, as described by Devlin: 'one man, one vote; a fair drawing of electoral boundaries; freedom of speech and assembly; repeal of the Special Powers Act (which gives the police almost unlimited power of arrest and detention); and a fair allocation of jobs and houses'.[10] The People's Democracy organised many protest marches calling for these aims. The now increasing unrest in Northern Ireland caused concern for the government at Westminster.

On 22 November, the government, under Labour Prime Minister Harold Wilson, announced a Five Point Reform programme. The programme recommended changing the system of housing allocation, the establishment of an ombudsman to oversee citizen complaints, and modernisation of local government elections. Devlin stressed that 'these were not reforms, but suggestions for reform' and did not include the central issue of one man, one vote.[11] The People's Democracy planned their largest action in response: a march from Belfast to Derry. The march would take four days, resembling Martin Luther King's American Civil Rights march from Selma to Montgomery in 1965. The Minister of Home Affairs, Captain Long, discouraged the organisers from this project, but he did not ban the march. Long feared that the march would incite further violence. Devlin and the other organisers ignored such warnings, and the march left Belfast on 1 January 1969. The scale of the violence that ensued could not have been foreseen. A large police contingent accompanied the marchers and launched intermittent charges on the group along their route. On the final day of the march, 4 January, a group of over 200 militant unionists were waiting at Burntollet Bridge on the outskirts of Derry and launched a violent attack on the protesters; the police did little to intervene. Devlin was attacked and beaten but received only minor injuries and proceeded with the march. The BBC reported that 13 people received hospital treatment, although Devlin maintained that 87 people were hospitalised.

The People's Democracy march finally arrived in Derry city, where the protesters were welcomed by a crowd gathered at Guildhall Square. A podium had been erected, and Devlin made an impassioned speech there, declaring:

> All over Northern Ireland people are suffering the same injustices as are suffered here in Derry. But you people in Derry have taken up the fight and we marched from Belfast to show that we would come to your aid, through all the other places who've suffered possibly in silence.[12]

The rally was eventually dispersed by the police, and riots broke out that evening in Derry. Police attacked Catholic areas of the city, causing concern once again about police impartiality. On 15 January, then Prime Minister of Northern Ireland, Terence O'Neill, established an official inquiry into the disturbances in Derry.[13]

There followed a month of violence and protests across Northern Ireland, and the Unionist party was in turmoil. When an election was called in March 1969 it was agreed that the People's Democracy would enter a candidate in the South Derry constituency, and Devlin stood unsuccessfully. She was defeated by Major Chichester-Clark, towards whom she directs much of her speech in this section. The following month, a by-election for the Mid-Ulster seat was held after the death of George Forrest, a Unionist MP. Forrest's wife, Anna, stood as the Unionist candidate, and Devlin contested the election. This time she stood as a Unity candidate, symbolising that she was a candidate agreed on by the socialist and republican parties. On 17 April there was a historically high turnout, with 91.5 per cent voting. Devlin secured the seat, returning 33,648 votes, over 4,000 more votes than the Unionist candidate. Five days later, Devlin gave her maiden speech at the House of Commons.

Devlin held her seat until 1974; in her autobiography, *The Price of My Soul*, published the year of her election, she is scathing about the political structure. She served a prison sentence just months after her election. Following a loyalist march in Derry on 12 August 1969, rioting broke out between nationalists and the Royal Ulster Constabulary (RUC) that became known as the Battle of Bogside, the Catholic area where the clash occurred. Devlin was sentenced for her involvement and served time in Armagh Gaol. At the request of the unionist government, led by Northern Ireland Prime Minister Chichester-Clark, British troops were deployed to Northern Ireland to support the RUC. Through Operation Banner, troops were deployed on the night of 14 August 1969 and remained in Northern Ireland until July 2007, becoming the longest continuous deployment of the British army in history. Rather than broker peace, the army's presence in Northern Ireland incited more violence over the coming years. Devlin remained a strong voice at Westminster, defending civil rights in the midst of the introduction of internment, which gave authorities the power to detain people without trial. The unionist government introduced internment in Northern Ireland on 9 August 1971, and British armed forces arrested mainly young Catholic men under this legislation.

On 30 January 1972, a peaceful protest against internment was organised by NICRA, and thousands of people gathered on the streets of Derry. The Northern Ireland Troubles reached a new height of violence when British paratroopers opened fire on the crowd, killing 13 people and injuring many more. Devlin was among those who were shot at on the streets of Derry. The following day, Devlin attended the House of Commons and requested to speak on the matter during the related parliamentary session. The Speaker of the House, Selwyn Lloyd, refused her request. During his three-minute statement to the house, Home Secretary Reginald Maudling did not issue any apology for the killings but defended the actions of the paratroopers, claiming they fired in self-defence. Devlin crossed the floor of the chamber and slapped Maudling across the face. When asked by BBC reporters outside of Westminster if she intended to apologise to Maudling, she replied, 'I'm just sorry I didn't get him by the throat.'[14] She was suspended from parliament.

Devlin married Michael McAliskey in 1973. She lost her seat in the general election of February 1974 and that year helped found the Irish Republican Socialist Party. Devlin ran for election to the European Parliament in 1979 but was unsuccessful. She remained politically active and became an organiser for the H-Block Committee, campaigning for political status for IRA prisoners in the Maze prison in Belfast. Her work on this high-profile campaign drew a bitter response from militant unionists. At 8.15 a.m. on the morning of Friday, 16 January 1981, three loyalist gunmen smashed through the front door of Devlin's Coalisland home and shot her and her husband. The couple's three young children were in the house at the time, and although traumatised they were not physically harmed. This was a well-orchestrated attack: sledge hammers were used to break the front

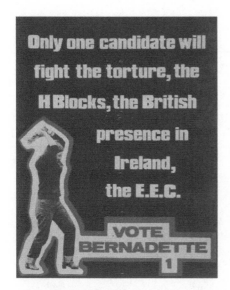

Only one candidate will fight the torture, the H Blocks, the British presence in Ireland, the E.E.C.

VOTE BERNADETTE 1

17. Bernadette Devlin's European election poster, 1979. Courtesy of Irish Election Literature.

door, and telephone lines to the house had been cut. Devlin was shot in the chest, arm and thigh. Her husband, Michael, was shot in the back and legs at close range. The couple were seriously injured but survived the ordeal. Three members of the extremist Unionist Ulster Defence Association were later sentenced for the attack. Devlin ran for election to Dáil Éireann in both general elections in 1982 but was unsuccessful.

Devlin is named in *A Century of Women*, a collaborative project 'developed in response to the general invisibility of women across historical narratives'. The authors of the project note that, since 1997, Devlin has been 'active in the South Tyrone Empowerment Programme – a community-based organisation that she founded which supports the rights of migrant workers'.[15] She remains a persistent voice campaigning for the rights of immigrant workers. In January 2020 she was one of the first to speak out against the UK's introduction of a new points-based immigration system, warning that 'the economy of Northern Ireland cannot survive without immigrant labour, and this points system will make it extremely difficult.'[16]

A fitting tribute to Devlin was installed in Derry in 1996. The Bogside Artists; brothers Tom and William Kelly along with Kevin Hasson, painted a series of 12 large murals on gable walls in the Bogside area of Derry between 1994 and 2006. The murals depict, what the artists describe as 'moments in the neighbourhood's history during the Troubles . . . which shaped the lives of them and their community'.[17] In 1996 the artists painted a mural of Bernadette Devlin addressing the crowd at the Battle of the Bogside in August 1969. In the foreground of the mural a woman can be seen banging a bin lid on the ground, which was a common alert signal used to warn people that British troops were approaching. The mural memorialises Bernadette Devlin's seminal role in the Northern Irish civil rights movement.

18. Bernadette Devlin mural by the Bogside Artists on Rossville Street, Derry. Photograph by Kenneth Allen. Creative Commons Attribution-ShareAlike 2.0 license.

'I understand that in making my maiden speech on the day of my arrival in Parliament and in making it on a controversial issue I flaunt the unwritten traditions of the House, but I think that the situation of my people merits the flaunting of such traditions.

I remind the hon. Member for Londonderry (Mr. Chichester-Clark) that I, too, was in the Bogside area on the night that he was there. As the hon. Gentleman rightly said, there never was born an Englishman who understands the Irish people. Thus a man who is alien to the ordinary working Irish people cannot understand them, and I therefore respectfully suggest that the hon. Gentleman has no understanding of my people, because Catholics and Protestants are the ordinary people, the oppressed people from whom I come and whom I represent. I stand here as the youngest woman in Parliament, in the same tradition as the first woman ever to be elected to this Parliament, Constance Markievicz, who was elected on behalf of the Irish people. . . .

The hon. Member for Londonderry said that he stood in Bogside. I wonder whether he could name the streets through which he walked in the Bogside so that we might establish just how well acquainted he became with the area. I had never hoped to see the day when I might agree with someone who represents the bigoted and sectarian Unionist Party, which uses a deliberate policy of dividing the people in order to keep the ruling minority in power and to keep the oppressed people of Ulster oppressed. I never thought that I should see the day when I should agree with any phrase uttered by the representative of such a party, but the hon. Gentleman summed up the situation "to a t". He referred to stark, human misery. That is what I saw in Bogside. It has not been there just for one night. It has been there for 50 years—and that same stark human misery is to be found in the Protestant Fountain area, which the hon. Gentleman would claim to represent. . . .

The people in my country who do not wish to join the society which is represented by the hon. Member for Londonderry are by far the majority. There is no place in society for us, the ordinary "peasants" of Northern Ireland. There is no place for us in the society of landlords because we are the "have-nots" and they are the "haves".

We came to the situation in Derry when the people had had enough. Since 5th October, it has been the unashamed and deliberate policy of the Unionist Government to try to force an image on the civil rights movement that it was nothing more than a Catholic uprising. The people in the movement have struggled desperately to overcome that image, but it is impossible when the ruling minority are the Government and control not only political matters but the so-called impartial forces of law and order. It is impossible then for us to state quite fairly where we stand.

How can we say that we are a non-sectarian movement and are for the rights of both Catholics and Protestants when, clearly, we are beaten into the Catholic areas? Never have we been beaten into the Protestant areas. When the students marched from Belfast to Derry, there was a predominant number of Protestants. The number of non-Catholics was greater than the number of Catholics. Nevertheless, we were still beaten into the Catholic area because it was in the interests of the minority and the Unionist Party to establish that we were nothing more than a Catholic uprising—just as it is in the interest of the hon. Member for Londonderry to come up with all this tripe about the I.R.A. . . .

We, the people of Ulster, are no longer to be fooled. . . .

I was in the Bogside on the same evening as the hon. Member for Londonderry. I assure you, Mr. Speaker—and I make no apology for the fact—that I was not strutting around with my hands behind my back examining the area and saying "tut-tut" every time a policeman had his head scratched. I was going around building barricades because I knew that it was not safe for the police to come in.

I saw with my own eyes 1,000 policemen come in military formation into an oppressed, and socially and economically depressed area—in formation of six abreast, joining up to form 12 abreast like wild Indians, screaming their heads off to terrorise the inhabitants of that area so that they could beat them off the streets and into their houses. . . .

The hon. Member for Londonderry said that the situation has got out of hand under the "so-called civil rights people". The one thing which saved Derry from possibly going up in flames was the fact that they had John Hume, Member of Parliament for Foyle, Eamonn McCann, and Ivan Cooper, Member of Parliament for Mid-Derry, there. . . .

Another solution which the Government may decide to adopt is to do nothing but serve notice on the Unionist Government that they will impose economic sanctions on them if true reforms are not carried out. The interesting point is that the Unionist Government cannot carry out reforms. If they introduce the human rights Bill and outlaw sectarianism and discrimination, what will the party which is based on, and survives on, discrimination do? By introducing the human rights Bill, it signs its own death warrant. Therefore, the Government can impose economic sanctions but the Unionist Party will not yield. I assure you, Mr. Speaker, that one cannot impose economic sanctions on the dead.'[18]

SIXTEEN

Betty Williams
1943–2020

Nobel Peace Prize acceptance speech
Oslo City Hall, Norway

II DECEMBER 1977

'War has traditionally been a man's work.'

On 11 December 1977 Betty Williams became the first and, as of 2021, only Irish woman to give a Nobel Peace Prize acceptance speech. She delivered her 40-minute speech the day after the award ceremony attended by 400 dignitaries from around the globe, including King Olav of Norway and members of his royal family. The Nobel Prize was jointly awarded to two Irish women, Betty Williams and Mairead Corrigan, in 1976. The award was made a year late, as the Nobel awarding committee did not find a suitable candidate the previous year.[1] Following Williams and Corrigan's actions in late 1976, the committee was motivated to award the women the prestigious prize for their 'courageous efforts in founding a movement to put an end to the violent conflict in Northern Ireland'.[2] The Nobel Prize for Peace had only been awarded to three women since its establishment in 1901. As of 2021 Williams and Corrigan remain the only Irish women to receive a Nobel prize in any category.

Corrigan did not deliver an acceptance speech, later recalling the prospect as daunting: 'the greatest difficulty I had was facing university professors and intellectuals and people like that.'[3] Williams delivered the speech on behalf of herself and Corrigan. She noted how women were removed from public affairs throughout history, which had resulted in women focusing on events close to home. This was certainly true for Williams and Corrigan, who on witnessing the horrendous consequences of the violence in Northern Ireland took direct action.

Williams' speech was passionate, coherent and inspiring. She described the events that led the women, along with Ciaran McKeown, to establish the Movement of the Peace People, a grassroots movement of Catholic and Protestant campaigners for peace. The movement later became known simply as the Peace People. On 10 August 1976, just after 2 p.m. on a sunny summer afternoon, a violent incident occurred between British troops and members of the IRA (Irish Republican Army) which resulted in the deaths of four young people in West Belfast. British troops pursued a car with two IRA occupants; Danny Lennon was driving with one passenger. Lennon had recently been released from prison on 30 April that year, after serving three years for IRA activity.[4] When Lennon's car reached Finaghy Road North, troops opened fire, fatally shooting Lennon. Lennon's car swerved onto a footpath, crashing into Anne Maguire who was walking with her four young children.[5] Joanne, aged eight, and Anne's six-week-old son, Andrew, were killed instantly. Anne and John, her two-and-a-half-year-old son, were seriously injured. Another son, Mark, aged seven, who had been walking a few feet ahead of his mother and siblings, escaped the impact. John underwent surgeries to amputate his legs but died in hospital the following day. Anne sustained serious brain and other injuries; she was eventually released from hospital. Anne Maguire never recovered from the ordeal and the violent loss of her children.[6]

Betty Williams, a 33-year-old receptionist and mother of two young children, was on her way home when she witnessed the horrendous scene and went to Maguire's aid. By 1976 the violence in Northern Ireland had escalated to its highest point; 1,600 people had been killed by violence related to the Troubles since they began in 1968. Witnessing this event stirred Williams, and she launched an intense campaign for peace. She phoned the local newspaper office of the *Irish News*, requesting that her phone number be distributed to anyone who wanted to support a peace march. While people across Belfast struggled to comprehend the Maguire tragedy, Mairead Corrigan, Anne Maguire's sister, accompanied her brother-in-law to formally identify the bodies of her niece and nephews. Corrigan was moved to go to the Ulster television station buildings and request that they broadcast an appeal from her for peace. Corrigan's appeal struck at the hearts of many across Northern Ireland and further afield when it aired on BBC. On learning about Williams' activities, Corrigan phoned her, and the two women later began working together in their campaign for peace.

An organised movement for peace would face condemnation from many quarters, especially those engaged in the violent conflict, as evidenced on 12 August, the day of Danny Lennon's funeral. That morning, 67 death notices appeared in the *Irish News* in Belfast for Lennon; in one notice he was described as having 'died in action against British occupation forces'.[7] The funeral of the Maguire children took place the following day. After the funeral, Williams and Corrigan were scheduled to take part in a current affairs programme, *Seven Days*, a joint broadcast by RTÉ and BBC Northern Ireland. Journalist Ciaran McKeown, an expert on paramilitary conflict in Northern Ireland, was also invited to speak. Corrigan and Williams met McKeown for the first time that day in the BBC's Belfast offices, and together they later founded the Peace People.

The day after the Maguire children's funeral, the peace march set off through the streets of Belfast. There was an unprecedented turnout, with over 20,000 people, including Catholics and Protestants, calling for an end to violence. The marchers were mainly women, but they were supported by large numbers of men. The march started in the Catholic area of Andersonstown, meeting outside the chapel of St Michael the Archangel, with hundreds of women from the Protestant areas of Shankhill and Sandy Row joining it. In the hours before the march, a 12-year-old girl, Majella O'Hare, had been killed at Ballymayer on her way to confession. Majella was caught in crossfire between British soldiers and members of the IRA. The killing of another innocent child caused the people in Northern Ireland to unite in a call to end violence. As Williams notes in her speech, there were some who opposed this peace movement. The Provisional IRA issued a statement of no surrender and dismissed the march 'as a "peace at any price" exercise'.[8] The *Sunday Independent* reported on IRA attempts to disrupt the march under the headline 'War goes on.' The article describes how when Williams was 'challenged at one stage with the question, "What about the thugs in uniform?" She answered: "We are against all men of violence."'[9]

As the Peace People gained support across the island of Ireland, members of the republican movement became concerned about losing support from within their own community. Gerry Adams, then imprisoned in the Maze Prison, also known as Long Kesh internment camp, wrote to the editor of the *Irish Press* defending the republican campaign. Adams was initially involved in the civil rights movement in Northern Ireland in the 1960s, but after the British army was deployed to Northern Ireland in 1969, he joined the republican movement, although he denies ever being a member of the Provisional IRA. Adams attempted to escape from internment on two occasions and was then serving time for these escapes.[10] In his letter Adams expressed his concern that three innocent Maguire children had been killed, stating that 'all I can do is offer my condolences to the Maguire family. If they refuse to accept this I will understand. If I am deemed as a hypocrite I will understand.'[11] Adams was clearly worried that the republican movement was being blamed for these killings, noting that 'the Maguire family understandably enough have condemned the IRA and Mr. Maguire whose wife still remains seriously ill in hospital has been forthright in his condemnation of the Republican Movement.' Adams attempted to distance the republican movement from blame, attesting that 'The Maguire family were not Danny Lennon's enemies and he was not their enemy. They were victims of circumstances created when he was shot dead.'[12]

Adams had overlooked a significant aspect of Williams and Corrigan's campaign: the women were not concerned about apportioning blame, and neither were their supporters. The Peace People wanted an end to all violence in Northern Ireland, and this message was clearly reaching many people across the island of Ireland, as was apparent in a letter printed beneath Adams' piece. The secretary of the Athlone Movement for Peace, U. O'Neill, applauded the Peace People, writing, 'The action of the women of Belfast in coming out against violence is the most encouraging development on the Northern Ireland scene for a long time. The vast majority of the people, whatever their religious beliefs or political aspirations, are unified in wanting peace.'[13] O'Neill concluded by asking people to contact the Athlone Movement to offer support.

The three co-founders of the Peace People harnessed the growing calls for peace and set about establishing a programme of peace rallies. McKeown wrote the movement's declaration, which remains on the Peace People's website and stays open for signatures. The declaration begins, 'We have a simple message to the world from this movement for Peace. We want to live and love and build a just and peaceful society. We want for our children, as we want for ourselves, our lives at home, at work, and at play to be lives of joy and Peace.'[14] Over 100,000 people signed the declaration within six months of the establishment of the Peace People. With a committed and driven focus, the movement continued raising awareness of the intolerable violence across Northern Ireland. Peace rallies and protests were staged across the island of Ireland and the United Kingdom. Within six months of establishing the peace movement, the rate of violence in Northern Ireland had decreased by an extraordinary 70 per cent. The work of Williams, Corrigan and McKeown undoubtedly contributed vastly to this decrease.

The Nobel committee were keen to award a prize to the Peace People because this award could help progress the work of establishing peace. Through the Nobel award, the movement's profile would be heightened globally. The award came with prize money, which could help the cause. However, as noted by Judith Hicks Stiehm, this 'selection was controversial because the prize was awarded so quickly that the impact of the movement could not be assessed'.[15] After receiving the award, Williams and Corrigan returned to Belfast to a public reception in their honour. A *Belfast Telegraph* article printed in advance of the reception pointed out a resistance from some quarters to support Williams and Corrigan, describing how 'local politicians have been notably backward about expressing their congratulations . . . perhaps this is because politicians feel that they themselves are empowered to hold the key that might open the door to peace. Such a view is arrogant and short-sighted.'[16]

The *Belfast Telegraph* article also noted that Bishop William Philbin had declined to attend the public reception. Due to protocol, this meant that there could be no representative from the Catholic hierarchy at the event. McKeown later explained that because the organisers of the Peace People had criticised Church leaders for 'not taking a more active stand against terrorism', Philbin was offended.[17] Despite their best efforts to reconcile with the Bishop, their relationship with him remained on difficult terms. While Bishop Philbin did not speak publicly on the matter, a Presbyterian minister, Desmond Mock, did make a damning comment on the Peace People's criticism of church leaders. Mock sent a stern warning to the Belfast community that anyone attending the civil reception for Williams and Corrigan 'will perhaps unwittingly be aiding and proclaiming political pacifism which is a most dangerous philosophy of weakness and disarmament'.[18]

Praise was forthcoming from Church leaders in the Republic of Ireland. The Church of Ireland Bishop of Clogher, Robert Heavener, made special mention of the women in his sermon at Monaghan Parish Church on 11 December.[19] With such lack of support from politicians and church leaders in Northern Ireland, the reception for Williams and Corrigan on their return from Oslo was described as a 'dismal welcome'.[20] This was a disappointing tribute to two women who were engaged in work to secure peace. Corrigan and Williams not only dedicated their time and energy to their campaign, they also endured many threats on their lives. During their time in Oslo, they were guarded closely by Norwegian police, and the hotel where they stayed was kept secret 'because of the ever-present possibility of a terrorist attack on the two peace women's lives'.[21]

By 1978 the movement lost momentum as it was surrounded by controversy often spread by hard-line nationalists and loyalists. Corrigan and Williams were accused of making money off the Peace People movement as, by then, they were working full-time for the organisation and being paid from funds raised. Corrigan and Williams resigned as chairpersons but remained active members of the group. In 1980 Anne Maguire died by suicide, and Corrigan married Jackie Maguire, previously her brother-in-law. Williams divorced her first husband in 1982 and married James Perkins in 1986; she moved with her new husband to Florida. Both women continued with peace work on a separate basis. Corrigan worked with the Peace People and on numerous other global peace initiatives. Williams became an active campaigner against the death penalty in the United States and against the production of nuclear weapons. Williams died on St Patrick's Day in 2020 in Ireland. Her last public appearance was only weeks before her death, when she signed the book of condolence for the late Northern Ireland politician Seamus Mallon in Belfast. Many high-profile newspapers carried her obituary. Corrigan's statement on Williams' death was printed in the *Irish Times* obituary, in which she said, 'Betty was a woman of great courage with a passion for peace and a love and compassion for all children. Betty will be sadly missed but remembered lovingly by all of us who knew Betty. I felt privileged to know her as a great peace activist and friend.'[22]

The two women did not end the violence in Northern Ireland, but they gave people the courage to stand up for their rights and demand peace. This momentous change of direction paved the way for the peace process and the signing of the Good Friday Agreement in 1998. The year after the agreement was signed, the Feminist Press of the City University of New York launched a series of books dedicated to women who changed the world; Corrigan and Williams feature as the subjects of a joint biography. The biographers best sum up the legacy of Corrigan and Williams, stating that 'they tapped into their country's longing for peace and gave people hope for a better future. They remain a timeless example of what the most ordinary of people can accomplish when they refuse to be governed by fear.'[23] Williams' speech remains as a testament to what they accomplished.

19. Peace Jam's 10th anniversary Nobel Peace Prize winners. Left to Right: Desmond Tutu, the 14th Dalai Lama Tenzin Gayatso, Betty Williams, Jody Williams, Rigoberta Menchú Tum, Adolfo Perez Esquivel, Shirin Ebadi, and Mairead Corrigan Maguire, 15 September 2006. Photograph by Ivan Suvanjieff, GNU Free Documentation License.

'I stand here today with a sense of humility, a sense of history, and a sense of honor.

I also stand here in the name of courage to give name to a challenge.

I feel humble in officially receiving the Nobel Peace Prize, because so many people have been involved in the campaign that drew such attention to our leadership that an award like this could justifiably be made. Mairead Corrigan and I may take some satisfaction with us all the days of our lives that we did make that initial call, a call which unlocked the massive desire for peace within the hearts of the Northern Irish people, and as we so soon discovered, in the hearts of people around the world . . . not least in Norway, the generosity of whose people to our cause is the main reason for our current ability to expand our campaign.

But unlocking the desire for peace would never have been enough. All the energy, all the determination to express an overwhelming demand for an end to the sickening cycle of useless violence would have reverberated briefly and despairingly among the people, as had happened so many times before . . . if we had not organized ourselves to use that energy and that determination positively, once and for all.

So in that first week Mairead Corrigan, Ciaran McKeown and I founded the Movement of the Peace People, in order to give real leadership and direction to the desire which we were certain was there, deep within the hearts of the vast majority of the people, . . . and even deep within the hearts of those who felt, perhaps still do, feel obliged, to oppose us in public.

That first week will always be remembered of course for something else besides the birth of the Peace People. For those most closely involved, the most powerful memory of that week was the death of a young republican and the deaths of three children struck by the dead man's car. A deep sense of frustration at the mindless stupidity of the continuing violence was already evident before the tragic events of that sunny afternoon of August 10, 1976. But the deaths of those four young people in one terrible moment of violence caused that frustration to explode, and create the possibility of a real peace movement. Perhaps the fact that one of those children was a baby of six weeks in a pram pushed by his mother made that tragedy especially unbearable. Maybe it was because three children from one family, baby Andrew, little John and eight-year-old Joanne Maguire died in one event which also seriously injured their mother, Anne, Mairead's sister, that the grief was so powerful. Perhaps it was the sheer needlessness of this awful loss of life that motivated people to turn out in protesting thousands that week. And we do not forget the young republican, Danny Lennon who lost his life that day. He may have been involved in trying to shoot soldiers that day and was himself shot dead, and some may argue that he got what he deserved. As far as we are concerned, this was another young life needlessly lost. As far as we are concerned, every single death in the last eight years, and every death in every war that was ever fought represents life needlessly wasted, a mother's labour spurned. . . .

I am also aware of a sense of history. I am aware of all the people who have stood here before to receive this award. . . . And with that sense of history, we feel a special sense of honor . . . honor for women, perhaps a little specially at this time. War has traditionally been a man's work, although we know that often women were the cause of violence. But the voice of women, the voice of those most closely involved in bringing forth new life, has not always been listened to when it pleaded and implored against the waste of life in war after war. The voice of women has a special role and a special soul force in the struggle for a nonviolent world. We do not wish to replace religious sectarianism, or ideological division with sexism or any kind of militant feminism. But we do believe; as Ciaran McKeown who is with us in spirit, believes, that women have a leading role to play in this great struggle.

So we are honored, in the name of all women, that women have been honored especially for their part in leading a nonviolent movement for a just and peaceful society. . . .

Because of the role of women over so many centuries in so many different cultures, they have been excluded from what have been called public affairs; for that very reason they have concentrated much more on things close to home . . . and they have kept far more in touch with the true realities . . . the realities of giving birth and love. The moment has perhaps come in human history when, for very survival, those realities must be given pride of place over the vainglorious adventures that lead to war. . . .

But I am also angry. I am as angry today, in a calm and a deep sense at the wastage of human life that continues each day, as I was when I saw young life squashed on a Belfast street. . . .

For us on that little area of the globe known as Northern Ireland, we know how much we have yet to do, indeed that we will have much to do for the rest of our lives. Today, we may be receiving the Nobel Peace Prize, which has been described as "the highest honor any human being can receive on this earth". Well that may be the case, and we tremble in the awful responsibility that such an honor places on us. But even as we receive it, we think of the blood that has been spilt, and may yet be shed on that beautiful landscape, from the majestic Mourne Mountains to the Glens of Antrim, from dear old suffering Belfast to the magnificent lakes of Co. Fermanagh, from lovely Derry on the banks of the Foyle to the orchards of Armagh. And we know, that for us, there is still a vast amount of work to be done to make the lives of the Northern Irish people as beautiful as our landscape is green.'[24]

SEVENTEEN

Siobhán McKenna
1922–86

Anti-Apartheid and the Actors' Equity
United Nations, Harlem State Office Building, New York

19 MARCH 1982

'The theatre should always be in the vanguard of liberty and democratic principles.'

Siobhán McKenna is best remembered as an enigmatic actress and theatre director; however, she was also a human rights activist and a forthright advocate for racial equality. On 19 March 1982 McKenna was invited to address a special meeting at the United Nations (UN) offices in New York to commemorate the Sharpeville massacre. The meeting, organised by the UN section of the Department of Public Information of non-governmental organisations, was held to show solidarity with people struggling against racism and racial discrimination.[1] In her speech McKenna outlined the strong and growing anti-apartheid movement in Ireland, emphasising how the arts community and individual performers were a key element in overturning the apartheid system then operating in South Africa. McKenna's speech highlights her commitment to ending the system of apartheid and the significance of cultural boycotts in overturning this racist legislation.

Apartheid, which in Afrikaans means *apartness*, was a policy that established racial segregation in South Africa. Racial segregation was widely practised in South Africa prior to 1948, but that year the National Party extended the policy that legalised racial discrimination. The South African government was controlled by a white minority, who accounted for only 15 per cent of the population. The majority Black population was denied an entitlement to vote, and through legislation they suffered immense economic and civil rights discrimination. The Population Registration Act of 1950 'classified all South Africans as either Bantu (all Black Africans), Coloured (those of mixed race), or white. A fourth category—Asian (Indian and Pakistani)—was later added.'[2] These classifications became the cornerstone of apartheid legislation. Pass laws forced Black South Africans to carry an identification pass with them at all times to control their movements, restricting where they could work, live and frequent.

In March 1960 a group called the Pan African Congress (PAC) organised a peaceful protest against apartheid in the Black township of Sharpeville. On 21 March thousands of Black South Africans marched to Sharpeville without their passes in defiance of the unjust law. Without warning, the police opened fire on the unarmed protesters, killing 69 people and injuring more than 180. It was reported later that over 700 bullets were fired by the police, who shot people in the back as they fled.[3] The government declared a state of emergency and outlawed the PAC and the African National Congress (ANC), a political party fighting to overthrow apartheid. Thousands of Black South Africans were arrested and tried for treason. Nelson Mandela, who later became the first democratically elected President of South Africa, was one of those tried. The year after this violent event, the government began forced removals of Black South Africans from their homes in rural areas, designating these areas as white only. Their confiscated land was sold at low prices to white framers. Between 1961 and 1994, more than 3.5 million people were forcibly removed from their homes in this way.

The Sharpeville massacre was the first major violent event stemming from apartheid in South Africa and one discussed by McKenna in her speech. The 21 March is now designated as International Day for the Elimination of Racial Discrimination in memory of those who lost their lives that day. In the immediate aftermath of the Sharpeville massacre, the UN Security Council met to consider what action should be taken, and on 1 April the council adopted a resolution calling for South Africa to 'abandon its policies of apartheid and racial discrimination'.[4] A special committee on the Policies of Apartheid was later formed and first met in April 1963. The South African government did not comply with any of the UN's directions, and a series of embargos against South Africa came into effect over the coming years. In November 1974 South Africa's membership of the UN was suspended in response to growing international opposition to the policy of apartheid. By 4 November 1977 a mandatory arms embargo prevented all UN member states from shipping or selling munitions or military vehicles to South Africa. In the midst of these embargoes, the UN General Assembly called on all states 'to suspend cultural, educational, sporting and other exchanges with the racist regime and with organisations in South Africa which practice apartheid'.[5]

McKenna's speech was part of the UN commemoration of the Sharpeville massacre, 22 years after the event. As noted by McKenna, the regime of apartheid had not weakened by 1982. Nelson Mandela had by then served 20 years in prison for attempting to overthrow the apartheid system, and Black South Africans continued to suffer immense injustices. McKenna played a central role in the cultural boycott of South Africa, endorsed by the UN. A list of all entertainers, actors and athletes who had performed in South Africa was published annually and distributed widely. The first register was published the year after McKenna's speech in October 1983 and listed all people who had performed in apartheid South Africa since 1981. Publication of performers' names who had appeared in South Africa had a direct effect on their future earning potential as well as their public profile. In the United Kingdom and Northern Ireland, for example, many local authorities introduced laws banning those listed artistes from per-forming in their jurisdictions. While 'in Norway, the Norwegian Council for Southern Africa requested the Norwegian Broadcasting Corporation not to transmit records, cassettes or tapes made by individuals whose names appear on the register.'[6] Such moves ensured that the number of artists agreeing to perform in South Africa dramatically reduced over the following years. The cultural boycott had an extraordinary impact on pressurising the white-controlled government of South Africa into ending the practice of racial separation.

On learning about what she describes as the 'brutal and dehumanising regime' of apartheid, McKenna signed a declaration promising never to perform in South Africa until the system was overturned. McKenna was a prestigious actress and a highly respected voice in Actors' Equity, the labour union representing theatrical actors. She was intimately aware of civil rights injustices. She was born in 1922 in a Catholic area of the Falls Road in Belfast, during a turbulent time in Ireland's history. The Anglo-Irish Treaty, which led to the partition of the country into the six counties of Northern Ireland and the 26 counties of the Irish Free State, had been signed just months before McKenna was born. During her first year of life, a civil war raged across Ireland. McKenna's Irish-speaking family moved to Galway in 1928, and McKenna first became involved in Irish-language theatre through Galway's Taidhbhearc. McKenna pursued an illustrious career in theatre. Historian Margaret MacCurtain credited her as being 'pre-eminent among the players who brought the dramatic works of the Irish literary revival to the national and international stage in the second half of the twentieth century'.[7] McKenna was a powerful voice in the world of performance, and she used this position to campaign against apartheid.

At the time of her speech, McKenna was a member of Ireland's Council of State, a prestigious body established to advise the President of Ireland on state matters. McKenna was nominated for this role in 1975 by President Cearbhall Ó Dálaigh and continued as a member of the council during President Patrick Hillery's term. She makes particular reference to President Hillery when discussing the Irish rugby tour of South Africa, which took place in 1981. This tour has been described by sports journalist David Coughlan as 'one of the biggest sagas in Irish sport', and this sporting engagement is a focus in McKenna's speech.[8] Despite the international call for an embargo against South Africa, the Irish Rugby Football Union (IRFU) accepted a request to tour the country and play seven games against South African teams. Taoiseach Charlie Haughey and Foreign Minister Brian Lenihan requested that the IRFU cancel the tour. When the IRFU refused, the government stopped a funding grant of £12,000 to them. The Irish rugby team was then not a professional team, and players held down full-time jobs. The government warned that those team members working for the civil service would not be granted holiday leave for the tour.

The IRFU proceeded with the tour, which was used by the South African government as a propaganda triumph; cabinet ministers hosted a highly publicised reception for the male Irish rugby players in Pretoria. The rugby tour caused Ireland international embarrassment, and some Irish athletes were banned from entering international sporting events. McKenna was determined to raise the issue in her speech. As McKenna outlines, there was intense opposition to the South African rugby tour throughout Ireland. Trade unions in Ireland opposed the tour, and the unions representing airport workers announced that flights for the team to South Africa would not be handled by their staff. Public demonstrations across the country were organised by the Irish Anti-Apartheid Movement, founded by Kader Asmal and Terence McCaughey. Public protests were planned to culminate in the largest demonstration at the squad's departure, which led the team to sneak out of the country. The 26 team members caught flights to London, without wearing any team identification, before departing for Johannesburg. Many of the players lost their jobs or were forced to resign. The national Irish broadcaster, RTÉ, refused to broadcast the games. President Hillery made a public statement against the South African tour, and when the Irish rugby team won the Triple Crown the following year in 1982, Hillery was not in attendance.[9]

The South African tour by the male Irish rugby team generated a heightened awareness in Ireland of the deplorable conditions imposed by apartheid. The movement in Ireland grew after that 1981 controversy. In 1984 Mary Manning, a worker in Dunnes Stores supermarket, followed her trade union advice and refused to handle South African goods. Manning was suspended from her job, and ten of her colleagues walked out on strike in support. McKenna wrote to the Dunnes Stores workers congratulating them 'for their magnificent stand'.[10] The Dunnes strike lasted until South African goods were banned from Ireland in April 1987.

McKenna did not live to see the success of the Dunnes Stores strike. She died at the age of 64 years on 16 November 1986 after suffering a heart attack following an operation in the Blackrock Clinic in Dublin. President Hillery issued a statement summarising the incredible impact of her work, stating, 'her lifetime contribution to the enrichment of so many aspects of Irish life at home and to the reputation of Ireland everywhere by her exceptional talents, has been immeasurable.'[11] Her popularity and her distinguished reputation are evident in the obituaries of her carried in local and national newspapers across the island of Ireland and in America and Britain. The *Ulster Herald* described her as 'the most distinguished Irish actress of her age'.[12]

According to her wishes, McKenna was buried at Rahoon Cemetery in county Galway. She was survived by her son, Donnacha. Her husband, the Abbey actor Denis O'Dea, predeceased her.[13] During her lifetime, McKenna received many awards and accolades, including honorary doctorates from the National University of Ireland, Galway; Trinity College Dublin; and the University of Ulster, Coleraine. There are numerous portraits of McKenna, perhaps most notably a print by Yousuf Karsh now held by the National Portrait Gallery in London. McKenna's personal and work papers are now most fittingly held in the archives department of NUI, Galway.

McKenna's speech at the UN remains as an important reminder of her steadfast work on human rights. By 1990 the South African government was under intense international pressure to remove the system of apartheid. Gradually, laws were overturned, including the Population Registration Act. Nelson Mandela was freed after being imprisoned for 27 years. One of Mandela's first international visits was to Ireland. He arrived in Ireland on 1 July 1990 and addressed Dáil Éireann the following day. In his speech, Mandela recognised the importance of Irish people in helping dismantle the apartheid regime, stating:

> For more than a quarter of a century your country has had one of the most energetic and effective anti-apartheid movements in the world. Irishmen and women have given wholehearted and often sacrificial support for our struggle in the fields of economic, cultural and sports relations. We, therefore, salute your sportspeople, especially the rugby players, your writers and artists and the Dunnes' and other workers.[14] They will not be forgotten by the masses of our people.[15]

In 1994 a new South African Constitution enfranchised Black South Africans and other racial groups. Mandela was elected as president in the first democratic election in South Africa, and apartheid was finally at an end. Siobhán McKenna's speech is a vital reminder of the horrendous apartheid system and of Irish efforts to overthrow this racist regime.

20. Siobhán McKenna, New York, 8 January 1959. Photograph by Talbot NY, Creative Commons.

'Mr. Chairman, and members of the United Nations Special Committee against Apartheid, I thank you for inviting me to share with you and all concerned people, the observance of International Day for the Elimination of Racial Discrimination; and also, to commemorate together the Anniversary of The Sharpeville Massacres.

I consider the invitation to be an honour for Ireland and for the very strong Irish Anti-Apartheid Movement there. As for myself, I feel privileged to have been asked to address this meeting. I do so, not only as a citizen of Ireland, but also as a member of Actors' Equity. It was as an actor that I first took a stand against Apartheid many years ago, when, together with other members of Actors' Equity, which included such illustrious names as Dame Peggy Ashcroft, we signed a declaration promising never to perform in South Africa until there was an end to their brutal and dehumanising regime.[16]

If we look up the word Equity in our dictionary, we find that it means the quality of being equal or fair. If we look up the word Apart we find equivalents such as . . . Asunder; Apartness = Aloofness; a part as in French — to a place apart from the general body; separate, separately in thought or consideration; aside, away from all employment. And thus, Apartheid, based as it is upon the alleged superiority of one race over others, and inseparably linked to man's exploitation of man, is everything which is the opposite of Equity.

Twenty-two years ago at Sharpeville the South African Government's police-force brutally gunned down sixty-nine defenceless men[,] women and children and seriously wounded another one hundred and eighty, all of whom were engaged in a peaceful demonstration against the racial policies of that government. To-day, twenty-two years later, the evils of Apartheid have not lessened. Due to the selfish attitudes of individuals, groups of people and of certain governments, South Africa continues to enjoy directly or indirectly, support for its disgusting divisiveness, its systematic deprivation and degradation of the black people, herded into reservations in their rightful homelands and either exploited as enforced labour or penned in in enforced idleness, each condition demeaning and ignominious to the human spirit. Despite these facts some Irish Rugby players accepted an invitation to play in South Africa last year and in the face of a vast turnout of the Irish people who marched in protests up and down the country leaving these players in no doubt as to the feelings and wishes of the majority of their own people. Our president Dr. Hillery spoke out against the tour, as did our churches, our trade unions, our City Corporation, the government and other politicians. Private citizens, men, women and children marched in a huge throng through the streets of Dublin, ending up outside the Department of Foreign Affairs in St. Stephen's Green. I had the task of handing in a letter requesting, as a last resort, that passports be withheld from the players. To do so, we were told, would be a violation of our Constitution which allows freedom of movement to all our citizens.

What an irony of situation.

All the same it was gratifying to see the great numbers of people who filled the streets on this occasion, and I remembered the first anti-Apartheid torchlight procession held in Dublin years before when only about two or three hundred of us walked from the Garden of Remembrance in Parnell Square, through O'Connell Street and ending up then as now in St. Stephen's Green. On that occasion someone gave me a box to stand on and a few poems to read by African poets with strange-sounding names. As is usual in Dublin, we had a small following of children, who chattered away as I read as best I could in the flickering light. It was hardly a captive audience. I could hear a scatted phrase or two from them "What is she saying?" "Who is she at all?" "What is she talking about?" Sometimes we must speak out even when we are met with seeming misunderstanding; but I like to think that some of those children at least were among the adults who marched in protest against our Rugby players' visit to South Africa. From small springlets come rivers.

It may seem unfair to expect such lofty principles for sport, from the arts and entertainers, when governments and the world of commerce fail to do their duty but two wrongs cannot make a right. Sports personalities and actors and artists and entertainers have a special closeness with the people and by placing themselves with the forces for good, they can do much to influence to-day's inter-dependent world. . . .

Are we actors exaggerating the extent of our own importance on this issue? No: according to Yvonne Bryceland, the South African actress whose husband was put in jail, and she herself can no longer return to work there. No: according to South African playwright Athol Fugard. No: according to Jonathan Kent, a young South African actor who played Nero with me in a London production of Brittanicus last summer. He misses his country but he says he can never feel comfortable working in the theatre there again until there is an end to Apartheid.

For most actors, to play in a society where exclusion of one group by another, makes inequality a blatant flouting of common human rights, is an absurdity of what life and liberty should mean to us all. Indeed the tradition of all good theatre has always been synonymous with the struggle to remove prejudice. The theatre should always be in the vanguard of liberty and democratic principles.

To-day is a day for us to reaffirm our support for all people struggling for their basic human rights. Article I of The Declaration of Human Rights declares all human beings are born free and equal in dignity and rights. Many countries as well as South Africa have still to introduce real changes through which all the people may exercise their right to self-determination and equality. Truly only a democratic state, founded on the will of all the people, can secure for all their birthright without distinction of colour, race, sex or belief.'[17]

EIGHTEEN

Nuala Fennell

1935–2009

Introduction of the Eighth Amendment to the Constitution
Dáil Éireann, Leinster House, Dublin

17 FEBRUARY 1983

'Because I am a feminist it has often been presumed that I must be in favour of abortion.'

Irish politics entered a new realm with the establishment of a Ministry of State for Women's Affairs and Family Law in December 1982. Nuala Fennell, a steadfast feminist campaigner, was appointed to this role. She took on the position amid a heightened debate on abortion in Ireland. On 17 February 1983, Fennell rose to address the Dáil regarding a proposed Eighth Amendment to the Constitution, which, if introduced, would prevent abortion from being legalised in Ireland. It may have come as some surprise to those in the Dáil chamber that Fennell's speech was in support of this amendment. Her speech is a powerful reminder that feminists cannot be categorised as homogeneous. Fennell put forward an argument against legalising abortion in Ireland from a feminist perspective, outlining how unwanted pregnancies highlighted gender inequalities and fundamental flaws in the structure of Irish society more broadly.

Fennell's background as a campaigner for women's rights ensured that feminist groups and individuals had high expectations for her new role. However, the ministry itself was not supported financially, and Fennell did not have a place in Cabinet. Fennell had an understanding of the political structure and an awareness of women's inequality within that system, a point she makes in her speech, noting how 'until recently very few Members of this House could become pregnant and actually give birth.' She was an impressive and a convincing orator, who brought a strong feminist voice into Dáil debates.

Fennell first came to public notice in Ireland in 1970, when she wrote about gender equality in the women's pages of the *Irish Press* and the *Evening Press* national newspapers. Through these endeavours she connected with other feminist journalists, including Mary Kenny, Mary McCutchan, Mary Anderson, Nell McCafferty and June Levine. This core group of women joined with other feminist campaigners in founding the Irish Women's Liberation Movement (IWLM), the most provocative second-wave feminist organisation in the Republic of Ireland. However, by October 1971, Fennell had resigned from the IWLM, viewing the organisation as too confrontational.

Fennell went on to co-found a pressure group campaigning for women's equality within marriage called Action, Information and Motivation (AIM). She tirelessly lobbied government for changes to legislation, including granting equal rights for women to ownership of the family home and access to free legal aid for women in difficult or abusive marriages. Through her many efforts, Fennell established Irish Women's Aid, becoming its first chair in 1975. Around this time, she became an executive member of the Council for the Status of Women, now the National Women's Council of Ireland.[1] Fennel wrote a number of books and pamphlets on issues surrounding women's legally subordinate position within marriage. In 1974 her book *Irish Marriage: How Are You!* included a chapter entitled 'Wife-beating: A husband's prerogative?'[2] In 1980 she co-wrote a self-help guide for women in broken marriages.[3] Fennell established good working relationships with key politicians, most notably Garret FitzGerald who became leader of Fine Gael in 1977. In his leadership role FitzGerald recruited a 'number of high-profile women activists' into the ranks of Fine Gael, including Fennell, Gemma Hussey and Monica Barnes.[4]

Fennell was first elected to Dáil Éireann, winning a seat in Dublin South, in the general election on 11 June 1981. A Fine Gael-Labour coalition government was formed under FitzGerald but fell some months later. After a brief change of government, the coalition was back in power following the November 1982 general election, and this government remained in place until 1987. Fennell held her seat throughout the tumultuous elections of 1981 and 1982, becoming Minister of State for Women's Affairs and Family Law, then a newly established ministry spread across the departments of Justice and the Taoiseach. The Eighth Amendment to the Constitution was one of the first debates in the Dáil that centred on women after Fennell took up her ministry. Legislating for termination of pregnancy continues to be a contentious issue globally, but the topic became even more controversial in the Irish context.

There was no mention of abortion in the Irish Constitution up to 1983. Abortion in Ireland was then legislated against through an interpretation of an old British law passed in 1861, the Offences Against the Person Act. This law stated that women who 'procure a miscarriage' would be subjected to the highest criminal punishment. Furthermore, the legislation criminalised any person assisting this 'miscarriage'. As noted by Aideen Quilty et al., the 1861 act was 'interpreted to criminalise abortion in all circumstances' under Irish law.[5] This interpretation seemed all the more ludicrous since women in Britain could legally access abortion through the Abortion Act 1967, which came into effect in April 1968. The Abortion Act, however, did not extend to Northern Ireland, ensuring that women throughout the island of Ireland could not legally access a termination of pregnancy. In their detailed study on the history of abortion in Ireland, Lindsey Earner-Byrne and Diane Urquhart testify that this British legislation 'had significant impact on the lives of women on the island of Ireland who could, and did, travel for legal and safe abortions'.[6] By 1983 it was recognised that many Irish women were seeking terminations of their 'unwanted or unviable' pregnancies abroad, facilitating 'Ireland's continued evasion of complex issues related to pregnancy'.[7]

During the 1970s many countries in Europe moved to update laws legislating for abortion on various terms, including Demark in 1973, Austria and France in 1975, and Italy and Luxembourg in 1978. Ireland had been a member of the European Community (EC) since 1973.[8] There were growing concerns among pro-life campaigners, leaders of the Catholic Church and conservative politicians that Ireland, as a member of the EC, would be forced to introduce legislation for abortion in line with other EC countries. In 1981 an organised group was established called the Pro-Life Amendment Campaign (PLAC), whose stated main aim was to seek protection for the unborn within the Irish Constitution. Politicians could no longer evade the issue. In November 1982 then Taoiseach Charles Haughey published the wording of a proposed Eighth Amendment to the Constitution: 'The State acknowledges the right to life of the unborn and, with due regard to the equal right to life of the mother, guarantees in its laws to respect, and, as far as practicable, by its laws to defend and vindicate that right.'[9] If passed, the Eighth Amendment would introduce the first Irish law making abortion illegal; this would supersede any other legislation and could only be altered through a further referendum.

The Fianna Fáil government fell shortly after publication of the amendment wording, and it was then up to the newly elected coalition government to pursue a referendum on the issue. In February 1983 the Attorney General, Peter Sutherland, advised the government that 'the wording of the proposed amendment to the Constitution would inevitably cause confusion and uncertainty among doctors, lawyers and the judiciary.'[10] Sutherland went further by concluding that 'if a doctor were faced under the proposed wording with a choice of saving the life of a mother or her foetus, the only logical course would be to do nothing because the wording declared each had an equal right to life.'[11] The day before Fennell's speech, the *Irish Times* published Sutherland's warning under the headline 'Attorney General rules out wording.'

Fennell does not focus on the wording of the amendment in her speech nor, indeed, on the pertinent issue of unviable pregnancies, rather she discusses her reasons for opposing abortion from a feminist perspective. Her experience of campaigning for women in abusive marriages and of women living in unsuitable environments is particularly evident throughout. Rather than see abortion as the answer to unwanted pregnancies, Fennell argued that legislation and social change were required to ensure the number of such pregnancies was reduced. In her speech she calls for access to proper family planning methods and for the provision of better sex education. Furthermore, Fennell draws men into this equation, describing how many unwanted pregnancies are the result of 'the immature and irresponsible behaviour of men'.

A particular strength of Fennell's argument is her focus on necessary legislative change to better the lives of unmarried mothers and their children. The categorisation of children born out of wedlock as illegitimate was embedded with negative legal and social implications. Nearly a decade previously, Mary Robinson, in her role as a senator, put forward draft legislation to abolish the category of illegitimacy in Irish law. During her 20-year period as a senator, Robinson, an authority on constitutional law, successfully campaigned on many issues of social injustice.[12] In her detailed and moving speech to the Seanad in 1974, Robinson described how:

> Children born out of wedlock are not equal before the law. Children born out of wedlock are discriminated against in that they do not have succession rights to their father's property; in that their family relationship is not given full recognition and protection, and in that they are burdened with the social stigma implied in being called illegitimate.[13]

The Illegitimate Children bill did not reach a full debate in the houses of Irish government, and despite Robinson's best efforts, the legal definition of illegitimacy remained.

As a minister of state, Fennell took up Robinson's campaign, which became a focus in her speech on the Eighth Amendment. In this context, Fennell was aware of the social stigma attached to children born out of wedlock and voiced concern that a pregnant unmarried woman may be forced to seek a termination of pregnancy due to this classification. She mentions the Law Commission's most recent report on illegitimacy, which had been published five months previously.[14] Fennell would continue to pursue this campaign, and in 1986 she described a proposed bill for change that 'for the first time gives rights and entitlements to a group of people, the children born outside marriage, who up to this have been left entirely outside the law in terms of guardianship, maintenance and succession'.[15] In 1987 the Status of Children Act finally abolished the state of illegitimacy in Irish law, and Fennell played a key role in this progression.

Despite her feminist approach in this speech, Fennell was attacked from several quarters for her support of criminalising abortion, with many claiming that she was working against feminist interests. Days after her speech, Fennell was subjected to what journalist Mary Maher described as a 'stormy session', when she was questioned by no fewer than 50 female journalists in Government Buildings. Fennell reiterated her support for the introduction of the Eighth Amendment. She was questioned on the wording of the amendment, which by then had also been condemned by Protestant church leaders for being too rigid. The fact that this wording would introduce a legal ban on terminating any pregnancy, regardless of the situation, was a focus of journalists that day. After several refusals to answer the question, Fennell eventually 'accepted the principle of the present legislation that all pregnancies should be brought to term, regardless of the circumstances or the wishes of the woman concerned'.[16] An article detailing Fennell's response appeared on the front page of the *Irish Times* the next day.

The letters pages of the *Irish Times* were awash with condemnation of Fennell in the following days and weeks. She was accused of posing 'as a feminist politician only to become upon appointment to her present position in government just another one of the boys'.[17] Such condemnation was particularly harsh. Fennell continued campaigning to introduce other legislation noted in her speech, legislation which protected women as wives and mothers and as individuals. In April 1983, in a speech to the Mothers' Union in Dublin, Fennell outlined her determination to secure legislation for divorce, for the removal of illegitimacy and for women's rights to ownership of their family home.[18] Days later, she addressed a conference of the Limerick Federation of Women's Clubs, setting out plans for a committee to consider how best to achieve gender balance in employment.[19] Fennell kept her promises and chaired an Inter-departmental Working Party on Women and Family Law Reform later that year which published a detailed report in 1985 entitled *Agenda for Practical Action*.[20]

The referendum on the Eighth Amendment was due to take place on 7 September 1983; five days before the ballot, a horrendous case was brought to the public's attention. Journalist Pádraig Yeats published an article in the *Irish Times* about Sheila Hodgers, a mother of two children. Hodgers was attending a private Catholic hospital, Our Lady of Lourdes in Drogheda, for cancer treatment. The hospital withdrew her cancer treatment because she was pregnant: 'On Saint Patrick's Day 1983, she gave birth in "agony" to a daughter who died immediately; she [Hodgers] died several days later.'[21] Despite the Hodgers case, the Irish public voted in favour of introducing the Eighth Amendment. 841,233 people voted in support, with a minority of 416,136 people voting against. The turnout at the poll was low however, possibly indicating a high number of undecided voters. Just over half of those entitled to vote in the referendum, 53.76 per cent, turned out to cast their votes.

Fennell continued to press for the introduction of divorce in Ireland, and she played a significant role in orchestrating a referendum on the issue on 25 June 1986, which was ultimately defeated. Despite her continued work in the area of social reform, she lost her seat at the next election in November 1987; 'She was immediately nominated by Taoiseach FitzGerald to the outgoing seanad, and was then elected to the new Seanad on the labour panel (1987–9), serving as a member of the Oireachtas committee on women's rights. She was returned to the Dáil for Dublin South in 1989.'[22] During Fennell's final term in the Dáil, the Eighth Amendment continued to have horrendous implications for women in Ireland – a fact that Fennell became most aware of.

In 1992 a 14-year-old girl became pregnant by rape; her case became known as the X case to protect her identity. The case was reported to Gardaí, and the girl's parents arranged travel to England for their daughter to undergo a termination of the pregnancy. The parents sought advice from the Gardaí about using the aborted foetus for DNA evidence in the rape charge. Attorney General Harry Whelehan sought an injunction under the Eighth Amendment preventing the girl from travelling to undergo the procedure. The injunction was granted by Declan Costello in the High Court on 17 February 1992. The following day, a debate on the ruling was initiated in the Dáil. During this debate the suppression of female voices was evident. Then Taoiseach Albert Reynolds invited only the leaders of political parties, all men, to comment. TD Madeline Taylor Quinn raised a point of order asserting, 'I want to put on the record my protest at this Government disallowing women to speak in this debate. The Taoiseach further compounded the exclusion of women by inviting only the leaders of all parties to address the general issues raised by the case.'[23] The then serving Ceann Comhairle, James C. Turney, dismissed the remark as not being a point of order. To which another Fine Gael TD, Monica Barnes, noted that the fact that women had been excluded from making statements was 'a reflection of the exclusion of women in all structures of our society.'[24] Fennell intervened as the Taoiseach began making his remarks. She stated clearly, 'I want to make a protest about the brevity of these proposed Statements which does not allow any woman or indeed fair-minded man in this House who wants to contribute to speak about this issue.'[25]

The following day, Fennell requested that the Taoiseach consult with the Council for the Status of Women, the Oireachtas Joint Committee on Women's Rights, or a cross-party group of women Deputies in this house. She questioned whether 'he intend[s] to consult with or discuss this issue with women's organisations or groups or does he see them as being irrelevant in his debate'?[26] Reynolds denied this request, recommending that the discussion would take place among party leaders. The High Court decision was eventually overturned in the Supreme Court based on the fact that there was a threat to the girl's life by suicide if she was forced to complete the full term of her pregnancy.

Fennell was appalled at her party's position on the X case, and she resigned as Fine Gael Spokesperson on Women's Rights in May 1992, stating that she had been silenced on these issues. Fennell told a journalist for the *Irish Press*, 'I want to speak on issues relating to abortion, to the area of the X case, and in relation to the Church.'[27] The X case had opened a new debate surrounding access to abortion in Ireland, and proposed amendments to the Constitution were put to a referendum scheduled for November 1992. The three items under consideration were the right to travel, the right for information and the risk of suicide as justification for abortion. Fennell supported the proposed amendments, and she was targeted by anti-abortion groups. Youth Defence picketed her house in Dalkey on the evening of 17 September. Fennell described this onslaught as 'outrageous behaviour' from 'people in a democracy of civilised people'.[28] When the current Dáil was dissolved on 5 November 1992, Fennell announced that she would not seek re-election at the general election later that month and resigned from politics.

Fennell established a political lobbying firm and continued to work in this practice. She was diagnosed with a blood disorder, myelodysplasia, in 2004. She set about writing her memoirs, which she completed on 23 July 2009. Fennell died in St Vincent's Hospital, Dublin, on 3 August 2009. She was survived by her husband Brian and their three children. She was buried in Shanganagh Cemetery, in south county Dublin. Her book *Political Woman: A Memoir* was published in September 2009 with a foreword by Mairead McGuinness, then a Member of the European Parliament.[29]

The public voted overwhelmingly to remove the Eighth Amendment from the Irish Constitution in May 2018.[30] This result was welcome in many quarters, and journalist Miriam Lord penned a celebratory article in the *Irish Times* on the announcement of the verdict. In her article, Lord claimed that 'some [feminist campaigners] never thought they would live to see the day. Some, like Monica Barnes and Mary Holland and Nuala Fennell and many more, didn't. The celebration was for them too.'[31] Fennell's speech is a reminder of the complex journey the feminist movement has travelled in Ireland.

'This debate . . . has engendered a considerable, and at times an emotive, if not shrill, public debate. This, I believe, is a reflection of the very deeply held public concern and conviction about abortion, the manner in which it touches our perception of right and wrong, and the way in which we regard life itself.

The concept of something in the order of 60 million abortions throughout the world each year is overwhelming in its magnitude, as one which, along with the increasing easy availability of abortion on demand, causes very great concern to many individuals and organisations. . . .

Because I am a feminist it has often been presumed that I must be in favour of abortion. There is an automatic assumption that if you work for, or have a commitment to, the campaign for women's rights, you would also be in favour of abortion legislation. I could never support this view because I believe that abortion is fundamentally wrong. I do not expect a citation for this fact, nor would I judge any woman who has had an abortion. I merely mention it because in terms of feminism, I am exceptional when it comes to the inter-national view of abortion legislation and its availability. I also mention it because many Opposition Deputies accused me last year of being pro-abortion, possibly because I have worked for women's rights.

Where abortion is resorted to, I regard it as an unfortunate violence against women, apart from the other violence against the foetus. I must further state that while my commitment to feminism does not include an acceptance of abortion as a woman's right, it very emphatically does include a commitment to ensuring that women have free and ready access to comprehensive family planning methods, which I do not regard is now the case, and it also includes a commitment to ensuring the protection and safety of a mother's life in pregnancy and childbirth. . . .

The Eighth Amendment to the Constitution is about people and specifically about pregnant women. I do not imagine that the subject of pregnancy in any specific detail is one which can have filled many pages of the Official Report in the past. This could be related to the fact that until recently very few Members of this House could become pregnant and actually give birth. It has not been a problem or a reality for TDs or for many Senators . . . it is very apparent that the pregnant woman has been kept at a distance from the main public debate. . . .

For many women the news of a pregnancy comes with very mixed feelings. Apart from the women who see it as a cause of celebration and happiness, there are others who feel absolutely shattered at the discovery. I am making this point in some detail because I wish to dispel the idea that women are a homogenous group whose circumstances are all the same and whose feelings are identical. Every woman is an individual. . . . These women include mothers with larger families than they can cope with, many living in very inadequate housing. They are women with health problems, for whom pregnancy is regarded as a hazard, wives in difficult marriages, women who are not married, girls from 14 upwards who are at school or at work – these are the women for whom an unwanted or unplanned pregnancy can be an unremitting nightmare and who are faced with the agonising decision about abortion.

I know that many of these pregnancies are because of lack of access to proper family planning methods or because of inadequate sex education – or due to the immature and irresponsible behaviour of men. Many Irishmen, I am sorry to say, do not accept responsibility for their sexuality, and it galls me to see how quickly many of them will point the finger at a woman who is the victim of an unwanted pregnancy. Can I say that I know that many a fee for an English abortion for an Irishwoman came out of the pigskin wallet of a respectable and upstanding member of Irish society, as a pay-off for his sexual indiscretion.

For a society and a country committed to the total exclusion of abortion legislation now and in the future, we have a pitiful record when it comes to the treatment, the needs and the role of the un-married mother in our society. . . .

I cannot see this constitutional issue in isolation from the lives of the people with whom it is concerned, women and children. We have to take into account the lives of many Irish women in Ireland today. We have an obligation here to tackle the problems confronting women. One of the most appropriate areas for legislative change is the abolition of the concept of illegitimacy, under which it will be possible for an expectant mother to make a declaration of paternity and I am examining the proposals of the recent Law Reform Commission on Illegitimacy with a view to the earliest possible legislation.

But we have other obligations – they entail making provision for childcare facilities, legislation to give access to comprehensive family planning, examining the availability of voluntary male and female sterilisation, and above all, to plan a programme of adequate housing for larger families, for those who need them and for single parents; so that no woman will be forced by circumstances to have to opt for abortion.

It is scandalous that we have families living in grossly overcrowded conditions, as I well know, with 15 and 16 living in a three-bedroomed house and young unmarried mothers with their babies living in damp, rat-infested basements.

We should not legalise abortion. I have given a commitment in any election I have ever stood for that I would never contribute to, or support, the decriminalisation of abortion. I support, with my party, the holding of this referendum, but would ask the House to spare a thought for thousands of our countrywomen – and they are our countrywomen – who go to England for abortion.'[32]

NINETEEN

Nan Joyce

1940–2018

Trócaire seminar
University College Galway[1]

17 JUNE 1983

'Hatred and evil that afflicts my people.'

Nan Joyce, a prominent voice for Traveller rights in Ireland, gave an impromptu address at the 10th anniversary Trócaire seminar in University College Galway on 17 June 1983. *Irish Times* reporter Patrick Nolan described how this oration had an 'extraordinary impact on the seminar receiving more applause . . . than anyone else who presented reports'.[2] Trócaire, the official overseas development agency run by the Catholic Church in Ireland, had raised over £33 million to fund overseas development in its first decade of existence. Joyce called on the agency to use some of this money to support Travellers and to educate settled people whose current viewpoint is often 'the same attitude of racism, and apartheid that they condemn in other countries'.[3]

The seminar was attended by 350 representatives from 22 countries, including 50 delegates from what was then termed Third World countries, 'a class of economically developing nations'.[4] Joyce was an eloquent orator, and her speech that day clearly outlined how the hardships experienced by Travellers in Ireland were aligned with the experiences of those living in developing countries. T. P. O'Mahony, religious correspondent for the *Irish Press*, summed up Joyce's challenge to her audience: 'can we as Irish Christians address ourselves with credibility to the problems of the Third World if we appear to be doing little or nothing about various forms of injustice on our own doorstep?'[5]

Joyce's speech was reported by a number of journalists, none of whom reprinted her full speech verbatim. It has been possible to piece together Joyce's main points, and many original lines remain which shed light on her thought-provoking plea for equality. The speech below is taken from two newspaper articles written by Joseph Power and T. P. O'Mahony, who attended Joyce's talk. Joyce did not leave an archive of papers behind and was known to speak off the cuff rather than from prepared notes. She did record her autobiography, which was transcribed and edited for publication by writer Anna Farmar in 1985. An author's note at the beginning of her book provides an explanation for the lack of written records kept by Joyce. In it, Joyce explains, 'it's an awful sad thing to have no education. If I knew how to write properly and had good spelling I wouldn't have done this book on tape.'[6]

The lack of educational opportunities available to Travellers is just one of the many injustices that this ethnic group experienced in the 1980s and, indeed, gross inequalities continue in education. Between November 2019 and January 2020, Maria Quinlan consulted with Traveller and Roma parents, students, teachers and principals for a government-commissioned report, *Out of the Shadows*, as part of the National Traveller and Roma Inclusion Strategy. Prior to publication of the report, it was confirmed that Quinlan found 'institutional and structural discrimination and racism within the education system', while Traveller children feel 'ignored' by many teachers.[7]

Patrick Nevin, manager of the Tallaght Travellers Community Development Project, traced the mistreatment of Irish Travellers back to the foundation of the Irish Free State in 1922. Nevin describes how the new state 'set its sights squarely on the project of creating a mono-cultural identity . . . we see the creation of an attempt to remove from history, any group or people that did not sit in with the new state's ideals of what it decided was the true Irish or valued Irish.'[8] The Irish Traveller did not fit the tidy categorisation of perceived Irishness and was certainly not appropriately valued in Irish society, a fact reflected in the first government-led commission. On 1 July 1960, a Commission on Itinerancy was established under Charles Haughey, then parliamentary secretary to the Minister of Justice. The use of the term *itinerant* was unacceptable when applied to a people who describe themselves as Traveller or Travelling people. The commission's terms of reference highlights how the government made no attempt to understand the history of Travellers in Ireland or to appreciate this group as having a distinct ethnicity. Instead, the commission was established to solve what they described as the 'problem arising from the presence in the country of itinerants in considerable numbers'.[9]

Rather than support Travellers by providing better access to health and education services or improving facilities at their sites, the commission sought ways to effectively eradicate this community by promoting 'their absorption into the general community'.[10] The commission was led by government officials and included representatives from groups thought to be affected by this so-called 'problem', such as the National Association of Farmers and an Garda Síochána, but did not include any representatives from the Traveller community. Nevin points out how this absence ensured that 'the content of the report was not about the problems faced by Travellers, but the problems caused by Travellers.'[11] The view that Travellers are problematic in Irish society is one that would continue through the decades following the report. Joyce became a spokesperson for her community in an attempt to redress this long-standing racist viewpoint.

The traditional nomadic lifestyle of Travellers was disrupted in the mid-twentieth century by an upsurge of commercial development and the construction of major new roadways and housing estates across Ireland. Added to this, the move towards disposable packaging caused hygiene issues in camps. New types of machinery also ensured that Travellers could no longer depend on earning an income from their traditional trades, which included tin-smithing, horse-trading and seasonal agricultural labour. Joyce described how 'years ago the travellers only stayed in small groups because you could pull a wagon in anywhere, there was no traffic and there were plenty of camps. We had baskets for food and cans for milk so there were no boxes and plastic bags and bottles from supermarkets for rubbish.'[12] In the 1960s small-scale Traveller organisations formed, seeking better rights; however, many of these groups did not include input from Travellers, which led to misunderstandings of the issues faced. The Irish Council for Itinerant Settlement was one such group; it was founded in 1965 as a result of the commission's report.[13]

It was not until 1980 that successful resistance was seen in Traveller rights from within. Traveller woman Roselle McDonald took a court action appealing to stop the, by then, persistent evictions of Travellers from their camp sites. Such disruptions ensured that Travellers were constantly forced to move, which had major ramifications for the community, including for children accessing schooling. McDonald won her case, and it was ruled that Travellers could not be evicted from local authority property without being offered an appropriate alternative. This case was hailed as a victory; however, the ruling led to an increase in harassment of Travellers by settled people, ultimately forcing them to move from their sites.[14] In January 1981 the Travelling People Review Body was established by the ministries for the Environment and Health and Social Welfare; it was tasked with reviewing 'current policies and services for the travelling people and to make recommendations to improve the current situation'.[15] The review body was a promising development; at its inaugural meeting, the group was directed by ministers to examine ways in which Travelling people could effectively be included in decision-making processes and to work towards breaking down 'barriers of mistrust between the settled and travelling communities'.[16] However, the Travelling People Review Body would not publish their findings until 1983, after which a task force was established.

In the meantime, Joyce and many other Travellers would experience increased hardships. In 1981 Joyce and her family were forced to move from their site at Clondalkin. She had experienced much suffering in the previous year. When her family lived in Priorswood in north county Dublin, there was a series of bin collector strikes, during which locals began dumping their waste at Traveller sites. Joyce recalls how their camp became infested with rats. Her first-born grandchild, Anna-Marie, was just one year old when she contracted meningitis, thought to be linked to the rat infestation. Anna-Marie died within days, and her mother, Mary, suffered a nervous break-down and was admitted to St Ita's mental health facility.[17] Joyce moved to a site in Clondalkin to escape the deplorable situation at Priorswood and was not long there when bulldozers forced the family out. The Joyce family moved to a camp in Tallaght alongside another eight families. Shortly after this move, Dublin County Council announced construction of a Tallaght by-pass road.

The site of the proposed by-pass was then home to approximately 100 Traveller families; legally, the council could not move these families unless they offered them an alternative place to reside. Sociologist Patricia McCarthy describes how local residents took the issue into their own hands: 'with the active support of some local politicians, including a Fianna Fáil councillor, [they] organised protest marches. Vigilante type gangs patrolled around all open space in the area in order to force Travellers out of Tallaght.'[18] Joyce recounts how a group of locals descended on the field where the families were living and demanded they vacate the area within 48 hours.[19] With nowhere to move to, the families remained at their site, and a bitter con-frontation followed. For the first time, Joyce experienced the support of many local settled people, who came out and stood beside the Traveller families in support.

The events in Tallaght attracted media attention from the highest quarters. Gay Byrne, then the most prominent Irish presenter on RTÉ radio and television, arrived at the Tallaght site and presented his morning radio show from there. Joyce spoke on the programme, and she was inspired to begin an organised campaign seeking civil rights for Travellers. Joyce wrote a Travellers manifesto detailing the needs and wants of the community that was distributed to local and national newspapers. Joyce established the Committee for the Rights of Travellers, a group which included Traveller and settled people as equal members.[20] Among the nine stated aims of the committee was the call for 'full Irish citizenship and civil and human rights for Travellers', through the establishment of 'a minister or government department'. A key aim was for Travellers to 'be consulted at all stages of any development programme to ensure that it does not conflict with cultural or family aspirations'.[21] The committee further noted that 'any programme must include a campaign to educate the settled community to take a more positive attitude towards Travellers.'[22] Joyce recognised that the only way to obtain equal rights for Travellers was to 'break down the barriers' between the communities.[23] With this goal, Joyce engaged in a public speaking tour across the country, addressing audiences at schools, universities, and community centres. She organised pickets outside government buildings, distributing information leaflets about the plight of Travellers.

In the midst of this vibrant activity, a general election was called in November 1982. Joyce stood as an independent candidate for her local Dublin South-West constituency under her official name Ann Joyce. She was the first Traveller to contest a seat in Dáil Éireann. Joyce did not presume that she would be elected but used this platform to get national publicity for Travellers' rights.[24] Her election leaflet described her in simple terms: 'Ann Joyce is a mother of eleven children, a grandmother and an Irish citizen.' The first page of the leaflet details Joyce's background and is a testament to the injustices faced by Travellers, especially noting, 'Joyce was educated for about three years at primary school in Ireland and England.' She offered 'the decent fair minded people of Dublin South West the opportunity to use their vote in a positive way for JUSTICE, ACCEPT-ANCE and FAIR PLAY'.

In the most public display of racism against Travellers, a local Tallaght man, Richard O'Reilly, ran as a candidate on an anti-Traveller platform, using the abusive campaign slogan 'Get the knackers out of Tallaght.' Unfortunately, the use of such offensive terminology still prevails, but in recent times, it is not viewed as acceptable language in general society. In 2014, Cathal O'Reilly, a Sinn Féin candidate in Ennis, was forced to resign from the Clare County Council elections and from the political party due to his use of anti-Traveller terminology.[25] While Richard O'Reilly was not admonished in this way, he did not gain public support, failing dismally in the election. Joyce returned an impressive vote count of 581, nearly double O'Reilly's 297 votes.[26] Joyce's vote count was all the more notable considering that most Travellers, being without a permanent postal address, could not vote.

Joyce's positivity was soon threatened when she was arrested in June 1983 on the charge of jewel theft. Joyce explains how for months after the election she was harassed by members of the Garda, who regularly arrived at their site and searched the Joyce family caravan. She was arrested on charges of stealing £500 worth of jewellery and receiving a stolen gold bangle.[27] The theft charge was dropped a week later due to lack of evidence, but the charge of receiving stolen goods remained an active case for a number of months. Eventually, Joyce was cleared of all charges. There was a sense among many in the settled and Traveller communities that Joyce was framed in an attempt to silence her campaign. Joyce was not a stranger to police mistreatment of Travellers: when she was only 12 years of age, her father, John Donoghue, died in police custody in Northern Ireland. The circumstances of her father's death have never been clarified.[28] Despite not being charged; Joyce's arrest was reported in many newspapers. Joyce recalls how she 'felt really down about the whole thing but then I said to myself, "If I give up, if I don't go on speaking out, people will think I was guilty."'[29]

It was at this point that Father Michael Mernagh, a committed supporter of Traveller rights, suggested that Joyce attend the Trócaire seminar in Galway. She participated in a workshop on human rights. Michael D. Higgins, then recently elected to the Seanad and later President of Ireland, was in Joyce's workshop group, as was the prominent human rights activist Seán MacBride.[30] Each workshop group voted for a spokesperson to address the seminar, and the human rights group voted for Joyce as their spokesperson. Joyce was advised to speak for five minutes but went over her allotted time. Her speech was passionate and articulate and caused her audience to question their own misperceptions of Travellers. Comparing the living conditions of Irish Travellers to conditions experienced by people in developing countries was a wake-up call for many audience members. In her speech she notes, for example, the use of the birth drug Depo-Provera on Traveller women. In a report for the Women's Health Council, Catherine Conlon observes that Depo-Provera was shown to be 'administered to women in Third World countries and ethnic minorities in Western countries despite being the subject of controversy regarding safety'.[31] Joyce's speech received the greatest media attention of any of those presented during the three days at the Galway seminar.

In 1983 the Traveller committee founded by Joyce evolved into the first Traveller-only organisation, Minceir Misli. This new organisation did not survive partly due to barriers imposed on its members, such as lack of access to formal political structures and high rates of illiteracy. In 1985 funding was received from the Industrial Training Authority, and the Dublin Travellers' Education and Development Group was established; this organisation later became Pavee Point, which in 2021 is Pavee Point: Traveller and Roma Centre, based in Dublin. Joyce's speeches brought the injustices faced by Irish Travelling people to a national platform, inspiring further activism by Travellers and educating settled people about this particular form of racism. Joyce moved to Belfast shortly after her speech in Galway and brought her vibrant campaigning style there. She co-founded and chaired the Northern Ireland Council for Travelling People. In her final years, Joyce returned to Dublin to live with family members.

In recognition of Joyce's steadfast work promoting Travellers' rights, the President of Ireland, Mary McAleese, presented her with a Lifetime Achievement Award at the presidential residence, Áras an Uachtaráin, in 2010. In March 2017, Joyce finally saw the fruits of her persistent campaign when Ireland 'conferred official recognition on Travellers as an ethnic group'.[32] Such recognition ensures that Traveller culture and identity is valued within the Irish legal system and makes Travellers a protected group within Irish equality legislation. Rosaleen McDonagh, a playwright from the Traveller community, applauded this move, highlighting how 'official acknowledgement of our minority ethnic status signifies a more hopeful future for our community. . . . Finally we can rejoice in being both Irish and a Traveller.'[33] Joyce died the following year, on 7 August 2018, at the age of 78; she was survived by eleven children. Nan Joyce's legacy continues to inspire those who campaign for full equality for Travellers.

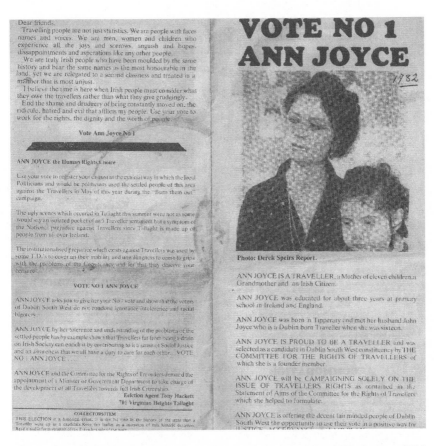

21. Nan Joyce election leaflet for Dublin South-West constituency, November 1982. Courtesy of Irish Election Literature.

'We are treated as outcasts in our own country. You people are very concerned about the Third World. I think you should also be concerned about us; we are the fourth world. We live among rats in camps or caravans. We are often in fields partly filled with water. Sometimes bulldozers come and dig big holes where a child could be drowned. . . .

Our children suffer from as many diseases as the children of the Third World. Some of them even suffer malnutrition. We may have a bit more food but we are treated in the same way as the unfortunate people of the developing countries.

The Irish travellers, she claimed, faced problems similar to those for which Trócaire were aiding people in the Third World. These included unjust treatment and lack of legal rights; lack of access to housing, or to serviced and approved sites, to water supply and sanitation.

Moreover, she said, the Irish travellers had inadequate health care, were subjected to the controversial birth drug, Depo-Provera, had little access to education, poor job opportunities and few future life chances.

As the oldest ethnic minority group in the country, the travellers, said Nan Joyce, faced living conditions in which they were treated as a blight on the image of Ireland. This was a contradiction to people's Christian beliefs. They were a marginal group, numbering 2,432 families, who occupied the last rung on the Irish social class ladder.

She complained that travellers were being used as the ultimate "whipping dog" and were looked down upon because they were poor, illiterate and had a malignant, negative, self image resulting from years of oppression and harassment. . . .

As with most poor marginalised people, travellers remained locked within the culture of silence, aloof, reticent and kept to themselves. They tended only to hit the headlines when they were stealing, or when a tiny minority of their children were seen begging or glue sniffing on O'Connell Bridge in Dublin.

She called on Trócaire . . . to use some of its resources in raising awareness and solidarity among travellers and in educating the Irish people to the fact that their attitude to and treatment of the travelling people was the same attitude of racism and apartheid that they condemn in other countries.[34]

Travellers . . . are not just statistics. "We are people with faces, names and voices — men, women and children who experience all the joys and sorrows, anguish and hopes, disappointments and aspirations like any other people."

Moreover, she added, travellers were truly Irish people who had been moulded by the same history and bore the same names as the honourable in the land, yet they were relegated to a second classness and treated in a manner that was most unjust.

"I believe the time is here when Irish people must consider what they owe the travellers rather than what they give grudgingly. End the shame and drudgery of being constantly moved on, the ridicule, hatred and evil that afflicts my people."

[T]he time had now come for the Irish bishops and the Government to respond to the plight of the travellers and to insist that they be given the same rights as members of the settled community.'[35]

TWENTY

Mamo McDonald

1929–2021

Speech on women in agriculture at European Economic Community seminar Dublin Castle

8 NOVEMBER 1984

'In Kerry you're better off to be a greyhound than a woman.'

On 8 November 1984 Mamo McDonald addressed a conference in Dublin Castle that garnered much national and European attention. McDonald was then president of the Irish Countrywomen's Association (ICA), the largest national women's organisation in Ireland. She was an influential, absorbing speaker with an easy-going approach. Her speech, based on her personal research, examined the significant inequalities faced by women in the agricultural sector in Ireland. The two-day conference was a European Economic Community (EEC) forum that focused on women in agriculture and self-employment, following publication of a draft directive on this topic. The conference was addressed by many high-profile politicians, including the Taoiseach and then President of the European Community, Garret FitzGerald; Nuala Fennell, Irish Minister of State for Women's Affairs; and Senator Mary Robinson. McDonald's speech received the most attention of all contributions to the conference and was widely reported in newspapers across the country.

Many newspaper articles cited McDonald's confronting remark that 'In Kerry you're better off to be a greyhound than a woman.'[1] The *Kerryman* printed a cartoon by artist Noreen Breen depicting a man drinking with a greyhound at a bar with the comment 'who really is the Kerryman's nearest and dearest?'[2] The thought-provoking line was used by McDonald to showcase how those controlling the agricultural sector in Ireland were more concerned about high profit than about the position of women in the sector. McDonald's speech provides an insight into the reality for females working in agriculture, which saw them forced into subsidiary roles, regardless of their expertise or organisational skills. Speaking at an EEC forum on this pertinent topic ensured that her message would have the utmost impact. Ireland then held membership of the EEC, which had significant benefits to the economic growth of the country.

In the wake of World War Two (1939–45), Robert Schuman, the French Foreign Minister, proposed a plan to ensure peace and cooperation between European States. In 1951 six nations – Belgium, France, West Germany, Italy, Luxembourg and the Netherlands – established the European Coal and Steel Community (ECSC). This cooperation succeeded and evolved into the EEC, now the European Union. From the outset, successive Irish governments had their sights firmly set on becoming a member of this community. After a process of applications and negotiations, the question of EEC membership was put to the people of Ireland to decide. Patrick Hillery, then Minister for External Affairs, was a strong force in leading the people of Ireland to join the European community. Hillery informed Irish citizens that membership of the EEC would support 'our national aims of full employment' and bring 'an end to involuntary emigration and a standard of living for all our people comparable to that enjoyed by our neighbours in Western Europe'.[3] In a referendum in November 1972, the people of Ireland voted by an over-whelming majority of 83 per cent in support of joining the EEC.

Ireland was one of three nations – the United Kingdom and Denmark were the other two – to join the six founding members of the EEC in 1973. Hillery served as Vice-President of the European Commission and European Commissioner for Social Affairs from that year until 1976. Ireland was then experiencing high unemployment, worsened by high inflation rates, which led to further waves of emigration and a national economic depression. Membership of the EEC ensured that Ireland was not as dependent on export trade with Britain, which was also experiencing an economic recession. Membership also provided Ireland with a host of benefits, including grant aids and later freedom of movement for its citizens across member states. A key advantage of membership for Ireland was the Common Agricultural Policy, providing a single European market for agricultural goods. The agricultural sector was crucial to the Irish economy at the time of membership, and this central importance continued through the 1980s. The significance of women's work in this sector was undervalued and, indeed, as can be seen in McDonald's speech, women's work in agriculture was often simply ignored.

McDonald gave her speech during Ireland's presidency of the EEC, when the Irish government was responsible for chairing EEC meetings, determining agendas, and facilitating dialogue between member states.[4] McDonald (née Bowen), originally from Galway, then lived in Clones in county Monaghan, where she became a central force in campaigning for gender equality. She was particularly aware of the injustices affecting women in employment. Due to the marriage bar, in place until 1973, she had been forced to leave her bank job when she married in 1950. McDonald joined the ICA, then a well-established national organisation. She later described how she originally joined the organisation to learn crafts and to make friends but soon 'discovered opportunities to voice opinions . . . and that working within the ICA, you could bring something about which you felt passionately and you could finish by walking into the office of a government minister about that cause.'[5] Political lobbying was precisely the route that McDonald pursued. She was an outspoken and articulate woman who represented the interests of women across the country. Her speaking skills were further honed through a public-speaking course at the ICA headquarters, An Grianán, in Termonfeckin, county Louth. She became president of the ICA in 1982 and held this post until 1985.

McDonald's speech at the EEC conference highlighted an aspect of Irish society that generated huge inequalities for many rural women. She began by examining the situation in the Irish Co-operative Organisation Society (ICOS) and recounted interviews with associated members. The ICOS, originally called the Irish Agricultural Organisation Society, as McDonald notes, was founded by Horace Plunkett to improve the economic position for farmers in Ireland. Plunkett 'began his efforts with the Irish dairy industry by persuading individual farmers to contribute a set amount of capital to establish a creamery. The farmers would then agree to supply all of their milk to this one creamery and in return receive a share of the profits.'[6] The plan was simple and extremely effective; as noted by Carla King and Liam Kennedy, dairy co-ops moved 'from creameries at the crossroads to multi-nationals'.[7] By 1992 the Kerry Co-op recorded a turnover of £827 million and then had subsidiary companies across the world.[8]

Women played a key role in the development of Irish co-op creameries, and as originally acknowledged by Plunkett, women should be represented on their co-op committees. In her speech McDonald provides a shocking example of how women were excluded from even attending co-op meetings. She recounts the case of Olivia Hughes, who was not welcome to attend an Annual General Meeting of the ICOS in place of her husband. Hughes founded Country Markets Ltd in Tipperary in 1946, and it was affiliated with the ICOS from the following year. The co-op continues to market locally produced farm, garden, and home produce. A plaque in honour of Hughes was unveiled in 2013 at the site of the first Country Market in Fethard; at the time of the unveiling, there were 60 branches of the co-op throughout Ireland.

McDonald was sure to voice her concern for all women in the agriculture sector who did not receive recognition for their work. The women affected were not just married women but thousands of single women who worked in farming. McDonald's concern was evident in her focus on Macra; that is, Macra na Feirme, which was founded in Kildare in 1944 as a support organisation for young farmers. McDonald quotes one male farmer as stating that female members of Macra had joined the organisation simply to look 'for rich farmer husbands'. Such a statement highlights how women in farming were not taken seriously. While women were not prohibited from joining or being on the committee of Macra, historically the presidential team was male-dominated. Through the work of activists including McDonald, this position has dramatically improved. In 2021 the Macra na Feirme president team comprises of one man and three women.[9]

The final and perhaps most significant organisation that McDonald examines is the Irish Farmers Association (IFA), founded in 1955. This association remains Ireland's largest representative organisation for farmers; the organisation was a firm supporter of Ireland's membership of the EEC. It is noteworthy that McDonald identifies clear barriers that prevented women from accessing full participation in IFA membership, describing a boys' club mentality in the organisation. Such barriers necessitated the formation of a women-only committee within the IFA: the National Farm Family Committee. Although one of McDonald's interviewees noted that this committee keeps women 'out of their [the IFA's] hair on the REAL issues', the Farm Family Committee remains in existence and now provides valuable leadership 'on social issues within the Association'.[10] Undoubtedly, such advances can be attributed to McDonald highlighting gender inequalities within agriculture and providing a voice for affected women.

McDonald's speech had the desired effect: she raised awareness of the issues faced by women in the agriculture sector in Ireland, and she delivered a powerful speech in a forum that could generate action. McDonald was supported in her assertions by the highest-ranking politicians at the conference. The Minister for Women's Affairs, Nuala Fennell, stressed that it was clear that 'a better deal for farm wives was called for',[11] while Mary Robinson declared that women 'played a secondary role and had a very low level of representation, if any at all, in agricultural co-operatives and occupational bodies'.[12] In concluding the conference, Taoiseach Garret FitzGerald stated his hope that the discussions would help the EEC adopt a positive action programme in favour of women.[13]

The following month, on 13 December 1984, the EEC published a recommendation on the Promotion of Positive Action for Women, which provided numerous resolutions and recommendations to achieve equality for self-employed women, including those working in agriculture. The recommendations were considered when Fennell oversaw the final report on *Irish Women: Agenda for Practical Action*, and one chapter of the report focused on women in rural Ireland. The report was published in January 1985, just weeks after McDonald's speech, and was later discussed in the Seanad.[14] In July 1985 Senator James Dooge, a Seanad representative of the Joint Committee of Women's Rights, described the report as 'an item of great importance'.[15] Dooge highlighted what he considered the key points of the report, including the position of married women who contributed to the family farm. Dooge noted that women's 'very real economic contribution is not reflected in our statistical system, for example in our estimates of gross national product. This is a distortion of what the real situation is in regard to all women who work in the home. It is an even worse distortion in the case of many women in rural Ireland.'[16]

The situation for Irish women in the agriculture sector in Ireland has greatly improved since McDonald's speech; however, women remain a minority in this sector. A report in *Today's Farm* confirmed that 'In Ireland, 2016 figures from the Central Statistics Office show that just under 13,000 women were employed in the agriculture, forestry and fisheries sectors. This is 10.8 per cent of the total and far below the UE-28 average of 28.5 per cent.'[17] In 2021 the Irish Farmers Association estimated this figure to have reached just 12 per cent.[18]

McDonald continued campaigning on social equality for the rest of her life. In 1986 she brought the World Tri-Annual Conference of the Association of Countrywomen to Killarney in county Kerry. She arranged addresses from the most prominent Irish feminists at the conference, including Mary Robinson, Margaret MacCurtain, Nell McCafferty, and Nuala Fennell. McDonald founded Age and Opportunity in 1988, an organisation to improve the quality of life for older people, which remains active in the community. In 1990 she co-founded the Cassandra Hand Summer school of Clones Lace, named after the woman who introduced the making of this lace to the area as a relief project during the Great Famine. McDonald remained connected with global feminist movements and attended the United Nations End of Decade Women's Conference in Nairobi in 1995.

A vivacious personality throughout her life, McDonald returned to education in her 70s and graduated with a master's degree in women's studies from University College Dublin. She was a keen writer and published her first poetry collection, *Circling*, in 2015.[19] Mamo McDonald died on 17 June 2021 in Monaghan. She was survived by ten of her eleven children, 32 grandchildren, 12 great-grandchildren and her two sisters.[20] Her husband Vincent predeceased her, dying prematurely in 1979. McDonald was mourned throughout the country, and her obituary was carried in many local and national newspapers. Her speech is a vivid reminder of her astute and effervescent campaigning, which helped establish a more equitable Irish society.

"'In Kerry you're better off to be a greyhound than a woman" — at least that's what I was told when researching the topic of women's representation in Occupational Organisations. It seems as far as Kerry Co-op are concerned greyhounds are high profile — they "Respond" you see! Fed on the Co-op produced Respond Greyhound Meal they thrive and sportingly compete in the Annual Respond Cup Race — prize fund £5,000. Women don't fare as well in that part of the country (maybe Kerry women are not rated as responsive).

The ICOS recommendation adopted in 1980 laying down that families, not individual farmers, should have membership of their co-ops would appear to have fallen on deaf ears — a southern Executive member of ICOS when asked about the recommendation claimed he had never heard of it. However, let us not suppose that this situation exists only in Munster and that it is Southern Co-ops alone who ignore the potential of women's participation.

Figures have never been my forte — so rather than glean information from statistical records I decided on a personal approach, talking to people North, South, East and West, and building up a picture from the facts given. But first the historical background. Sir Horace Plunkett founded the Co-operative Movement in the late 1800's. The Irish Agricultural Organisation Society gained in strength and influence, but in 1910 Sir Horace admitted to a basic error when he said, "We men, having to deal with a problem that embraces the whole of rural life, have attempted to enlist only half the rural population — the male half."

Again he said, "We should insist upon far more women being elected upon the Committees of any societies, whose operations directly or indirectly affect their share of the home work."

However, Jack Hughes, a South Tipperary farmer, unable to attend the AGM of his Co-op in the early 1940's, sent his wife Olivia to represent him, and the other members present — all men — turned her out. This was a shocking blow but Olivia Hughes — a long-time member and later also president of the Irish Countrywomen's Association — was a very determined lady. Rallying the members around her she established Country Markets Ltd. . . . a Co-operative especially to cater for the needs of the small producer. . . .

By the 1960's there were over 200 Creameries all over the country. . . .

Progress of course, but small wonder that the ICOS recommendation of 1980 did not create a tidal wave of womanly involvement — scarcely a ripple indeed.

My survey covered four Co-ops, North Connacht Farmers in Sligo, Bailieboro in Cavan, Avonmore in Kilkenny and Kerry Co-op. Those people I questioned were all actively involved in farming. The majority were women who not only provided essential back-up services to the farm home enterprise, but were themselves involved in calf rearing, cattle breeding, dairy management and record keeping — women of intelligence, enterprise and the will to be involved.

The answers to my questions were very similar. No, there were few, if any, women active in the Co-ops, none on Committees or Boards of Management. One told me of the time she was the only woman at the AGM, a situation she found both daunting and embarrassing. She did not speak but ventured back the following year to find another shareholding widow like herself, and a number of farm wives — "a small beginning," she said, "but heartening." Increasingly farm wives attend the Co-op AGMs but so far have not participated in debate. It does not occur to farmers, I was told, to put shares in the names of their family members which would boost their confidence and encourage interest and involvement.

The women I spoke to said they have not encountered hostility, but then neither have they been made to feel particularly welcome. "It takes motivation," one commented, "we get that from the ICA, but I know a widow who was refused the right to vote, though she had inherited the farm and the Co-op shares — she did not come back."

In general, I was told, women tend to play a passive role and so their non-election to office is as much the fault of women themselves as of traditional male attitudes towards them.

Questions on participation in other farm organisations elicited some interesting answers. "Oh loads of women in Macra," one man said, "all looking for rich farmer husbands." He was half joking whole in earnest but surely they are on a fruitless quest — rich farmers being "as scarce as hen's teeth" if Joe Rea is to be believed. His wife added her comments, "Well, whatever they are there for the women in Macra get the hard jobs — like secretary, they find them more reliable and efficient than the men."

Since membership of the Irish Farmers Association is composed of families rather than farm heads women are free to attend meetings — here again they seldom if ever attain executive rank, with the exception of the National Farm Family Committee (one of 16 within the IFA) which is an all woman committee. One remarked, "It's like a safety net, keeping us out of their hair on the REAL issues", and another said, "Well, it's a sort of Cinderella committee — before the ball."

A down to earth western woman said, "Well that IFA dues are deducted from my creamery cheque so I have every right to be there. They don't notify me about ordinary meetings but I always go to the AGM. The men always welcome me as the ICA representative and sure I'm as much a farmer as any of them. It's a bit annoying though — the meeting scheduled to start at nine usually gets started nearer ten and they are very centred around 'Bar activities'." One can imagine if this situation prevails in many places how inhibiting it would be for women's participation.

Many of the bright new stars in the sphere of cattle breeding are women — for too long they have played a subsidiary role but increasingly are involving themselves in Cattle Breeding Societies and again many of them take on secretarial office. A Department of Agriculture official said he knows a number of women involved in cattle breeding with considerably more expertise, interest and involvement than their husbands but acknowledgement on a joint basis is never given — it's always the husbands gain the laurels. . . .

I once listened to a dissertation (dare I say diatribe) by a very "macho" man of my acquaintance. "All nature upholds the principle of male dominance," he said, "look at the bull, the lion, the eagle." Tentatively I mentioned the Queen Bee . . . "The exception which proves the rules," he said.'[21]

TWENTY ONE

Alice Glenn

1921–2011

Dáil debate on constitutional amendment to introduce divorce
Dáil Éireann, Leinster House, Dublin

14 MAY 1986

'Any woman voting for divorce is like a turkey voting for Christmas.'

Alice Glenn, often described by media sources as a rebel TD, addressed the Dáil on 14 May 1986 and outlined her opposition to the introduction of divorce legislation to Ireland.[1] Glenn's speech attracted vast attention in advance of a referendum on the issue, mainly due to her assertion that 'Any woman voting for divorce is like a turkey voting for Christmas.' Her speech was in direct opposition to the government's recommendation for a tenth amendment to the Constitution, which, if introduced, would remove the prohibition on divorce in Ireland. As noted by historian Diane Urquhart, 'The period from 1969 to 1984 saw divorce reform in the majority of Western countries.'[2] By the time of Glenn's speech, Ireland was the only Western European country that did not have a provision for marital divorce. The proposed referendum on divorce would take place in Ireland on 26 June amid a heated debate on the topic, on which Glenn was particularly vocal.

Glenn was first elected in 1981 as a Fine Gael TD for Dublin Central, following two unsuccessful election attempts. She regained her seat at the November 1982 election and served in the Fine Gael-Labour coalition government. Glenn was notably the first woman member of the Dublin Port and Docks Board (1979) and the first female chair of the Eastern Health Board (1982). Glenn was born in Dublin and raised in the inner city area of Usher's Quay. She was one of ten children and was educated at the Convent of Mercy, Stanhope Street. Glenn made a remarkable progression into politics: she was a working-class woman who did not have the opportunity to complete her education. Glenn was obliged to work from a young age in order to supplement the family income, and her accomplishments are therefore all the more noteworthy. Glenn was described as 'a staunch upholder of traditional values whose politics were rooted in concepts of "family, faith and motherland"'.[3] Terry Calvin notes that this was evident from as early as 1978, when she gave a 'speech urging the 10,000 married women working in the public sector to alleviate unemployment by quitting their jobs'.[4]

As a TD she quickly became a cause of concern for the Taoiseach and Fine Gael party leader, Garret FitzGerald, during his campaign to liberalise the laws on contraception and divorce. In April 1983 Glenn was among a group of TDs who objected to a 'pro-life amendment because it failed to prohibit future legislation for abortion, and instead forced a more broadly phrased clause through the Dáil'.[5] In 1985 she voted against her party on contraception legislation that made non-medical contraceptives, including condoms, available to people over 18 without prescription. On 20 February, a vote on this bill in the Dáil was only narrowly won by the coalition government at 83 votes in support to 80 votes against. Glenn voted against the bill and therefore lost the party whip, which saw her temporarily expelled from the parliamentary party.[6] She attracted intense national media attention over these years and infamously became a focus in Christy Moore's song 'Delirium Tremens', which concluded with the lines, 'I dreamt I was in a jacuzzi along with Alice Glenn / 'Twas then I knew I'd never ever, ever drink again.'[7]

Months later, Glenn launched an attack on Fine Gael when she opposed the government proposal to reduce the family tax allowance. She recorded her outrage in a newsletter, *The Alice Glenn Report*, which was published by an organisation called the Family Forum, established by Glenn's supportive husband, William. Over 10,000 copies of the four-page newsletter were distributed to households across her constituency. In it, Glenn remarked that 'the tax burden on families may very well be the cause of many social problems, which have developed in Ireland in recent years – marital breakdown, crime, drug abuse and child abuse.'[8] The newsletter included an application form to join the Family Forum, which was described as 'a non-profit organisation formed "to carry out non-partisan education concerning matters of vital interest to Irish families"'.[9] Reporting on the appearance of this literature, the *Sunday Independent* newspaper carried the headline 'Alice and Fine Gael head for divorce'. The choice of the newspaper's terminology pointed not just to her potential permanent ousting from the Fine Gael party but also to the current debate on divorce then reaching a climax.

The question of introducing divorce to Ireland escalated in July 1983, when a joint committee comprising members of the Seanad and the Dáil were tasked with considering 'the protection of marriage and of family life, and to examine the problems which follow the breakdown of marriage'.[10] Seanad members on the committee included two notable legal experts: Mary Robinson and Catherine McGuinness, who were both avid supporters of progressive legal reform. As part of the committee's method of enquiry, they placed advertisements in national newspapers over the coming months seeking submissions from interested parties pertaining to divorce. Over 700 written submissions were received from a range of individuals and 24 organisations. The divorce debate intensified and became the focus of a panel discussion on the *Late Late Show* on 3 March 1984, then the most popular chat show on Irish television. Glenn joined the panel and began by adamantly expressing her position that she was in total opposition to divorce being introduced to Ireland. She continued by making a surprising assertion that divorce was worse than the death of a spouse. Glenn maintained that:

> the death of love between a man and woman and in a home is the most traumatic thing that can happen ... I would go so far as to say that the effects of it are probably more devastating that the natural demise of either one or the other because in that circumstance they are supported by friends and relatives and their grieving period has some end in sight; for these other people they live in a permanent limbo.[11]

The audience retaliated to this suggestion; one man claimed that people like Alice Glenn have a 'very poor opinion of the Irish people, and in fact they have a very low opinion of Irish marriage'.[12]

The report of the Joint Committee on Marriage Breakdown was published on 27 March 1985; it recommended a referendum on the issue. The committee noted particularly that the Constitution had then been in place for 48 years, and 'Irish people have never been afforded a democratic opportunity to express their views as to whether they wish the current constitutional prohibition on divorce to be retained.'[13] The proposed referendum was made public on 23 April 1986: the electorate would vote on the question of removing an article from the Irish Constitution that legislated that 'No law shall be enacted providing for the grant of a dissolution of marriage.'[14] If agreed by a majority vote in the referendum, an amendment would be inserted into the Constitution that a divorce could be passed by a court if a marriage had failed but only under the condition that this failure amounted to at least five years.

The day after the public announcement of the referendum, Senator Mary Robinson appeared on RTÉ's *Today Tonight* political affairs programme alongside Glenn. Robinson applauded the decision to hold a referendum but was clear that she considered the proposed change too restrictive as the government had indicated that the process would require 'a period of five years separation before proceedings can be initiated'.[15] The reasoning behind such restrictive legislation may well have been to convince voters that a yes vote would not lead to on demand divorce. Additionally, the tight control was undoubtedly linked to the Taoiseach's own thinking on the issue. In her detailed study of political reform during this time period, Ciara Meehan reveals that although FitzGerald is remembered as a 'modernising, progressive figure . . . his proposals were shaped by conservative thinking'.[16] Meehan describes the 1986 divorce referendum as 'a liberal measure conceived within a conservative framework'.[17] Regardless, Glenn was concerned that the wording was not firm enough for her to support this proposed legislative change.

The Tenth Amendment of the Constitution Bill was put to the Dáil for approval of the referendum on 14 May 1986 by the Minister for Justice, Alan Dukes. In his opening address, Dukes noted that 'this is one of the most important proposals to come before the Oireachtas and the people in recent years.'[18] The next person to speak was Fianna Fáil TD Michael Woods, whom Glenn refers to in her speech. The Fianna Fáil party was against the proposed legislation. Woods proceeded to give a detailed speech for over an hour on the negative implications of the proposed divorce bill. Glenn began her speech by complimenting Woods on his excellent contribution to the debate. She continued by outlining her main objections to the introduction of divorce and the potential negative consequences for women in Ireland through this legislation. Such results, Glenn maintained, stretched from placing young girls at risk of sexual abuse from a new father figure to a discarded wife becoming economically dependent on the state.

Much of Glenn's speech played on the fears felt by many married women in Ireland at that time. However, these fears were not without ground as many women had been pushed out of the labour market due to numerous social and legal restrictions. An Economic and Social Research Institute report identifies issues facing women in employment during the 1980s in Ireland.[19] A marriage bar in place until 1973 meant that women were forced out of employment upon marriage, and many found it difficult to re-enter employment after the bar was lifted. In 1980, the Supreme Court found that married women were unfairly discriminated against under Irish tax law, which clearly disadvantaged them in employment. The average age of mothers giving birth for the first time was under 25 during the 1980s, and childcare issues were and remain a central concern for working mothers. Although women were, on average, better educated than men at this time, restrictions on employment placed married women with children in a vulnerable situation if their husband left them.

Glenn followed her speech with the publication of another issue of *The Alice Glenn Report*, which carried the headline of her then well-known line 'A woman voting for divorce is like a turkey voting for Christmas.'[20] Glenn's

speech and associated newsletter may well have inspired the Labour Party's
National Women's Committee to express their concern about what Urquhart
describes as 'gender-based scaremongering'.[21] The committee wrote to the
National Referendum Committee the week after Glenn's speech, saying,
'[T]his campaign aimed at planting worries in people's (especially women's)
minds has been very successful, since the arguments are emotional ones,
aimed at creating a level of fear and insecurity.'[22]

The proposed referendum was passed by the Dáil on 21 May and by
the Seanad on 24 May. A referendum date was set for 26 June, when the
question of introducing legislation for divorce was put to a public vote. The
introduction of divorce was overwhelmingly rejected by voters, with 63
per cent against the constitutional change and only 36 per cent voting in
support. The result attracted global media attention, with the *New York Times*
announcing, 'the Irish uphold ban on divorce by 3-to-2 margin'.[23] The ban
on divorce in Ireland remained for a further decade. Another referendum on
the issue would not take place until 24 November 1995.

Glenn undoubtedly contributed to the defeat of the referendum, but
this ensured that her position in Fine Gael was now unsustainable. With
a general election looming, Fine Gael established its selection committees
in November 1986 to decide on election candidates. At the Dublin Central
selection convention, held on 28 November, Glenn was not selected despite
warnings that the party would not gain two seats in that constituency without
her on the ballot. Her determined nature was evident on the evening of
the convention, with the *Evening Herald* reporting that 'Glenn emerged as
the iron lady of Irish politics.'[24] Such comparisons with Margaret Thatcher
had previously been made by media sources due partly to Glenn's 'sharply
tailored dress sense'.[25]

Glenn stood as an independent candidate in the February 1987 general
election. *The Alice Glenn Report* published before the election carried the
headline 'Why Fine Gael Divorced Alice Glenn.' Glenn was unsuccessful
at the election, and she remained an independent member on Dublin City
Council. In 1991 she was selected as the first woman chair of the Dublin
Port and Docks Board. Glenn engaged in low-level campaigning in later
referendums on abortion and divorce. The Fifteenth Amendment of the
Constitution Act eventually removed the prohibition on divorce through a
referendum in 1995, with a minute majority of 50.28 per cent in favour and
49.72 per cent opposed.

There were many challenges to the referendum result. Des Hanafin,
chair of the anti-divorce campaign, brought the first challenge to both the
High Court and the Supreme Court, 'alleging that the use of public monies
to fund the government's "yes" referendum campaign influenced the vote
by between 3 per cent and 5 per cent – and was therefore sufficient to have

impacted the close result.'[26] Hanafin's challenge was unsuccessful. After much public and political debate, the Family (Divorce) Law Act of 1996 was deemed to have passed the Seanad in September 1996. The final amendments to the bill were passed on 20 November and divorce was signed into law by the President of Ireland on 27 November 1996. It was particularly poignant that Mary Robinson was then president and signed the legislation.

The law included a provision that couples must have been living separately for four of the previous five years before applying for a divorce.[27] The restrictive measures for securing a divorce were not removed until a referendum in 2019, when people overwhelmingly voted to reduce the separation period. Despite warnings from Glenn and her supporters that removing the ban on civil divorce would lead to a rise in marital breakdowns, Ireland continually reports the lowest rates of divorce in Europe.[28]

Glenn faded from the political realm soon after this. She died the day before what would have been her 90th birthday, on 16 December 2011, at Our Lady's Manor Nursing Home in the Dalkey suburb of Dublin. She was survived by her two sons: Gary and Liam. Her son Liam gave a eulogy at her funeral service that focused on Glenn's resilience and her colourful character. He described how one day, as his mother was leaving a bank a motorbike pulled up beside her and a man grabbed her handbag. Liam recounted, 'Alice immediately used her umbrella, and the getaway driver got away. By the time the security men came along, Alice had the man on the ground and he was shouting "get her off me, she's mad."'[29]

As noted in the *Irish Times* obituary to her, Alice Glenn was a 'Conviction politician whose patriotism was defined by her faith'.[30] Even those who may have disagreed with Glenn's traditional values and approach to politics cannot deny that she was a determined and courageous woman. Her speech remains as a testimony to the strength of women's voices during a turbulent time in Irish social reform.

Alice Glenn

The Alice Glenn Report

Vol. 2 No.1   Box 1690 ● Dublin 8   January / Feburary 1987

WHY FINE GAEL *DIVORCED* ALICE GLENN

THE TWO MANIFESTOES

When you elected me to Dail Eireann in 1981, and again in 1982, I was not aware, nor could you have been that there was ONE MANIFESTO FOR PUBLIC CONSUMPTION AND A HIDDEN AGENDA.

Had the Party Leadership stuck to its Public Manifesto I probably would have remained a quiet normal back-bencher. However, when the Party came into power it seemed to embark on what has come to be known as the Taoiseach's "Crusade", or as I prefer to call it THE HIDDEN AGENDA known only to the inner circle or which I have never been a part.

Many programmes or policies never mentioned by the Fine Gael Party, before being elected, were produced in the years of this Government which I felt were against the best interests of the majority of the people, their Christian values and family life.

Alarm bells sounded for me at the 1985 Ard Fheis when Dr.

Fitzgerald warned that anyone who wished to be GAELIC AND CATHOLIC would get no support from him. I have been in the Party all of my life - emotionally as well as factually - and tradition counts with me. My dilemma was how to remain on the national scene as an outspoken promoter of traditional and family values while being a member of a Party I felt was led by persons opposed to these values.

PARTY UNITY BEFORE MORAL PRINCIPLES?

I found myself in constant conflict with the Party Leadership on fundamental Constitutional issues, affecting every family in the land, viz:-

◆ THE PARTY STANCE ON THE PRO-LIFE AMENDMENT

◆ THE CONTRACEPTIVES BILL FOR TEENAGERS

◆ DIVORCE

◆ NATIONAL SOVEREIGNTY

In the fading twilight of this administration Dr. Fitzgerald was pushing two items I felt were contrary to our National sovereignty: the Extradition Bill and the ratification of the Single European Act.

I oppose violence - all violence - no matter how worthy the political end may be. Therefore I support extradition in principle. However, I believe that when a sovereign State turns over its citizens to stand trial in another country there must be complete trust that those citizens will get a fair trial. I still believe the Government ought to have deferred action on the Extradition Bill until the Guildford and the Birmingham Cases have been reviewed and the Stalker Case has been cleared to our satisfaction.

Likewise, before ratification of the Single European Act, the Government should have included a clause of reservation which would ensure Articles 40-44 of our Constitution could never be interfered with by legal action in the courts of the EEC. Dr. Fitzgerald did not agree with me on either of these issues and I had to vote against the

22. *The Alice Glenn Report*, Jan/Feb 1987. Courtesy of Irish Election Literature.

'A factor which is emerging more and more in Great Britain and elsewhere is the risk to young girls in particular where the new father figure, a stranger, no blood relation, enters the household. An increasing number of headlines are appearing in the British newspapers of sexual abuse of young girls in their own homes. We all agree that this is horrifying but these are consequences of the divorce culture and these facts cannot be denied. The world is a sociological reservoir where evidence of this sort abounds and anyone who is not prepared to accept this is not prepared to face reality.

The effects on women especially warrants some comment, and Deputy Woods mentioned them. The Minister said the children will have succession rights but no account is taken of the woman who is discarded. The woman will be the victim of this legislation, the cast aside spouse. Evidence proves that her status in society is seriously diminished. A very small percentage of Irish women are in the workforce – I think around 12 per cent – and an even smaller percentage are professionals. The rest would be employed in shops or offices and would not have job security. It follows from this that most of the people affected by this legislation would have to fall back on the resources of the State.

As I said, these women are denied succession rights but the position as regards family home protection is self evident. If a husband leaves his wife and children, what family home are we talking about? Reason would suggest that the family home is that of the second liaison. The Constitution is to protect the family but a wom[a]n cas[t] aside is not a family. She becomes a non-person. She loses all protection under the Constitution. The wife and the children are diminished. But the opposite happens to the male. He will have formed an alliance with somebody in the workforce who is bringing in plenty of money. That is all he is interested in. This is what has happened everywhere else and it will happen here. It occurs to me that any woman voting for divorce is like a turkey voting for Christmas.

The important point here is that the children of the divorced spouse are at risk. They are living with their mother and she is not part of a family. Article 42 says the duty of parents is to "provide, according to their means, for the religious and moral, intellectual, physical and social education of their children". She probably does not have the resources to do that and she is left in a very vulnerable position. . . .

I am not going to go into the difference between the words "failure" and "separation" because there is no connection. I reiterate that to include what is suggested here – that a marriage has failed, that the failure has continued for a period or periods amounting to at least five years and that there is no reasonable possibility of reconciliation and that any other condition prescribed by law has been complied with – is a recipe for the most liberal form of divorce ever introduced. It took England 100 years to legislate to the point from which we are starting. Can you visualise a situation in these costly courts which will be set up where a couple are confronted with a judge who is handing down a judgement on his interpretation of that section? Who can say what failure is. Can any of us? I believe that would be extremely difficult to do. I honestly believe a confidence trick is being played on our people with this suggestion.

. . . it would appear that no fault divorce is what we are talking about, and that almost on demand. Great Britain has supposedly a two year embargo before a divorce is granted, and in Belgium it is three years. Those times were written into the legislation, but of course the people concerned all go to the courts and now there is no longer even any pretence that that has any validity. They can get divorce almost on demand. I have heard lately that it may be possible shortly to get divorces by post. Anybody who believes that we cannot go down that road is just not prepared to face reality. . . .

I would like to comment about the proposed courts. There will be judges specially qualified to deal with marriage breakdown cases, but where are they likely to look for guidance in these cases? I suggest that they will look where they have been looking in the recent past for cases of this nature. They will look to America, the only other country governed by a constitution as we are, and it is of assistance in this matter to see what the Americans are doing. What are they doing in America at the moment? One marriage in three breaks down in divorce. Thousands of men are incarcerated in jails because they will not or cannot pay alimony. When the women go into court in pursuit of their alimony they are told in effect by the judges "Do not waste our time. You are an able-bodied woman. Go and work for yourself. He is not married to you any longer and cannot afford to keep two homes." That is the situation in a nutshell.

. . . I am concerned about the common good and the people of this nation. Not only will I vote against the introduction of divorce when I get to the ballot box, but I will work night and day to inform and to encourage everyone I can to do the same, to go out in throngs and say "No" to this evil recommendation.'[31]

TWENTY TWO

Inez McCormack

1943–2013

Symposium on Feminism – Our early Years
Forum Hotel Belfast

I MARCH 1986

'Express our hate in a manner in which we can face it.'

In the midst of the Troubles in Northern Ireland, there was an expansion of women's organisations across the six counties. In 1985 there was an interest in the early years of the women's movement in the north, which partly stemmed from a course run by the Workers' Education Association and delivered by Christina Loughran. The course inspired Joanna McMinn, coordinator for the Women's Education Project, and Margaret Ward, then women's officer for Belfast City Council, to organise an event that members of all the different women's groups, past and present, would be invited to contribute at.[1] This took shape in a one-day symposium held in Belfast on 1 March 1986.

The symposium provided an opportunity for representatives from women's organisations to reflect on their achievements to date and to assess their future goals. The afternoon involved a general discussion, which became extremely heated at times, complicated by sectarian divides. Inez McCormack addressed these divides in her concluding speech at the symposium. Symposium co-organiser Ward described how the discussion became 'divisive in parts, and she [McCormack] had to think on her feet when speaking'.[2] McCormack's remarks on that day were powerful and insightful, calling on those gathered to acknowledge their differences rather than attempt to ignore them.

The symposium venue, now the Europa Hotel, was labelled by international media as the most bombed hotel in Europe, having been subjected

186

to frequent attacks and bomb threats during the Troubles.[3] The proceedings were later edited by Ward for publication in a pamphlet *A Difficult, Dangerous Honesty: 10 Years of Feminism in Northern Ireland*, which included the unabridged text of McCormack's contributions. The symposium was a momentous event, bringing together feminist representatives from across Catholic and Protestant communities. Yet the event was not reported in local or national newspapers. McCormack's remarks were only recorded in the pamphlet distributed among interested parties in 1987 and have therefore been overlooked. Details of this symposium and of McCormack's remarks provide an insight into a key time of feminist activism in Northern Ireland.

The feminist symposium took place during a time of heightened awareness of women's inequalities across the island of Ireland. However, the experiences of women in Northern Ireland differed immensely from those in the Republic of Ireland. Northern Ireland was then under direct rule from Westminster, a position established in 1972 when the British Prime Minister, Edward Heath, suspended the parliament in Belfast.[4] Ward notes that despite being ruled from Westminster, the women of Northern Ireland did not enjoy the same resources or legislation as the rest of the United Kingdom. Northern Ireland did not 'have divorce law reform, in deference to the strength of religious feeling in the province; abortion was still subject to life in prison, and of course there were no refuges, no rape crisis centres, no women's centres, [and] homosexuality was illegal'.[5] While legislative reforms in these areas progressed in Britain, Northern Ireland was often excluded. A prime example of this was the 1967 Abortion Act, which provided access to abortion in Great Britain but was not extended to Northern Ireland.

The continued violence in the north of Ireland brought an added traumatic dimension for women living in the six counties. During the 1980s, 57 women in Northern Ireland were killed through republican and loyalist brutality.[6] As the primary caregivers, women carried the weight of caring for family members injured, killed or imprisoned during the conflict. As Loughran testified, 'feminism does not develop easily in a war situation.'[7] With these issues in mind, Ward recognised that it was time to examine 'any unifying potential that feminism might have to offer a divided society'.[8]

McCormack was the ideal person to chair the one-day symposium; in both her personal life and her work as a trade unionist, she was dedicated to a non-sectarian approach. She was born into a Protestant family in county Down and attended Magee College in Derry before studying at Trinity College Dublin. After graduating she met Vincent McCormack, a Catholic man from the Bogside area of Derry and later a founding member of the Derry Labour Party. The couple became involved with the civil rights movement and took part in the People's Democracy march from Belfast to

Derry in 1969.Violent attacks were made on the marchers at that civil rights demonstration, and Inez McCormack was injured.[9] Around this time, Inez married Vincent despite her parents' objections; she later recalled that 'mixed marriages weren't exactly popular or acceptable.'[10] McCormack described how prior to her involvement in the civil rights movement, she worked as a clerk in the Stormont civil service and had 'accepted as part of the natural order that Catholics should not proceed beyond the most junior grades. No statutory instrument underpinned this discrimination, unlike Birmingham, Alabama, where the law required blacks to give up their seats on buses to whites, but it was applied with the same rigour.'[11]

From the 1970s, McCormack dedicated herself to securing a more equitable society in Northern Ireland. In 1972 she was employed as a social worker in the poor Catholic area of Ballymurphy in West Belfast. Residents of the Ballymurphy estate were traumatised in the wake of a massacre that happened just months before McCormack took up her job. In August 1971 following the introduction of internment, which allowed the arrest and detention of paramilitary suspects without trial, British troops killed ten unarmed civilians in the Ballymurphy area.[12] McCormack worked amid violent disturbances, and when an attempt was made to close her offices, she contacted the National Union of Public Employees (NUPE), now UNISON, for support. She took on the role of shop steward with NUPE, and by 1976 she had become a full-time trade unionist, serving as the union's regional officer. In this role McCormack represented women who worked in hospitals and schools, many of who were low-paid cleaners. In her speech, McCormack describes the women she worked with as very poor. She worked tirelessly to improve women's working conditions, describing how her 'greatest achievement is seeing the glint in a woman's eye who believed she was nobody and now knows she is somebody'.[13]

McCormack ascended through the ranks of the trade union movement, becoming the first female chair of the Northern Ireland committee of the Irish Congress of Trade Unions (ICTU) from 1984 to 1985. She successfully campaigned on many employment issues and most famously broke a stalemate at Belfast's Royal Victoria Hospital in 1985. Journalist Susan McKay describes how McCormack and 'the striking laundry workers she represented, sternly overlooked by a statue of Queen Victoria, pushed trolleyloads of festering laundry out of the hospital's corridors and into the offices of senior management who had, up until then, managed to ignore the smell.'[14] She was one of four sponsors of the MacBride Principles, which established nine fair employment principles for American companies trading with Northern Ireland, launched in November 1984.[15] The employment principles included measures to increase the employment of under-represented religious groups and were described by Fr Seán McManus as encouraging 'non-discriminatory

U.S. investment in Northern Ireland'.[16] Within a decade, the principles
had been adopted across 16 American states and endorsed by key political
leaders, including President Bill Clinton.[17] Sinn Féin's magazine *An Phobhlact*
credited the nine principles as 'one of the most effective anti-discrimination
campaigns undertaken since the creation of the Six-County state'.[18]

By the time of the symposium in March 1986, McCormack was a highly
respected figure in Northern Ireland who successfully campaigned for social
and economic reform across religious and political divides. She opened the
event with a call for attendees to share their stories about their feminist
work. Describing the current problems in Northern Irish society, McCormack
asserted that 'I think women and the women's movement has the chief
contribution to make to changing the nature of that society. I think it's time
we took power and did it.'[19] Following McCormack's invitation, a number
of feminist leaders spoke, including Eileen Eavson of the Coleraine Women's
Group, Lynda Edgerton of NI Women's Rights, Patricia Morgan of Craigavon
Women's Group, members of the Socialist Women's Group, Marie-Therese
of the Belfast Women's Collective, Karen McMinn of the Noreen Winchester
Campaign, and representatives from lesbian and other groups. The morning
session was a time to reflect on the achievements of feminist activity in the
last decade and was described by Ward as 'informative and enjoyable'.[20]

The afternoon session, which involved a general discussion, saw a
change of mood, at times revealing 'disillusion and anger'.[21] One contributor
maintained that 'women should be organising solely in their own areas,
even if this restricted them to their respective ghettos', which would isolate
feminist groups from each other.[22] The discussion became very heated,
and McCormack stepped in to provide an honest and frank evaluation of
these sectarian and political divides. McCormack's speech was delivered in
response to the heated debate and was therefore spontaneous. Her remarks
were insightful and calmed the situation; she described the collaborative
style of NUPE members, who could work with other women despite their
religious, political, or personal differences.

McCormack employed this diplomatic style during the peace treaty debates;
she played a vital background role in the 1998 Good Friday Peace agreement,
demanding the inclusion of human rights and equality provisions. She became
the first female president of the ICTU in 1999, a position she held until 2001.
Despite growing demands on her time, McCormack remained actively involved
in feminist and human rights organisations, joining numerous boards and
committees. She served on the board of directors of InterTrade Ireland and
as a member of the Northern Ireland Human Rights Commission.[23] In 2006,
McCormack founded Participation and the Practice of Rights (PPR) to fight
injustice by challenging systems that enable inequality through exclusion.

In 2007 McCormack was one of seven women portrayed in a documentary play *Seven*, which Vital Voices Global Partnership commissioned to reveal the stories of women who had worked for change around the globe.[24] The play premiered in January 2008 in New York City and continues to be performed in towns and cities around the globe.[25] A production was staged in the Hudson Theatre, New York, on the opening night of the Women in the World Summit on 12 March 2010; it was introduced by Hillary Clinton. Clinton's husband, Bill, had played a central role in the Good Friday Agreement negotiations, and Hillary had met McCormack on a number of occasions during this process. Hillary Clinton's connection with Belfast remained strong long after the agreement was signed; she was appointed as Chancellor of Queen's University Belfast in 2020, although her formal inauguration was postponed until 2021 due to Covid-19 restrictions. Before the 2010 New York production, Clinton described how the play 'powerfully portrays the transformative way that seven courageous women have changed their societies for the better – from peace-building, to fighting corruption to combating violence against women'.[26] Hollywood actress Meryl Streep played McCormack in this production.

In September 2012 McCormack was diagnosed with inoperable colon cancer, which had spread to secondary areas of her body. Aware that she did not have long to live, McCormack recorded her final interview with her friend Susan McKay. McCormack left the Foyle Hospice in Derry to go home for a few hours to take part in the interview.[27] McKay was keen to document McCormack's important work and legacy. McCormack agreed to contribute to a documentary that McKay later produced and narrated based on this final interview. *Inez: A Challenging Woman* includes interviews with friends and colleagues, including President Michael D Higgins, former President Mary Robinson, former US Secretary of State Hillary Clinton, former president of the ICTU Patricia McKeown, and human rights lawyer Michael Farrell.

Inez's husband, Vincent, was interviewed for the documentary and described how his wife's 'political awareness arose really from very direct experience of extreme poverty and extreme exclusion and extreme humiliation'.[28] In her interview, Clinton was clear about the impact McCormack had made on the lives of people in Northern Ireland, stating that although 'her name is not on the [Good Friday] agreement, it's someone like Inez who has made it possible for people to find a way of actually living these agreements'.[29] Perhaps the most poignant comment came from President Higgins, who described her human rights work as globally significant, noting that 'Inez McCormack doesn't belong to just any one region or belong indeed to Ireland but belongs to the world.'

McCormack died on 21 January 2013, before the documentary was completed. She was survived by her husband and her daughter, Anna. Obituaries of McCormack were carried in local and national newspapers in Ireland, the United Kingdom and America. The *Belfast Telegraph* published her obituary under the aptly titled headline 'A true champion of the down-trodden'.[30] Her funeral processed from her home to Belfast City Cemetery, where hundreds of people attended her burial. At the time of the funeral, Mark Durkan, MP for Foyle, addressed the House of Commons, stating that 'someone who espoused the ethic that no minority was too small to be protected or cherished was Inez McCormack, whose funeral takes place today.'[31] He called on the British Secretary of State, Theresa Villers, to join him in paying tribute to McCormack; Villers enthusiastically joined this tribute.

Thirteen weeks after McCormack's death, Meryl Streep gave a moving tribute to Inez at the Women in the World Summit on 4 April 2013. She opened her tribute by describing McCormack as 'a tall woman and a towering figure in the movement for civil rights in Northern Ireland, a feminist, a humanitarian, a human rights advocate and one of the great peacemakers of Northern Ireland'.[32] Tributes to her continued over the coming years. In March 2014 *Seven* was performed in the Great Hall of Parliament in Belfast and in the Guildhall, Derry. *Inez: A Challenging Woman* won the Best Documentary Award at the prestigious Galway Film Fleadh in July 2014. It has since been screened in Ireland, Britain and America. On 21 January 2015 BBC Northern Ireland showed the documentary in tribute to McCormack on the second anniversary of her death.

McCormack's former colleague Patricia McKeown observed that McCormack 'was internationally recognised – not always so recognised at home, but I think in recent years it has become very clear that we all owe a debt to a woman who broke the mould and never gave up'.[33] The text of McCormack's speech provides an insight into how she challenged people in Northern Ireland to accept their political differences and work together in the interest of improving human rights.

23. Inez McCormack (left) with Margaret Ward at the first Reclaim the Night protest in Belfast, November 1987. Courtesy of Margaret Ward.

'If we cannot articulate that difficult, dangerous honesty between us, that we are beginning to touch on, because what we are beginning to touch on is a bit of hate, which is surfacing. Now we shouldn't deny it's there, but we shouldn't also deny that we are capable of facing it and dealing with it, and that is the lesson, as women, that we must do. I'm going to tell you something else, where I learned my discipline from. I work for very poor women. I work for women from West Belfast, I work for women from Protestant areas, and I'm thinking of them when they came together – we call it a committee because that's how we get the money – and there was a women's liberation conference organised by gay women, by Women Against Imperialism, and god knows what women, and there was an invitation [–] would we send women to it. And our women's committee met and they are mostly quite old, and they decided to send a delegation – 20 – virtually the whole committee, as nobody was going to be excluded.

I explained that this conference would be organised, not by the trade union movement but would be organised by gay women, it would be organised by women who would have different politics to some of them, and who would have the same politics as some of them. Now these were women, some of them have become politicised, some are very conservative (with a small "c" and a big "c"), some came from strongly loyalist backgrounds, some came from very strongly republican backgrounds. And they went in their delegation of 20, and they went to the workshops on the national question and they went to the workshops on drug and alcohol abuse (that by the way set them all bubbling), and some of them came from country areas and there was a social that night and mostly it was gay women at that social, and one of the women was sitting beside me – she must be about 58, and I wish she was here because she's magic, she's a school meals supervisor in County Tyrone – and she came to the social that night.

Some of the younger gay women in fact found our members more difficult to handle than the other way round because the thing that intrigued our members all day was Irish gay lesbians were difficult to grasp, but Australian lesbians were something else! I'm trying to make this humorous because there needs to be a capacity in us to express our hate in a manner in which we can face it, and a capacity for us to express our prejudice because the division in Ireland is not easy, but by god, we are women in Ireland and we have got to face it. There were gay women necking in front of her – she was 58 and it was her first conference – and I said to her "Do you find this difficult, would you rather we just went?" And she just said, "Well Inez, they spend their life living at the edge of my world, I should spend an evening living at the edge of theirs."

Now, there is a capacity to take responsibility for women who are different from her, women from a different background that I found very, very humbling. And what I am saying to you is very simply this, that there is a capacity within women in Ireland, not to "rise above our divisions", because that just denies our reality, but I do not actually think in this discussion, to be honest, that we have trusted enough in the belief that we are women in Ireland. I don't think we can deny our political allegiances, I don't think we can deny our backgrounds, I don't think we can deny any of that, because that is part of what we are, and if we deny any of that then we are no longer relevant to the women in Armagh jail, or to the women in the Shankill. We're not relevant if we deny that division, but there is a capacity to face it there, and to be frank, if a 58-year-old woman from a country area can, in one night in her life make a mature and tolerant remark like that, then we have got a duty to serve that woman. We have got a duty to empower her to speak in Ireland because if we are not capable of speaking in Ireland, she is and what she stands for is. She is capable and those women were capable, of facing the national question within each other. . . .

All I'm saying is that the maturity and discipline which is not mine, but which I've learnt over the years, comes from working with very poor women who have no space and who, from when they get up in the morning and go to bed at night, have to have a strategy for survival. That's not just working-class politics, you cannot deny the reality of West Belfast politics either, or the reality of gay politics. But it puts upon us a responsibility which frankly today, I think we have only begun to exercise. And that is to talk about our divisions in a manner which makes us face them and not deny them. And that's all I've got to say.'[34]

TWENTY THREE

Mary Robinson

B. 1944

Presidential Inauguration speech
Dublin Castle

3 DECEMBER 1990

'Come dance with me in Ireland.'

In 1990 the people of Ireland instigated change when they elected Mary Robinson, a young woman from county Mayo, as the seventh president of Ireland. Robinson's inauguration speech was a powerful expression of what she described as passing 'the threshold to a new pluralist Ireland'. This was the first time that a woman addressed the Irish nation as president. To that date, she was the youngest person to hold the highest office in the land and the only candidate to be elected without the support of the Fianna Fáil party. Robinson's inauguration speech outlined the new and innovative approach that she would take to fulfil her role as president, including reaching out to Irish emigrants abroad and to all communities in Northern Ireland. Her speech marks a significant time in Ireland's history, when the role of the presidency would be reimagined with new purpose.

The choice of Robinson (née Bourke) as president was noteworthy as from the 1960s she was a stalwart supporter of progressive social reform in the country. She was born in Ballina, county Mayo, in May 1944, the third of five children in a privileged Catholic family. Robinson was afforded the best educational opportunities, studying for a four-year legal science degree at Trinity College Dublin. Robinson went to Trinity during a time when Catholics were prohibited from attending the Protestant founded university. On 7 February 1944 John Charles McQuaid, Archbishop of Dublin and the Catholic Primate of Ireland, issued a stipulation that no

Catholic could attend Trinity College unless they received permission from him. He decreed that 'any Catholic who disobeys this law is guilty of mortal sin and while he persists in disobedience is unworthy to receive the Sacraments.'[1] This ban remained in place until June 1970, when it was lifted by the Catholic Bishops in Ireland.

Robinson disregarded the Catholic hierarchy's opposition to Trinity, and she excelled at her studies there. She was elected auditor of the prestigious Dublin University Law Society in 1967. Her inaugural address as auditor in February 1967 reveals her early drive to achieve legislative reform in Ireland and her confidence in speaking at public forums. Robinson spoke on the topic of 'Law and Morality in Ireland', advocating for the decrim- inalisation of suicide and homosexuality and for the removal of bans on divorce and contraception. Her speech was radical, which was most evident in her focus on the '"special position" afforded to the Catholic church in the Irish Constitution'.[2] She later described how this address was a 'seminal moment' for her.[3] Robinson would passionately pursue reforms on divorce and contraception as well as the decriminalisation of homosexuality and suicide over the coming three decades. Her 1967 address received attention and was reported in detail in the *Irish Times*.[4]

Robinson graduated from Trinity College later in 1967, receiving first class honours. During her final two years at Trinity, Robinson studied for her Barrister-at-Law degree through the Honorable Society of King's Inns where she also received first class honours, and she was called to the Irish bar in 1967. She received a fellowship to pursue a Masters of Law at Harvard Law School and moved to Boston in August 1967 for one year of study. This was a remarkable time for Robinson to study in America, which was then witnessing intense student protests regarding civil rights and the Vietnam War (1955–75). While she was studying in Boston, Martin Luther King was assassinated in Memphis, Tennessee. The assassination of such an influential civil rights leader in America had a devastating effect on students at Harvard University. Robinson described how the civil rights movement had 'a great influence' on her; she was 'distraught' about King's murder.[5] Robinson graduated from Harvard with her Master's degree in 1968.

Robinson returned to Ireland and was employed by University College Dublin as a tutor in law. In 1969 she applied for the Reid Professorship of Constitutional and Criminal Law at Trinity, a part-time professorship open to applicants practising at the Irish bar. Robinson was successful and took up the position in October 1969 at the age of only 25; she was the youngest person to hold this prestigious professorship. Meanwhile there was a general election in Ireland in June 1969. Robinson stood for election to the Seanad as an independent candidate for a university seat.[6] She was successfully elected, taking the third seat for Trinity College. Robinson attended her first

Seanad session on 5 November 1969, at which the first order was to elect a new Cathaoirleach (chair of Seanad Éireann). Senator Michael Yeats, son of the poet W. B. Yeats and a member of Fianna Fáil, was proposed. While nominations for the chair were rarely contested, there was an objection in this instance. Senator Owen Sheehy Skeffington, son of Hanna and Frank Sheehy Skeffington, objected on the ground that Yeats could not be objective as he complied to the Fianna Fáil party line without question.[7] Robinson was the only senator to support Sheehy Skeffington, and with the majority in his favour, Senator Yeats was elected as Cathaoirleach. Robinson's first attendance at the Seanad was reported by journalist John Healy in the *Irish Times* under the heading 'Two Trinity senators vote against Cathaoirleach'.[8] Healy's article noted that Robinson 'promises to be the most charming dissenter in the House'.[9] The journalist could not have envisaged just how significant Robinson's career in the Seanad would become.

Robinson served as a senator for 20 years, having been successfully elected in seven successive Seanad elections. She served as an independent senator, besides a period from 1977 to 1982 when she joined the Labour Party. From the outset, Robinson was determined 'to implement law reform'.[10] She began her campaign by compiling a private member's bill to repeal the Criminal Law (Amendment) Act of 1935, which outlawed the sale or advertisement of contraceptives. The ban on contraceptives in Ireland was detrimental to women's rights; as historian Sandra McAvoy observes, this ban delayed 'the emancipation of Irish women – not least by subordinating their rights to life and health to their reproductive functions'.[11] In October 1970 Robinson called a public meeting, inviting members of the Irish Family Planning association, general practitioners, and interested citizens. The meeting sparked the first of many clashes she would have with the Catholic hierarchy. In response to Robinson's activities, Archbishop McQuaid issued a letter to be read at every mass the following Sunday. The letter stated that contraception 'would be, and would remain, a curse upon our country'.[12]

In 1970 Robinson married Nicholas Robinson (Nick); the couple met while they were both studying law at Trinity. Robinson's choice of partner caused controversy for some, including her parents, as Nick was Protestant. Nick remained an unfaltering supporter of Robinson's work, which was particularly important during her early career; she was subjected to attack for her progressive views. Robinson's senate colleague John Horgan maintained that 'Robinson paid a heavy personal price for her liberalism. Her family refused to attend her marriage to a Protestant and she was the recipient of hate mail of the most vulgar kind.'[13] Horgan believed that much of this hate was directed at Robinson because of her gender.

Despite pressures from conservative and religious quarters, Robinson continued to be a progressive voice calling for legislative reform in Ireland.

She campaigned for the abolition of the category of illegitimacy in Irish law and ending discrimination against women in the selection of jurors. Robinson campaigned in two of the most controversial referenda in Ireland, battling against the introduction of the Eighth Amendment to criminalise abortion in 1983 and in support of providing for divorce in 1985. She also led numerous legal cases seeking reform, perhaps most notably Norris v Ireland. Robinson took the case for David Norris, a colleague at Trinity College, a gay man who sought to decriminalise homosexuality in Ireland. Her legal support of Norris eventually led to the decriminalisation of homosexuality in Ireland in 1993.[14] It is fair to say that during 20 years as a senator, Robinson was at the forefront of the most progressive campaigning for legislative reform.

In the summer of 1989 a general election was called, and Robinson decided not to stand for re-election. She reasoned that she was able to bring about change more effectively by pursuing legal cases than through her position in the Seanad.[15] Added to this, she had recently established the Irish Centre for European Law with her husband Nick in 1988, to produce independent education on European Directives and European law. By that stage, the couple had three children: Tessa, William and Aubrey. On 14 February 1990 former attorney general John Rogers asked Robinson to meet with him. Rogers invited Robinson to stand for the upcoming presidential election as the Labour Party candidate. After much consideration Robinson agreed to stand as an independent candidate nominated by Labour. Her presidential campaign was formally launched on 1 May 1990 in Limerick city. The probability of Robinson being elected as the next president of Ireland was low, reflected in an Irish bookmaker offering odds of 100/1 against her winning the election.[16]

Robinson stood for election as the President of Ireland (Uachtarán na hÉireann), the head of state of the Republic of Ireland. The role of president was established through the Irish Constitution of 1937, with the first president, Douglas Hyde, taking position in 1938. Following Ireland's withdrawal from the Commonwealth, which came into effect on 18 April 1949, the role of the President of Ireland became more significant from an international perspective. The president is elected by the people of Ireland; however, if agreed by all party consent, a president can be placed in office without a public election. Hyde was inaugurated as president without an election and served until 1945. The following five presidents were all Fianna Fáil candidates: Seán T. O'Kelly (1945–59), Éamon de Valera (1959–73), Erskine Childers (1973–4), Cearbhall Ó Dálaigh (1974–6) and Patrick Hillery (1976–90). With the sudden death of President Childers in office, Ó Dálaigh was nominated for the office unopposed. Ó Dálaigh resigned from the position two years later, and Hillery was nominated unopposed for two consecutive terms, serving until 1990. The presidential election held on 7 November 1990 was the first time in 17 years that the people of Ireland had the opportunity to vote for their president.

Robinson stood against two candidates in the 1990 election: Brian Lenihan and Austin Currie. Lenihan, the Fianna Fáil candidate, served as Tánaiste until a week before the election and was perceived as a sure winner. Currie, a civil rights leader in Northern Ireland, stood as the Fine Gael candidate and was seen as only having an outside chance of winning. There was a decent turnout at the polls, with 64 per cent of the electorate casting their votes. On the evening of 9 November 1990, Robinson and Lenihan were invited to the count centre at the Royal Dublin Society (RDS) for the result declaration.[17] The returning officer read the final count, declaring Robinson's victory with 52 per cent of the vote. Robinson, flanked by Lenihan and Taoiseach Charles Haughey, gave a rousing acceptance speech, which she had prepared with the help of Eoghan Harris an Irish journalist and political advisor. In her speech, she declared:

> Today is a day for victory and validation. Even as I salute my supporters, as Mary Robinson, I must also bid them farewell as President-elect. They are not just partisans, but patriots, too. They know that as president of Ireland I must be a president for all the people, but more than that, I want to be a president for all the people. Because I was elected by men and women of all parties and none, by many with great courage who stepped out from the faded flags of the Civil War and voted for a new Ireland, and above all by the women of Ireland mná na hÉireann, who instead of rocking the cradle, rocked the system, and who came out massively to make their mark on the ballot paper and on a new Ireland.[18]

This was indeed a vote for a new Ireland. Robinson was refreshingly different from the Irish presidents who had gone before her. The previous six presidents were older men, who were apparently rewarded with the esteemed office for their political service. Robinson's acceptance speech suggested that during her term in office she would not simply attend national events or remain quietly in the presidential residence, Áras an Uachtaráin. Robinson was one of the women of Ireland who 'rocked the system', and she would continue to do so throughout her term in office and beyond.

Robinson's presidential inauguration was scheduled for 3 December 1990 in St Patrick's Hall in Dublin Castle. It was traditional for the newly elected president to deliver a speech to the nation after taking the formal declaration. Robinson described how the 'inauguration speech was an opportunity to consolidate in a single document my own ideas of the presidency, and my plans for it. . . . I wanted to capture the idea of an Ireland that was opening up, that was able to elect a woman with a track record like mine, and that at the

24. President-elect Mary Robinson, with defeated candidate Brian Lenihan (left) and Taoiseach Charles Haughey, R.D.S., Dublin, 9 November 1990. Courtesy of the National Library of Ireland.

same time needed to be reminded of its own history.'[19] Robinson prepared her speech over the coming four weeks and sought advice from friends, including Richard Kearney, then a professor of philosophy at UCD. She also sought input from Eavan Boland, a renowned Irish poet. It was her husband Nick who was her 'primary collaborator in drafting the speech'.[20] Robinson was aware that 'there had been no great tradition of significant inaugural addresses.'[21] Robinson's speech established a new tradition. Her inaugural presidential address has become one of the most referenced speeches in Ireland. She gave the address in front of 500 invited guests, and the proceedings were broadcast live across the nation by RTÉ television.

Robinson's opening lines echoed her acceptance speech, describing a new progressive Ireland. Her mention of being a president for all Irish people around the globe marked a new direction for the presidency. Robinson was moved to highlight the plight of the forgotten Irish: the generations of Irish emigrants who often lived in poverty abroad. Robinson's consideration of the emigrant Irish continued throughout her term as president. This aspect is most evident in the light she installed in the front window of Áras an Uachtaráin as a symbolic light for Irish emigrants and exiles. She was greatly influenced by Boland's poem 'The emigrant Irish', which includes the lines 'Like oil lamps we put them out the back / of our houses, of our minds.'[22] This light remains in a window of the Áras as a beacon for the Irish diaspora. This symbolic move was extended in December 2020 by President Michael D. Higgins, who lit a 'river of light' for all the Irish abroad who could not make it home for Christmas due to Covid-19 travel restrictions then in place. As president, Robinson continued to value Irish literature and culture and promote it to a global audience, and her speech is sprinkled with references to great Irish authors. Although Robinson was not a fluent Irish speaker, she believed it was important to incorporate the native language into her speech, choosing to talk about her travels around Ireland during her campaign tour in Irish.[23]

After giving her inauguration speech, Robinson was escorted by the Taoiseach, Charles Haughey, to inspect the guard of honour in the forecourt of Dublin Castle. This was a particularly significant image for the people of Ireland to witness: a woman, now commander-in-chief of the defence forces, inspecting Irish troops. Robinson's speech was generally well received by people in Ireland. Many newspapers carried detailed accounts of her speech, including the *Evening Herald* in their afternoon edition that same day.[24] The following day, her speech was printed in full by numerous newspapers.[25] A number of newspaper articles on 4 December examined the significance of Robinson's campaign and subsequent election. Emily O'Reilly, then political correspondent with the *Irish Press*, described Robinson's campaign as 'an attempt to kick-start the liberal agenda back into life. It had been flattened by the events of the 80s, by the results of the abortion and divorce referenda, by the stunning success of a highly motivated conservative elite who trampled the liberals into the ground.'[26]

Some journalists attempted to quell the excitement of the election of the first female Irish president. The *Evening Herald* warned that Robinson 'will be gagged firmly and securely both by the Constitution and politicians who want to ensure she doesn't use her considerable intellectual ability to make this a unique Presidency'.[27] Previous presidents had indeed been controlled through such constitutional and political measures, but Robinson established a new course for her term as president. Many of the duties assigned to the President, as outlined in the Constitution, relate to the formalities associated with the passing of bills and the dissolution and reassembly of Dáil Éireann. Within months of her inauguration, Robinson had a meeting with the Taoiseach, Haughey. He presented Robinson with an interpretation of the Constitution, suggesting that the 'President could not give press interviews or speak independently of the government – it would be considered "addressing the nation" – without approval of the government'.[28] Robinson, a constitutional lawyer, refused to accept this position and successfully presented her legal arguments against this opinion. From this point on, it was agreed that Robinson had the right to speak directly to the press and at public meetings without seeking government approval.

Robinson remained President of Ireland for seven years, and during that time she followed through on the promises she set out in her inauguration address. She engaged with nationalist and unionist communities in Northern Ireland, developed relationships within the European Union, and reached out to countries in need. She resigned from the office of president on 12 September 1997 to take up the position of the United Nations High Commissioner for Human Rights, a role she held until 2002. She has been a member of the Elders, an independent body of global leaders working for human rights, since 2007. She is president of the Mary Robinson Foundation for climate justice established in 2010. Robinson has been the recipient of numerous prestigious awards for her humanitarian work, including the Presidential Medal of Freedom, which she received from the President of the United States, Barack Obama, in 2009. Mary Robinson continues to successfully campaign for human rights for people around the globe.

25. Mary Robinson, UN Special Envoy for the Great Lake Region during a press point in Goma, 30 April 2013. Photograph by MONUSCO/Sylvain Liechti, Creative Commons.

'The Ireland I will be representing is a new Ireland, open, tolerant, inclusive. Many of you who voted for me did so without sharing all of my views. This, I believe, is a significant signal of change, a sign, however modest, that we have already passed the threshold to a new pluralist Ireland. . . .

My primary role as President will be to represent this State. But the State is not the only model of community with which Irish people can and do identify. Beyond our State there is a vast community of Irish emigrants extending not only across our neighbouring island – which has provided a home away from home for several Irish generations – but also throughout the continents of North America, Australia and of course Europe itself. There are over 70 million people living on this globe who claim Irish descent. I will be proud to represent them. And I would like to see Áras [an] Uachtaráin serve – on something of an annual basis – as a place where our emigrant communities could send representatives for a get together of the extended Irish family abroad.

There is yet another level of community which I will represent. Not just the national, not just the global, but the local community.

Within our State there are a growing number of local and regional communities determined to express their own creativity, identity, heritage and initiative in new and exciting ways. In my travels throughout Ireland I have found local community groups thriving on a new sense of self-confidence and self-empowerment. Whether it was groups concerned with adult education, employment initiative, women's support, local history and heritage, environmental concern or community culture, one of the most enriching discoveries was to witness the exten[t] of this local empowerment at work.

As President I will seek to the best of my abilities to promote this growing sense of local participatory democracy, this energising movement of self[-]development and self[-]expression which is surfacing more and more at grassroots level. This is the face of modern Ireland.

Ba mhaith liom a rá go bhfuair mé taithneamh agus pléisiúr as an taisteal a rinne mé le míosa anuas ar fuaid na hÉireann. Is fíor álainn agus iontach an tír atá againn, agus is álainn an pobal iad muintir na hÉireann.

Fuair mé teachtaireacht ón bpobal seo agus mé ag dul timpeall: "Teastaíonn Uachtarán uainn gur féidir linn bheith bródúil aisti, ach, níos mó ná sin, gur féidir linn bheith bródúil lena chéile - toisc gur Éireannaigh sinn, agus go bhfuil traidisiúin agus cultúr álainn againn".

Is cuid án tábhachtach don gcultúr sin an Ghaeilge – an teanga bheo – fé mar atá a labhairt sa Ghaeltacht agus ag daoine eile ar fuaid na hÉireann.

Tá aistear eile le déanamh anois agam – aistear cultúrtha, leis an saibhreas iontach atá sa teanga Ghaeilge a bhaint amach díom féin.

Tá súil agam go leanfaidh daoine eile mé atá ar mo nós fhéin – beagán as cleachtadh so Ghaeilge – agus go raghaimíd ar aghaidh le chéile le taithneamh agus pleisíur a fháil as ár dteanga álainn féin.

TRANSLATION

[I want to say how much I enjoyed travelling around Ireland over the last few months. Ours is a truly beautiful country and the Irish people are a wonderful race.

I got a message from the people that they wanted a President they could be proud of, but more than that, that we could take pride together – in our Irishness and our wonderful heritage and culture.

The Irish language is an important part of that culture, as spoken in the Gaeltacht areas and around the country. I am about to embark on another journey – a cultural voyage of discovery of the wealth and beauty of the Irish language. I hope others who, like myself, are somewhat out of practice, will join me on this journey, and that we will progress together to enjoy to the full our own beautiful language.]

The best way we can contribute to a new integrated Europe of the 1990s is by having a confident sense of our Irishness. Here again we must play to our strengths – take full advantage of our vibrant cultural resources in music, art, drama, literature and film; value the role of our educators; promote and preserve our unique environmental and geographical resources of relatively pollution-free lakes, rivers, landscapes and seas; encourage and publicly support local initiative projects in aquaculture, forestry, fishing, alternative energy and small-scale technology.

Looking outwards from Ireland, I would like on your behalf to contribute to the international protection and promotion of human rights. One of our greatest national resources has always been and still is, our ability to serve as a moral and political conscience in world affairs. We have a long history of providing spiritual, cultural, and social assistance to other countries in need – most notably in Latin America, Africa and other Third World countries. And we can continue to promote these values by taking principled and independent stands on issues of international importance.

As the elected President of this small democratic country I assume office at a vital moment in Europe's history. Ideological boundaries that have separated East from West are withering away at an astounding pace. Eastern Countries are seeking to participate as full partners in a restructured and economically buoyant Europe. The stage is set for a new common European home based on respect for human rights, pluralism, tolerance and openness to new ideas. The European Convention of Human Rights – one of the main achievements of the Council of Europe – is asserting itself as the natural Constitution for the new Europe. These developments have created one of the major challenges for the 1990s.

If it is time, as Joyce's Stephen Dedalus remarked, that the Irish began to forge in the smithy of our souls "the uncreated conscience of our race" – might we not also take on the still "uncreated conscience" of the wider international community? Is it not time that the small started believing again that it is beautiful, that the periphery can rise up and speak out on equal terms with the centre, that the most outlying island community of the European Community really has something strange and precious to contribute to the sea-change presently sweeping through the entire continent of Europe? As a native of Ballina, one of the most western towns in the most western province of the most western nation in Europe, I want to say – "the West's awake".

I turn now to another place close to my heart, Northern Ireland. As the elected choice of the people of this part of our island I want to extend the hand of friendship and of love to both communities in the other part. And I want to do this with no strings attached, no hidden agenda. As the person chosen by you to symbolise this Republic and to project our self[-]image to others, I will seek to encourage mutual understanding and tolerance between all the different communities sharing this island.

In seeking to do this I shall rely to a large exten[t] on symbols. But symbols are what unite and divide people. Symbols give us our identity, our self[-]image, our way of explaining ourselves to ourselves and to others. Symbols in turn determine the kinds of stories we tell; and the stories we tell determine the kind of history we make and remake. I want Áras an Uachtaráin to be a place where people can tell diverse stories – in the knowledge that there is someone there to listen.

I want this Presidency to promote the telling of stories – stories of celebration through the arts and stories of conscience and of social justice. As a woman, I want women who have felt themselves outside history to be written back into history, in the words of Eavan Boland, "finding a voice where they found a vision".

May God direct me so that my Presidency is one of justice, peace and love. May I have the fortune to preside over an Ireland at a time of exciting transformation when we enter a new Europe where old wounds can be healed, a time when, in the words of Seamus Heaney[,] "hope and history rhyme". May it be a presidency where I the President can sing to you, citizens of Ireland, the joyous refrain of the 14th Century Irish poet as recalled by W. B. Yeats:

"I am of Ireland. . . come dance with me in Ireland."

Go raibh míle maith agaibh go léir.'[29]

TWENTY FOUR

Máire Geoghegan-Quinn

B. 1950

Speech marking the decriminalisation of homosexuality
Dáil Éireann, Leinster House, Dublin

23 JUNE 1993

'Genuine tolerance is not achieved by the turning of a blind eye.'

The Minister for Justice, Máire Geoghegan-Quinn, brought a Sexual Offences bill to the Dáil in 1993. The bill proposed decriminalising male homosexual activity. The passing of this legislation had momentous consequences for gay rights in Ireland. On 23 June 1993 a second stage reading of the bill was debated in the Dáil. Geoghegan-Quinn opened the debate with a speech highlighting the injustice that gay men in Ireland had lived under since the foundation of the state. Colm Tóibín, a prestigious Irish author and a gay man, described how Geoghegan-Quinn's speech was 'a new sort of utterance in Ireland, high idealism which was matched by swift action in the form of legislation. She spoke of ideals from a position of power. So much Irish eloquence before her had arisen from powerlessness.'[1]

In 1993 Ireland was the only remaining member of the European Economic Community (EEC) to retain criminal penalties against male homosexual activity. An archaic law introduced while Ireland was under British rule, the Offences Against the Person Act 1861, meant that homosexual men could face imprisonment of between ten years and life for engaging in consensual sexual activity.[2] As Geoghegan-Quinn noted in her speech, 'in practice these laws are rarely if ever implemented', and therefore it was argued that the law did not need updating. Geoghegan-Quinn's engagement with this argument was unambiguous: she maintained that leaving such a criminal law in place 'would be grossly and gratuitously offensive to those who happen to be homosexual'. This was the first organised attempt to decriminalise male homosexual activity through the Department for Justice in Ireland. In her contribution to the debate, Fine Gael TD Nora Owen noted the significance of this reform being introduced by a female Minister for Justice. Owen surmised that 'it is easier for women to cope with the reality of the discrimination homosexuals suffer. I say that from the heart because women have had to face such enormous discrimination in their lives.'[3]

Geoghegan-Quinn was the first female Minister for Justice in Ireland; she was appointed to the position in January 1993 on the establishment of the Fianna Fáil–Labour coalition government. She was born in Connemara, county Galway, in 1950 and first entered politics in 1975 following the death of her father, Johnny Geoghegan, a Fianna Fáil TD for Galway West. Geoghegan-Quinn contested the by-election for her father's seat, also representing Fianna Fáil. She was returned as TD for Galway West in the 1975 by-election and was elected to that constituency for eight successive Dáil assemblies. Geoghegan-Quinn represented a liberal aspect of the Fianna Fáil party during a significant time for social reform in Ireland. She was first appointed to a Cabinet position in 1979 as Minister for the Gaeltacht; notably, she was the first woman to hold a Cabinet post in Ireland since Countess Markievicz had served as Minister for Labour (1919–21).

While there was pressure on the Irish government to decriminalise male homosexual activity, Geoghegan-Quinn was undoubtedly the driver behind the legislation that finally brought forward this reform. In her speech Geoghegan-Quinn notes the pressure for Irish reform in the wake of a European Court decision in the Norris case. David Norris, a lecturer at Trinity College Dublin, had launched his campaign to decriminalise homosexuality nearly two decades previously. In 1977 Mary Robinson led Norris's case at the High Court, arguing that the Offences Against the Person Act was 'repugnant to the Irish Constitution of 1937[;] [the laws] were not continued in force at the time of the Constitution's enactment and therefore did not form part of Irish law'.[4] In theory, all laws from before the introduction of the Irish Constitution in 1937 should have been replaced. The High Court ruled against Norris in *Norris v. The Attorney General*. On 10 October 1980 Justice McWilliam concluded that 'one of the effects of criminal sanctions against homosexual acts is to reinforce the misapprehension and general prejudice of the public and increase the anxiety and guilt feelings of homosexuals leading, on occasions, to depression and the serious consequences which can follow from that unfortunate disease.'[5] Regardless of the negative consequences of criminalising male homosexual activity, the case was dismissed on legal grounds.[6]

Robinson issued an appeal to the Supreme Court on behalf of Norris. In 1983 the Supreme Court appeal was denied, with the majority judgement given by Chief Justice O'Higgins, stating that 'Homosexuality has always been condemned in Christian teaching as being morally wrong. It has equally been regarded by society for many centuries as an offence against nature and a very serious crime.'[7] This was a fundamentally flawed statement coming from the highest court in Ireland. Norris persisted with his aim to overthrow the criminalisation of homosexuality, and Robinson took his case to the Court of Human Rights in Strasbourg. While the Strasbourg case was ongoing, Norris was elected to Seanad Éireann in 1987; he became an independent senator for the University of Dublin Constituency. The election of the first openly gay senator was a testament to growing support for LGBT rights.[8] In October 1988 the Strasbourg court ruled that Ireland had breached Article 8 of the European Convention on Human Rights, 'which provided that everyone had the right to respect for his private and family life, and that that right could not be interfered with by the state except for a legitimate aim, such as for the protection of health and morals or a pressing social need'.[9]

A clear statement was made by the European Court that criminalisation of homosexuality was in violation of human rights, yet no immediate action was taken by the Irish government to redress this; no action would be taken for another five years. During this time, Robinson had been elected as President of Ireland, and she used her position to send a message that gay and lesbian people were equal citizens. On 12 December 1992 Robinson invited 32 representatives from Irish lesbian and gay organisations to a reception at Áras an Uachtaráin. It was reported in the *Evening Herald* that Ireland has 'an immense distance to travel to attain justice and equality for gay and lesbian people[;] the President's gesture is at least proof that the journey is beginning'.[10] Kieran Rose, founder of the Gay Lesbian Equality Network (GLEN), attended the reception and later recalled how 'Being welcomed into the symbolic home of all Irish people was very important and significant. It seemed to me that those years of struggle, exclusion and abuse were being put behind us.'[11]

In January 1993 Geoghegan-Quinn was appointed as Minister for Justice, only weeks after the LGBT reception at Áras an Uachtaráin. Norris maintained that prior to this point, the issue of decriminalising male homosexual activity was not regarded as a priority by the Irish government. Norris further noted that 'it was fortunate in that, by the time it came around, Maire Geoghegan Quinn was Minister and, as a woman, she was less subject to taunts from her male colleagues.'[12] Geoghegan-Quinn was concerned that Irish legal reform regarding homosexuality was behind other European legislation. Her bill was therefore progressive in many aspects, including in establishing an equal age of consent for heterosexual and homosexual activity. Imposing an equal age of consent was an advance on the British legislation that had been introduced in 1967, and Geoghegan-Quinn clarified why the Irish legislation should not include such a distinction, stating that

> there is no logical reason for assuming that, while persons of 17 are capable of giving valid consent to heterosexual activity, persons of homosexual orientation do not acquire such capacity until they are older. Underlying any such proposition would be the idea that homosexual orientation carries with it the burdens of lack of maturity or lower intellect.[13]

Her speech was well received in the Dáil. Mary Harney, a Progressive Democrats TD, responded by asserting that this 'is about freedom, tolerating difference and respecting the rights of other consenting adults. . . . As Daniel O'Connell once said: "By extending freedoms to others you enhance and not diminish your own."'[14] The Criminal Law (Sexual Offences) bill, 1993, also included provisions for the 'prosecution of women found guilty of soliciting clients for the purpose of prostitution'.[15] The aspect regarding prostitution faced some condemnation during the Dáil debate, while the sections of the bill relating to decriminalising homosexuality faced objection from only a minority of TDs. The bill was passed in the Dáil the following day, on 24 June 1993.[16]

On 7 July 1993 the bill was signed into law; most appropriately, it was signed by President Robinson. Decriminalisation of male homosexual activity marked a significant point for LGBT rights in Ireland. The passing of this bill ensured that activists could dedicate their time and resources in pursuit of broader equality issues. Legislative reform over the coming years included protection against discrimination in employment on the grounds of sexual orientation through Employment Equality Acts introduced in 1998 and 2004. The Equal Status Act in 2000 ensured that individuals could not be 'treated less favourably' in the provision of goods and services, based on nine grounds, including sexual orientation.[17] In 2015 Ireland became the first country in the world to extend marriage to same-sex couples through a public vote.

Geoghegan-Quinn had risen quickly through the ranks of Fianna Fáil, and she proved to be a forthright Cabinet minister, applauded for her handling of the decriminalisation of homosexuality bill. In 1994 when Labour Party minister Mervyn Taylor resigned, she took over the role of Minister for Equality and Law Reform. The Fianna Fáil–Labour coalition government was in turmoil due to numerous political scandals, and in November 1994, Taoiseach and Fianna Fáil leader Albert Reynolds resigned.

Geoghegan-Quinn stood in the party leadership contest, opposing Bertie Ahern. It seemed possible that Ireland was on course for its first female Taoiseach. However, with Ahern receiving much support from his Fianna Fáil colleagues, Geoghegan-Quinn withdrew from the contest. In 2021 Ireland remains one of the few European countries never to have had a female head of government. In an unprecedented move, a new government was formed without the need for a general election. Fianna Fáil, under Ahern's leadership, was now an opposition party, and Geoghegan-Quinn no longer held a Cabinet seat.

The government was led by a rainbow coalition of Labour, Fine Gael and Democratic Left. The government remained in place until 1997, and during this time Geoghegan-Quinn became an effective opposition TD and the Fianna Fáil Spokesperson on Health. She played a central role in holding the government to account during the Hepatitis C scandal, when it was exposed that at least 1,000 women had been given contaminated blood products. She also wrote her first novel, *The Green Diamond*, a story based around the lives of four young women renting a house together in Dublin.[18] One of the characters, Derva, could be seen to reflect Geoghegan-Quinn; she is from Galway and is the daughter of a politician. In January 1997, with a general election looming, Geoghegan-Quinn announced her retirement from politics. She cited 'concern about media intrusions into the privacy of her life'. The *Belfast Telegraph* said that Fianna Fáil was 'stunned by the announcement from prominent front bencher Máire Geoghegan-Quinn'.[19] Ahern described how 'he had tried to persuade her not to resign, and indicated that she would have a position at his Cabinet table if Fianna Fáil were returned to power.'[20] Many newspapers, including the *Irish Times*, commented that Geoghegan-Quinn's resignation was regrettable for a 'woman who might have been Taoiseach'.[21]

Geoghegan-Quinn took up a position as a non-executive director of Aer Lingus and began writing columns for the *Irish Times*. In 1999 she was nominated to the European Union Court of Auditors; she was appointed for a subsequent term in 2006 and resigned in 2010 to take the position of European Commissioner for Ireland for research, innovation, and science. Tributes were paid to Geoghegan-Quinn in the Seanad on the twenty-fifth anniversary of the decriminalisation of homosexuality in Ireland on 19 June 2018. In his speech to the Seanad, Senator Jerry Buttimer moved a motion of apology:

That Seanad Éireann: acknowledges that the laws repealed in the Criminal Law (Sexual Offences) Act 1993 that criminalised consensual sexual activity between men:
- were improperly discriminatory, contrary to human dignity and an infringement of personal privacy and autonomy,

- caused multiple harms to those directly and indirectly affected, namely men who engaged in consensual same-sex activities and their families and friends, and
- had a significant chilling effect on progress towards equality for the Lesbian, Gay, Bisexual, Transgender and Intersex (LGBTI) community, acknowledging in particular the legacy of HIV/AIDS within the context of criminalisation.[22]

The apology was welcomed by those present in the Seanad and applauded by LGBT activists in the public gallery. Buttimer's statement was a stark reminder of the horrendous injustice that gay men in Ireland experienced. His words also highlight the courageous stand Geoghegan-Quinn took to overturn this homophobic legislation. Her speech is a testament to the no-nonsense approach of a female politician who had the potential to be Taoiseach.

26. Máire Geoghegan-Quinn, EU commissioner for research, innovation and science, European Commission's headquarters, Brussels, 17 July 2012. Photograph by Terje Heiestad / NordForsk, Creative Commons.

'The primary purpose of this Bill, which forms part of a comprehensive programme of reform of the criminal law which I have under way at present, is to decriminalise sexual activity between consenting mature males. . . .

While it is the case that the main sections of the Bill arise against a background of the European Court decision in the Norris case, it would be a pity to use that judgment as the sole pretext for the action we are now taking so as to avoid facing up to the issues themselves. What we are concerned with fundamentally in this Bill is a necessary development of human rights. We are seeking to end that form of discrimination which says that those whose nature is to express themselves sexually in their personal relationships, as consenting adults, in a way which others disapprove of or feel uneasy about, must suffer the sanctions of the criminal law. We are saying in 1993, over 130 years since that section of criminal law was enacted, that it is time we brought this form of human rights limitation to an end. We are recognising that we are in an era in which values are being examined and questioned and that it is no more than our duty as legislators to show that we appreciate what is happening by dismantling a law which reflects the values of another time.

That process of change is not easy and, understandably, many people worry that the traditional values which they hold so dear, and many of which are fundamentally sound, are under siege from emerging modern realities. But, of course, it is not a matter of laying siege to all the old certainties, nor is it a matter of jettisoning sound values simply to run with a current tide of demand, which may or may not be a majority demand. It is, rather, a matter of closely looking at values and asking ourselves whether it is necessary, or right, that they be propped up for the comfort of the majority by applying discriminatory and unnecessary laws to a minority, any minority.

As a people we have proved our ability to adopt a balanced and mature approach in dealing with complex social issues. In this context I am particularly pleased to note that, by and large, the public debate which has taken place in relation to the area covered by the Bill has been marked by a lack of stridency and by a respect for the sincerity of the views held by others. . . .

This House needs no reminding of the tragedy which ensues when difference is deprived the right of expression and suppressed.

Returning specifically to the theme of the Bill, does anybody believe that if the laws from the last century which we are now seeking to repeal did not in fact exist, we would now be seriously suggesting that they would be enacted? How can we reconcile criminal sanctions in this area with the fact that there is a whole range of other private, consenting behaviour between adults which may be regarded by many as wrong but in which the criminal law has no part to play?

Some parents, in particular, may be uncomfortable about what is being proposed and I fully understand what gives rise to that discomfort. That is why it is so important that we understand precisely what is being proposed. It is the removal of discrimination in the case of consenting adults in respect of their sexuality, not the removal of protection in the case of children and other vulnerable members of society. In fact, the Bill seeks to protect the vulnerable where protection did not exist heretofore.

I know too that there are parents who will know what it means in practice to have a child whose very nature it is to be homosexual. Very few of them would, I believe, be likely to regard it as helpful if in later life one of their own children was an active homosexual, liable to imprisonment – under the present law up to life imprisonment – for giving expression to his sexual orientation.

I do not believe that it is any answer to say that in practice these laws are rarely if ever implemented and we would be best to leave well enough alone. Such an approach would be dishonest, could bring the law generally into disrepute and, it seems to me, would be grossly and gratuitously offensive to those who happen to be homosexual. Genuine tolerance is not achieved by the turning of a blind eye. The social acceptability of homosexuality is not something which by our laws we can decree; the hurt which homosexuals feel at their treatment as outcasts by some members of the community is not something which we can dispel by the use of some legislative magic wand. What we can do under the terms of this Bill is leave those of homosexual orientation free to come to terms with their lives and express themselves in personal relationships without the fear of being branded and being punished as criminals.

There is also, of course, the concern expressed by those who feel that removal of the criminal sanction in effect may be seen as a form of encouragement to engage in homosexual activity, that removal will in practice have this result and that this, in turn, will lead to the spread of disease. There is nothing to support the proposition that removal of the criminal sanction in the case of consenting adults – I repeat that what we are talking about are consenting adults – will lead to an increase in promiscuity. Nor is there any evidence that it inevitably follows that removal of the criminal sanctions will foster the spread of disease.

I have no doubt that the disease issue, specifically the question of AIDS, will be raised in the course of the debate on the Bill. For now, I will confine myself to two comments. First of all, the right course in dealing with the possible spread of disease through sexual intercourse is to encourage safe sexual practices, not criminalise one form of sexual activity. Secondly, there is no doubt that disease can be, and is, spread by unsafe heterosexual activity but nobody seriously suggests that the right course, therefore, is to criminalise heterosexuality. I am not being dismissive of the AIDS issue – the subject is far too serious for a dismissive approach – what I am saying is that the solution is not a ban on homosexual activity. . . .

It is right that we should take the opportunity, now, of rolling back over 130 years of legislative prohibition which is discriminatory, which reflects an inadequate understanding of the human condition and which we should, rightly, see as an impediment, not a prop, to the maintenance and development of sound social values and norms. I am pleased, therefore, to commend the Bill to the House.'[23]

TWENTY FIVE

Nora Owen

B. 1945

Speech on women in politics
Colmcille Winter School, Gartan, Donegal

27 FEBRUARY 1994

'Are political candidates chosen according to sex or ability?'

On 25 November 1992 a general election returned the highest percentage of female TDs to date in the history of the Irish state. Alongside this advance, the President of Ireland was a woman, and the significant portfolio of Minister for Justice was held by a female. Nora Owen argued that women still remained grossly underrepresented in Irish politics and that female politicians were viewed as an oddity. In February 1994 Owen addressed the fifth annual Colmcille Winter School, a forum where experts discussed topics of consequence for Ireland. The theme of the school that year was local government. Experts spoke on a range of topics, including recent developments in Northern Ireland and in Dublin as well as the role of education and the Irish language in local government. Owen's topic of choice was simply titled 'Women and local government'. Her session was chaired by Mary Coughlan, then a Fianna Fáil TD for Donegal South-West.[1] Owen's choice of focus was brave, considering that all the other speakers over the weekend event were men. Her speech was straightforward, engaging and timely. Owen outlined factors preventing women from entering politics and spoke of the importance of a gender-balanced government, arguing that this was in the interest of political parties.

Nora Owen (née O'Mahony) was born in 1945 in Dublin. She was first elected into public office in 1979 as a councillor for Malahide. In 1981 she was elected as a TD representing Fine Gael in the North Dublin constituency.

She lost her seat in the 1987 general election. Owen was returned as a TD in the 1989 general election, and she excelled in the political environment. Owen descended from notable political stock: her grandfather was Johnny Collins, brother to Michael Collins. Owen's mother, Kitty O'Mahony, was one of the last family members to see Michael Collins alive.[2] Owen's older sister, Mary Banotti, also joined Fine Gael and served as a Member of the European Parliament (MEP) from 1984 to 2004. Owen maintained that her childhood made her particularly aware of gender discrimination in Ireland. Her father died when she was only four years old, and her mother returned to work in order to raise her six young children. In an interview with journalist Andrea Smith, Owen recalled that 'At that time, a man who became a widower was allowed a tax break to enable him to go to work and employ someone to look after the kids, but women weren't given that when their husbands died.'[3] Nora married Brian Owen in 1968, and the couple had three children. She received much support from Brian throughout her political career.

At the time of her speech, Owen was deputy leader of Fine Gael; she was the first woman to hold this position in the party. The general election held in November 1992 witnessed a marked increase in the number of female candidates standing for election. However, this increase only amounted to 20 women being elected as TDs, equating to a mere 12 per cent of the total number of TDs in the Dáil.[4] In her speech, Owen notes that the rate of female councillors elected to local government that year was even lower, at just 11 per cent. A Fianna Fáil–Labour coalition entered government, and a Seanad election followed in February 1993. Only seven women were elected to the Seanad, and it was hoped that this number would be increased by the Taoiseach's nominations. In her assessment of women in politics, Frances Gardiner describes how 'the Taoiseach's nominees were awaited with great expectancy by women's groups, and there was understandable consternation when Albert Reynolds nominated only one woman and ten men.'[5] Reynolds' only female appointment was Marian McGennis, a Fianna Fáil candidate. His decision ensured that only 13 per cent of senators were female. This was a most disappointing move as the Seanad nominations coincided with the publication of the *Report of the Second Commission on the Status of Women*. The report strongly recommended a commitment to gender balance in politics.

The report by the Second Commission on the Status of Women was published in January 1993, and Reynolds was presented with a copy on 11 February. The second commission had been established in 1989 to examine gender inequalities in Ireland. Their 500-page report set out recommendations to reduce gender inequalities and was 'strongly critical of the absence of women in political positions of influence'.[6] In her assessment, Yvonne

Galligan highlighted a main recommendation of the report, which was for 'speedy redress of gender imbalance at all levels of political activity through various means to secure a minimum of 40 per cent representation of any one sex'.[7] Furthermore, the commission recommended that 'Legislation should be implemented if this is not reached within 10 years.'[8] The commission proposed the implementation of gender quotas, through which political parties would be required to recruit a set percentage of female and male election candidates. The commission emphasised that quotas were 'a temporary compensatory measure of the kind provided for in the United Nations Convention on the Elimination of all Forms of Discrimination against Women, to which Ireland is party'.[9]

The main political parties attempted to redress gender imbalance, but the measures they proposed were weak and had no major impact. In 1993 an internal report organised by Owen's party, Fine Gael, determined that gender quotas would not be introduced to their party 'because of the danger of compromising democratic principles'.[10] Owen's speech highlights why a political system dominated by men is in fact a threat to obtaining true democracy. Fine Gael recommended the formation of a women's group and the appointment of a women's officer alongside training and mentoring of female party members. Gender politics expert Fiona Buckley asserts that 'the impact of these measures was negligible. During the period 1989 to 2002, women's membership on the Fine Gael national executive hovered between 20 and 30 per cent, male office holders dominated party leadership positions (chair and vice-chair), and only four new women TDs were elected.'[11]

When the rainbow coalition came to government in December 1994, the leader of Fine Gael, John Bruton, became Taoiseach. Owen was appointed as Minister for Justice, taking over from Máire Geoghegan-Quinn. The media initially responded positively to this choice. Tom Brady, security editor with the *Irish Independent*, described how 'Owen's star has been rapidly on the rise during the past couple of years after emerging as a highly effective performer in the Dail and the media at a time when the fortunes of her party were at a very low ebb.'[12] Owen remained Minister for Justice until 1997, during which time she oversaw progressive criminal law reform. She instigated a referendum in 1996 on the issue of bail, which included a provision for a court to refuse bail 'to a person charged with a serious offence'.[13] The referendum was carried and led to the introduction of the Bail Act 1997, which had a positive impact on the legal justice system in Ireland.

The 1990s were particularly difficult years to oversee the Department of Justice. There was a marked increase in criminal activity in Ireland. In 1995 Veronica Guerin, an investigative journalist with the *Sunday Independent*, warned of the 'ever-rising crime problems in Ireland'.[14] At an awards ceremony in New York, Guerin described how 'a number of reporters – not just myself – have been subjected to death threats and to intimidation on a daily basis.'[15] Guerin was subjected to numerous threats from individuals when she exposed their criminal activities through her journalism. On 30 January 1995 a gunman called to Guerin's home, and in a failed murder attempt, she was shot in the leg. On 7 June 1996, Detective Garda Jerry McCabe and Detective Garda Ben O'Sullivan were escorting an An Post van transporting money through Adare in county Limerick.[16] During an armed raid on the van, attackers fired 15 rounds of ammunition into the garda car; Detective McCabe was killed, and his partner severely injured. This killing was followed weeks later, on 26 June, by the murder of Guerin. She was shot six times by two members of a criminal gang while she was stopped at traffic lights on a main road outside of Dublin. Owen retaliated quickly and effectively.

Owen established the Criminal Assets Bureau (CAB) on 15 October 1996. The CAB is now a central force through which the Irish state tackles criminal activity. The bureau has the power to seize money and goods earned through illegal activity. This force swiftly became active, ensuring that criminal activity was shut down after financial resources were seized. Despite proving herself to be a resourceful and successful Minister for Justice, Owen was often subjected to attack due specifically to her gender. She recalled the ridiculousness of media comments when reports proposed that 'there would be less criminal activity if there was a male Minister for Justice.'[17] The fact that female politicians are viewed differently is addressed by Owen in her speech in Donegal. In 2002 Owen lost her seat in the general election. She volunteered with Special Olympics Ireland and became a regular political commentator on radio and television.

A new generation of female politicians took up Owen's cause to improve gender balance in Irish politics. In 2009 Senator Ivana Bacik authored a report on 'Women's Participation in Politics' for the Joint Oireachtas Committee on Justice. The report identified key reasons for increasing women's political representation, including 'a more representative democracy' and 'international obligations'.[18] The report also identified the challenges women face when entering politics at local, national, or European level, named as the five *c*'s: childcare, cash, confidence, culture and candidate selection procedures.[19] Bacik's report added to the argument in favour of implementing gender quotas in Irish national politics. In 2012 Ireland adopted a gender quota system, obliging political parties to select at least 30 per cent female and 30 per cent male candidates to contest general elections. This threshold was set to rise in 2023 to a 40 per cent minimum. Political parties will be financially penalised, in terms of their state funding, if they do not meet the quota. While gender quotas have had a positive impact, women remain grossly underrepresented in Irish politics.

In 2019 Dáil Éireann celebrated its centenary. In the first one hundred years of government, just 114 women served as TDs as opposed to 1,190 men who had taken a seat in the Irish national parliament. In the following general election in 2020, only 22.5 per cent of elected TDs were women. The senior Cabinet positions were predominantly granted to male politicians with, initially, only four women occupying senior posts out of the 14 available. In a by-election in July, Bacik was elected as a TD for the South Dublin constituency, adding another strong female voice to the Dáil chamber.

A stark reminder of the inequalities that a male-dominated political system can produce was seen in April 2021. For the first time in the history of the Irish State, a serving cabinet minister announced that she was pregnant. It was quickly realised that there was no structure in place for maternity leave for TDs, senators or cabinet ministers. After much debate, the Minister for Justice, Helen McEntee, was granted maternity leave. Her female colleagues agreed to take on her duties, with extra responsibilities. McEntee then officially became a minister without a portfolio, with the expectation that she would be reassigned as the Minister for Justice in November 2021. McEntee's predecessor, Nora Owen left a considerable legacy as a politician and as a Minister for Justice. Her speech challenged political parties to tackle gender imbalance, and her words continue to resonate for women in Irish politics in 2021.

'I want to pose a question . . . should we be concerned that the percentage of women getting elected to Local Authorities still stands only at 11 per cent? We have to ask, are political candidates chosen according to sex or ability? We still very often hear people referring to politicians and women politicians. As long as these distinctions are made we do not manage to treat people on a fair and democratic basis, then this difference in language will continue to keep the percentages small and men and women on separate lists, as it were. We must remember that women are people, men are people and our aim as women, who wish to participate in all aspects of life, must be to strive to reach a situation where I am not described as a "woman politician" but as a politician who happens to be a woman, whilst my two colleagues Dinny McGinley and Paddy Harte are politicians who happen to be men. . . .[20]

With women forming more than half the electorate in any election, why isn't the woman's vote more effective in getting more women into local Government and into Parliament?

The chief reason could be tradition and custom that politicians were always men but surveys have shown that women's indifference and lack of interest and the scarcity of suitable women candidates have also been reasons for the low number of elected women. The Party system and the structures of selection conventions and the rules governing such things as length of service etc. are also listed as part of the impeding factors that keep women out of politics.

Less and less women are voting the same way as their husbands which tended to be a pattern for a long time and this I feel is an explanation why a higher number of women got elected to the Dáil in 1992.

We cannot under-estimate either the enormous importance of the election of Mary Robinson as our President. A very high percentage of women came out to vote for her and this I feel woke more women up to the realisation that a good woman candidate can succeed and can be a very good representative for their constituents. . . .

There are many women in Ireland who genuinely do wish to vote for a woman candidate and would also like to vote for a particular Party. This is why it is so essential for political parties to make it possible to have a balanced ticket to offer to the electorate. A gender balance as well as a talent balance are necessary ingredients for an attractive ticket for the electorate and the Parties that make an effort to do this have reaped their rewards. . . .

With the European elections looming in June this year and indeed, the urban elections and two by-elections, there has been a great deal of talk of "parachutes" and "glamour candidates" and "imposed candidates" and nearly all of these are women. I am somewhat concerned about the preoccupation of political party gurus who . . . have drawn up an identikit photo for a typically winning candidate and this year the identikit picture is that of a woman, not too old, attractive looking with a profile in some other facet of life other than politics and who is considered to portray that certain something that will sweep her into being elected. . . . Why should a woman get involved at a basic level in a political party, gain experience, work to understand the political system and indeed the mechanics of how one learns the political ropes of a political party if she can carry on with some other job of work and be around to be catapulted into an easily winnable seat without any effort on her part? A balance must be struck between choosing women who have something to offer the electorate and the potential constituents once elected by way of experience and ideas, commitment etc. and using a woman because she happens to match the particular flavour the electorate is seduced into thinking they want.

I read somewhere, sometime ago about the fact that traditionally people will ask what a woman candidate looks like. Back in 1975 the French Secretary of State for the Conditions of Women, Françoise Giroud was described on Norwegian radio in the following way: "She has all the qualifications which men at the top demand from such ladies. Not so young that she distracts and not so old that she is overlooked. Not too beautiful or too ugly. Not too intelligent but on the other hand not too stupid. Well dressed and well prepared, but not too sharp. If in addition she will concentrate on the very small problems and not the big serious questions of society which the men themselves will handle, she will certainly be a success.'"[21]

TWENTY SIX

Bríd Rodgers

B. 1935

Speech on women and the Good Friday Agreement
National University of Ireland, Maynooth, Kildare

16 OCTOBER 1998

'A time of unprecedented opportunity presented by the Good Friday Agreement.'

In 1998, the National Women's Council of Ireland (NWCI) celebrated its
25th anniversary with its annual conference themed 'Women Mapping the
New Millennium'.[1] The event at Maynooth University included workshops
and speeches from high-profile female politicians, community activists, journalists and feminist campaigners. Bríd Rodgers of the Social Democratic and
Labour Party (SDLP) opened the two-day event. Rodgers delivered an astute
address comparing the struggle for women's equality with the struggle for
equality in Northern Ireland between nationalists and unionists. It was a
pointed move for the NWCI to invite Rodgers to open the conference that
year as the Good Friday Agreement had recently been ratified through a
referendum on 22 May 1998. In her speech Rodgers describes this momentous agreement as an 'unprecedented opportunity' to achieve equality
for all people on the island of Ireland. Rodgers played a significant role
in developing the Good Friday Agreement, and her speech highlights the
importance of women's roles in the path towards achieving political reform
through peaceful means.

Rodgers was firmly committed to delivering this speech, evident by the
fact that she had to forgo attending celebrations in Derry for John Hume's
Nobel Peace Prize. Hume was then leader of the SDLP, a political party
founded in Northern Ireland in August 1970. The establishment of the
SDLP was a landmark event in Northern Irish politics as the party was

'distinguished from the province's other leftist and Republican groups by its commitment to political and nonviolent means of uniting Northern Ireland with the Irish republic'.[2] The SDLP gained electoral support and was the first nationalist party to occupy a government position in Northern Ireland when it won four seats in the short-lived power-sharing executive body of 1973–4.[3] Rodgers was a founding member of the SDLP and became chair of the party in 1978, becoming the first woman to chair a political party in Ireland.

Bríd Rodgers (née Stafford) was born in the Gaeltacht area of Gweedore in county Donegal and is a fluent Irish speaker. She moved to Northern Ireland in 1960, where she lived in Lurgan with her husband, Antoin Rodgers; the couple had six children together. Rodgers became involved in the civil rights movement in Northern Ireland from 1965 and worked with Conn and Patricia McCluskey who founded the Campaign for Social Justice. Rodgers painstakingly collected statistics in the Lurgan area to help Conn McCluskey provide evidence that Catholics were being discriminated against in housing and employment. She went on to become a member of the executive of the Northern Ireland Civil Rights Association (NICRA).

Through civil rights work, Rodgers realised that political reform was necessary to establish equality between Catholics and Protestants in Northern Ireland. In an interview with RTÉ presenter Padraic Ó Catháin, Rodgers described how 'it was the desire to help vulnerable people in that minority of Northern Irish nationalists that drew [her] to social justice in the first place.'[4] After serving as chair of the SDLP from 1978 to 1980, she became general secretary of the party until 1983. She was nominated by Taoiseach Garret FitzGerald to Seanad Éireann and served as a senator from 1983 to 1987. During her time as a senator, Rodgers contributed to the Action Plan for the Irish language, making recommendations to the government on future Irish language policy.[5]

Rodgers became a much-needed voice representing Northern Irish issues on the floor of the upper house of Irish government. On 3 April 1984, RUC constable John Robinson was cleared in a Belfast Crown Court of murdering Seamus Grew. Grew was shot while attempting to get out of his car at Mullacreevie housing estate on 12 December 1982.[6] Grew was unarmed and was shot by Robinson on suspicion of being a member of the Irish National Liberation Army (INLA), a republican paramilitary organisation. The day after the court ruling, Rodgers proposed a suspension of standing orders in the Seanad to discuss what she described as 'a specific and important matter of public interest requiring urgent consideration, that is the implications for peace and stability in this country of the decision handed down yesterday in the Northern Ireland court in the case involving the shooting dead of an unarmed civilian in County Armagh'.[7] Her discussion was ruled out by the chair; however, she received support from fellow senators and appropriately highlighted an issue of importance for the country.

Rodgers was a senator during the signing of the 1985 Anglo-Irish agreement, known as the Hillsborough agreement, a treaty between the British and Irish governments seeking an end to the violence in Northern Ireland. The treaty was signed by British Prime Minister Margaret Thatcher and Taoiseach Garret FitzGerald, on 15 November. Rodgers gave a detailed account of the treaty and its implications and restrictions during the Seanad debates that followed. The treaty gave the Irish government a role in an advisory capacity for the running of Northern Ireland. Rodgers applauded the fact that for the 'first time' there was 'a framework within which the Nationalists in Northern Ireland are given equality of status with the Unionists'.[8] The agreement was rejected by unionist parties in the north, with the Ulster Unionist Party (UUP) and the Democratic Unionist Party (DUP) leading a campaign with the now infamous slogan popularised by Ian Paisley 'Ulster Says No.' In her address to the Seanad, Rodgers described how 'fears are being whipped up unnecessarily by leaders who ought to know better.' The treaty did not establish an end to violence or lead to a power-sharing government in Northern Ireland, but the process ultimately generated greater co-operation between the British and Irish governments, which laid a foundation for the Good Friday Agreement.

Rodgers played a central role during the process towards the Good Friday Agreement. She was the SDLP delegate at the Brookes/Mayhew talks, a series of talks established by Northern Ireland Secretary Peter Brookes in 1991 to help restore a devolved government in Northern Ireland. The talks continued under the leadership of Brookes' successor, Patrick Mayhew, in 1992. On 15 December 1993, the Joint Declaration on Peace, also known as The Downing Street Declaration, was released by British Prime Minister John Major and Taoiseach Albert Reynolds. The agreement established a charter for all-party peace talks. In 1994 a ceasefire by the IRA was followed by a ceasefire among loyalist paramilitary groups. Duncan Morrow, a specialist in conflict resolution, describes how 'the ceasefires of 1994 marked a sharp change of course in Northern Ireland, ushering in the first lengthy period free of the threat of political violence since the 1960s.'[9] Although sporadic violence erupted that year, the path to peace was on course. Rodgers was selected as a SDLP delegate at the Forum for Peace and Reconciliation talks in Dublin Castle, chaired by Judge Catherine McGuinness. The forum was established by the Irish government as part of the Northern Irish peace process and first met on 28 October 1994, continuing with regular meetings until the end of 1995.

On 30 May 1996, Rodgers was elected to the Northern Ireland Forum in the Upper Bann constituency. One hundred and ten delegates were elected from across all political parties to engage in peace talks. Rodgers chaired the SDLP talks team from 1996 to 1998. The peace talks led to the Good Friday Agreement being reached on 10 April 1998. The British and Irish governments agreed on the central issues, as did the four major parties in Northern Ireland: the SDLP, Sinn Féin, the UUP and the Alliance Party. The only major party to abstain from agreement was the DUP. The agreement provided for a power-sharing Northern Ireland Assembly, including nationalist and unionist representatives. The new assembly would operate with devolved power from Westminster, deciding over local policy matters. While the agreement recognised Northern Ireland as being part of the United Kingdom, it also established a provision that Ireland could be reunited through a majority public vote in Northern Ireland and the Republic of Ireland.

On 22 May 1998, a referendum was held across the island of Ireland. The agreement was overwhelmingly accepted by 94 per cent of voters in the Republic of Ireland and favoured by a lesser but still significant majority of 71 per cent in Northern Ireland. The referendum established the Northern Ireland Act 1998. Prior to the Good Friday Agreement, the Irish Constitution maintained a territorial claim to the entire island of Ireland, including Northern Ireland. The Constitution was therefore amended after the referendum to include new provisions. The Constitution confirmed that people born in any area of the island have 'the entitlement and birthright' to be considered Irish citizens.[10] A further article described the process through which a united Ireland could be achieved:

> It is the firm will of the Irish nation, in harmony and friendship, to unite all the people who share the territory of the island of Ireland, in all the diversity of their identities and traditions, recognising that a united Ireland shall be brought about only by peaceful means with the consent of a majority of the people, democratically expressed, in both jurisdictions in the island.[11]

The peace process and later enactment of the Good Friday Agreement caused paramilitary organisations in Northern Ireland to abandon violence and instead join the political process. Elections were held for the New Northern Ireland Assembly on 25 June, and Rodgers was elected in the Upper Bann constituency. The assembly met on 1 July 1998 in Castle Buildings at Stormont, Belfast. David Trimble of the UUP was elected as First Minister with Seamus Mallon of the SDLP as Deputy First Minister. During the first months of its establishment, the assembly drew up plans for a devolved government and an outline of ministries. The Nobel Peace Prize for 1998 was awarded jointly to John Hume and David Trimble for their work in establishing the Good Friday Agreement.

While celebrations for Hume's award were planned in Derry by the SDLP, Rodgers travelled to Maynooth to open the NWCI conference. The conference did not gain appropriate media attention and, when it was reported, newspaper articles reflected a general public aversion for feminism. The *Sunday Independent* reported that 'the idea of a feminists' conference is not a pretty one for many people. Feminism, especially the North American variety, has a bad public image; it has become a caricature – the aggressive, dungaree-wearing man-hater with a penchant for workshops on how to find her own G spot.'[12] The article did, however, conclude that 'there was nothing scary in Maynooth, just a group of women who had made some major changes in society and were planning a few more.'[13] Indeed, there was an impressive contribution from numerous feminists who led change in Irish society and who would greatly continue to impact on equality reform in the country.

Speakers included Ann Louise Gilligan, co-founder of the Shanty Project in Tallaght, a project to empower through education, now called An Cosán. Gilligan and her partner Katherine Zappone, who co-founded the Shanty project, would later become instrumental in bringing marriage equality for same-sex couples to Ireland. Niamh Breathnach, a former Minister for Education, addressed the conference as did *Irish Times* journalist Kathryn (Kate) Holmquist, who was later described as a 'Luminous writer who became a voice of the voiceless'.[14] Rodgers was not the only Northern Irish politician to attend: Jane Morrice chaired a workshop. Morrice was elected in the North Down constituency in the June 1998 elections for the Northern Ireland Assembly as a Women's Coalition candidate. Morrice and the Northern Ireland Women's Coalition played a central role in achieving the Good Friday Agreement.

In her speech opening the conference, Rodgers describes how women were then represented at the highest level of key sectors, including government. This was certainly true for Northern Ireland. Historian Mary O'Dowd notes that the years from 1993 to 2000 'witnessed significant developments in the nature of women's involvement in the political life of Northern Ireland'.[15] Mo Mowlam was then Secretary of State for Northern Ireland and had contributed greatly to advancing the peace talks. In 1997 political parties adopted moves to further women's participation in politics: the SDLP and Sinn Féin introduced a system of positive discrimination to increase female membership in their parties and provided training for women interested in pursuing a political career. The progression of women in politics could be seen in many other countries. Rodgers mentions Madeleine Albright in her speech, who had been appointed as the United States Secretary of State in 1997, the first woman to hold this position. Rodgers' inclusion of the Vital Voices conference, which was held in Belfast from 31

August to 2 September 1998, pointed to a significant American government initiative to promote women in leadership.[16] She was careful to note that the increasing inclusion of women in politics must continue.

On 2 December 1999 the full process of establishing a devolved government of Northern Ireland was concluded. Rodgers was nominated as Minister for Agriculture and Rural Development and became deputy leader of the SDLP in November 2001. She lost her ministry in 2002 with the suspension of the Executive that October. The suspension occurred after the Sinn Féin offices at Stormont were raided as part of an alleged IRA spy ring. The action caused a major political crisis, and the Northern Ireland Secretary, John Reid, suspended devolution. Rodgers decided not to stand in the forthcoming election in May 2003, but she remained as deputy leader of the SDLP until February 2004.[17] Rodgers celebrated her 69th birthday on 20 February 2004 and had served her time in Northern Irish politics. Northern Ireland remained governed through Westminster until 2007, when then DUP leader Ian Paisley and Sinn Féin's Martin McGuinness entered a power-sharing government.

Despite intermittent violence in Northern Ireland, peace was obtained through the Good Friday Agreement. Some politicians feared that the UK's departure from the European Union through Brexit would threaten the stability of the Good Friday Agreement. The DUP was the only major party in Northern Ireland to support Brexit in the 2016 referendum. Although the overall result carried the motion for Britain to leave the EU, a majority of 56 per cent of people in Northern Ireland voted to remain. There was concern that establishing checks and borders between the Irish Republic, an EU member state, and Northern Ireland, a non-EU state, would reignite violence. In an interview on RTÉ's radio programme *Country Wide*, Rodgers described the issue of a potential border on the island of Ireland as a 'dreadful' uncertainty.[18] Declan Kearney, Sinn Féin's national chairperson, warned that because of Brexit 'the entire basis of the Good Friday Agreement is now faced with its most serious threat in the history of the peace process.'[19] After much negotiation, the Northern Ireland Protocol was agreed to prevent a land border on the island of Ireland. This protocol became law on 1 January 2021, ensuring that Northern Ireland continued to follow EU rules as part of the single market, with checks taking place on goods entering Northern Ireland from England, Scotland or Wales.[20]

The Good Friday Agreement remains a significant framework for the continuation of peace on the island of Ireland. On 10 May 2021 Senator Niall Blaney presented a motion to the Seanad 'to reaffirm our commitment to this historic document that has put an end to decades of violence'.[21] During the debate, Senator Fiona O'Loughlin paid tribute to the women who were instrumental in the Good Friday Agreement; she named Rodgers along with Monica McWilliams, Mo Mowlam and Liz O'Donnell. O'Donnell was then Minister of State at the Department of Foreign Affairs and negotiated on behalf of the Irish government in the peace talks. McWilliams co-founded the Northern Ireland Women's Coalition (NIWC) in 1996 with Pearl Sagar, Bronagh Hinds and Jane Morrice. [22]

Bríd Rodgers remains vocal on Northern Irish issues and is respected for the role she played in establishing peace in Ireland and providing a power-sharing government for Northern Ireland. Her speech at the National Women's Council of Ireland conference is a powerful reminder of the significant contributions made by women in the shaping of modern Ireland.

'The struggle for women's rights is in many ways comparable to the struggle for equality of rights between nationalist and unionist in Northern Ireland. The essential and often the most difficult first step is to get society to recognise that there is a problem. It is never easy to break the cosy consensus that invariably exists for those who benefit from the status quo. Generally speaking people become aware of injustice only when it touches their own lives. And so 25 years ago the gross injustices suffered by women in Irish society were not seen for what they were. Rather they were seen as the norm, the natural way of things. Violence against women or children in the home was a private family matter. One did not interfere.

Those who suffered in silence had nowhere to turn. The fundamental issue of human rights was not considered. Indeed tragic incidents in very recent years would indicate that such a culture has not yet been totally eradicated. The myth that "the hand that rocks the cradle rules the world" clouded the reality that the hand in question was often underprivileged as a result of its nurturing responsibilities and was invariably disadvantaged in later life as well.

Much remains to be done. The challenge facing us as we enter the new millennium, at a time of unprecedented opportunity presented by the Good Friday Agreement, is to establish a society in Ireland where women and men, regardless of class, creed, political belief, national identity, race, sexual orientation or disability can enjoy equality of treatment and equality of opportunity, a society which accepts difference for what it is, the essence of humanity. To be different is not to be better or worse. It is to be human.

Those women who are now playing a part at the highest levels of government, in public office, in business, in the trade unions, in the media, in the world of work generally have demolished the myth that women are in some ways inferior to or not quite as capable as their male counterparts. It is now recognised worldwide, as Madeleine Albright reminded us in a message to the recent Vital Voices Conference in Belfast, that it is not just right to encourage and facilitate the participation of women in all spheres of economic and social activity, it is the smart thing to do. Equality for women is not just good for women, it is good for families, it is good for the economy, it is good for society. It is good for our country.

So what next? The Good Friday Agreement has given us a framework within which we can, all of us together using our talents, build a New Ireland — an Ireland where our differences can become a source of enrichment not of division. An Ireland where its people of both nationalist and unionist traditions can begin to appreciate the benefits of co-operating in the many areas of mutual interest for the benefit of all. In the section of the agreement dealing with Rights, Safeguards and Equality of Opportunity the British Government commits itself to pursuing "broad policies for promoting social inclusion, including in particular community development and the advancement of women in public life".

That commitment will be measured by the manner in which the present Northern Ireland Bill deals with the establishment of the new Equality Commission. Anything which would diminish the effectiveness or downgrade the importance of the Equal Opportunities Commission is simply not in keeping with this commitment and is not acceptable. We want to go forward, not backward.

We live in exciting and challenging times. Ireland needs to harness the talents of all her people. Mná na hÉireann have already made an invaluable contribution to society and to their country. We will all be the poorer if society as a whole fails to enable and empower women in the years ahead.'[23]

TWENTY SEVEN

Monica McWilliams

B. 1954

Distinguished lecture – From peace talks to gender justice
Joan B. Kroc School of Peace Studies,
University of San Diego, California

29 SEPTEMBER 2010

'We moved the margins to the mainstream.'

Women's central role in the Northern Ireland peace process has yet to be fully acknowledged. Monica McWilliams ensured that women's voices were included in peace negotiations that ultimately shaped the terms of the Good Friday Agreement in 1998. In September 2010 McWilliams, then chief commissioner for human rights in Northern Ireland, was invited to address the Joan B. Kroc Institute for Peace & Justice at the University of San Diego. Her talk, 'Precarious progress: From peace talks to gender justice,' was part of the distinguished lecture series, first established by the institute in 2003. The series offers the wider community an opportunity 'to engage with leaders who are working to forge new dialogues with parties in conflict and who seek to answer the question of how to create an enduring peace for tomorrow'.[1] McWilliams delivered a compelling speech, providing an incisive assessment of the formation and activities of the Northern Ireland Women's Coalition (NIWC). Ultimately, her talk illustrated how feminist interventions in Northern Ireland can inform global peace initiatives.

McWilliams is an engaging and an impassioned orator, who has experience in addressing a vast range of audiences from students in lecture theatres to engaging with hostile politicians at political assemblies. The forum for this speech is a prestigious one, with distinguished lectures delivered by prominent international leaders and policymakers at the Institute. Previous speakers included Mary Robinson in 2005, then UN High Commissioner for Human Rights; Shirin Ebadi in 2006, a Nobel Peace Laureate; and Jane Goodall in 2008, founder of the Jane Goodall Institute and UN Messenger of Peace. Two years after McWilliams delivered her lecture, Senator George J. Mitchell, the independent chair of the Northern Ireland peace talks, also delivered a distinguished lecture.[2]

McWilliams incorporated images into her one-hour talk, which she described as a 'picture series'. She used photographs, newspaper clippings and posters to animate her talk tracing women's campaigns for peace and social reform during the Troubles as well as the formation of the NIWC. Her speech reached a wide audience, well beyond those gathered at the University of San Diego that evening. This full speech was recorded and uploaded on the University of California Television site, a channel that has just under 900,000 subscribers.[3] An edited version of her lecture was also published as a pamphlet by the Joan B. Kroc Institute, including a transcription of the post-lecture discussion and an interview with Dee Aker, Deputy Director of the Institute.[4]

Monica McWilliams was born in the small town of Ballymoney in county Antrim and was raised in Kilrea, county Derry. From an early age, she proved herself to be a skilled orator winning several awards for debating. After graduating from Queen's University, Belfast in 1975, she was awarded a scholarship to pursue a postgraduate degree at the University of Michigan. McWilliams accepted a position as a lecturer in the University of Ulster in 1978. She was keen to educate women from disadvantaged areas and to develop a feminist awareness which she partly achieved by introducing a Certificate in Women's Studies to the university. McWilliams progressively became more active with campaigns and organisations demanding equality for women. Among her numerous roles, she served on the committee of the first Women's Centre in Belfast and established the Northern Ireland Poverty Lobby seeking rights for prisoners' wives and one-parent families during the Troubles. McWilliams is named in *A Century of Women*; the authors highlight the findings of a major study she completed in 1992 'as seminal, leading to the first government policy in the UK on domestic violence'.[5]

Focussed negotiations on peace in the early 1990s offered the people of Northern Ireland renewed hope and McWilliams followed these developments closely. The Joint Declaration on Peace, established on 15 December 1993, provided a charter for all-party peace talks. It was decided that in order to participate in the talks, parties must abide by the six principles set out in the Mitchell Report on Decommissioning, published in January 1996.[6] Introducing the report to the House of Commons, British Prime Minister John Major described how 'The key to progress in Northern

Ireland is confidence—confidence to enable the parties to sit down together without threat of force. The retention of arms by the paramilitaries on both sides is the biggest single factor in holding back that confidence.'[7] With the Mitchell principles as a guide to establishing a democratic forum for all-party peace talks, Major and Taoiseach John Bruton announced that talks would begin on 10 June that year.[8]

Proximity talks began in March 1996. These talks involved intense meetings with the leaders of the main parties in Northern Ireland, all male: David Trimble, Ulster Unionist Party; Ian Paisley, Democratic Unionist Party; John Hume, Social Democratic and Labour Party; and Gerry Adams, Sinn Féin. In her speech, McWilliams describes how the British and Irish governments 'wanted the small paramilitary parties to be included, and so they made a list'. However when the women looked at the list of parties to be involved in the talks, they said, 'this isn't very democratic. Where are we on this list?' McWilliams was moved to establish the Northern Ireland Women's Coalition in April 1996 with Pearl Sagar, Bronagh Hinds, Jane Morrice and others. The all-female, non-sectarian political party, was formed to ensure a greater inclusion of female politicians in the formal peace negotiations.

The core group of organisers impressively mobilised 70 female candidates in a short time frame. The NIWC campaigned to be included on the electoral lists for the all-party peace talks. Members agreed that they would have two party leaders, one Protestant and one Catholic, to ensure that cross-community views were equally represented. McWilliams, a Catholic, and Sagar, a Protestant woman who worked as a community worker, were nominated as leaders. Twenty-four political parties in Northern Ireland competed for inclusion in the peace negotiations; seats would be allocated to the ten parties that secured the most votes in constituency elections. The NIWC adopted the slogan 'Wave goodbye to Dinosaurs', identifying their members as a new wave of politicians. The NIWC polled ninth in the elections on 30 May 1996, receiving more votes than the Labour party.

The NIWC secured two seats at the peace talks which opened in Stormont on 10 June, less than two weeks after the elections. McWilliams and Sagar took their seats in the negotiations chaired by George Mitchell, the United States special envoy who had overseen the Mitchell Report. Nell McCafferty, a feminist journalist and author, described this significant development. She highlighted how:

> Until the [Women's] coalition came along, the dreary integrity of the quarrel between feminism and patriarchy in the North seemed destined to remain forever intact, unchanged, and unchangeable. Even as Britain's war with the Irish Republican Army (IRA) stumbled to a close in August 1994, it seemed that women would not have a voice in the peace-time settlement.[9]

This was the first time that a women's political party had successfully organised in Northern Ireland. NIWC members focussed on ensuring that human rights, equality and inclusion would shape the Good Friday Agreement.

In her speech, McWilliams describes how involvement with the NIWC placed the women in a dangerous position. She notes particularly an attack on a women's centre following a visit by President Mary Robinson. Robinson visited the Windsor Women's Centre in the loyalist area of Broadway in Belfast on 12 September 1996. During her visit, protesters gathered outside and heckled Robinson saying 'Stay out of Ulster.'[10] Robinson had been invited to the centre as part of a series of engagements in Belfast that day. Hours later, the premises was firebombed, causing a reported £20,000 worth of damage.[11] Annie Campbell, the NIWC press officer, observed that this was 'the first time a women's centre has been targeted but that reflects the very progressive approach women's centres have taken regarding cross-cultural dialogue'.[12] The attack showed that women were now taking important steps in cross-cultural politics but as McWilliams notes in her speech, this meant they were now seen as a threat.

The women of the NIWC persisted in their work despite hostility from male politicians and sometimes receiving animosity from female politicians in other parties. Elsewhere in her speech, McWilliams credits older women who got behind the campaign to form the all-female party and who expertly managed media interest. She particularly highlights the involvement of May Blood, a founder member of the NIWC, who acted as campaign manager. Blood, originally a mill worker from Belfast, had gained exceptional experience organising at community level. She had received an MBE in 1995 for the immense contributions she made towards social reforms in Northern Ireland. Blood was a significant voice behind the NIWC and described how the group wanted 'to get women to where decisions were being made. Two women [McWilliams and Sagar] were elected and those two women had the most horrendous time over two years, physically and mentally they were abused. But if the guys thought that were going to get rid of them, they picked on the wrong two women.'[13]

McWilliams and Sagar remained vocal throughout the two years of demanding talks. McWilliams signed the Good Friday Agreement on 10 April 1998. Shortly after this momentous agreement was signed, artist Raymond Watson took bronze casts of the hands of the key signatories including John Hume, David Trimble, David Ervine and most fittingly, McWilliams.[14] As McWilliams testifies in her speech, without the inclusion of NIWC leaders in the peace talks 'there would have been nothing [in the agreement] on victims, integrated education, mixed housing, children and nothing about the importance of rebuilding lives, dealing with the past.' Through their negotiations, McWilliams and Sagar also ensured the release of 2,000 prisoners within two years of the agreement being reached. Additionally, as noted by transitional justice expert Catherine O'Rourke, the Good Friday Agreement acknowledged 'the right of women to full and equal political participation and committed the British government to advancing the position of women in public life pending the establishment of a regional assembly in Northern Ireland'.[15]

McWilliams and Jane Morrice were elected as NIWC candidates in the elections for the assembly on 25 June 1998. There were delays implementing the agreement which O'Rourke maintains 'led to the polarization of politics in the region and significantly improved the political fortunes of the more-extreme political parties. That left little political space for a cross-community party organized on the basis of gender.'[16] The NIWC failed to keep their seats in the assembly elections in November 2003 and the party disbanded in 2006. However, the NIWC had changed the face of politics in Northern Ireland which encouraged more women to join political parties. Former members of the NIWC became active in institutions that were established through the peace agreement. McWilliams was appointed as chief commissioner of the Northern Ireland Human Rights Commission in 2005. The establishment of this position, as McWilliams notes, directly stems from the terms of the Good Friday Agreement. In this role she was tasked with drafting the advice on a Bill of Rights for Northern Ireland. Shortly before delivering this speech at the University of San Diego, McWilliams submitted her report to the Westminster government. She aptly described the Bill of Rights as 'one of the foundational documents coming from the Good Friday Agreement.'[17]

McWilliams served two terms as chief commissioner but resigned one year early 'in protest against the Conservative government's lack of support for the Commission'.[18] In 2011 she transferred to the Transitional Justice Institute at Ulster University to fully engage with research on human rights and the following year she was appointed as oversight commissioner for prison reform in Northern Ireland.[19] McWilliams engages with peace initiatives globally offering advice and insights through workshops for women in other conflict areas, including Colombia and the Middle East, on UN Security Council Resolutions on Women, Peace and Security.[20]

McWilliams has published widely in the area of domestic violence and on women's roles in peace and conflict.[21] She was one of nine politicians involved in the peace process who were jointly awarded the John F. Kennedy Library Profile in Courage Award in 1998. The following year she was given the Frank Cousins Peace Award. In 2017 BBC Northern Ireland first aired a documentary described as 'the extraordinary story [of the NIWC,] a cross-community party formed in 1996 by local working- and middle-class women. Frustrated with the stalemate of local politics, the women ran a door-to-door campaign to win two seats at the historic peace talks, which culminated in the Good Friday Agreement.'[22] The documentary, titled *Wave Goodbye to Dinosaurs*, after the party's campaign slogan, features interviews with McWilliams.[23] The documentary also includes Bernadette Devlin McAliskey who 'observes that the NIWC's role has been largely invisible in retelling the story of the Good Friday Agreement. "Not because women get written out of history," she concludes; "they never get written in."'[24]

McWilliams has been awarded a number of honorary doctorates in recognition of her work and accomplishments, including Doctor of Humane Letters from Lesley College in Cambridge. On 24 September 2021, Hillary Clinton was formally inaugurated as Chancellor of Queen's University, Belfast. After her inauguration, Clinton oversaw honorary doctorates for McWilliams, Morrice, Sagar and Hinds. In her address, Clinton celebrated the key role these women had played. She declared that, before the NIWC was established, 'women did not have a seat at the table. A quarter century of bloodshed and strife and embedded sexism had discouraged most women from politics. But not these four, they were relentless in their commitment to peace and they had a slogan too, wave goodbye to the dinosaurs.'[25]

McWilliams has written a book recounting her life and work for women's rights, peace and equality. This publication will undoubtedly inspire further research into women's central position in the Northern Irish peace process. It is most appropriately titled *Stand Up, Speak Out.*[26] Monica McWilliams continues to speak out on behalf of generations of women in Ireland and beyond. Her speech in this section is a vital record of her inspiring work, which continues to impact us so greatly.

'[When] political leaders asked us, "Where did those women come from?" – [it was] as if we'd fallen out of the air. Well, we came from somewhere. We started as accidental activists. What do I mean by "accidental activists"? We accidentally fell into activism. If something awful was happening, we rose up; we took to the streets; we marched; we demanded that the situation change, and we responded. And sometimes that was the only way that we could do it.

[Some of us had] cut our teeth on civil rights activism. . . . The whole civil rights movement that was happening [in the United States] came right across the Atlantic in waves and [when it] hit Europe, it certainly hit us in Northern Ireland, when we watched on our television screens what was happening. . . .

Feminist activism was much smaller but rose and grew and became a snowball and made connections with all this various type of activism, and some of it was welcomed and some of it wasn't. And eventually this led us to party political activism, and we eventually decided, building on all of what went before, that the time was right to form a party. And today I work in human rights as the Chief Commissioner for Human Rights, and I have to say that if I die, I do not want anyone to say that I suddenly switched and became a human rights defender and forgot all of what went on before in terms of women's activism, no more than we could have said that about the peace agreement. That when we went in and we read on the final nights what was in the agreement, we asked ourselves, "And how does this speak to the women in the country? Can they also see themselves in this agreement?" . . .

But the combatants were still very suspicious of women's rights. The combatants – and there were many female combatants – were saying, "The issue here is the constitutional issue of having a united Ireland", or on the Protestant side [where] there were many fewer female combatants who said, "It's the union with Britain that's the most important, and women's rights can wait." How many times have you heard that all over the world – that these are the priority issues? And so, they were suspicious of those of us who were trying to bring [other] issues like domestic violence and rape and sex discrimination to the fore. . . .

The women took to the streets over and over. . . . Eventually, 1994 came; we had the first ceasefires, and they were reinstated eventually in 1997. [And the *Belfast Telegraph* headline declared] "It's over. It's time to [re]build, not time to tear down." And that's what we focused on as women. We said, "There's been enough tearing down. Now we have to move." And we moved quickly. All this time women were growing as civic leaders, and in fact we became better known outside the country than we did in the country. . . . We knew that peace had to be consolidated at the grassroots. And what we also knew was that there was no point in us being recognised outside the country for what we were doing. We had to do something inside, and so we moved the margins to the mainstream.

The talks were declared in 1996. The British and Irish governments decided which parties should go. They wanted the small paramilitary parties to be included, and so they made a list. And we looked at it and said, "This isn't very democratic. Where are we on this list?" And so [we] made a phone call to the British official and said, "By the way, there's a group of women here who want to stand for election." It wasn't true; [we were] just testing the system. And he said, "Oh, that's fine. What's the name of your party?" . . . And [we] dreamed up this word called "Women's Coalition", and then [we] thought, "Hmm. That's a 'W'. That means we'll be at the bottom of the ballot sheet, which isn't a good idea." So [we] stuck "Northern Ireland" in front of it. And [we] put the phone down, and [we] thought, "What have [we] just done?"

. . . the women felt protected by the fact that it was going to be parties that were going to stand, and so we decided this was possible. Peace processes can move rapidly. They can create new opportunities. Of course, it could have been destabilising. We were very protective [of each other]. Indeed, one of the women's centres got burned down because Mary Robinson came to visit, and they [the paramilitaries in that area] decided this wasn't a very nice thing, the President of Ireland coming to a women's centre in Belfast. And what was the response? They simply threw in a petrol bomb and burned the centre to the ground.

And we were very worried about the fact that if we organised politically, we might end up [with paramilitaries] burning more centres to the ground. Because if you weren't in politics, you weren't seen as a big threat. We decided anyway that we were going to go for it. . . .

We took two aims: to get more women into politics and to work and strive for workable solutions. Very simple; no big policy statements, not loads and loads of papers – just simple aims of human rights, equality, and inclusion. We were Protestant and Catholic and women of no religion. We were across the classes; we were cross sector; there [were] professional women; there were women who were unemployed. We were urban and rural. And we came with that disparity and that mix and said, "We will work hard to get to the[se] talks." . . .

It was an enormous personal journey for some of the women because it was difficult and at times dangerous, what we were asking them to do. . . . Sometimes our offices did get . . . windows broken, but we didn't want women in their own homes to have their windows broken every night. There was a backlash from women in the other parties, who felt that they had been around for years and suddenly we had appeared on the scene. But . . . they discovered that the male leaders in their parties were so worried about us that they said to them, "well we promise that we'll put you further up in profile in future, as long as you stay with us." . . .

We did reach an agreement two years later. The agreement was declared. . . . That night, at quarter past five on Good Friday, thousands of people suddenly crowded in – mostly ex-combatants, because they wanted to make sure that what was being signed . . . could stand up afterwards. We were exhausted and exhilarated, and we were viewed as valued contributors. Senator Mitchell then wrote and said we were a significant factor. He said that we were treated very roughly at the beginning, but through perseverance and talent we became recognised as valued contributors. I didn't know this until recently that an Irish government official said we were the most efficient and focused [party] throughout the talks. . . .

These are the things that we succeeded in getting in, but there were things that we lost. And I learned some bitter lessons. If we hadn't been at the table, there would have been nothing on victims, integrated education, mixed housing, children, and nothing about the importance of rebuilding lives, [and] dealing with the past. Some of the other big issues we did negotiate: prisoner releases – 2,000 prisoners walked out of jail two years later in the year 2000. . . .

The lessons we learned [were to] rejoice . . . but fundraising must go on and on and on, if women are going to get into politics or stay in politics or be active in the community. . . . And learning in retrospect, collective decision-making takes time. You need cash. You need confidence. You need childcare. You need a good culture, and you need to have good candidates, selected as women. You need to have a good media strategy. If they tell you you're not real politicians, ask, "What does a real politician look like?" Keep optimistic but realistic. And keep the back channels open. Keep an eye on those support measures because they will disappear after a peace process, and they have, and that was a disappointment for us. . . .

The final pieces are, for me, [that] foundational rights have to be written in[to peace agreements] and [they] have to be enforced. That's my job now as Chief Commissioner; [and with my fellow commissioners] I've drafted the bill of rights. I took the words from UN 1325 into the preamble, and I said, "Our bill of rights must value the role of women in public and political life and their involvement in advancing peace and security.'"[27]

TWENTY EIGHT

Adi Roche

B. 1955

Address to the United Nations General Assembly
UN Headquarters, New York

26 APRIL 2016

'A new word, Chernobyl, entered into the history of language.'

In the early hours of 26 April 1986, Reactor Number 4 at the Chernobyl Nuclear Power Plant in northern Ukraine ruptured, causing a steam explosion. One plant worker, Valeriy Khodomchuk, was killed instantly, and a second worker, Vladimir Nikolayevich Shashenok, died hours later. Thirty workers from the site died within days of the explosion.[1] Over the weeks that followed, an incalculable number of people were exposed to extremely high levels of radiation. An unofficial test on the reactor went profoundly wrong, causing a meltdown that damaged its core. Radioactive contamination over 400 times greater than that resulting from the atomic bomb dropped on Hiroshima was released.[2] Within four days of the explosion, high radiation levels were recorded across Europe, including Poland, Germany, Romania, Italy, Belgium, the Netherlands, Great Britain and Greece. Within one week, gaseous airborne particles had travelled around the globe, reaching Japan, India, the United States, and Canada.[3] Radioactivity was first recorded in Ireland on 2 May at Glasnevin in Dublin through a sample air filter. William Reville, Professor of Biochemistry at University College Cork, maintained that the radioactive level remained acute in Ireland for two weeks after the accident.[4]

The border to the Eastern European country of Belarus is situated just 20 kilometres from the site of the Chernobyl plant. Seventy per cent of the released radiation from the accident fell over Belarus, affecting more than seven million people. On the thirtieth anniversary of the Chernobyl disaster, a special general assembly of the United Nations (UN) was convened on 26 April 2016. The Belarusian government made the unprecedented move of inviting a representative from a Non-Governmental Organisation (NGO) to lead the address during the time allotted to their country at that assembly. The founder and Chief Executive Officer of Chernobyl Children International (CCI), Adi Roche, was invited to lead the address on behalf of Belarus.[5]

Roche, originally from Clonmel in county Tipperary, first became aware of issues concerning nuclear power in 1979, after the nuclear accident at Three Mile Island, Pennsylvania, near where her brother Donal then lived. She joined anti-nuclear protest rallies against a nuclear plant proposed for Carnsore Point, Wexford.[6] Roche took voluntary redundancy from her job at Aer Lingus in 1984 and worked as a volunteer for the Irish Campaign for Nuclear Disarmament (CND). At the time of the Chernobyl disaster, Roche was a full-time volunteer for the CND, through which she supported people living in areas affected by the Chernobyl explosion. Five years after the explosion, Roche received a fax from doctors in Belarus and Ukraine imploring, 'SOS Appeal. For God's sake help us get the children out.'[7] The fax was signed 'we are a team of doctors and we can no longer be silent.'[8] The ongoing contamination in these areas was detrimental to the health of children especially. Roche was deeply affected by this plea and immediately responded by organising practical and life-changing aid. In 1991 she founded CCI, which has vastly enhanced the lives of thousands of people from affected areas. In recognition of the organisation's continuing humanitarian work, the UN granted CCI official NGO status in 2004.

The speech by Roche in this section is a powerful reminder not only of the devastation caused by the initial explosion at Chernobyl but also of the continuing damaging impact on human life. Her address had an impact on those attending the UN general assembly and raised public consciousness about Chernobyl more broadly. By the time Roche addressed the UN, she had personally led 30 missions to the highly contaminated area around the Chernobyl plant, an area now termed the 'Zone of Alienation'. At the time of the disaster, the worst affected countries – Belarus, Ukraine and Russia – were within the Union of Soviet Socialist Republics (USSR). The USSR was governed from Moscow, and Mikhail Gorbachev was then General Secretary of the Communist Party of the Soviet Union. Two-and-a-half weeks would pass before Gorbachev publicly announced details of the nuclear explosion. Appearing on television, broadcast to an estimated audience of two hundred million viewers, Gorbachev maintained that 'the Soviet Government will take care of the families of those who died and who suffered.'[9] Gorbachev would later claim that the nuclear disaster caused the collapse of the USSR in 1991.[10]

When the USSR collapsed, Roche was by then immersed in a highly organised support mission to provide help to those affected by the Chernobyl disaster. In a radio interview in 2018 Roche described how she initially was 'activated through the kind of non-violent direct action movement of the time. Really during the time of the height of the cold war, when East and West were ... threatening mutual annihilation, we were like the piggies in the middle, [a] small island nation, what could we do? But we could be a beacon of hope.'[11] Roche ensured that, through her organisation and activities, Ireland became a beacon of hope for those affected by the Chernobyl disaster.

The USSR had been ill equipped to deal with this catastrophe; there was no plan in place to deal with a nuclear explosion of this magnitude. A military task force was established within hours of the disaster happening, assigned with cleaning up and containing the radioactive area. Men were drafted from across the USSR to protect their motherland through an assignment formally known as the 'Liquidation of the Consequences of the Chernobyl Accident'. In his award-winning research on the disaster, Adam Higginbotham details how 'young men in Kiev, Minsk, and Tallinn had been summoned from their workplaces—or roused by a knock on the door in the middle of the night—and taken to be issued uniforms, sworn under oath, and told they should consider themselves to be at war.'[12] This team grew to 700,000 men, who became known as the liquidators. Research estimates that 40,000 liquidators died and 70,000 more were disabled through their work to clean up and make safe the area surrounding Chernobyl; these casualties included soldiers, miners, firemen and helicopter pilots.[13]

Three weeks before her speech, Roche travelled again to the Zone of Alienation and met with a group of liquidators. Her first call on the UN assembly was to recognise the heroism of these men, whom she compared to the first responders at New York's 9/11 attack. Through their tireless work, the liquidators of Chernobyl protected much of Europe and further afield from experiencing a further nuclear catastrophe. Support for the liquidators, medically or financially, has been sadly inadequate. One such liquidator, a senior plant engineer Yuri Andreyev, worked in the immediate aftermath of the explosion. Despite losing consciousness on a number of occasions, he managed to cool the switched-off reactors numbers 1 and 2; otherwise they could have triggered another explosion. His vocal cords were burned from radiation exposure, and he acquired a blood disorder.[14] The health consequences for the liquidators exposed to radioactive material were immense. As well as working on the immediate clean-up operation, liquidators worked in the 30-mile radius on mitigation activities on a large scale until 1990.

In her speech Roche also made a plea on behalf of citizens living in the affected areas: she requested, among other things, uncontaminated food and provisions, the monitoring of radiation check-ups, and for contaminated zones be kept population free. Roche's plea was significant considering the findings of a World Health Organisation (WHO) report in 2006, which exposed the high number of people living in the affected areas. After the explosion, 116,000 people living in the area surrounding the nuclear plant and 220,000 people in the surrounding territory were relocated. However, the report found that another five million people living in territories 'contaminated to a substantial level' were not relocated.[15]

The importance of ensuring that food remains uncontaminated is evident from the stark findings published in an updated WHO report in 2016. This research confirmed that for:

> Young children and adolescents who were exposed to radioactive iodine through contaminated food and milk in 1986, an increase of thyroid cancer incidence was reported. By 2006, more than 5,000 cases of thyroid cancer were diagnosed among those who were children at the time of the exposure. By 2015, the total number of cases in the three affected countries has reached 20,000.[16]

Over one million children still live in contaminated zones, and food remains under threat of being contaminated. Greenpeace Russia reported on the largest forest fires ever recorded in the Chernobyl exclusion zone in April 2020. Campaigner Rashid Alimov described how 'Cities like Kyiv are exposed to the health impact of inhaling smoke in the short term and in the longer term, risk internal irradiation through contaminated berries, mushrooms and milk bought on the local markets.'[17]

Roche's warning 'to prevent Chernobyl becoming the next Chernobyl' is hauntingly accurate. It is estimated that 220 tons of radioactive material remain in Reactor 4. In order to contain this material, construction of a giant cover made from concrete and steel, known as the Chernobyl sarcophagus, began less than a month after the accident. Due to the high levels of radiation workers were exposed to during construction, robots were used to seal the joints of the building. Unfortunately, not all openings were fully sealed, which caused corrosion to the structure over the following years. The sarcophagus soon began to exhibit structural issues and needed to be replaced with a new safe confinement structure. Construction began near the site in 2010, and the completed structure was brought into position in November 2016, just months after Roche delivered her speech to the UN. It would take another three years to finalise the structure, and in July 2019, it was first displayed to the public. Roche's assertion about the importance of dismantling the sarcophagus was affirmed in July 2020 by the company contracted to remove it. A company spokesperson announced that 'only gravity had been keeping the structure tethered to its supporting blocks.'[18]

Roche delivered her speech with the objective of being 'a voice for the forgotten victims and survivors of the Chernobyl disaster'.[19] She not only accomplished her objective but also raised awareness of the continuing issues attached to the Chernobyl disaster and initiated action. On 8 December 2016 the UN officially declared 26 April International Chernobyl Disaster Remembrance Day. This significant move was in response to Roche's request to the UN general assembly. The President of Ireland was the first head of state to officially recognise the Remembrance Day. In his International Chernobyl Disaster Remembrance Day message in 2017, President Michael D. Higgins declared:

> Ireland's response was unique; we were one of the first countries to respond to the humanitarian crisis by providing support for and meeting the needs of thousands of Chernobyl's victims. Adi Roche's Chernobyl Children International has become a world leader in supporting and advocating for the children who were affected by the Chernobyl disaster across the stricken regions.[20]

Roche travelled to Belarus and Ukraine along with Ali Hewson, board director of CCI, to commemorate the first official Remembrance Day.

This remembrance day ensures that Roche and CCI will continue to raise awareness and receive support for her steadfast work on behalf of people affected by Chernobyl. As of 2020 CCI has delivered over €107 million worth of medical and humanitarian aid to those in the affected regions of Belarus, Ukraine and Western Russia. Under Roche's management, CCI has vastly improved the lives of thousands of children in Belarus through numerous ground-breaking schemes. CCI pioneered an adoption agreement between Ireland and Belarus, which has sanctioned the adoption of hundreds of children from Belarus to Ireland. The organisation purchased and renovated 30 houses as it developed its Home of Hope Programme, which provides alternatives to state orphanages. CCI also established the only fully equipped baby hospice in Belarus. Under Roche's influence the Belarus government is establishing an independent living programme for teenage boys and girls residing in institutions, in place of moving such teenagers to adult units when they reach 18 years of age. CCI medical interventions include over 4,000 cardiac surgeries performed by Irish-funded cardiac surgeons and the development of a child cardiac surgery programme for children with congenital heart defects due to radiation exposure.

The Chernobyl accident continues to affect the lives of millions of people in the most debilitating ways, and the threat of further contamination across Europe is indisputable. Adi Roche has ensured that a new generation is aware of and responsive to this ongoing crisis through publications, visual arts and documentaries, most recently through the highly acclaimed HBO and Sky Television series *Chernobyl* (2019).[21] Roche has been given numerous humanitarian awards, including the Pride of Ireland Lifetime Achievement Award in 2016, the Princess Grace Humanitarian Award in 2015, the David Chow Humanitarian Award in 2008 and the Robert Burns Humanitarian Award in 2007. She has been awarded honorary degrees from the University of Limerick, jointly with Ali Hewson, in 2016; NUI Galway in 2002; and the University of Alberta, Canada, in 2001.

27. Adi Roche addressing the United Nations General Assembly in New York, 26 April 2016. Photograph courtesy of Adi Roche.

'Thirty years ago today at exactly 1:23 a.m. on the morning of the 26th of April 1986, a chain of events in Reactor No. 4 at the Chernobyl Nuclear Power Station led to a massive explosion spewing deadly radioactive contamination into that beautiful night sky, where the blowing winds scattered it far and scattered it wide, unfolding at terrifying speed and thus triggering what has become the world's worst nuclear disaster.

A new word, *Chernobyl*, entered into the history of language, the history of world disasters, and the history of the world with deadly and frightful force. The sun shone, the wind blew, rain fell down, and so did the radioactive poison. . . .

I cannot speak to you with the authority of a scientist or with the authority of a doctor; I cannot prove my statements with laboratory or field test experiments, for I have no medical or scientific academic qualification to endorse my remarks to you. But, in humility, I can offer you my truth, my witness, and my evidence of the heart.

I have visited and worked in the Chernobyl area for thirty long years, and I am still haunted by the stories of people I've met over that time – women like Tanya from a demolished village in southern Belarus called Lipa. I remember she talked about how she was forever "rooted like a tree" to the earth of her ancestors, but how she was now "withering away and dying". . . .

248

Chernobyl, and now sadly Fukushima, is very, very bleak and dark forever![22] A sin against the beauty and wonder of our beautiful planet Earth, a sin against ordinary decent people. There may be an impression that 30 years on Chernobyl is something from the past: it no longer poses a threat to the world, but the reality is very, very different. Chernobyl is not from the past: Chernobyl is sadly forever; the impact of that single shocking nuclear accident cannot be undone; its radioactive footprint is embedded in our world forever, and countless millions of people are still being affected by its deadly legacy. Friends, we may never know the full extent of the contamination; we may never be able to prove it as if it were a simple geometry proposition, but the tragedy that is Chernobyl is very, very real.

Three weeks ago, I returned to the highly contaminated 'Zones of Alienation' – zones of exclusion, as they are called – that surround the Chernobyl plant and beyond. I was there on a fact-finding mission, and while there, I was asked by some of the men who heroically fought for days and months to contain the spreading of that radioactive fire, the men who carried out the evacuation of towns and villages, the men who had to demolish and bury and burn two thousand towns and villages. They asked me to bring to you their story and to bring their voices to this gathering today.

And today, I wear this Chernobyl service medal with great pride and with deep respect and a deep sense of responsibility, and this photograph has been given to me by a liquidator military officer called Valerii Zaitsev. I hold the photograph here in acknowledgement of the work that the men like Valerii and others did in order to protect our planet. Seven hundred thousand of these men, the liquidators, were ordinary people. They were soldiers; they were civilians; they were helicopter pilots, firemen, miners, engineers. They were sent into the Chernobyl nuclear conflagration. [For] Valerii and his gallant comrades, fighting this highly radioactive fire in Chernobyl was their Ground Zero. And like the brave rescue services, the heroes of 9/11 in New York's terrible catastrophe, they, the Chernobyl liquidators – these noble, these self-sacrificing men – ought to be rightly honoured and recognised as the heroes who not just saved Europe but really saved the world from greater catastrophe!

Many of the Chernobyl liquidators feel that they have not been so honoured. In fact, they feel they have been dishonoured, neglected, abandoned, forgotten by the world. And so my first appeal to this great assembly is that these heroic men – these first responders of a nuclear accident age – the liquidators, . . . be recognised and that the world would set up a global fund to ensure their medical and social needs are taken care of. In honouring my pledge to Valerii and to thousands of other brave fighters, I respectfully place this request before the floor of this house.

[Secondly,] I also respectfully propose that this day, the 26th of April, be pledged and designated as an official United Nations Chernobyl Day, a day that would always be honoured, commemorated, and be a day for renewal and recommitment to discover new initiatives to alleviate further the suffering of the people in the affected, stricken lands.

Thirdly, I would like to say that to prevent [Chernobyl becoming the next Chernobyl], I ask that the United Nations urgently use their power and their influence to propel forward the completion of the new sarcophagus, that vital safety shield over the exploded reactor, which is critical to ensure that we can contain the highly radioactive material which is rumbling and lurking still in Reactor 4 and that we move swiftly to the next phase – phase two – of dismantling the reactor and safely finding a way to remove and store what will be hundreds of tons of highly radioactive material. Now this is a challenge, this project, because it has never been done before. . . . It will require new technology, new thinking, and new expertise.

[Fourthly,] I also humbly ask for the provision to be made to fund access to clean food and adequate food monitoring, in order to protect the citizens still living in the stricken regions.

And fifthly, that monitoring and radiation check-ups of people be reinstated throughout the stricken regions along with the provision of the most up-to-date medical and scanning equipment, ensuring extensive ongoing monitoring, particularly for children and pregnant mothers living in the contaminated area.

And finally, that the contaminated zones of highly radioactive land be kept free of cultivation and re-population. . . .

While other disasters are, yes, vying for all of your attention, Chernobyl, unfortunately, often is [relegated] to the realms of history and to the past. Probably because the images from this tragedy are so different to the deeply disturbing images of war, of famine, of other disasters, where we can see the immediacy of a bomb, a bullet, or starvation.

However, the war that has been waged since 1986 by Chernobyl is a silent, invisible but nonetheless deadly one. It has no smell, no taste, nothing to forewarn you of danger. There was no "safe haven", no escape, no emergency exit. Yet, my friends, it beats in the hearts of every innocent man, woman, and child still living. It beats in their rivers, their towns, their streams, and their forests. The deadly radiation clicking endlessly, ferociously in Geiger counters into the silent numbness that is and always will be Chernobyl.'[23]

TWENTY NINE

Saffa Musleh

B. 1978

Speech on redefining the Irish person
Wexford Arts Centre

23 SEPTEMBER 2016

'Reflect on what you perceive to be an Irish look.'

Saffa Musleh took the stage of the Arts Centre in Wexford town in September 2016, challenging her audience to re-evaluate their preconceived notions about what constitutes an Irish person. Her talk was personal, sensitive and well grounded. Musleh's speech was a pertinent reminder for her audience to embrace Ireland as a forward thinking, multicultural society. Musleh represents a new Irish generation of skilled, vocal women who are leading social reform. She delivered her speech as part of a TEDx evening event themed 'Tomorrow imagined', organised by educator and entrepreneur Denise Whitmore. Musleh's speech carried a powerful message appropriate to many societies but especially relevant to Ireland in the twenty-first century.

The forum for Musleh's speech ensured that her message was heard well beyond the Wexford venue at which she spoke. TEDx talks are now spreading around the globe through independent, community-organised events. Talks are held at local venues, where an audience hears from a selection of speakers, focusing on a set theme. As part of the process, speeches are recorded and uploaded to the TED (Technology, Entertainment, Design) site and streamed across social media platforms, reaching audiences worldwide. The TEDx format highlights the changing forums in which women can make their voices heard. Unfortunately, online forums are also targets for far-right groups and individuals with unscrupulous intentions. Musleh's talk was uploaded on 22 November 2016 and was watched online by nearly 10,000 people. Her focus fitted most appropriately into the theme 'Tomorrow imagined', as she stressed the need to improve Irish society for the next generation.

Musleh was born in Dubai and moved to Ireland in 2003, where she has worked across government and private sectors. She has contributed vastly to Irish society, especially in terms of healthcare education. Musleh is a qualified nurse and healthcare trainer, who worked in the Mater Private and Tallaght Hospitals before taking a position as a healthcare trainer with Comfort Keepers and other companies.[1] In 2007 she won the Ireland AM/ Mothercare writing competition, with a short story on her experience of motherhood. Her story featured in a book published later that year, *Mum's the Word: The Truth About Being a Mother*.[2] The book was edited by Sarah Webb, who organised the publication as a fundraiser for cystic fibrosis research at the National Children's Hospital in Tallaght. Authors, including Musleh, donated all profits from the book sales to the cystic fibrosis cause. The volume comprises short stories by prestigious Irish women writers, including Cathy Kelly, Anne Enright, Sinéad Moriarty, and many others. Musleh was the only non-professional writer to be included in this volume, and her story was highly applauded. In her review of the book, journalist Sinéad Desmond noted that 'Among the stories is one from Saffa Musleh, a nurse who won an Ireland AM comp[etition]. . . . I read her story and I smiled, I cried but above all I was moved by her searing honesty.'[3]

After living in Ireland for five years, Musleh was legally entitled to apply for Irish citizenship. She became an Irish citizen at a ceremony in the Four Courts in Dublin. In her speech Musleh celebrates her Irish citizenship status while examining what this means for her within Irish society. She describes how she was driven to give this talk because of

> a personal experience that I felt needed to be shared. As an educator, I believed in spreading knowledge and, perhaps naively, thought that raising awareness about what was a very common turn of phrase in Irish daily life meant for the recipient, as well as shedding some light on the thoughts underlying that phrase 'where are you really from?'[4]

Musleh's discussion of the question 'where are you *really* from?' is insightful.

Musleh's speech sheds light on a positive new direction for Ireland, a country which has broken free from previous waves of emigration to become a place which attracts migrants. Ireland has a deep and disturbing history of forced emigration, especially from the nineteenth century. The Great Irish Famine forced over a million Irish people to seek refuge in Britain, North America, Australia and beyond. Later economic crises ensured that emigration continued well into the twentieth century. It is estimated that between 1850 and 1913, over four and a half million people left Ireland.[5] Waves of emigration continued throughout the twentieth century for numerous reasons, most often due to a lack of work but also during times of escalated political violence.[6] By the end of the twentieth century, this pattern began to reverse. A study in 2008 by Piaras Mac Éinrí and Allen White identified that 'Over the past decade, years of emigration and exile have been supplanted by sustained immigration of a multiplicity of different groups including returning Irish emigrants, refugees, asylum seekers and labour migrants.'[7] In more recent years, immigration into Ireland has far exceeded emigration outwards; in the year ending April 2020, there was a net migration of 28,900 people.[8]

The story of Ireland's reversed migration trend is a positive one. From a fiscal perspective, Ireland is now a popular destination for immigrants due to a strong economy. The fact that the immigration system is not points based ensures that highly skilled immigrants, such as Musleh, can obtain a visa to work in the Republic of Ireland, adding greatly to the Irish economy. From a social perspective, the benefits are manyfold and include a multi-cultural community on the island of Ireland. The change in migration patterns and in Irish society has happened relatively fast. Therefore, what Musleh describes as the stereotypical Irish look has quickly become an outdated and inaccurate one. Perceptions of a supposed Irish look cause deep concerns for Irish people who do not fit this tidy categorisation of a freckle-faced white person. These concerns are expressed by Musleh in a clear and sensitive manner, describing the implications not only for her as an Irish citizen but also for the next generation, including her own daughter. Musleh's speech is therefore noteworthy, representing an Irish person who does not fit a narrow and inaccurate idea of Irishness.

Musleh gave her talk in Wexford just three months after the Brexit referendum, when Britain voted to leave the European Union. When the results of the referendum were announced on 24 June 2016, the UK was already experiencing heightened racist violence. In the 38 days following the referendum, more than 2,300 racist incidents were reported to the police, with Metropolitan police chief Bernard Hogan-Howe describing the rise as a 'horrible spike'.[9] Such racist incidents were connected to anti-immigrant views perpetuated by far-right groups. When Musleh gave her speech, no far-right group had managed to gain a platform at local or national level in Ireland, but these groups were emerging. The same month that Musleh's speech was uploaded to *YouTube*, another far-right group, the National Party, was founded. Bryan Fanning, a Professor of Migration and Social Policy, best describes the rationale of these 'far-right parties and groups that oppose immigration, promote narrow definitions of Irishness and look for inspiration to populist nativist movements in other English-speaking and European democratic countries'.[10]

Musleh's assessment of this narrow definition of Irishness was therefore timely. She called on her audience to consider how they view and question Irishness. When Musleh's speech reached the internet, she was the victim of a horrendous backlash. She recalled that 'I did not anticipate the attacks from the far right and nationalist movements that took place a few months after the talk was published on YouTube, and have since been more and more aware of the futility of education and knowledge in circles where racism and xenophobia breed.'[11] Musleh's TEDx speech remains online, but unlike other talks on the site, the comments section is disabled due to such bigoted reactions. Unfortunately, similar anti-immigration and racist views circulated online with more organisation when Ireland was placed into lockdown during the onset of the Covid-19 pandemic in early 2020. Far-right groups seized the opportunity to organise street protests against government restrictions to curtail the spread of the pandemic. While such groups gained supporters through these actions, their 'attempts at anti-immigrant populism . . . in advance of the 2020 election did not strike a chord with the electorate.'[12] In the Irish general election in February 2020, far-right individuals and two groups, the Irish Freedom Party and the National Party, entered election candidates in 21 different locations. The parties failed dismally, and no far-right candidate was elected to Irish government. The news site *The Journal* celebrated these results with the headline 'Far-right parties barely register after polling less than 1% in most constituencies'.[13]

Musleh's important message reached a vast audience. Since giving her speech in Wexford, she has been told by many people that after listening 'they reassess how they address that query [where are you *really* from?] when talking to others.'[14] In her speech Musleh acknowledges that people often ask this question not with an anti-immigrant or racist intent. However, posing such a question denies many people their Irishness. Her speech was a brave attempt to redress what could become a problem in Irish society. The negative repercussions of denying people their Irishness were witnessed in a devastating way in Dublin in 2021.

In January 2021 the Lord Mayor of Dublin, Hazel Chu, suffered racial abuse outside her home, the Mansion House. Chu was born and raised in Dublin and lived in Firhouse as a child. Her parents, originally from Hong Kong, emigrated to Ireland, where they met each other and married in the 1970s. Chu has been involved in politics since 2014 and was elected Lord Mayor of Dublin on 29 June 2020.[15] The incident in January was certainly not the first episode of racial abuse suffered by Chu in her own country. Following her election as Lord Mayor, Chu recounted how she and her young daughter had been targeted. Chu told a political correspondent for the *Irish Examiner*, 'if it comes down to one thing – you don't like a woman of colour in this office – then we have a huge problem. We have a vocal minority in this country we have to tackle.'[16] While such racist abuse is most certainly hurled only by a minority of people in Ireland, Musleh's assertions echo Chu's warning that this issue needs to be tackled now. Chu, an Irish woman serving the community of Dublin as Lord Mayor, was placed in a situation where she feared for herself and for her daughter, based on the colour of their skin.

Far-right groups with anti-immigrant platforms continue in their attempts to infiltrate Irish politics. In July 2021 the leader of the National Party, Justin Barrett, contested a by-election in the Dublin Bay South constituency. Barrett has stood in previous campaigns, including the 2004 European Parliament elections, on an anti-immigrant platform. He announced his candidacy for the Dublin by-election in an online *YouTube* video on 9 June 2021.[17] Barrett received less than two hundred votes, and Ivana Bacik topped the polls to take her seat as TD for Dublin Bay South. This election result is significant in relation to immigration: Bacik is a steadfast campaigner for equality and has played a part in many reforms. In December 2020 Bacik made a public call for citizenship applications to be fast-tracked for foreign frontline medical workers fighting the Covid-19 pandemic.[18] She continues to contribute greatly to Irish society, and she is the granddaughter of an immigrant. Her grandfather, Karel Bacik, moved to Ireland from Czechoslovakia in 1946. He was a glass manufacturer, who had been imprisoned by the Nazis during World War Two. In Ireland he established a crystal factory that later became Waterford Glass, the largest employer in the county. Such is the vast contribution that immigrants have made and continue to make to the development of Irish society.

The current population of the island of Ireland reached just under seven million in September 2021.[19] This is the highest recorded population of the country since the 1851 census. After the years of the Great Famine, death and emigration devastatingly depleted the population of Ireland. The rate of immigration into the country continues to outnumber the rate of people emigrating out of Ireland. It is high time, indeed, that Musleh's message is taken seriously; there is no stereotypical Irish look. The diversity of the Irish population was underscored on 5 September 2021, when Pamela Uba was crowned Miss Ireland. Uba made history as the first black woman to hold this title, the *New York Post* declared 'The Irish have something to celebrate.'[20]

Musleh continues to use her education and expertise to improve Irish society and remains vocal on issues that cause concern. Writing in the *Irish Times* in 2018, she noted that 'I had been attacked by far right movements in Ireland, and kept reassuring myself that these are the minority, that we are not people who hate or promote hatred.'[21] Her speech delivers a powerful message that should be read by people across Ireland and those who face similar threats from far-right groups in other countries.

'I am the daughter of second-generation Palestinian immigrants. I was born in Dubai, but I am not a citizen of the United Arab Emirates because you do not acquire citizenship in Dubai unless your parents were original nationals. So I'm not Palestinian either because of the political situation in Palestine; nobody got any Palestinian identification in the last few decades. . . . When I got a chance to move to Ireland, I jumped at it. It was an opportunity to start a new life, to build a family, and I did, and within a year of moving to Ireland, I knew I was home. . . .

So I applied for the citizenship but also decided that I had to do my homework and become a real Irish person. . . . I eventually got my day in the Four Courts, where I stood and took the oath and obtained the right to become an Irish citizen. Since that day, I get asked on [an] almost weekly basis, "Where are you from?" And I reply, "I'm Irish", knowing fully well that an inevitable second question was on the way. "Ah no, where are you *really* from?" And that second question, ladies and gentlemen, is what I'm going to talk about today.

The question of where I'm really from stems from a mind-set that identifies the Irish look as one that stereotypically [is] monochromatic, probably freckled. More importantly, it's a look that is outdated, and I'll tell you why it's outdated. Over the last ten to fifteen years, we have been welcoming into our country people from all over the world: immigrants, foreign workers, EU citizens, a lot of whom have left as soon as the Celtic Tiger crumbled, but a lot of whom have stayed; and the Central Statistics Office proves that many of them actually claim this country as their second home, stayed, built a new life, became Irish citizens, had Irish children. In the same period of time, we have also been loving and adopting children from African and Asian countries, *sans* freckles. And we've been bringing these children up as our own, as Irish children, who wouldn't know themselves to be anything else. If we do not have the conversation now, and if we do not start redefining what the look of the Irish is, these children, these Irish children, my own daughter included, are going to very shortly move into secondary education, higher education, the job market, and get asked where they really come from; and that isn't fair.

We have lots of theories about the Irish identity. We like to romanticise. . . . Joyce saw a modern, contemporary country; Yeats wanted the revival of the traditions of the Celtic; each one of them unique in their Irishness and yet all Irish. We can no more deny a unionist, for example, his Irishness than we can a republican. So what I'm saying is if we can accept such differing views of what an Irish person is or believes, how can we let something like the colour of our skin change our perspective of what an Irish person is?

We are a far more contemporary country than we give ourselves credit for, and I know we don't like boasting about how great we are, but we are great. We voted for gay marriage, the first country in the world to do so. We embrace the rainbow flag on Pride Week in every single street, in every city of this country. We love it; we accept it; we are happy about it, so let's apply that same love, acceptance, and happiness to those of us who have a different colour skin than the porcelain hue that we've attached to the old-fashioned look of the Irish. So what I'm asking of you today is to just reflect on what you perceive to be an Irish look. What do you think an Irish person should look like? Because this is something we need to do now, before it's too late; before the conversation happens around fixing a problem that we could have sorted out from the very beginning. And the next time you meet somebody who is Irish and maybe looks like me – or maybe a bit darker – please don't deny them that Irishness; please don't ask them where they *really* came from. Affirm it, and accept it, and if you are really curious – because I know we are nosy, and we like to get our noses in everybody's business – ask them about their heritage. "I can see that you're Irish, or I know you're Irish. Tell me about your heritage; tell me about your background; tell me about your ancestry." It's only a little step, a very small one, but it's where change begins.'[22]

THIRTY

Mary McAleese

B. 1951

Keynote address at 'Why Women Matter' conference
Jesuit Curia, Rome

8 MARCH 2018

'The tidal wave is quickly approaching the Vatican walls.'

In February 2018 former President of Ireland Mary McAleese was banned from speaking at a conference in Vatican City. The conference, themed 'Why Women Matter', was organised by the Voices of Faith group. The group's mission is to 'empower and advocate for a prophetic Catholic Church, where women's voices count, participate and lead on equal footing with men'.[1] The conference was scheduled to take place in the Holy See on International Women's Day, 8 March 2018. Chantal Götz, the conference organiser and managing director of Voices of Faith, was required to submit a complete list of speakers to the Vatican for approval in advance of the event. For four years, the annual Voices of Faith conference had taken place in the Vatican without any issue. In 2018 Cardinal Kevin Farrell, a Dubliner and then the most senior Irish person at the Vatican, opposed speakers on the conference programme without providing justification. McAleese and Ssenfuka Joanita Warry, an LGBT rights advocate in Uganda, were barred from attending the conference in the Vatican.[2]

The organising committee made the decision to move the conference to another venue. The Jesuit Curia, based outside the Vatican wall, offered their premises for the conference. The conference organisers invited McAleese to give the keynote address in a gesture of solidarity; she was originally scheduled to contribute to a panel discussion. McAleese delivered a powerful and passionate keynote address on 8 March 2018. Her speech demanded the equal inclusion of women in the full structures of the Catholic Church. During her speech, McAleese laid out clear reasoning on how the hierarchy of the Catholic Church operated from within a misogynistic and homophobic culture. Her speech gained global attention, and McAleese later described how 'Cardinal Farrell's intervention ensured that a routinely overlooked conference became the subject of huge international press interest.'[3] Undoubtedly, Farrell's decision generated much interest in the conference in the weeks before it was due to take place. However, it was McAleese's forthright attack on the misogynistic basis of the Church that garnered global interest. McAleese was best placed to address this subject as an experienced diplomat with an advanced comprehension of canon law.

Mary McAleese (née Leneghan) was born in Ardoyne, north Belfast, in 1951. She was the eldest of nine children, and her Catholic family witnessed much violence and hostility during the Troubles in Northern Ireland. McAleese described how Ardoyne 'became the area with the highest per capita incidence of sectarian murders and gained a reputation as a place apart'.[4] In her speech McAleese describes how education liberated many people 'out of poverty, out of powerlessness, and into opportunity'. Education undoubtedly liberated McAleese. She graduated from Queen's University Belfast with a first-class honours degree in law in 1973, and after a further year of study, she was called to the Northern Irish Bar in 1974. During her time at Queen's, McAleese's family was subjected to sectarian attacks both at their home and at her father's pub, the Long Bar on the Falls Road. With violence in the area mounting, her family moved to county Down.

McAleese practised as a barrister for one year before being appointed as Reid Professor of Criminal Law, Criminology and Penology at Trinity College Dublin, at the age of just 24, in 1975. In an article aptly titled 'A high-achieving Northern Catholic', journalist Catherine Cleary described how McAleese's 'research brought her to the attention of the media when she trenchantly criticised the criminal justice system, especially the largest prison in the State, Mountjoy, and the juvenile prison, St Patricks'.[5] In 1976 she married Martin McAleese, and the couple later had three children together: Emma, Justin and Sara-Mai. McAleese steadily became involved with progressive legal reform, including the Campaign for Homosexual Law Reform, which she co-founded with David Norris and others. McAleese remained committed to the Catholic Church, and in 1984, she was invited by Cardinal Ó Fiaich and Archbishop Ryan to be a Catholic Church delegate in the New Ireland Forum taking place at Dublin Castle. McAleese described how she 'raised with Archbishop Ryan the problem that if I was asked about Church teaching on LGBTI issues in a public forum, I would not be able to defend it. He simply said, "Did I ask you to?" The answer was "no", and so I went to the forum.'[6] In 1987 McAleese returned to Queen's

University to take up a position as Director of the Institute of Professional Legal Studies, and in 1995, she became the first female Pro-Vice Chancellor of the University.

In 1997 McAleese was Fianna Fáil's chosen candidate in the presidential election to succeed Mary Robinson. McAleese was opposed by four other candidates: Mary Banotti (Fine Gael); Adi Roche (Labour, Democratic Left, and the Green Party); Dana Rosemary Scallon (Independent); and Derek Nally (Independent). McAleese received a record majority of first preference votes and was inaugurated as the eighth President of Ireland on 11 November 1997. She became the first person from Northern Ireland or, indeed, from Ulster to occupy the Head of State role in Ireland. The theme of McAleese's presidency was Building Bridges, and she actively embraced both communities in Northern Ireland during her term as president. On 7 December 1997, less than one month after her inauguration, McAleese generated controversy when she received communion at Christ Church Cathedral in Dublin. The image of a Catholic woman receiving communion in an Anglican Cathedral caused much public debate in Ireland. The Catholic Archbishop of Dublin, Cardinal Desmond Connell, maintained that 'Catholics who receive Communion in a Protestant Church are engaging in a "sham" and a "deception".'[7] Taoiseach Bertie Ahern was quick to point out the irony of this reasoning, he noted that 'the Church was condemning an act of reconciliation and bridge-building between the denominations.'[8]

With her term of office coming to an end in 2004, media speculation about the next president began early that year. An *Irish Times* poll conducted in February 2004 showed that McAleese 'would receive overwhelming endorsement in all regions, age cohorts and social groups' in a presidential election.[9] With such a high satisfaction rating for McAleese as president, opposition parties did not put forward candidates against her bid for a second term in office. McAleese was returned for a second term unopposed. She was inaugurated on 11 November 2004. McAleese hosted Queen Elizabeth II to Ireland in May 2011. This was the first official visit of a British monarch to the country since independence and it was immensely successful; the *Irish Independent* declared the 'Queen's historic visit hailed as a massive success'.[10] McAleese served a total of 14 years as President of Ireland, until November 2011. In June 2013, an iconic bridge near Drogheda was renamed the Mary McAleese Boyne Valley Bridge, symbolising the success of McAleese's building bridges theme of her presidency.

In 2012 McAleese returned to study and received a master's degree and licentiate in canon law from the Pontifical Gregorian University in Rome. She then pursued a PhD in Canon Law at the Gregorian University's Faculty of Canon Law.[11] Her thesis focused on Children's Rights and Obligations in Canon Law. McAleese was due to defend her 500,000-word PhD thesis in an oral examination in 2018. In the months before her oral defence, she delivered her keynote address at the Jesuit Curia, a venue that she was familiar with. As a student, she had regularly attended supervisory meetings in that same building. When McAleese took the podium to deliver her address, she first thanked Götz and members of the Voices of Faith group for changing the venue to ensure 'that no woman's voice would be excluded on their watch'.[12] In her speech, McAleese directed a clear challenge to Pope Francis 'to develop a credible strategy for the inclusion of women as equals throughout the Church root and branch'.

Her speech traces the history of previous Popes on the question of the ordination of women priests in the Catholic Church. McAleese mentions Pope Paul VI, who commissioned a report on women in the Church on 3 April 1973. She describes the subsequent decision, not to introduce the ordination of women priests, as a tool used to lock women out of leadership and decision-making power within the Church. The *Declaration on the Question of Admission of Women to the Ministerial Priesthood* was authorised by Pope Paul VI and concluded that 'one cannot see how it is possible to propose the admission of women to the priesthood.'[13] The declaration was officially released on 15 October 1976, in honour of the feast of Saint Theresa. Such sentiments echo McAleese's assertions that the Catholic Church has simply marginally increased 'the visibility of women in subordinate roles'. McAleese's argument was clear, focused, and embedded in an insightful assessment of canon law and theological history.

McAleese's keynote address resonated with many people in Ireland. Four days after her speech, RTÉ's radio programme *Claire Byrne Live* commissioned a poll to assess how the public viewed her speech.[14] Over 1,000 people contributed to the survey, which found that 78 per cent agreed with McAleese's views. That same day, 12 March, a headline in *The Journal* announced that the 'Vast majority of people agree that Catholic Church is an "empire of misogyny".'[15] Members of the Catholic Church in Ireland spoke out in support of McAleese, including Iggy Donovan, an Augustine priest based in Fethard. In an interview for the Tipperary-based newspaper *The Nationalist*, Donovan stated his full support of McAleese's 'call for women to be ordained and [for] her right to express that view'.[16] Donovan noted that McAleese 'is highly qualified in canon law and theology. If it came to a boxing match most bishops would not be able to lay a glove on her in theology.'[17]

McAleese did face some condemnation for her speech from other members of the Catholic clergy. Brendan Hoban, a Catholic priest and a columnist, wrote his assessment of McAleese's speech in the *Western People*. In his full-page article, Hoban did not disagree with the sentiments expressed by McAleese, but it is telling that he commented on how 'the robust and angry tone of former President Mary McAleese's speech may have diverted somewhat from her message.'[18] A similar speech delivered by a man would possibly be described as passionate and powerful rather than with negative terminology of 'robust and angry'. Significantly, when Hoban expressed this same assessment to a female friend, 'her immediate response was that, in present circumstances and in past memory, women had every right to be angry.'[19] While Hoban's article was a veiled attack, others were more direct. Vincent Twomey, a priest and a retired professor of moral theology, was a panel member on Marian Finucane's Sunday radio programme when the issue of McAleese's speech was discussed. Twomey described how 'when I read the report from her speech, I found it, as a cleric, amusing; she was just over the top quite frankly.'[20] Finucane queried his reaction, and Twomey responded that McAleese 'is misusing her position as an ex-president. . . . It undermines the dignity of the office.'[21]

McAleese had previously faced this same argument: that as an ex-president she should remain silent on public matters. She had been criticised for backing the 2015 Marriage Equality referendum and for publicly supporting her son, Justin, who came out as a gay man during the referendum campaign. Journalist Bruce Arnold maintained that McAleese 'had broken the convention that former presidents don't get involved "on any matter that affects the public"'.[22] McAleese later responded to such criticism by saying, 'I firmly believe in freedom of speech as long as I have power of speech.'[23] She continues to be vocal, especially on matters relating to systemic problems within the structures of the Catholic Church, including its stance on LGBT rights.

After delivering her keynote address, McAleese became concerned about the World Meeting of Families, which was due to be held in Dublin in August 2018. The meeting, which is held every three years, was established by Pope John Paul II in recognition of the importance of marriage and the family. The Catholic organisers made a clear decision early in 2018 not to include LGBT families in this celebration. A booklet announcing the World Meeting of Families was amended in January 2018, removing all images of same-sex couples. Text was also deleted from the original booklet, which had noted that 'while the Church upholds the ideal of marriage as a permanent commitment between a man and a woman, other unions exist which provide mutual support to the couple. Pope Francis encourages us never to exclude but to accompany these couples also, with love, care and support.'[24]

Pope Francis announced his intention to visit Ireland as part of the World Meeting of Families. McAleese decided 'that one way of showcasing Ireland's egalitarian and inclusive attitude to families in advance of the papal visit would be to make the annual Gay Pride event into a family celebration'.[25] The Pride festival is celebrated in Dublin every June and was therefore scheduled to take place two months before the papal visit. McAleese suggested to her son Justin and to journalist Ursula Halligan that the theme of the 2018 festival should be 'We Are Family.' Justin and Halligan approached the Pride Committee, who instantly agreed. McAleese describes how 'the [Pride] festival was an outstanding success, with twice the anticipated number attending – mothers, fathers, grannies, grandads, babies in buggies toting their rainbow flags.'[26] Pope Francis's visit was not such a success; McAleese described it as 'a bit of a damp squib'.[27] McAleese was recipient of the inaugural Vanguard award at the Gaze LGBT film festival in Dublin on 5 August 2018, in recognition of her 'unwavering support for the advancement of the LGBT+ community'.[28]

McAleese returned to Rome in September 2018 for the oral defence of her PhD, as is the usual practice for many universities. On 28 September, McAleese successfully defended her thesis, in Italian, in front of three members of her examination panel. The *Irish Independent* pointed out that the 'three-person panel [was] (all male, of course).'[29] On 5 November 2019, McAleese delivered the annual Edmund Burke lecture at Trinity College Dublin. Her lecture, entitled 'The future of Ireland: Human rights and children's rights', called for 'a clear acknowledgment from the Catholic Church that the canon laws which constrict children's rights have now been overtaken by the [United Nations] Convention and our Constitution'.[30]

Mary McAleese remains a prominent voice demanding a thorough reform of the Catholic Church and the eradication of misogyny, anti-Semitism and homophobia within its structures. During the Root and Branch Synod, a lay-run international gathering, held at Bristol in September 2021, McAleese criticised Pope Francis for publication of a report from the Vatican's doctrinal office 'banning priests from blessing same-sex unions, on the grounds that God "cannot bless them"'.[31] McAleese addressed the synod on 10 September 2021, with her talk, 'No Synodality Without Freedom of Speech — Canon law must acknowledge the human rights of Church members.' In her talk, she was scathing of the report released from the Vatican in March 2021, describing how 'this was a document that never had to be written, but it was, and he [Pope Francis] authorized it. That tells me just how ultra conservative he really is.'[32]

Mary McAleese is currently Professor of Children, Law and Religion at the University of Glasgow. She has held numerous prestigious scholarships and fellowships including at Boston College, the University of Notre Dame and at St. Mary's University London. She has received many honorary doctorates including from the University of Otago, University of Aberdeen, Trinity College Dublin and the University of Ulster. McAleese's speech at the Jesuit Curia is a warning that 'The tidal wave is quickly approaching the Vatican walls', and her words are inspiring a movement seeking to reform the Catholic Church.

28. President Mary McAleese meeting with United States President Barack Obama, Áras an Uachtaráin, Dublin, 23 May 2011. Photograph by Pete Souza, Official White House Photographer, Creative Commons.

'The Israelites under Joshua's command . . . they circled Jericho's walls for seven days; they blew trumpets; and they shouted to make the walls fall down. We don't have trumpets, but we have voices, voices of faith, and we are here to shout to bring down our Church's walls of misogyny. . . .

At the second Vatican council, Archbishop Paul Hallinan of Atlanta warned his fellow bishops to stop perpetuating "the secondary place accorded to women in the Church of the twentieth century" and to avoid the Church becoming, in his words, "a latecomer in their social, political and economic development". . . .

Paul VI even commissioned a now long forgotten study on women in church and society. Those of us who were youngsters then, we surely thought that the postconciliar Church was well on the way to full equality for our 600 million female members. And yes, it is true that since the council, new roles and jobs have opened up to the laity, including women. But these have simply marginally increased the visibility of women in subordinate roles, including in the curia. They have added nothing to their decision-making power or their voice, because visibility and voice are not the same thing, and visibility without voice can actually reinforce one's silence. Remarkably, since the council, roles which were specifically designated as suitable for

264

the laity have been deliberately closed to women. I find this just totally perplexing. . . .

Back in 1976, we were told that the Church does not consider herself authorised to admit women to priestly ordination. This, of course, has served to lock women out of any significant role in the Church's leadership, doctrinal development, and authority structure since these have all been historically reserved to or filtered through ordained men. Yet, in divine justice, it seems to me that the very fact of the permanent exclusion of women from priesthood and all its consequential exclusions, that very fact should have provoked the Church's hierarchy to insist on finding innovative ways, radical ways, of including women's voices as of right, not in trickles of tokenism by careful tapping. . . .

Just imagine this normative scenario: imagine for a moment that as a result of this the Pope decides to call a synod on "Women in the Church" (some chance), and 350 male celibates turn up to advise the Pope on what women really want. That is how ludicrous our Church has become, because that is our system.

How long can the hierarchy sustain the credibility of a God who wants things this way, who wants a choice, wants a church, where women are invisible and voiceless in church leadership, in legal and doctrinal discernment, and decision-making but actually are expected to do all the hard work that keeps the Church going from generation to generation. . . .

Now this regrettable situation arises because the Catholic Church has long since been a primary global carrier of the toxic virus of misogyny. Its leadership has never sought a cure for that virus, though the cure is freely available. Its name is equality.

Down the 2,000-year highway of Christian history came the ethereal divine beauty of the Nativity, the cruel sacrifice of the Crucifixion, the hallelujah of the resurrection, and the rallying cry that wakens me up and gets me through the day each day of the great commandment to love one another. But, down that same highway came these man-made toxins of misogyny, of homophobia, to say nothing of shameful anti-Semitism, with their legacy of damaged and wasted lives and deeply embedded institutional dysfunction.

The laws and cultures of many nations and faith systems were also, of course, deeply patriarchal and excluding of women; many still are. But today the Catholic Church lags noticeably behind the world's advanced nations in the elimination of the discrimination against women, a disgrace for an organisation which claims to have been created by God or love in the universe. Worse still, because the

Catholic Church is, to quote Ban Ki-Moon, "the pulpit of the world", its overt patriarchalism acts as a very powerful brake on dismantling the architecture of homophobia and of misogyny, wherever they are found in the world.[33] There is an irony here, for education has been crucial, crucial, to so many of us; to the advancement of women in the world, it has been a *sine qua non*.

And for most of us – I imagine many of us here – the education which liberated us was provided by the Church's frontline workers, those wonderful people, clerical and lay, who have done so much to lift men and women and children out of poverty, out of powerlessness, and into opportunity. . . .

Today, we challenge Pope Francis to develop a credible strategy for the inclusion of women as equals throughout the Church root and branch, including in its decision making. A strategy with targets, with pathways, with outcomes, regularly audited, independently audited. I noticed Cardinal Farrell said that women's progress in the Church was a process. Well, we challenge them: start the process, get it going, put the fuel in the engine, hit the button, because the failure to include women as equals has deprived the Church of fresh and innovative discernment. It has consigned it to recycled thinking among a hermetically sealed, cosy, male clerical elite, regrettably often flattered by carefully chosen token lay people, among them women. . . .

At the start of his papacy, Pope Francis said, "We need to create still broader opportunities for a more incisive female presence in the Church."[34] These are words, which, regrettably I have to say, a church scholar described as evidence of Francis's magnanimity. Let us be very clear – at least let me be very clear – women's right to equality in the Church arises organically from divine justice. It does not and should not depend on ad hoc Papal benevolence, magnanimity. It is our right. . . .

Just four months ago, the Archbishop of Dublin, Diarmuid Martin, felt compelled to remark that the low standing of women in the Catholic Church is *the* most significant reason for the feeling of alienation towards the Church in Ireland today. Yet Pope Francis has said that women are more important than men because the Church is a woman. Holy Father, Holy Father, why not ask women if they feel more important than men in the Church? I certainly don't. . . .

Back in this hall in 1995, the Jesuit congregation asked God for the grace of conversion from a patriarchal church to a church of equals where women truly matter, because only that church is really worthy of Christ, and only such a church can credibly make Christ matter.

The time for that Church is now, Pope Francis; the time for change is now. Let me just finish with a line that might be familiar to you, from a very famous Irish poet, and it's so often used in the context of the Irish Peace Process, but it seems to me so relevant here today; it's from Seamus Heaney's "The Cure at Troy", where he says, . . .

> History says, Don't hope
> On this side of the grave.
> But then, once in a lifetime
> The longed-for tidal wave
> Of justice can rise up,
> And hope and history rhyme.

The tidal wave is quickly approaching the Vatican walls.'[35]

THIRTY ONE

Clare Daly

B. 1968

Speech on the Repeal of the Eighth Amendment to the Constitution
Dáil Éireann, Leinster House, Dublin

29 MAY 2018

'A ball and chain that dogged us all our adult lives.'

On 25 May 2018 the people of Ireland voted overwhelmingly in favour of repealing the Eighth Amendment to the Constitution. The Eighth Amendment prohibited abortion in Irish law and had then been in place for 35 years. This was the first opportunity in over three decades for Irish people to vote on the legal provision of abortion services. There was a large turnout at the polls, and 66.4 per cent voted in favour of repealing the Eighth Amendment and replacing the related text. The Irish Constitution would now include a section simply stating, 'Provision may be made by law for the regulation of termination of pregnancy.'[1] Four days after the referendum, time was allotted in Dáil Éireann for statements from the floor regarding the referendum result. During the five minutes allocated to her, Clare Daly, an Independents 4 Change TD, responded with a speech that captured the mood of people in Ireland at that time.

In her speech Daly described the immense wrongs that had been perpetrated against women who experienced crisis pregnancies and fatal foetal abnormalities under the terms of the Eighth Amendment. Daly acknowledged that campaigners had worked tirelessly for 35 years to support women in crisis situations, noting the work done by the Well Woman Centre, the Irish Family Planning Association, and the Abortion Support Network in the UK. Along with these groups, student activists attempted to support women who required access to abortion services. Ivana Bacik described how, as a student activist in the 1980s, she 'was taken to court and threatened with prison for distributing information to Irish women on where to access abortion'.[2] Daly also pays tribute to Ailbhe Smyth, who became a major force in achieving the repeal of the Eighth Amendment.

Daly's speech focuses on what she calls 'the beginning of the final phase', which began in 2012, on the twentieth anniversary of the X case.[3] In February 2012 the National Women's Council of Ireland (NWCI) held a meeting that 'highlighted the inaction by successive governments to legislate for the constitutional right to an abortion in life threatening pregnancies'.[4] Orla O'Connor, director of the NWCI, observed that the 'Supreme Court directed that legislation should be passed to allow women to end pregnancies when their lives are in danger' during the X case in 1992.[5] Consecutive governments had failed to introduce such legislation over the course of the following 20 years. This argument reinvigorated the pro-choice campaign in Ireland, and politicians faced escalated pressure to legislate for access to abortion services. Sociologist David Ralph attests that 'having languished on the political fringes for a considerable time, this was the year [2012] that the vexed question over what to do about Ireland's strict and—as it would transpire—at times fatally dangerous abortion ban moved decisively back centre stage.'[6]

In April 2012 Daly introduced the Medical Treatment (Termination of Pregnancy in Case of Risk to Life of Pregnant Woman) bill to the Dáil.[7] The bill, presented on behalf of Daly and two other TDs, Mick Wallace and Joan Collins, was an attempt to bring about the legislation proposed by the Supreme Court. If passed, legislation would allow for the termination of pregnancy if there was a substantial risk to the life of the pregnant woman. On 17 April, a full-page article appeared in the *Irish Times* that fundamentally changed the basis of the pro-choice campaign.

Journalist Kathy Sheridan interviewed four women about their experiences of travelling to the UK for abortions due to fatal foetal abnormalities. Jenny McDonald, Ruth Bowie, Amanda Mellet and Arlette Lyons made a courageous decision to be named and photographed for that *Irish Times* article. Sheridan described why the women chose to be identified and assessed the possible impact of this:

> Only hours before, each was still deciding whether to appear in this picture. Such is the silence and stigma surrounding their stories, the mere fact of revealing their real names and faces would most likely give them a place of sorts in Irish social history. The decision was not taken lightly. 'But we're just being hypocrites if we don't,' decided Ruth Bowie, 'What are we ashamed of?'[8]

The women described the circumstances through which they were forced to seek medical help abroad. All four women had planned pregnancies and were devastated when their foetuses were diagnosed as having 'an abnormality incompatible with life'.[9] Medical practitioners were not legally permitted to assist with terminations of pregnancy, and therefore the women travelled to hospitals in England to undergo procedures. The four women met for the first time just weeks before the *Irish Times* interview. They came together to form a support group, Terminations for Medical Reasons.

The second stage reading of Daly's bill was due to take place on 18 April 2012. Daly and the NWCI facilitated a meeting in Leinster House before the Dáil debate. McDonald, Bowie, Mellet, and Lyons met with TDs to share their experiences and discuss Daly's proposed bill. The four women were present in the public gallery during the Dáil's second reading of the bill when Daly proclaimed that:

> we are humbled to be moving this motion on the Bill on behalf of the 150,000 Irish women who have been exported from this country since the 1980s to access safe abortions in Britain, without adequate support, away from their families and friends and at significant financial cost, additional emotional trauma and stigma, and whose voices have been sidelined for decades and ignored.[10]

Daly's bill was voted down the following day, when only 20 TDs voted in favour of it as opposed to an overwhelming 111 votes against its introduction.[11] The four co-founders of Terminations for Medical Reasons appeared on the *Late Late Show* the following evening, 20 April. They were interviewed by Ryan Tubridy about the need for legislative reform to provide access to abortion. In her speech in this section, Daly is clear about the vast contribution these women made towards the eventual repeal of the Eighth Amendment. Their brave move to identify themselves changed the basis of the pro-choice campaign, when women were encouraged to share their stories about abortions.

In October 2012 a shocking case occurred that highlighted the urgent need for abortion legislation in Ireland. Savita Halappanavar and her husband, Praveen, lived in Galway and were expecting their first child. Halappanavar attended University Hospital, Galway, on 21 October complaining of severe back pain spreading to her lower pelvic area. She was 17 weeks pregnant. The following day, it was confirmed that there was 'an inevitable/impending pregnancy loss', and she was admitted to the hospital to manage the impending miscarriage.[12] Halappanavar's condition deteriorated over the coming days, and she became extremely ill. Halappanavar and her husband requested a termination, which was denied to them by the medical team, due to the legal implications of the Eighth Amendment. Without medical intervention, Halappanavar's blood became infected, and she died of severe sepsis on 28 October at the age of just 31.

When details of Halappanavar's death became known publicly, Ireland's restrictive laws became the focus of international media attention. In India, Halappanavar's country of origin, the *India Times* website carried the headline 'Ireland murders pregnant Indian dentist.'[13] The BBC announced on its web site, 'Woman dies after abortion request "refused" at Galway hospital'.[14] There was a public outcry in Ireland, and the tragic case undoubtedly caused many more people to question the ethics of the Eighth Amendment. On 14 November, the front page of the *Irish Times* was dedicated to Halappanavar's case under the headline 'Woman "denied a termination" dies in hospital'.[15] Thousands of people took to the streets across Ireland to protest against the Eighth Amendment in the wake of Halappanavar's death, including in protests outside government buildings.

Pro-choice campaigners established a five-year plan of action and continued to lobby government demanding the repeal of the Eighth Amendment. With such intense pressure, political opinion gradually began to sway. Ivana Bacik notes that 'the political momentum for change led to the establishment in 2017 of two processes to review the amendment: a citizens' assembly and a cross-party parliamentary committee.'[16] Both reviews recommended the repeal of the Eighth Amendment, which resulted in the announcement of a referendum by Taoiseach Leo Varadkar on 14 June 2017. On 9 March 2018, debate began on the Thirty-Sixth Amendment of the Constitution bill 2018 in the Dáil. Pro-choice activists immersed themselves in an intense campaign in the lead-up to the referendum. Undoubtedly, the most successful organisation was conducted by Ailbhe Smyth, Gráinne Griffin and Orla O'Connor through their umbrella group called Together For Yes. This group included 70 organisations from across Ireland who called for the repeal of the Eighth Amendment.

The three co-directors of Together For Yes had an impressive record of social justice campaigning. Smyth, a seasoned activist, had campaigned on all previous abortion referendums; she had been a member of the Strategic Executive of the successful referendum campaign for marriage equality in 2015 and had co-founded the Coalition to Repeal the Eighth Amendment. Griffin was a founding member of the Abortion Rights Campaign and had amassed much experience working with NGO and community organisations. O'Connor, as director of the NWCI, had played a key role in re-invigorating the pro-choice campaign in 2012 and had led numerous successful campaigns on behalf of women's rights.[17] Smyth described the effective strategy of their campaign, noting, 'from as early as 2013 activists were told women's personal stories about the Eighth Amendment coupled with clear medical information were the only way to fight the battle to come.'[18] This approach combined with the group's support of pro-choice politicians, including Daly, was highly effective as the referendum results testify.

The day before the polls opened for the repeal referendum on 25 May, street artist ACHES painted a mural of Savita Halappanavar on a wall in Portobello in Dublin city. Many people visited the mural and paid tribute to Savita after casting their votes.[19] By the time the results of the referendum were announced, the mural was encircled with flowers and notes. One note read, 'For Savita, you made us fight. Never again.'[20] The notes were later removed by Together For Yes members, to avoid weather damage. Digital images were taken to preserve the hundreds of messages, which were then sent to Savita's parents.[21] The image of Savita Halappanavar remains a powerful memory of the horrendous consequences of the Eighth Amendment on the lives of so many women and couples in Ireland. Clare Daly's speech in the Dáil marks a vital point in modern Irish history when, finally, women would be granted access to abortion.

The Health (Regulation of Termination of Pregnancy) Act 2018 passed through both houses of the Oireachtas and was signed into law by President Michael D. Higgins on 20 December 2018. The act allows for termination during the first 12 weeks of pregnancy. Other sections of the bill include provision for terminations after the 12-week term, if there is a risk to the life of the pregnant woman or if the foetus has not reached viability.[22] By October 2019 it was reported that over 300 General Practitioners (GPs) and 10 out of 19 maternity hospitals in Ireland were providing free and legal access to abortion in Ireland.[23]

Women in Northern Ireland remained in limbo in regard to abortion access. The 1967 abortion law in the UK did not extend to Northern Ireland. Stormont collapsed in January 2017, when the two main parties in the power-sharing agreement, Sinn Féin and the Democratic Unionist Party (DUP), split over a political disagreement. With Northern Ireland being governed through Westminster, Labour MP Stella Creasy proposed the decriminalisation of abortion in Northern Ireland in July 2019. The proposal was supported by 332 votes to 99. In October 2019, with Stormont still not restored, the law was passed to decriminalise abortion in Northern Ireland; it came into effect on 31 March 2020.

29. Savita Halappanavar mural by street artist ACHES, outside the Bernard Shaw Pub, Portobello, Dublin, 26 May 2018. Creative Commons.

'Yesterday, we were walking across Dublin and we met a Donegal man on a bicycle who was mad to talk. He said abortion had been an issue all his adult life and he could not believe it was over. He said he never wanted to hear the word again. I felt an enormous sympathy. What he said summed up exactly the way I felt about it myself. For so many, the weekend's vote was like an enormous weight being lifted. A ball and chain that dogged us all our adult lives was finally gone. I cannot believe that I am 50 years of age and it has taken this long. It has taken my daughter to come home for her first vote to get us here. For so many women, it represented so much. It is almost like society atoning for everything it has done to women in this country; atoning for how we stigmatised women faced with crisis pregnancies, the Magdalen laundries, the mother and baby homes, the shaming, the forced adoptions and the robbed identities about which we will hear later this afternoon. It still goes on.

The biggest sentiment behind the "Yes" vote and the question people asked most often was "Who am I to judge?" They said it was not their decision. So many people in our society have acknowledged that life is hard and that there are choices a lot of people have to make, including today, which they would really rather never having to make. It is not easy to parent alone in this State. It is not easy to raise a child or children with disabilities with the lack of support that is there. It is not easy to find out one is pregnant to a violent man. It is not easy, of course, to hear that one's much-wanted pregnancy has a fatal anomaly which is incompatible with life. As a society, we were never going to be able to end that pain, but we could make sure we did not add to it.

When Deputies Mick Wallace, Joan Collins and I introduced our legislation in 2012, only 20 Deputies voted with us. At that time, four incredible women went on the "Late Late Show". It was the first time people in this State openly identified themselves as having travelled for terminations. They were Amanda, Arlette, Jenny and Ruth who later founded the group Terminations for Medical Reasons. Is it not appalling that they and their colleagues had to lay bare their most appalling pain and tragedy in order to turn that into a social movement which changed history? They should not have had to do that. I am in awe of them and all of their colleagues who took part in the campaign. When we assembled here and Deputy Wallace moved the legislation on fatal foetal abnormalities, those women were in the Gallery. Afterwards, their hearts were broken that the House had voted against them again. There were people who travelled that day and there is probably someone who is travelling today also. We should not have compounded their pain but the fact that they stepped forward was huge.

It was not the beginning of the campaign. Some rewriting has taken place in that regard. However, it was the beginning of the final phase. We had the founding then of the abortion rights campaign and the first march for choice, which was the first openly pro-choice activity in the State. It was only after the march that, sadly, Savita died and the move to repeal gained a greater urgency. Many people came on board the repeal movement then and I am delighted they did. However, we should remember the time before the glory days when it was the Well Woman Centre, the Irish Family Planning Association and the Abortion Support Network in the UK which took in our women and girls and paid for their fares. If I had to name one person more than anyone else, it was Ailbhe Smyth, a giant of this movement who stood there when there was no glory to be had.

I acknowledge genuinely the role the Taoiseach and the Minister for Health, Deputy Harris, played albeit it took them a while to get there. . . . Let us be honest however and point out that politicians have not led on this issue. We have not even followed until recently.

This has been an uphill battle. A boulder has been pushed up a hill for decades and no one here was behind it. Let us be honest about it for once. No one was involved. In fact, a lot of people here were sitting on the boulder, making it even more difficult for those outside who wanted to push for change. Others, of course, decided to jump ahead and claim some of the glory once the boulder was at the top of the hill and about to go down the other side, even though they had done none of the pushing. I do not say that to score points, but to learn the lesson because there is going to be a next time. Perhaps we can learn something next time around. We need to move to enact the legislation. Even today, however, I have heard people trying to out-posture each other as to who will be the most radical, claiming we should cancel all holidays between now and forever and bring in legislation tomorrow or even yesterday. It is nonsense. Can we please cop on with the games, which are despicable?

My last point is for students and young people. I am proud of the student movement. I was one of those students years ago but we did not succeed in changing the world. I hope this generation will. The young people who mobilised and enfranchised their peers are the legends in this. I hope they make a better job of changing the world than we did.'[24]

THIRTY TWO

Elizabeth Coppin

B. 1949

Speech on how the Catholic Church can never pay for its sins
Oxford Union, Oxford University

28 FEBRUARY 2019

'The Catholic Church continue in their abusive treatment.'

Elizabeth Coppin (née Riordan) was committed to an industrial school in county Kerry at the age of just two. She spent her childhood and teenage years incarcerated in religious-run institutions, including three Magdalene Laundries where she was subjected to abuse and forced labour. The last Magdalene Laundry, run by the Sisters of Our Lady of Charity on Sean MacDermott Street in Dublin, closed in Ireland in 1996. The following year, Coppin walked in to a Garda Station in Kerry and filed an official complaint about the treatment she had received from 1964 to 1968. Although no action came from this initial complaint, Coppin continued on a legal course seeking justice and recognition for the abuse she endured. Her determined campaigning has had a positive influence on survivors of abuse in Irish religious institutions across the world. In 2019 Coppin was invited to participate in an Oxford Union debate on the motion 'the Catholic Church can never pay for its sins.' Her speech was honest, direct and passionate. This speech provides an insightful account of how the lives of women were impacted when they were incarcerated in state-endorsed institutions in Ireland and of the complex systems of redress they have been forced to endure.

Coppin was born on 21 May 1949 in Killarney, county Kerry. In 1951 she was committed to an industrial school, under orders to be held there until she reached her sixteenth birthday. She was committed by Listowel District

Court on the grounds that she was illegitimate and her mother could not care for her. Coppin spent her earliest years in an industrial school in Tralee, operated by the Sisters of Mercy. She describes how she 'was subjected to horrific emotional and physical abuse there by the nun in charge'.[1] Coppin remained in the industrial school until she reached 14 years of age, at which point she was transferred to St Vincent's Magdalene Laundry in Peacock Lane, Cork, operated by the Religious Sisters of Charity. Coppin recalled the fear she felt when she entered the Magdalene laundry: 'I was so scared. I had been always with children and babies. Seeing all these old women and hearing them crying out at night was terrifying.'[2] Coppin was forced to work unpaid in the laundry six days a week. Her living conditions were prison-like, existing in a small cell containing only a bed and a basin. The cell door was kept bolted, and the windows were fitted with bars. Coppin was 'forbidden to speak and was generally deprived of human kindness. She lived in conditions of deliberate deprivation, with inadequate food and heating.'[3]

The first Magdalene asylum in Ireland opened on Leeson Street, Dublin, in 1765. By the end of the nineteenth century, there were 22 asylums across the country. The asylums were originally established as philanthropic refuges for fallen or destitute women at risk of entering into prostitution. The name *Magdalene* asylums evoked the biblical figure Mary Magdalene, a prostitute who is redeemed. In the 1830s the running of the asylums was assumed by religious orders in Ireland. By the twentieth century Magdalene asylums in Ireland were mainly controlled by congregations of Catholic nuns. Such institutions were not confined to Ireland, and Magdalene laundries operated across the United Kingdom, in the United States, Canada and many sites across Europe.

The Irish asylums were not state funded, and the nuns operated commercial laundries, worked by mainly unpaid inmates, to fund their operation. The original aim of the institutions, to rehabilitate prostitutes or to shield others from this route, was soon forgotten. Women involuntarily entered Magdalene Laundries for numerous reasons and not simply, as is often assumed, because they were pregnant outside of wedlock. Many women on remand or probation were sent by an order of the court. Young women and children who were in abusive or neglectful households were often routinely incarcerated in the laundries or industrial schools. Numerous young women were transferred from industrial schools, as in Coppin's case. In his groundbreaking research on the history of Magdalene Laundries, James M. Smith describes how 'transferring women and children from the care of one Catholic religious congregation to another facilitated Ireland's architecture of containment.'[4]

Coppin spent two years at St Vincent's Magdalene Laundry before escaping in August 1966. She was soon apprehended by officers from the

Irish Society for the Prevention of Cruelty to Children (ISPCC) and taken to a different Magdalene Laundry, the Good Shepherd in Sunday's Well, Cork. The ISPCC, a society that originally operated under the auspices of the British National Society for the Prevention of Cruelty to Children (NSPCC), became an independent society in Ireland in 1956.[5] The society was established to protect the welfare of children; initially, the patrons were the President of Ireland, the Archbishop of Dublin, and the Church of Ireland and Catholic Primates of All Ireland.[6] Inspectors were appointed from the ranks of retired police and army personnel to oversee child welfare in the community. These inspectors were generally men and became known colloquially as cruelty men. The fact that Coppin was apprehended by cruelty men and taken to a Magdalene laundry highlights the role of the ISPCC in the incarceration of young women at this time. A Commission to Inquire into Child Abuse, established in 2000, published its findings after a nine-year investigation. The report, written by Justice Seán Ryan and known as the Ryan Report, found that 'the extent of the ISPCC involvement in committing children to industrial schools cannot be accurately ascertained but it can be stated as significant.'[7]

Coppin spent one year in the Good Shepherd laundry at Sunday's Well, where she was subjected to even worse treatment. While there, her hair was shorn, she was dressed in sackcloth and renamed Enda, a male name associated with the nun who mistreated her in the industrial school. In March 1967 Coppin was transferred to another Magdalene Laundry, also run by the Sisters of the Good Shepherd, St Mary's, in Waterford. During her time in these institutions, Coppin was never given information about when or, indeed, if she would be released. Smith notes 'that many women remained confined for life',[8] a fact of which Coppin was fully aware, and she became increasingly concerned that she would die in a Magdalene Laundry and be buried in a mass grave on its site.

Coppin was eventually released in April 1968, one month before her nineteenth birthday. Like many survivors of Magdalene institutions, she emigrated to the United Kingdom as soon as she could afford the fare. She moved to England in 1969, where she met Peter Coppin, and the couple married in 1973. Coppin stayed living in England, settling in Cambridgeshire with her husband and their two children. She remained traumatised by her early life. In 1997 and again in 1998, Coppin filed charges with An Garda Síochána. There was no outcome from these charges. In 1999 she launched civil proceedings with the High Court against the religious orders that managed the industrial school and the Magdalene laundries where she was held. The proceedings were struck out by the High Court on 23 November 2001 'on the ground of "inordinate and inexcusable" delay'.[9]

Coppin was determined to continue her pursuit of justice and to shed light on the abuse suffered by so many women and children incarcerated in Catholic institutions in Ireland. In 2002 she testified before the Commission to Inquire into Child Abuse. In 2005 she applied to the recently established Residential Institutions Redress Board, which decided on award payments to victims of industrial schools. Coppin accepted the award of payment, as she 'felt she had no choice but to do so'.[10] The payment was given without admission of liability from the religious congregations or from the Irish state.

In 2011 Coppin received hope that survivors of the Magdalene laundries would receive justice. In July the United Nations Committee against Torture (CAT) issued a report that included a damning statement about the Irish government's lack of action regarding survivors:

> The Committee is gravely concerned at the failure by the State party to protect girls and women who were involuntarily confined between 1922 and 1996 in the Magdalene Laundries, by failing to regulate and inspect their operations, where it is alleged that physical, emotional abuses and other ill-treatment were committed, amounting to breaches of the Convention. The Committee also expresses grave concern at the failure by the State party to institute prompt, independent and thorough investigations into the allegations of ill-treatment perpetrated on girls and women in the Magdalene Laundries.[11]

The CAT recommended that the Irish government immediately launch thorough, independent investigations into all complaints concerning the Magdalene laundries and where possible 'prosecute and punish the perpetrators with penalties commensurate with the gravity of the offences committed'.[12] Furthermore, the committee stressed that all survivors should be offered compensation and rehabilitation.

In response, the Irish government established an Inter-Departmental Committee to investigate the state's involvement with the Magdalene laundries. Coppin submitted a statement to the chair of the committee, Senator Martin McAleese, outlining details of the state's involvement in her forced detention. The voluntary group Justice for Magdalenes (JFM) submitted a report to McAleese along with supporting material of survivor testimonies, totalling 795 pages, and archival and legislative documentation, totalling 3,707 pages.[13] The committee headed by McAleese examined ten laundries operated by four Catholic orders: Sisters of Our Lady of Charity, Sisters of Mercy, Religious Sisters of Charity, and Sisters of the Good Shepherd. Coppin had spent time in three of the institutions examined.

The McAleese report was published in 2013: it reported that 10,000 women had spent time in the Magdalene laundries from the foundation of the Free State in 1922 until the closure of the final laundry in 1996.[14] Of this number, at least 26.5 per cent were incarcerated through facilitation by the state.[15] After the publication of this report, Taoiseach Enda Kenny addressed Dáil Éireann, issuing an unreserved apology: 'I, as Taoiseach, on behalf of the State, the Government and our citizens, deeply regret and apologise unreservedly to all those women for the hurt that was done to them and for any stigma they suffered as a result of the time they spent in a Magdalene Laundry.'[16] Many survivors of the Magdalene laundries were in the public gallery to witness a national apology for the wrongs they had experienced. Kenny summed up the mood of the country by saying, 'The Magdalene laundries have cast a long shadow over Irish life and over our sense of who we are.'[17]

The government established a Magdalene Laundries Restorative Justice Scheme in July 2013 headed by Justice John Quirke. Payments to survivors were determined by the length of time that a woman had spent in a Magdalene laundry. Coppin was awarded a payment through this scheme; the payment did not include an admission of liability. In order to receive payment, Coppin was required to 'agree in writing to waive any right of action against the State arising out of her admission to and work in the laundries'.[18] This was not the justice that Coppin sought. She wrote to the Minister for Justice and Equality, Alan Shatter, in December 2013, seeking more time to consider whether to accept these terms. Coppin also requested that the government address the human rights violations against survivors of Magdalene laundries. After further engagement with the Restorative Justice Implementation Unit of the Department of Justice and Equality, Coppin received the response that 'she either accept or reject the ex gratia payment.'[19] She accepted the payment on 21 March 2014 and signed the waiver but did not give up her campaign. When the government launched the Commission of Investigation into Mother and Baby Homes and Certain Related Matters in 2015, Coppin wrote to the related authorities, including the Minister for Children and Youth Affairs, Katherine Zappone.[20] Coppin sought an extension of their terms of reference to include an investigation into the Magdalene laundries. She did not receive a reply.

In 2017 the CAT considered a progress report, assessing what actions the Irish state had taken based on their recommendations. The UN committee 'expressed its deep regret that the State party had not undertaken an independent, thorough and effective investigation into the allegations of ill-treatment of women and children in the Magdalene laundries or prosecuted and punished the perpetrators'.[21] Reports of the state's failure to act in the interests of Magdalene survivors caused public concern. In response, a two-day event was organised by the voluntary group Dublin Honours Magdalenes on 5 and 6 June 2018. Two hundred and thirty survivors from around the globe gathered in Dublin, accompanied by over two hundred of their family members.[22] The women, including Coppin, were enthusiastically welcomed by crowds gathered on the streets of Dublin. Coppin later visited Áras an Uachtaráin, where her group was greeted by President Michael D. Higgins and Sabina Higgins.

In his speech to the survivors Higgins was clear that 'Ireland failed you. When you were vulnerable and in need of the support of Irish society and its institutions, its authorities did not cherish you, protect you, respect your dignity or meet your needs and so many in the wider society colluded with their silence.'[23] The landmark event was the basis for a documentary, *Coming Home: When Dublin Honoured the Magdalenes*.[24] Coppin features in the documentary and describes how 'It was very emotional going back to a country that treated you like nothing, like nobody.'[25] The following month, in July 2018, Coppin lodged an Individual Communication with the CAT, a procedure similar to court proceedings. Through this process, Coppin and her legal team submitted arguments and evidence that the Irish state was refusing to fully investigate her charges of torture and mistreatment during her time at Magdalene laundries.[26] The Irish government was given time to respond and submit their evidence against Coppin's claim. By this stage, Coppin had exhausted all routes to have her case investigated, including the Gardaí, the courts, redress bodies, and appeals to government ministers. The United Nations was her final hope.

Coppin was invited to address the Oxford Union Society, a debating society founded in 1823 and with a prestigious reputation. The Oxford Union has hosted significant speakers, including the Dalai Lama, Desmond Tutu, Mother Theresa and Malcolm X. Debates on current affairs held by the Oxford Union have been credited with influencing public thinking. In 1975 the motion 'This House would say yes to Europe' was carried by 493 ayes to 92 noes. Days before the referendum on Britain's entry into the EEC took place, the union's debate was broadcast and is credited with influencing the high yes vote. The debate on the motion 'This House believes the Catholic Church can never pay for its sins' was held on 28 February 2019 at 8.30 p.m. Three speakers were for the motion, including Coppin, Mitchell Garabedian, the lawyer who represented survivors of sexual abuse by Catholic clergy in Boston, and Thomas Reilly, the former Attorney General in Massachusetts who led the investigation. Two speakers were against the motion: Jay R. Feierman, a former psychiatric consultant to a treatment programme in New Mexico for clerical sexual offenders, and Marci Hamilton, academic director of CHILD USA, an organisation working to prevent child abuse.[27] After compelling speeches in defence of the motion, most notably Coppin's courageous account of her personal experiences and of her long struggle for justice, the motion was carried.

On 20 January 2020 the CAT issued a landmark decision, finding that they had 'full jurisdiction to decide Elizabeth Coppin's complaint alleging that Ireland has failed to investigate or to ensure accountability or comprehensive redress for the abuse that she suffered in three of Ireland's Catholic Church-run Magdalene Laundries'.[28] The announcement came in the wake of yet another delay in the publication of the Mother and Baby Homes report, which had been due on 7 January 2020.[29] Commentators suggested that the UN announcement would force the government to speed up publication.[30] On 9 September 2021 *Ireland and the Magdalene Laundries: A Campaign for Justice* was published, documenting the ongoing work of the Justice for Magdalenes group, including an examination of the Irish state's investigation processes.[31]

Elizabeth Coppin's case is ongoing as of 2021. Whatever the outcome, Coppin's campaign has given hope and recognition to hundreds of survivors of Magdalene laundries. As noted in the pages of the *Irish Examiner*, 'Even if Ms Coppin is not successful in her case, she will have done herself, and the hundreds of other survivors of the Magdalene Laundries, a great service by raising awareness, once again, of the horror of those institutions.'[32] Coppin's speech is testimony to her lively determination and steadfast resilience.

30. Elizabeth Coppin, March 2010. Photograph courtesy of Elizabeth Coppin.

'My name is Elizabeth Coppin, and I'm a survivor of Irish institutional abuse. I'm going to share with you some of my own life experiences as a ward of the Irish state. I am now approaching my seventieth year. I'm a wife, a mother, a grandmother, a trained nursery nurse, a qualified teacher, and a survivor and activist for civil liberties, specifically for the Magdalene women survivors. To gain these achievements in life was not an easy journey. I struggled, made great sacrifices, and with no thanks to the Catholic Church. In fact, it was in spite of the Catholic Church and their representatives, who had been placed in important positions of power to look after helpless children and women. The nuns were assigned to protect, care, and educate me; in fact, they abused me and violated my human rights, and they were funded by the Irish government. From the ages of two to eighteen plus, I was reminded constantly I was a nobody and would amount to nothing. I believe the Catholic Church can never pay for their sins.

The Catholic Church continue in their abusive treatment by *not* respecting survivors of their institutions today. They refuse to open our personal records, and the Irish government has said, we cannot instruct the religious to open the records they have on all survivors. These personal records are kept in the Catholic Church's archives. We have no knowledge of our childhood illnesses, diseases, the types of injections we received, or any information of hereditary illnesses. The few generic bits of information *I* received from the Church and State records are redacted, and the same applies for the majority of survivors today.

I was born in a county home in Killarney; illegal adoptions took place, and the children who were not adopted were sent to the industrial schools, and the majority of the mothers were sent to the Magdalene laundries. I was put into an industrial school and orphanage owned by the Catholic Church. The Irish government gave the nuns funding to oversee to our wellbeing and education. My education finished six weeks into my thirteenth birthday. Because of the sheer magnitude of abuse carried out in the industrial schools by the nuns – whipping with a leather strap, name calling, being swung around the room by my hair, starvation, scrubbing and sanding long corridors on my knees from the age of ten to eleven – I decided I would finish my life even though I was still a child. I set fire to myself by lighting paper and setting light to my clothes. I never received proper medical attention. I did not see a doctor or receive a painkiller. I was left to suffer the burns in sheer agony. From the age of fourteen years and ten months, until one month before my nineteenth birthday, I was trafficked to and arbitrarily detained in three different Magdalene laundries. This was approved by the Irish government.

We slaved in the laundries daily. I am very conscious I'm using the word *slave*. We never got a penny for our slave labour. Women died of old age in these laundries. Various types of abuse [were] inflicted on me: I was trafficked, arbitrarily detained, physical abuse, hard labour daily, starvation, a ritual of silence daily while slaving, using a pot instead of a toilet, mental abuse, and solitary confinement. I was forced to spend three days and nights in solitary confinement in a padded cell. I was wrongly accused of stealing someone's sweets. I wish I had. The nun in question unlocked this cell and pushed me inside; no words were spoken by either of us. I was alone and petrified. The floor was bare; there was no bed, no mattress, and no blankets or a chair. However, there was a tin plate with a slice of stale bread on it, also a tin mug filled with water, and a pot for my toilet. Can you imagine how anyone would feel in this situation, let alone a seventeen year old? I was scared, very frightened, and so alone. It was then it dawned on me that this was how my life was going to be forever: I would die in this laundry as other women had done. I decided to try and run away or I would grow old and die in here, which I did. Then they've taken me back, so now by agents of the State and the Church, the NSPCC, and they've brought me back to number two. In laundry number two, my name was changed; I was given the nun's name who abused me in the industrial school at an earlier age, and it was a man's name. My hair was shorn; the same slavery continued. I was eighteen years and eleven months when I was finally released from the third Magdalene laundry. All my childhood and teenage years were in the care of the abusive Catholic Church representatives.

I have been seeking justice since 1997, when I first tried to pursue criminal proceedings. I have tried to get my case heard on an international level. I can't bring any case against the Vatican because they have not signed the right treaties. Ireland is fighting to have my case thrown out of the UN; they have fought every step of the way. I believe the Catholic Church had and still have influential followers in places of power and will always escape justice. There was no hope given to me by these God-fearing representatives of the Catholic Church, only abuse, inhumane and degrading treatment. I agree wholeheartedly with this house: the Catholic Church can never pay for their sins. What the Church did to me has shaped my life and affected me beyond belief, but not in a good way. I struggle every day. Yes, perhaps we should practise forgiveness in day-to-day life, but for me I can never forgive because I can never forget. I feel I am in a very fortunate position today here in Oxford, to be given this opportunity by all of you to speak of some of my personal experiences and to be part of this debate. I mentioned at the beginning that I was always told I was a nobody, but now, from being here, I know I am a somebody.

Thank you, all.'[33]

THIRTY THREE

Catherine Connolly

B. 1957

Speech on the publication of the Mother and Baby Homes report
Dáil Éireann, Convention Centre, Dublin

13 JANUARY 2021

'The language of the patriarch and the three unwise men.'

The final report of the Commission of Investigation into Mother and Baby Homes was compiled on 30 October 2020; it was not made available to survivors until 12 January 2021, when the report was also distributed to TDs.[1] The following day, 13 January, Taoiseach Micheál Martin addressed Dáil Éireann with a statement on the report. He began by declaring that 'This detailed and highly painful report is a moment for us as a society to recognise a profound failure of empathy, understanding and basic humanity over a lengthy period.'[2] He formally apologised to survivors of Mother and Baby Homes 'on behalf of the Government, the State and its citizens'. Martin also appropriately recognised that those victims of institutionalisation had done 'nothing wrong'. In his address, Martin did not explain why publication of the final report had been delayed or refer to the unacceptable way the report was distributed to survivors.

Catherine Connolly was the Leas-Cheann Comhairle (deputy chairman) of Dáil Éireann during these initial statements and chaired the session. In the latter half of the session, Cheann Comhairle Seán Ó Fearghaíl assumed the chair, and Connolly made the final statement that day on the Mother and Baby Homes report. Her speech was well considered, detailed and at times heated. She was scathing about the government's mishandling of the release of the report and about its format. She was particularly critical of the three male politicians in charge of releasing the report – the Taoiseach; the Tánaiste, Leo Varadkar; and Roderic O'Gorman, Minister for Children, Equality, Disability, Integration and Youth – describing them as 'three unwise men'.

The Commission of Investigation into Mother and Baby Homes and Certain Related Matters was established by the Irish Government in February 2015 and tasked with providing a full account of what happened to women and children in these institutions from the foundation of the state in 1922 until the closure of the last home in 1998. During these years, unmarried pregnant women were sent to these institutions to have their babies; most of the women had no support from the child's father or their own families, and some had been impregnated through rape or incest. A pregnant unmarried woman was thought to bring shame on their families, and Mother and Baby Homes were therefore veiled in secrecy. In numerous instances, children born in Mother and Baby Homes were placed for adoption without the consent of their mothers.

The commission was established as a result of the work of historian Catherine Corless, whom Connolly praises in her speech.[3] Corless spent a number of years, at her own cost, researching babies who died at the Mother and Baby Home in Tuam, county Galway. The building, a former workhouse, was owned by Galway County Council, and the home was operated by a French order of Catholic nuns, the Bon Secours. Corless discovered the names of 798 children who died in the home between its establishment in 1925 and its closure in 1961. In 2012 she published an article in a local history society publication, *Journal of the Old Tuam Society*, detailing her findings.[4] She found that the majority of deaths were of children under three years of age. While Corless acknowledged that Ireland had a high infant mortality rate during this time, the horrendous figures she discovered proved the death rate was considerably higher at the Tuam home.

Corless later secured death certificates for the 798 children, but she could not trace burial records for 796 of these children. Through painstaking research of old maps and accounts from local people regarding bones discovered in the area of the home, Corless found that the bodies of children had been placed in a concrete underground container on the grounds of the home. This underground structure was later confirmed to be 20 chambers 'built within the decommissioned large sewage tank'.[5] Corless set up the Children's Home Graveyard Committee to erect a memorial to the children at the unmarked site. Corless' article in the local history journal did not reach a wide audience. She contacted journalist Alison O'Reilly to help disseminate her findings nationally. On 2 June 2014 O'Reilly's article was published in the *Daily Mail* detailing Corless' findings under the headline

'Mass septic tank grave "containing the skeletons of 800 babies" at site of Irish home for unmarried mothers'.[6] Not surprisingly, the article attracted wide attention, and the shocking discovery became known as the Tuam scandal. Two days after the newspaper article was published, Taoiseach Enda Kenny announced the establishment of a government enquiry into Mother and Baby Homes in Ireland. Then Minister for Children, Charlie Flanagan, clarified that 'it is fully recognised by me and my Government colleagues that we need to establish the truth.'[7]

The Commission of Investigation into Mother and Baby Homes was chaired by Judge Yvonne Murphy, who had previously led investigations into clerical abuse in Ireland. Murphy authored the final report along with the two other commission members: William Duncan, an international legal expert on child protection and adoption, and Mary E. Daly, Emeritus Professor of History at University College Dublin. The report totals 2,865 pages and includes details of 14 Mother and Baby Homes and a representative sample of County Homes. There were 56,000 unmarried mothers and approximately 57,000 children in these homes during the time investigated by the commission.[8] It was estimated that a further 25,000 women and many more children were held in County Homes not included in the report during that same time period. The report was due to be published in February 2020, but publication was delayed; the commission stated that the delay was due to '"complex issues" which had arisen in the course of its investigations'.[9] A new date of submission was scheduled for 26 June 2020, but this was delayed further when the commission cited problems due to the Covid-19 pandemic. The commission submitted their final report to the government on 30 October 2020. The report was held until January 2021 before the Cabinet approved it for release.

In her speech Connolly attacks the delay and manner in which the report was launched. As an independent TD for Galway West / South Mayo, Connolly was familiar with the Tuam scandal. Prior to her election as a TD, she served as a Galway City Councillor for 17 years. She was first elected to Galway City Council in June 1999 and served as Mayor of Galway from 2004 to 2005. She was elected as an Independents 4 Change TD in 2016 and re-elected in 2020 as an independent TD. Connolly was appointed as Leas-Cheann Comhairle on 23 June 2020; she was the first woman to hold the office of either Leas-Cheann Comhairle or Cheann Comhairle in the Dáil. Connolly is a trained barrister and a clinical psychologist, which gave her insight into the issues surrounding the launch of the Mother and Baby Homes report.

The main findings of the report were leaked to the media before survivors had access to them. On 10 January 2021, the *Sunday Independent* newspaper reported on the main findings. The article included the stark statistics that 9,000 children had died in the 18 institutions investigated by the commission. Philomena Lee described her dismay that key findings were printed by the media before survivors had 'sight of [the report] and digest[ed] its findings'.[10] She voiced her concern that this will 'undoubtedly add to the heartache and trauma of those directly affected'.[11] Lee was sent to the Sean Ross Abbey in Roscrea, a Mother and Baby Home included in the report, when she became pregnant at the age of 18. She gave birth to a son, who was taken from her and sent to America for adoption without her consent. Lee spent years searching for her son; her story was written by journalist Martin Sixsmith, and in 2013 it was adapted as an Oscar-nominated film, *Philomena*.[12] Lee has since been an active campaigner seeking redress for women and children affected by Mother and Baby Homes.

The leaking of the report most certainly caused trauma for survivors and relatives; a point made clear by Connolly in her speech. This error was compounded by the format in which the government launched the report to survivors. Due to Covid-19 restrictions then in place, survivors could not attend an event in person, and they were instead invited to an online webinar for the report launch. The webinar was described by journalist Hugh O'Connell as a dismal event: 'When some 500 survivors of mother and baby homes logged onto a webinar last Tuesday lunchtime, they were confronted with an image of two besuited men either side of an oval table in the Sycamore Room of Government Buildings. Officials wearing facemasks sat socially distanced behind the two men.'[13] The social distancing restrictions then in place meant that many survivors were watching a computer screen with no support from friends or family. This format was worsened by the fact that survivors were advised to download the large report electronically. Connolly was conscious that many survivors may never have access to a hard copy, and to make this point, she held her copy of the report up during her speech to show survivors.

Connolly was further disappointed by the quality of the report, describing the writing as 'unprofessional and amateurish in parts'. She pays tribute to the survivors who came forward to speak with the confidential committee as part of the investigation. It later transpired those testimonies given by 550 survivors were not included in the final report. The government requested that members of the commission should appear before an Oireachtas Committee to clarify their treatment of survivors' testimonies. This request was denied. On 2 June 2021, Mary E. Daly took part in an online Oxford University seminar to discuss the methodology and terms of reference of the Mother and Baby Homes report. Daly noted that testimonies from the confidential enquiry could not be integrated into the report for a number of reasons. She stressed that it 'would have taken hundreds of hours cross-checking, rereading against . . . the other evidence available from registers and so on'.[14] Daly's remarks in the seminar intensified the situation. Speaking on RTÉ's *Drivetime* radio programme, Connolly asserted that 'It is extraordinary that one of the commissioners chose to talk about this, to a college, a privileged one, in this manner but yet all three commissioners refused to come before an Oireachtas Committee.'[15] In the wake of the Oxford seminar, a group of leading historians called for the rejection of the report, as the enquiry 'made no attempt to be survivor-centred'.[16]

Connolly's speech was powerful in providing a background of what James M. Smith has termed 'the nation's architecture of containment'.[17] She listed the numerous reports commissioned in the past three decades by the Irish state. Connolly mentions the Ferns report in 2005, which was the result of an inquiry into 100 allegations of child sexual abuse made between 1962 and 2002 against 21 priests from the Diocese of Ferns in county Wexford.[18] The inquiry found that 'before 1990 there appears to have been reluctance on the part of individual Gardai to investigate properly some cases of child sexual abuse that came to their attention.'[19] The Ryan report in 2009 was the result of the first inquiry by the Commission to Inquire into Child Abuse in reformatory and industrial schools. In that instance, survivors gave evidence of physical and sexual abuse perpetrated against them in industrial schools. The report concluded 'that the Catholic religious orders that ran the schools colluded in covering up abuse, and the Department of Education responsible for monitoring them was "deferential and submissive" to the religious orders'.[20] The Murphy report, published in 2009, was chaired by Yvonne Murphy and investigated 'the handling by Church and State authorities of a representative sample of allegations and suspicions of child abuse against clerics operating under the aegis of the Archdiocese of Dublin over the period 1975 to 2004'.[21] Murphy chaired a further investigation into child sexual abuse allegations in Cloyne, with publication of that report in 2011.

In 2013, after the publication of the Magdalene report, chaired by Martin McAleese, Taoiseach Enda Kenny issued an official apology to survivors in Dáil Éireann. Such inclusions in Connolly's speech highlighted the depth of institutional abuse in Ireland since the foundation of the state. As Connolly observed, many apologies have been made by Taoisigh over the last three decades, but little action has been taken by government to offer survivors support or compensation or to appropriately honour the women and children who suffered institutional abuse.

Connolly was one of the first politicians to question the rigour of the final report of the Mother and Baby Homes commission, and her concerns were unfortunately prophetic. In the following weeks, once survivors, politicians and academics had time to fully assess the report, many issues with the content became evident. Eight survivors sought judicial reviews of the report. One of those seeking a review was Mari Steed, who was born in the Bessborough Mother and Baby Home in 1960. During her time at Bessborough, Steed was subjected to a Quadrivax vaccine trial. The commission's report determined that seven vaccine trials took place at the Mother and Baby Homes examined during the period from 1934 to 1973. The commission noted that 'It is clear that there was not compliance with the relevant regulatory and ethical standards of the time as consent was not obtained from either mothers of the children or their guardians and the necessary licences were not in place.'[22] Yet the report concluded that 'There is no evidence of injury to the children involved as a result of the vaccines.'[23] Steed claimed that her rights were damaged as she was unlawfully subjected to a vaccine trial, and she sought 'an opportunity to address the commission's finding[s]'.[24]

Minister O'Gorman attempted to suppress action to repudiate the report, claiming that 'the report cannot be set aside as it will form the basis of a redress scheme currently being finalised for those who were resident in these institutions.'[25] Legal experts and campaigners pointed out that the government did not need a report in order to initiate a redress scheme for survivors. Maeve O'Rourke, a human rights lawyer and co-founder of the Clann Project, described O'Gorman's assertion as an attempted 'smoke-screen'.[26] The Clann Project, established in 2015, is a joint initiative by the Adoption Rights Alliance, Justice for Magdalenes Research and the global law firm Hogan Lovells. Clann is led by O'Rourke and Claire McGettrick who strive to 'establish the truth of what happened to unmarried mothers and their children in 20th century Ireland'.[27] In an attempt to rectify the inaccuracies in the Mother and Baby Homes report, Clann sought contributions through the Adoption Rights Alliance website from those affected on matters 'of incorrect facts or misrepresentation of testimony or not including matters that should have been investigated'.[28]

The cases of two survivors, Philomena Lee and Mary Harney, were scheduled for 17 and 18 November 2021 at the High Court. Harney was born in Bessborough Home in 1949 and spent two and a half years there before being fostered. Her foster parents were neglectful, and she was sent to Good Shepherd Industrial School in Sunday's Well at the age of five and remained there until she reached 16.[29] Lee and Harney pursued legal challenges against the Minister for Children, the Government of Ireland, and the Attorney General, claiming that 'the Commission's final report does not accurately reflect their evidence to it and breaches their rights to fair procedures and natural and constitutional justice.'[30]

The government cannot reverse the harm that was done to Lee and Harney or other survivors of Mother and Baby Homes, but it has the power to give survivors a voice and to initiate an appropriate redress scheme. In his address to the Dáil on the report, the Taoiseach stressed that 'The Government accepts and will respond to all of the recommendations made by the commission, and this response will centre on four pillars of recognition, remembrance, records and restorative recognition.'[31] The 'three unwise men' would do well to listen again to Catherine Connolly's speech.

'This document I have to hand is what the report looks like. I hold it up to show survivors because they do not have it. It is the executive summary with the recommendations and one or two other things. Not a single survivor has it. I have it since yesterday, when it was put in the pigeonholes of Deputies.

I am not sure whether the media colluded with the Government or whether it was pure ignorance on their part but in every bulletin, they said the report would be made available to survivors prior to us getting it. That has not happened. I see two female Ministers of State are present here today and I would love them to address this point. No report was ever given to the survivors. They were invited to a webinar, where they were told the Government's version and then they were invited to download 3,000 pages.

The Government has had the report since October. Members were told there was urgency to the legislation that went through the Dáil and the Government forced the legislation through. That report has sat with it since then. The three wise men running the country - in a worse moment I might refer to the three unwise men - decided to hold on to that report, to still not give it to the survivors and to stand up here today with sweet words and tell us they are apologising.

I welcome the Taoiseach's apology but I will place it in perspective. I will deal with 21 years very quickly. In 1999, we had an apology from Bertie Ahern for the treatment of 15,000 to 20,000 children in industrial schools, reformatory schools and what were called orphanages.

I am only picking some of the reports across those 21 years. That apology was followed by the Ferns report in 2005 and the Ryan report in 2009, which found that sexual abuse was endemic in industrial and reformatory schools for boys. Girls and boys suffered emotional abuse on a great scale. In 2009, we had the Murphy report; in 2011, we had the Cloyne report; and in 2013, we had the Magdalen report of an interdepartmental committee, follow[ed] by a review under Mr. Justice Quirke and the establishment of an *ex gratia* scheme, which was subsequently found by the Ombudsman to have been maladministered. We then set up Caranua. It was appalling to name it that and call it a "new friend" when it was really the old enemy in disguise. This was followed in 2017 by a technical report on the Tuam site, since which nothing has happened. . . .

Leading to this report was Ms Catherine Corless's discovery through painstaking work paid for by herself that there were 798 bodies. What was the response from the Sisters of Bon Secours at the time through Ms Terry Prone, the organisation's PRO? It was that not a single bone would be found and that not a single child would be found. There was a longer press release from the organisation. . . .

I look at this report and struggle for words, but I owe it to the survivors to find words. The Government has heaped abuse on abuse through the manner in which this subject has been addressed. . . . My trust is stretched, and if I am just a Deputy, how does the Government think the survivors who were sitting in on the webinar yesterday were left feeling when the Government's language and the language of the media told them that they had the report when they did not? The language of the patriarch and the three unwise men continues to tell women what is good for them and, indeed, the men who spent time in these homes.

Regarding this report, I will pay tribute to the survivors who came forward. Deputy Kelly mentioned a figure of more than 1,000. It has been difficult for us all to come to terms with this report quickly, but there were not 1,000. Rather, just over 500 came forward to the confidential committee and told their stories. My experience is that people who spent time in institutions rarely talk about it. . . .

The story jumps off the pages - the role of the church, the priest and the county council. Indeed, the Tuam home distinguishes itself by being one of the worst in the country, and although the county council was not actively involved, the home was under its control. It was also under the control of the county manager, who took an active role. There was even a policy there whereby if the woman got pregnant a second time, she was destined for the Magdalen laundry, not the mother and baby home. Can the Taoiseach imagine that? Listen to what I am saying about the county manager being actively involved.

The women tell a story in this report of rape and sexual assault. Nearly 12% of the women in the homes were under 18 years of age. Some were as young as 12. However, the commission found that there was no evidence that they were forced by the church or the State. It is incomprehensible to draw that conclusion or the many other conclusions I have great difficulty with based on the testimonies of the women when they told their stories. The priest jumps off the page. Solicitors jump off the page. GPs who phoned the doctors and priests jump off the page. Some of the sexual abuse was carried out by family members, including cousins and uncles, and priests. All of that is set out in this report, but according to the commission's conclusions, there was no evidence of compulsion. Either we believe the women or we do not. If we do not, then we are adding to their hurt and their fear that they would not be believed. I will use my few minutes in this debate to say that I absolutely believe the survivors who have come forward despite these difficult memories. The commission tells us that there was no evidence of compulsion or forced adoption. All of the evidence given confirms there was.

I would like the Taoiseach to have dealt with this issue in a more nuanced manner in his contribution. I do not expect him to have read all of the report - none of us could have in the time allowed - but the inconsistencies in it are nothing short of shocking. The writing is unprofessional and amateurish in parts and there are inconsistencies in how people are referred to. Sometimes they are called "people", sometimes they are called "witnesses", sometimes they are called "other witnesses", sometimes they are called "a woman", sometimes they are called "a survivor". There is no consistency. If something bad was said, the narrative sought to balance it by finishing on a positive note. . . .

The spin continues as regards the way this report was undertaken. That spin came from the then Taoiseach in 2017, which the current Taoiseach is continuing with today. . . . The powers that be were the church, with politicians playing a subservient role. I will use the county council in Galway as an example because it jumps off the pages. It held its meetings in the home. The absence of records and the appalling mortality rate were known at the time, but the Taoiseach is saying now that we are all responsible. I am not responsible. My family is not responsible. The people I know are not responsible. Those least responsible were those put into the homes. The Taoiseach should not stand here today and expect me to listen to him with patience when he tells us that society did that. It was done by a society composed of the powerful against the powerless. As with the old distinction between public and private medicine, if someone had the money to pay and came from a middle-class family, she was treated differently. She paid her way and did not spend as long in the home.

. . . I find the report's narrative disturbing. I accept the Taoiseach's apology. I would like to see it being accompanied by meaningful action, including swift redress, and learning from the debacle of the Magdalen redress scheme and Caranua. . . .

I hope this is the start of a truly meaningful debate and action where language means something and the Government actually listens to the people on the ground and never, ever repeats a webinar or the leaking of a report so it can control the narrative. It is simply disgraceful.'[32]

NOTES

INTRODUCTION

1. For example, Charles Philips, *Specimens of Irish Eloquence* (New York, 1820); Charles Philips, *Irish Eloquence: The Speeches of the Celebrated Irish Orators, Philips, Curran and Grattan* (Philadelphia, 1833).
2. Reflected in titles such as T. D. Sullivan, *Speeches from the Dock; or, Protests of Irish Patriotism* (New York, 1904).
3. Richard Aldous, *Great Irish Speeches* (London, 2007).
4. Ibid., p. xxii.
5. Angela Bourke et al. (eds), *The Field Day Anthology of Irish Writing, Volume 5: Irish Women's Writings and Traditions* (Cork, 2002), p. 59.
6. The Parliament of Northern Ireland was created under the Government of Ireland Act 1920 and sat from June 1921 until it was disbanded in 1972.
7. Aldous, *Great Irish Speeches*, p. 10.
8. Mary Robinson, *Everybody Matters: A Memoir* (London, 2012), p. 145.

CHAPTER I – PARNELL

1. *Census of Scotland 1881*: Report Vol. II, pp xxiv, 326–35, 362–71.
2. Paul Bew, *Ireland: The Politics of Enmity, 1789–2006* (Oxford, 2007), p. 568.
3. Noel McLachlan, 'Davitt, Michael', in *Dictionary of Irish Biography* (hereafter *DIB*) (www.dib.ie).
4. *Celtic Monthly*, May, June, and July 1880.
5. Margaret Ward, 'Historical overview', in Anna Parnell, *The Tale of a Great Sham*, Dana Hearne (ed.) (Dublin, 2020), p. xv.
6. 'Mr. Parnell in Sligo', *Nation*, 29 Nov. 1879.
7. Sonja Tiernan, *Eva Gore-Booth: An Image of Such Politics* (Manchester, 2012), p. 14.
8. Marie O'Neill, 'The Ladies' Land League', in *Dublin Historical Record* 35:4 (1982), p. 123.

9. Ward, 'Historical overview', p. xvi.

10. Ibid.

11. Detailed records of eviction forms completed by members of the Ladies' Land League are held in the National Library of Ireland, Dublin. For example, see Ms 17,714, which includes 100 forms relating to evictions in counties Cavan, Clare, Kildare, Longford, Mayo, Monaghan, Roscommon, Tyrone and Westmeath relating to the year 1881.

12. O'Neill, 'The Ladies' Land League', p. 124.

13. McCabe was elevated to Cardinal on 27 Mar. 1882.

14. O'Neill, 'The Ladies' Land League', p. 125.

15. John Redmond took over as leader of the Irish Parliamentary Party in 1900.

16. 'Bill to further amend law relating to occupation and ownership of land in Ireland', 19th-Century House of Commons Sessional Papers, CH Microfiche Number: 87.12, *ProQuest UK Parliamentary Papers*, https://parlipapers.proquest.com/parlipapers/docview/t70.d75.1881-056880?accountid=14700, accessed 19 Apr. 2021.

17. Bill Power, *Mitchelstown Through Seven Centuries* (Cork, 1987), p. 76.

18. House of Commons Debate, 20 August 1881, vol 265 cc552–76, *Parliament UK*, https://api.parliament.uk/historic-hansard/commons/1881/aug/20/class-iii-law-and-justice, accessed 16 Apr. 2021.

19. Margaret Ward, 'Parnell, Anna Mercer (Catherine Maria)', in *DIB*.

20. Ibid.

21. Margaret Ward, 'Parnell, Fanny Isabel', in *DIB*.

22. *Ilfracombe Chronicle*, 23 Sep. 1911, as cited in Lucy Keaveney, 'Media reports on tragic death of Anna Parnell', *WordPress.com*, https://luighseachblog.wordpress.com/2016/04/10/media-reports-on-tragic-death-of-anna-parnell-september-1911/, accessed 19 Apr. 2021.

23. *Ilfracombe Chronicle*, 30 Sep. 1911, as cited in Keaveney, 'Media reports on tragic death of Anna Parnell'.

24. National Library of Ireland, Dublin, 'The Tale of a Great Sham', a history of the Land League by Anna Parnell, with some associated letters from Miss Parnell to Miss H. Molony, 1909–11, Ms 12,144.

25. Dana Hearne, 'Updated introduction', in Anna Parnell, *The Tale of a Great Sham*, Dana Hearne (ed.) (Dublin, 2020), p. xxxi.

26. Department of Housing, Local Government and Heritage, 'Charles Stewart Parnell monument', *National Inventory of Architectural Heritage*, https://www.buildingsofireland.ie/buildings-search/building/50010557/charles-stewart-parnell-monument-oconnell-street-upper-parnell-street-dublin-dublin, accessed 19 Apr. 2021.

27. *Irish Examiner*, 15 Sep. 2021.

28. *Glasgow Herald*, 30 Aug. 1881.

29. Ibid.

CHAPTER 2 – MORISON

1. With thanks to historian Dorothy Page for her detailed research and talk on Harriet Morison at Toitū Otago Settlers Museum, Dunedin, on 11 April 2021, which provided a foundation for this section.

2. The census taken the previous year records a total population of 22,376 in Dunedin city, of which 1,378 were Irish born; 898 of whom were women. 'Results of a census of the colony of New Zealand', 5 Apr. 1891, *Statistics New Zealand*, www3. stats.govt.nz/historic_publications/1891-census/1891-results-census/1891-results-census.html, accessed 5 Aug. 2021.

3. Morison is recorded as being from Donegal on the Archives New Zealand, 'Passenger Lists, 1839–1973', Record Number 162, Immigration Date 21 Nov. 1874, *FamilySearch*, https://familysearch.org/ark:/61903/1:1:FS1W-W3V, accessed 27 Apr. 2021. Although she is noted as being born in Derry by Melanie Nolan and Penelope Harper, 'Morison, Harriet Russell', *Te Ara: The Encyclopedia of New Zealand*, https://teara.govt.nz/en/biographies/2m57/morison-harriet-russell, accessed 27 Apr. 2021.

4. Including in the *Evening Star*, 13 Apr. 1892; *Otago Daily Times*, 13 Apr. 1892; *Western Star*, 16 Apr. 1892; and *Patea Mail*, 25 Apr. 1892.

5. Barbara Brookes, *A History of New Zealand Women* (Wellington, 2016), p. 117.

6. Ibid., p. 113.

7. Ibid., p. 123.

8. 'Ten reasons why the women of New Zealand should vote', *New Zealand History*, https://nzhistory.govt.nz/media/photo/ten-reasons-for-vote, accessed 23 Apr. 2021.

9. Melanie Nolan and Penelope Harper, 'Dunedin Tailoresses' Union: 1889–1945', *New Zealand History*, https://nzhistory.govt.nz/women-together/dunedin-tailoresses-union, accessed 23 Apr. 2021.

10. Brookes, *A History of New Zealand Women*, p. 126.

11. Ibid., p. 127.

12. Ibid., p. 128.

13. The votes were 15 in favour and 17 against. *Feilding Star*, 10 Sep. 1891.

14. *Evening Star*, 7 Sep. 1891.

15. *Poverty Bay Herald*, 20 Apr. 1892.

16. *Evening Star*, 13 Apr. 1892.

17. Dorothy Page, 'Women's suffrage: The Dunedin story', in *Otago Settler News* 130 (Spring 2016), p. 3.

18. In 1896 Anna Stout became the first National Council of Women vice-president. Stout, who was born in Dunedin to Scottish parents, was most aware of the difficult campaign for women's suffrage in Britain. While living in England from 1909 to 1912, Stout became a significant ally of the Women's Social and Political Union then at their height of suffragette militancy. Anna was married to Sir Robert Stout.

19. *Evening Star*, 29 Apr. 1892.

20. The number of women who enrolled to vote in the general election on 28 November 1893 was 109,461.

21. However, women in New Zealand would not be entitled to stand for election to parliament until the passing of the Women's Parliamentary Rights Act in 1919.

22. The Suffrage Petition is digitised and fully searchable and is hosted by *New Zealand History*, https://nzhistory.govt.nz/politics/womens-suffrage/petition, accessed 30 Apr. 2021.
23. Figures quoted from Brookes, *A History of New Zealand Women*, p. 129.
24. *Auckland Star*, 20 Aug. 1920.
25. *Evening Star*, 20 Aug. 1925; *Stratford Evening Post*, 20 Aug. 1925.
26. *Poverty Bay Herald*, 20 Apr. 1892.

CHAPTER 3 – MARKIEVICZ

1. For an incisive assessment of Markievicz's gradual conversion to Irish nationalism see, Lauren Arrington, *Revolutionary Lives: Constance and Casimir Markievicz* (Princeton, 2016).
2. Senia Pašeta, 'Markievicz, Constance Georgine Countess Markievicz Gore-Booth', in *Dictionary of Irish Biography* (hereafter *DIB*) (www.dib.ie).
3. For example, George Sigerson's talk 'England's penal system', *Donegal News*, 3 Feb. 1912.
4. The male dominance of the society is evident from the board elections in 1909: Denis Gwynn (president); Mr P. J. Nolan (treasurer); Mr O. G. Fisher (correspondence secretary). The only woman to be elected was to the position of record secretary, a Mrs McHugh.
5. Founded by Douglas Hyde in 1893.
6. A plaque commemorating this meeting now adorns the building.
7. See Agnes O'Farrelly's speech in this volume.
8. For example, 'Girls to boycott soldiers', *Irish Independent*, 29 Mar. 1909; 'Irishwomen and nationality', *Donegal News*, 3 Apr. 1909; 'Where the Irish women scored', *Munster Express*, 3 Apr. 1909.
9. Constance de Markievicz, *Women, Ideals and the Nation: A Lecture Delivered to the Students' National Literary Society* (Dublin, 1909). National Library of Ireland, Dublin, pamphlet volume AA17502.
10. See Anna Parnell's speech in this volume.
11. For a critical contemporary biography of Maud Gonne see, Trish Ferguson, *Maud Gonne* (Dublin, 2019).
12. Hanna Sheehy Skeffington, 'Constance Markievicz – Stray memories and reflections', *Irish Press*, 9 Feb. 1940.
13. Margaret O'Callaghan and Caoimhe Nic Dháibhéid, 'MacBride, (Edith) Maud Gonne', in *DIB*.
14. 'Countess Markievicz as Joan of Arc', photography by Roe McMahon, 1914. NPA POLF200, NLI.
15. *An Phoblacht*, 16 Jul. 1932.
16. This issue is addressed by Theresa, 6th Marchioness of Londonderry in her speech 'Ulster will not let herself be cut adrift' in this volume.
17. James Connolly, *The Re-Conquest of Ireland* (Dublin, 1917), p. 243. This pamphlet was written by Connolly on 6 October 1913 and published by the Dublin press Maunsel the year after his execution. Connolly dedicated Chapter Six to the

299

plight of woman. The full text is available through CELT, University College Cork's electronic texts project, https://celt.ucc.ie//published/E900002.002.html, accessed 19 Feb. 2021.

18. 'Proclamation of Independence', *Government of Ireland*, www.gov.ie/en/publication/bfa965-proclamation-of-independence/, accessed 12 Mar. 2021.

19. For more information about Cumann na mBan, see Agnes O'Farrell's speech in this volume.

20. Mary McAuliffe and Liz Gillis, *Richmond Barracks 1916:We Were There: 77 Women of the Easter Rising* (Dublin, 2016).

21. See Mary MacSwiney's speech in this volume for more information on the Anglo-Irish Treaty and the 1922 general election.

22. Markievicz, *Women, Ideals and the Nation*.

CHAPTER 4 – LONDONDERRY

1. The Ulster Women's Unionist Council archives are held in the Public Records Office of Northern Ireland (hereafter PRONI), D1098.

2. PRONI, 'Introduction: Ulster Women's Unionist Council Papers', November 2007, *nidirect*, www.nidirect.gov.uk/sites/default/files/publications/ulster-women-unionist-council-papers-d1098.pdf, accessed 2 Dec. 2020.

3. Ruth Taillon and Diane Urquhart, 'Women, politics and the state in Northern Ireland, 1918–66', in Angela Bourke et al. (eds), *The Field Day Anthology of Irish Writing:Volume 5* (Cork, 2002), p. 353.

4. Diane Urquhart (ed.), *The Papers of the Ulster Women's Unionist Council and Executive Committee, 1911–1940* (Dublin, 2001), p. xii.

5. Referred to as Lady Londonderry throughout.

6. Taillon and Urquhart, 'Women, politics and the state in Northern Ireland', p. 353.

7. A term coined by MP John Bright, who opposed Gladstone's Home Rule bills.

8. Rachel E. Finley-Bowman, 'An ideal unionist: The political career of Theresa, Marchioness of Londonderry, 1911–1919', in *Journal of International Women's Studies* 4:3 (2003), pp 15–29.

9. H. Montgomery Hyde, *The Londonderrys:A Family Portrait* (London, 1979), p. 63.

10. The National Portrait Gallery, Photographs Collection, 'T. M. The King & Queen & House Party at Mount Stewart', taken by Mrs Albert Broom (Christina Livingston), NPG x196926.

11. *Belfast News-Letter*, 24 Jan. 1911.

12. Ibid.

13. 'Lady Londonderry', *Globe*, 24 Jan. 1911.

14. 'Ulster Unionist Women: Address by Lady Londonderry', *Irish Independent*, 24 Jan. 1911; 'Ulster Women's Unionist Association', *Dublin Daily Express*, 25. Jan. 1911.

15. Finley-Bowman, 'An ideal unionist', p. 17.

16. Draft Constitution of the Ulster Women's Unionist Council, Jan. 1911, as cited in Urquhart, *The Papers of the Ulster Women's Unionist Council*, p. 215.

17. PRONI, 'Minute book of the UWUC Executive Committee', 28 Jan. 1919, D1098/1/3.

18. PRONI, Lady Londonderry, *My Visit to Antrim*, 20 Sept. 1913, D2846/1/2/7.

19. Officially established as the Ulster Volunteer Force (UVF) in January 1913, a paramilitary organisation to resist the introduction of home rule in Ireland.

20. The 1638 National Covenant was signed by the people of Scotland in protest against King Charles I's right to decide how the Scottish Church should be governed.

21. PRONI, 'Ulster Solemn League and Covenant', 28 Sep. 1912, D877/28.

22. With thanks to Margaret Ward for raising this point.

23. PRONI, 'The Ulster Women's Unionist Council Declaration on Home Rule', 28 Sep. 1912, D1892/81. The Women's Declaration is fully searchable for individual signatures of women, including Lady Londonderry's own signature, through digitised imagery at *nidirect*, www.nidirect.gov.uk/services/search-ulster-covenant, accessed 4 Dec. 2020.

24. PRONI, 'About the Ulster Covenant', *nidirect*, www.nidirect.gov.uk/articles/about-ulster-covenant, accessed 4 Dec. 2020.

25. PRONI, 'Speech of Lady Londonderry', UWUC Annual Report of 1919, 28 Jan. 1919, D1098/1/3, as cited in Finley-Bowman, 'An ideal unionist', p. 24.

26. Diane Urquhart, 'Political herstories', June 2000, *BBC*, www.bbc.co.uk/northern ireland/schools/agreement/society/support/soc1_c021.shtml, accessed 7 Dec. 2020.

27. The South Africa Act 1909 saw the foundation of the Union of South Africa in May 1910, unifying the British colonies of the Cape, Natal, Transvaal and Orange River headed by Prime Minister Lois Botha.

28. PRONI, Belfast, 'Speech by Lady Londonderry at a meeting in Belfast for the purpose of forming an Ulster Women's Unionist Association', 23 Jan. 1911, D2846/1/2/2.

CHAPTER 5 – HINCHEY

1. Sheridan Harvey, 'Marching for the vote: Remembering the woman suffrage parade of 1913', *Library of Congress*, https://guides.loc.gov/american-women-essays/marching-for-the-vote, accessed 20 Aug. 2020.

2. 'Took 60 cups o' tea for as many votes', *New York Times*, 5 Sep. 1915.

3. Lara Vapnek, 'Hinchey, Margaret (1870–1944), suffragist and labor leader', *American National Biography*, www.anb.org.

4. The other three co-founders were fellow immigrant garment workers: Rose Schneiderman from Poland; Clara Lemlich from the Ukraine; and Mollie Schepps, a Jewish immigrant. Annelise Orleck, *Common Sense and a Little Fire: Women and Working-Class Politics in the United States, 1900–1965* (Chapel Hill, 2017), pp 87–113.

5. Primary sources related to the Triangle Factory Fire – including the trial transcript, victim and witness statements as well as supplemental resources – are held in the Kheel Center for Labor-Management Documentation and Archives at Cornell University, New York. https://trianglefire.ilr.cornell.edu/index.html, accessed 25 Aug. 2020.

6. A complete list and details of those who died was compiled by Michael Hirsch for the Kheel Center. https://trianglefire.ilr.cornell.edu/victimsWitnesses/victimsList.html, accessed 25 Aug. 2020.

7. Orleck, *Common Sense and a Little Fire*, p. 96.

8. Caryn E. Neumann, 'Woman Suffrage Party (WSP)', in Peter R. Eisenstadt and Laura-Eve Moss (eds), *Encyclopedia of New York State* (New York, 2005), p. 1,709.

9. The meeting convened between 29 Nov. and 5 Dec. 1913.

10. Jane Addams was awarded the Nobel Peace Prize in 1931, the first American woman to achieve that honour. Helen Ring Robinson was the first female State Senator of Colorado and the second female Senator in the United States; she was elected in 1912.

11. Sections from Hinchey's speech were included in a celebratory publication after women's suffrage was achieved in the USA. Ida Husted Harper (ed.), *The History of Woman Suffrage: Volume V 1900–1920* (New York, 1922), p. 365.

12. The Child Labor Society was a private organisation founded in 1904 to promote children's rights and protect them from child labour. The society's name is spelt here using the original American version.

13. 'She uses wit to win vote', *New York Call*, 13 Jun. 1915, as cited in Liam Hogan, 'Margaret Hinchey: Immigrant, labour leader, suffragette', in *Old Limerick Journal* 53 (Winter 2018), p. 16.

14. 'Margaret Hinchey tells of Wilson', *New York Times*, 5 Feb. 1914.

15. Letters between Hinchey and O'Reilly are contained in the Schlesinger Library, Radcliffe Institute, Harvard University, Cambridge, MA, 'Papers of the Women's Trade Union League and Its Leaders, Collection V: Leonora O'Reilly Papers'.

16. 'Margaret Hinchey comes to talk suffrage', *Daily Missoulian*, 22 July 1914.

17. The Indian Citizenship Act was enacted on 2 June 1924, granting citizenship to Native Americans born in the United States. Their right to vote remained governed by state law. It would take until 1957 before Native Americans were granted full voting rights nationally. 'Indian Citizenship Act', *Library of Congress*, www.loc.gov/item/today-in-history/june-02/, accessed 28 Aug. 2020.

18. For further reading on these connections, see Tara M. McCarthy, 'Woman suffrage and Irish nationalism: Ethnic appeals and alliances in America', in *Women's History Review* 23:2 (2014), pp 188–203.

19. 'Suffragists form a trench brigade', *New York Times*, 27 June 1915.

20. *New York Times*, 5 Sep. 1915.

21. Schlesinger Library, Radcliffe Institute, Harvard University, Cambridge, MA, 'Papers of Margaret Foley and Helen Elizabeth Goodnow', reference MC 404.

22. *New York Times*, 8 Sep 1915.

23. Mary Harris Jones, *The Autobiography of Mother Jones*, Mary Field Parton (ed.) (Chicago, 1925), p. 50.

24. Alan Singer, 'Jones, Mary Harris ("Mother Jones")', in *Dictionary of Irish Biography* (www.dib.ie).

25. *New York Times*, 7 Oct. 1916.

26. *New York Tribune*, 6 Oct. 1916.

27. *Gaelic American*, 27 Oct. 1917.

28. In reality this did not give African American women across the United States a vote; they were subjected to restrictive state laws prohibiting many from voting. The majority of Black women would only secure a vote in America when the Voting Rights Act was introduced in 1965.

29. 'A vote for women', *United States Senate*, www.senate.gov/artandhistory /history/ minute/A_Vote_For_Women.htm, accessed 7 Jul. 2020.

30. Meredith Tax, *The Rising of the Women: Feminist Solidarity and Class Conflict, 1880–1917* (New York, 1980), pp 174–6.

31. As cited in Hogan, 'Margaret Hinchey', p. 19.

32. 'Working women ask Coolidge's aid', *New York Times*, 18 Jan. 1926.

33. Hogan, 'Margaret Hinchey', p. 19.

34. 'Coolidge sees duty to women workers', *New York Times*, 19 Jan. 1926.

35. Albany, the capital city of New York State.

36. Those campaigning against granting women the vote, the anti-suffrage movement.

37. *Erin go Bragh* is an anglicisation of *Éire go Brách*, meaning Ireland to the end of time.

38. The 'Big Six' was the nickname of Christy Mathewson, the New York Giants' legend (major league baseball).

39. George B. McClellan Jr served as mayor of New York from 1904 until 1909.

40. *New York Times*, 5 Feb. 1914.

CHAPTER 6 – O'FARRELLY

1. The name of the organisation directly translates into English as the *Women's Council*, although the term used by members is the *Irish Women's Council*.

2. Founded in Dublin on 11 November 1913.

3. For more information, see Lady Londonderry's speech in this volume.

4. *Irish Independent*, 26 Nov. 1913.

5. Margaret Ward, *Unmanageable Revolutionaries: Women and Irish Nationalism* (London, 1995), p. 90.

6. National Library of Ireland, Dublin, 'Manifesto of the Irish Volunteers', 25 Nov. 1913, Ms 11396.

7. Ibid.

8. 'The Volunteers', *Sinn Féin Weekly*, 29 Nov. 1913.

9. Ward, *Unmanageable Revolutionaries*, p. 92.

10. *Irish Volunteer*, 18 Apr. 1914, p. 2, *Military Archives*, www.militaryarchives.ie/ ma/ ma/datafiles/pdf/1914.04.18%20-%20Vol%201%20No%2011%20The%20Irish% 20Volunteer_2.pdf, accessed 26 Feb. 2021.

11. Francis Phillips was secretary and vice-president of the Cashel Sinn Féin branch.

12. See Mary McAuliffe, 'Cumann na mBan founded in Dublin', *RTÉ*, www.rte.ie/ centuryireland/index.php/articles/cumann-na-mban-founded-in-dublin, accessed 25 Feb. 2021.

13. 'Cumann Na mBan Constitution', 1913, *South Dublin County Libraries*, http:// source.southdublinlibraries.ie/handle/10599/10463, accessed 25 Feb. 2021.

14. The provisional committee was Mrs John MacNeill, Mrs Wyse Power, Madame O'Rahilly, Miss Agnes O'Farrelly, MA, Mrs Tuohy, Mrs MacDonagh O'Mahony and Miss Gavan Duffy, BA.
15. 'Defence of Ireland fund', *Freemans Journal*, 21 Apr. 1914.
16. 'A new organisation', *Irish Independent*, 3 Apr. 1913.
17. Through Stopford Green's activities, a shipment of a thousand rifles to arm the Irish Volunteers was successfully landed at Howth in Dublin on 26 July 1914. See William Murphy, 'Green, Alice Sophia Amelia Stopford', in *Dictionary of Irish Biography* (hereafter *DIB*) (www.dib.ie).
18. *Irish Independent*, 5 May 1914.
19. Ibid.
20. *Irish Independent*, 6 May 1914.
21. Ibid.
22. 'Letter to editor', *Irish Independent*, 8 May 1914.
23. Bureau of Military History, 1913–21, 'Statement by Miss Louise Gavan Duffy' (joint secretary of Cumann na mBan Dublin 1914), p. 2, *Military Archives*, www. militaryarchives.ie/collections/online-collections/bureau-of-military-history-1913-1921/reels/bmh/BMH.WS0216.pdf#page=3, accessed 25 Feb. 2021.
24. Due to her anti-recruitment activities during World War One, Somers' mother was sacked from her position as postmistress in Dalkey, county Dublin. Somers wrote under the Irish version of her name 'Lasarfhiona Ní Shamhraidin'. Patrick Maume, 'Somers, Elizabeth', in *DIB*.
25. *Irish Volunteer*, 17 Oct. 1914.
26. Ward, *Unmanageable Revolutionaries*, p. 103
27. Ibid.
28. 'Woman's work: In the national cause', *Irish Volunteer*, 18 Apr. 1914, p. 2, as cited in Margaret Ward, *In Their Own Voice: Women and Irish Nationalism* (Dublin, 2001), pp 38–41.

CHAPTER 7 – GORE-BOOTH

1. Esther Roper (ed.), *The Prison Letters of Countess Markievicz* (London, 1987), p. 48.
2. Patrick Pearse, *Collected Works of Pádraic H. Pearse: Political Writings and Speeches* (Dublin, 1916), p. 87.
3. National Library of Ireland (NLI), Dublin, 'Surrender notice signed by Pearse, Connolly and MacDonagh', 29 Apr. 1916, Ms 15,000 (2).
4. 'Statements concerning civilian deaths in the North King Street area of Dublin, between 6 p.m. April 28 and 10 a.m. April 29, 1916', in Roger McHugh (ed.), *Dublin 1916* (New York, 1966), pp 220–39.
5. Roper, *The Prison Letters of Countess Markievicz*, p. 24.
6. Ibid.
7. For more detail on this case, see Hanna Sheehy Skeffington's speech in this volume.
8. NLI, 'Letter from EGB to Hanna Sheehy Skeffington', May 1916, Ms 33,605 (1).

9. NLI, 'Article on Francis Sheehy Skeffington by Eva Gore-Booth', Ms 22,654.
10. Ibid.
11. Ibid.
12. See Karl Spindler, *Gun Running for Casement*, trans. W. Montgomery (London, 1921).
13. Parliamentary Archives, Houses of Parliament, London, 'The case of Roger Casement; A confidential report', 21 July 1916, Lloyd George Papers, E/9/4/12.
14. Eva Gore-Booth, *Broken Glory* (Dublin, 1918).
15. Ibid., p. 7.
16. Ibid., p. 14.
17. Including 'To Constance – In prison' and 'To C. M. on her prison birthday', in *Broken Glory*, pp 10–11.
18. James Connolly was a committed socialist and trade unionist; his many campaigns helped workers in America, Britain and Ireland. One of the greatest influences on Connolly was Keir Hardie, originally a miners' leader in Ayrshire. Fergus A. D'Arcy, 'Connolly, James', in *Dictionary of Irish Biography* (www.dib.ie).
19. Roper, *The Prison Letters of Countess Markievicz*, pp 42–53.

CHAPTER 8 – SHEEHY SKEFFINGTON

1. Margaret Ward, *Hanna Sheehy Skeffington: Suffragette and Sinn Féiner: Her Memoirs and Political Writings* (Dublin, 2017), p. 144.
2. J. F. Byrne, *Silent Years: An Autobiography* (New York, 1953), p. 139.
3. Margaret Ward, *Fearless Woman* (Dublin, 2019), p. 233.
4. For more information on Skinnider's life, see Mary McAuliffe, *Margaret Skinnider* (Dublin, 2020).
5. See Agnes O'Farrelly's speech in this volume.
6. British National Archives, Kew, 'Report on anti-militarist meeting held at Beresford Place by Patrick J. McCarthy Constable 36G', 23 May 1915, Colonial Office Record Series Vol. 1, Dublin Castle Special Branch Files, CO 904/215/408.
7. Ibid.
8. Ibid.
9. *New York Times*, 5 Oct. 1915.
10. National Library of Ireland, Dublin, 'Francis Sheehy Skeffington', Ms 22,654. See Eva Gore-Booth's speech in this volume.
11. Details of the enquiry were printed in *1916 Rebellion Handbook* (Dublin, 1917).
12. Hanna Sheehy Skeffington, 'A pacifist dies' (Dublin, 1916), in Roger McHugh (ed.), *Dublin 1916* (London, 1966), pp 276–88.
13. Esther Roper (ed.), *The Prison Letters of Countess Markievicz* (London, 1987), p. 29.
14. Arthur Mitchell and Pádraig Ó Snodaigh (eds), *Irish Political Documents, 1916–1949* (Dublin, 1985), p. 42.
15. Éamon de Valera, *Ireland's Case Against Conscription* (Dublin, 1918).
16. For further details, see Sonja Tiernan, '"No Conscription Now! Or after the harvest": Women and anti-conscription in Ireland and England', in Oona Frawley (ed.), *Women and the Decade of Commemorations* (Bloomington, 2021), pp 107–23.

17. Hanna Sheehy Skeffington, *British Militarism As I Have Known It* (Tralee, 1946).
18. 'Women teachers case', *Irish Press*, 6 Mar. 1946.
19. Maria Luddy, 'Skeffington, (Johanna) Hanna Sheehy-', in *Dictionary of Irish Biography* (www.dib.ie).
20. US National Archives, Washington DC, 'Hanna Sheehy Skeffington speech', Department of Justice, National Archives Record Group No 60, Case File Number 9848-10204, as cited in Ward, *Hanna Sheehy Skeffington*, pp 169–72.

CHAPTER 9 – MACSWINEY

1. TD is an abbreviation of Teachta Dála, a member of the lower house of the Irish Parliament.
2. *Irish Times*, 11 Sep. 2021.
3. 'Parliament (Qualification of Women) Act', *UK Parliament*, www.parliament.uk/about/living-heritage/transformingsociety/electionsvoting/womenvote/parliamentary-collections/nancy-astor/parliament-qualification-of-women-act/, accessed 16 Dec. 2020.
4. Patrick Maume, 'MacSwiney, Terence James', in *Dictionary of Irish Biography* (hereafter *DIB*) (www.dib.ie).
5. 'Muriel and Mary MacSwiney give evidence before US Commission on Ireland', 13 Dec. 1920, *RTÉ*, www.rte.ie/centuryireland/index.php/articles/muriel-and-mary-macswiney-give-evidence-before-us-commission-on-ireland, accessed 11 Mar. 2021.
6. *The American Commission on Conditions in Ireland: Interim Report* (London, 1921), p. 9, *Cork City Council*, www.corkcity.ie/en/cork-public-museum/learn/online-resources/2019-20-55report-interim-the-american-commission-on-conditions-in-ireland-british-edition-1921.pdf, accessed 12 Mar. 2021.
7. M. A. Hopkinson, 'Collins, Michael', in *DIB*.
8. Dáil Éireann debate, Vol. T, No. 7, 20 Dec. 1921.
9. Dáil Éireann debate, Vol. T, No. 15, 7 Jan. 1922.
10. Ibid.
11. Dáil Éireann debate, Vol. S2, No. 3, 2 Mar. 1922.
12. 'Proclamation of Independence', *Government of Ireland*, www.gov.ie/en/publication/bfa965-proclamation-of-independence/, accessed 12 Mar. 2021.
13. 'Mary MacSwiney', *Irish Press*, 9 Mar. 1942.
14. 'Miss Mary MacSwiney; Irish republican extremist', *Belfast Newsletter*, 9 Mar. 2021.
15. *Irish Times*, 11 Sep. 2021.
16. Ibid.
17. Dáil Éireann debate, Vol. T, No. 8, 21 Dec. 1921.

CHAPTER 10 – WYSE POWER

1. 'Constitution of the Irish Free State (Saorstát Eireann) Act, 1922', *Irish Statute Book*, www.irishstatutebook.ie/eli/1922/act/1/enacted/en/print, accessed 23 Mar. 2021.

2. William Murphy and Lesa Ní Mhunghaile, 'Power, Jennie Wyse', in *Dictionary of Irish Biography* (hereafter *DIB*) (www.dib.ie).

3. Michael Laffan, 'Griffith, Arthur Joseph', in *DIB*.

4. Biographical details from William Murphy and Lesa Ní Mhunghaile, 'Power, Jennie Wyse', in *DIB*.

5. Dáil Éireann debate, Vol. 18, No. 8, 23 Feb. 1927.

6. Ibid.

7. 'Constitution of the Irish Free State'.

8. Caitriona Beaumont, 'Women, citizenship and Catholicism in the Irish Free State, 1922–1948', in *Women's History Review* 6:4 (1997), p. 570.

9. Ibid.

10. Department of Justice, 'Report of the Inter-Departmental Committee to establish the facts of State involvement with the Magdalen Laundries', 5 Feb. 2013, *Government of Ireland*, www.gov.ie/en/collection/a69a14-report-of-the-inter-departmental-committee-to-establish-the-facts-of/, accessed 23 Mar. 2021.

11. Saorstát Éireann, *Juries Bill, 1927*, p. 28.

12. The law was examined under the 1937 Irish Constitution, then in place.

13. Conor Hanly, 'Why were women absent from Irish juries for 50 years?', *RTÉ*, 19 Feb. 2020, www.rte.ie/brainstorm/2020/0219/1116230-ireland-women-juries/, accessed 23 Mar. 2021.

14. Murphy and Ní Mhunghaile, 'Power, Jennie Wyse', in *DIB*.

15. *Irish Independent*, 7 Jan. 1941.

16. *Irish Press*, 6 Jan. 1941.

17. *Nationalist and Leinster Times*, 20 Dec. 1991.

18. Seanad Éireann debate, Vol. 8, No. 14, 30 Mar. 1927.

CHAPTER 11 – PARKER

1. Brendan Lynn, 'Introduction to the electoral system in Northern Ireland', *Conflict and Politics in Northern Ireland*, https://cain.ulster.ac.uk/issues/politics/election/electoralsystem.htm, accessed 18 Mar. 2021.

2. 'Mr. Devlin's Flapper Bill', *Belfast Telegraph*, 16 Nov. 1927.

3. See Theresa Londonderry's speech in this volume.

4. Yvonne Galligan, 'Women MPs from Northern Ireland: Challenges and contributions, 1953–2020', in *Open Library of Humanities* 6:2 (2020), p. 20, doi: http://doi.org/10.16995/olh.591.

5. Ibid.

6. Ian Aitken, 'Stormont suspended', *Guardian*, 25 Mar. 1972.

7. 'Dehra Parker', in Angela Bourke et al. (eds.), *The Field Day Anthology of Irish Writing, Volume 5* (Cork, 2002), pp 363–5.

CHAPTER 12 – PATTERSON

1. David Bleakley, *Saidie Patterson: Irish Peacemaker* (Belfast, 1980), p. 12.

2. Ibid., p. 23.
3. Ibid., p. 31.
4. Ibid., p. 34.
5. *Northern Whig*, 2 Feb. 1940.
6. Ibid.
7. Bleakley, *Saidie Patterson*, p. 39.
8. Ibid.
9. *Belfast Telegraph*, 22 Feb. 1940.
10. Bleakley, *Saidie Patterson*, p. 40.
11. Labour Party, *Report of the Thirty-Ninth National Conference of Labour Women, Spanish Hall, Winter Gardens, Blackpool, May 29, 30 and 31, 1962* (London, 1962).
12. 'Peace Award recipients', *World Methodist Council*, https://worldmethodistcouncil.org/recipients/, accessed 30 Mar. 2021.
13. 'Peace heroine's bitter blow', *Birmingham Post*, 14 Sep. 1977.
14. Bleakley, *Saidie Patterson*, pp 34–5.

CHAPTER 13 – CHENEVIX

1. *Irish Times*, 5 Mar. 1963.
2. Including the *Irish Independent*, 26 July 1951; *Evening Herald*, 25 July 1951; *Irish Press*, 26 July 1951; *Evening Echo*, 25 July 1951; *Irish Examiner*, 26 July 1951.
3. *Irish Independent*, 26 July 1951.
4. Siobhán Marie Kilfeather, *Dublin: A Cultural History* (Oxford, 2005), p. 93.
5. Frances Clarke, 'Chenevix, Helen Sophia', in *Dictionary of Irish Biography* (hereafter *DIB*) (www.dib.ie).
6. Diarmaid Ferriter, 'Larkin, Delia', in *DIB*.
7. Clarke, 'Chenevix, Helen Sophia'.
8. The founding member countries were Belgium, Cuba, Czechoslovakia, France, Italy, Japan, Poland, the United Kingdom and the United States.
9. 'R090 – Equal Remuneration Recommendation, 1951 (No. 90)', *International Labour Organisation*, www.ilo.org/dyn/normlex/en/f?p=1000:12100:::NO:12100:P12100_INSTRUMENT_ID:312428, accessed 6 May 2021.
10. *Evening Echo*, 25 July 1951.
11. Margaret Ayres, 'Equal pay for women: Words not deeds?', in *Saothar* 36 (2011), p. 89.
12. As cited in Sylvia Walby, *Globalization and Inequalities: Complexity and Contested Modernities* (London, 2009), p. 391.
13. For example, Helen Chenevix, 'Women in local government', in *The Irish Housewife*, 1946, p. 34, and 'In memory of Louie Bennett', in *The Irish Housewife*, 1959, p. 34.
14. *Roscommon Herald*, 12 Apr. 1952.
15. *Irish Independent*, 26 Jul. 1951.
16. Ibid.
17. Diarmaid Ferriter, '"I was not a human being": A history of Irish childhood', *Irish Times*, 19 Jan. 2019.

18. Clarke, 'Chenevix, Helen Sophia'.
19. *Irish Independent*, 5 Mar. 1963; *Evening Herald*, 5 Mar. 1963; *Irish Press*, 5 Mar. 1963; *Irish Times*, 5 Mar. 1963.
20. *Evening Herald*, 7 Mar. 1963.
21. *Irish Times*, 5 Mar. 1963.
22. The extract from Chenevix's speech presented here has been taken from a number of sources, including Donal Nevin (ed.), *Trade Union Century* (Cork, 1994), pp 199–200; *Evening Echo*, 25 July 1951; and *Irish Press*, 26 July 1951. Speech reproduced courtesy of Deirdre Mannion, Irish Congress of Trade Unions.

CHAPTER 14 – CONDELL

1. Limerick was the first city in Ireland to appoint a mayor, a right granted by Prince John, Lord of Ireland, on 19 December 1197. Paddy Hoare and Denis M. Leonard, *Limerick: An Appreciation* (Limerick, 1992), p. 1.
2. For example, the possibility of having President Kennedy visit Wexford was raised by Sir Anthony Esmonde TD during a Dáil Éireann debate, Vol. 196, No. 8, 3 Jul. 1962.
3. Ian McCabe, 'JFK in Ireland', in *History Ireland* 1:4 (Winter 1993), p. 42.
4. There was a quota of compulsory landings at Shannon airport for transatlantic flights until Minister of Transport Martin Cullen brokered a deal that phased out this requirement by 2008. Denis Staunton, 'Airlines welcome phasing out of Shannon stopover', *Irish Times*, 12 Nov. 2005.
5. Dáil Éireann debate, Vol. 204, No. 2, 3 Jul. 1963.
6. John F. Kennedy Presidential Library and Museum (hereafter JFK Library), Boston, 'The Fitzgerald Family Bible, Gift of Thomas A. Fitzgerald Jr', Accession number MO 78.224.
7. 'Limerick's persistent lady', *Irish Independent*, 15 Jun. 2013.
8. O'Malley went on to become a pioneering minister for education in 1966. Patrick Maume, 'O'Malley, Donogh', in *Dictionary of Irish Biography* (hereafter *DIB*) (www.dib.ie).
9. 'U.S. President's visit', *Limerick Leader*, 25 May 1963.
10. Ibid.
11. JFK Library, 'Oral history interview by Joseph E. O'Connor with Frances Condell', 31 July 1966, Limerick, Series 1: 1964–2012.
12. Ibid.
13. 'Racecourse site inspected', *Limerick Leader*, 24 Jun. 1963.
14. 'Another sister will join presidential party', *Limerick Leader*, 26 Jun. 1963.
15. There are conflicting accounts of the numbers attending the Limerick reception. In her interview for JFK Library, Condell notes the number in attendance as 60,000, which is the number given here.
16. Patrick Bouvier Kennedy, Jackie and John F. Kennedy's son, was born five weeks prematurely on 7 August 1963 and died just 39 hours later.
17. Ryan Tubridy, *JFK in Ireland: Four Days That Changed a President* (London, 2010), p. 240.

18. 'Historic visit', *Limerick Chronicle*, 29 Jun. 1963.

19. De Valera's mother, Catherine Coll, emigrated from Bruree, Limerick, to the United States in 1879. Ronan Fanning, 'de Valera, Éamon', in *DIB*.

20. JFK Library, 'Remarks of the President, Greenpark Racecourse, Limerick', 29 June 1963, Speech Files, Box 43, President's Office Files.

21. The University of Limerick Special Collections (hereafter ULSC), Limerick, 'Letter from Ambassador McCloskey to Frances Condell', 10 July 1963, The Frances Condell Papers, reference IE 2135 P3.

22. ULSC, 'Letter from President John F. Kennedy', 22 July 1963, The Frances Condell Papers.

23. Ibid.

24. Rachael Kealy, 'Frances Condell: Limerick's first female mayor', *Limerick Life*, 19 Oct. 2016.

25. ULSC, The Frances Condell Papers.

26. This paragraph in *Limerick Chronicle*, 29 Jun. 1963.

27. President Kennedy was then in West Germany, where he delivered his now famous 'Ich bin ein Berliner' speech.

28. John Francis Fitzgerald, known as Honey Fitz, was John F. Kennedy's maternal grandfather. Honey Fitz was an American politician and the son of Thomas Fitzgerald from Bruff, county Limerick. In 1938 Honey went to Limerick to trace his ancestors. Tubridy, *JFK in Ireland*, p. 239.

29. Footage and text of this speech from 'Mayor Frances Condell's welcome to John F Kennedy 1963', *Limerick's Life*, https://limerickslife.com/john-f-kennedy/, accessed 14 Feb. 2020. Text of speech reproduced courtesy of Sharon Slater, *Limerick's Life*.

CHAPTER 15 – DEVLIN

1. Also referred to as Bernadette Devlin McAliskey after her marriage in 1973.

2. *Irish Examiner*, 23 Apr. 1969.

3. *Strabane Chronicle*, 26 Apr. 1969.

4. Bernadette Devlin, *The Price of My Soul* (London, 1969), p. 39.

5. Ibid., p. 73.

6. Ibid., p. 97.

7. Ibid.

8. Paul Arthur and Kimberly Cowell-Meyers, 'Ian Paisley', *Encyclopaedia Britannica*, www.britannica.com/biography/Ian-Paisley, accessed 27 Jun. 2021.

9. Devlin, *The Price of My Soul*, p. 102.

10. Ibid., p. 101.

11. Ibid., p. 113.

12. 'Northern Ireland: The Civil Rights Movement', *BBC*, www.bbc.co.uk/bitesize/guides/z3w2mp3/revision/7, accessed 27 May 2021.

13. The Honourable Lord Cameron, D.S.C., 'Disturbances in Northern Ireland: Report of the Commission appointed by the Governor of Northern Ireland' (Belfast, September 1969).

14. 'Bernadette Devlin attacks British Home Secretary', *BBC One*, 31 Jan. 1972, www.bbc.co.uk/programmes/p00nm166, accessed 27 Jun. 2021.
15. Margaret Ward, Myrtle Hill and Lynda Walker, 'Bernadette Devlin McAliskey (1947–)', *A Century of Women*, www.acenturyofwomen.com/bernadette-devlin/, accessed 27 Jun. 2021.
16. Freya McClements, 'Bernadette McAliskey: "The North's economy cannot survive without immigrant labour"', *Irish Times*, 20 Feb. 2020.
17. Bogside Artists Exhibition, www.bogsideartistsexhibition.org/the-murals-on-site, accessed 29 Sep. 2021.
18. House of Commons debate, Vol 782, cc262-324, 22 Apr. 1969, Hansard.

CHAPTER 16 – WILLIAMS

1. *Irish Examiner*, 10 Dec. 1977.
2. 'Betty Williams – Facts', *Nobel Prize Organisation*, www.nobelprize.org/prizes/peace/1976/williams/facts/, accessed 28 Jun. 2021.
3. 'A woman of peace', *The Scotsman*, 28 Jul. 2006.
4. 'Letter from Gerry Adams to editor', *Irish Press*, 23 Aug. 1976.
5. 'History', *Peace People*, www.peacepeople.com/history/, accessed 2 Jul. 2021.
6. *Evening Herald*, 12 Aug. 1976.
7. Ibid.
8. *Sunday Independent*, 15 Aug. 1976.
9. Ibid.
10. Gerry Adams' conviction was overturned by the British Supreme Court in 2020 for being unlawful. *Irish Times*, 13 May 2020.
11. *Irish Press*, 23 Aug. 1976.
12. Ibid.
13. Ibid.
14. 'First Declaration of the Peace People', *Peace People*, www.peacepeople.com/declaration/, accessed 4 Jul. 2021.
15. Judith Hicks Stiehm, 'Women and the Nobel Prize for Peace', in *International Feminist Journal of Politics* 7:2 (2005), p. 265.
16. *Belfast Telegraph*, 15 Dec. 1977.
17. Ibid.
18. Ibid.
19. *Belfast Telegraph*, 12 Dec. 1977.
20. Ibid., 20 Dec. 1977.
21. *Irish Independent*, 10 Dec. 1977.
22. *Irish Times*, 18 Mar. 2020.
23. Sarah Buscher and Bettina Ling, *Mairead Corrigan and Betty Williams: Making Peace in Northern Ireland* (New York, 1999), p. 17.
24. 'Betty Williams – Nobel Lecture', *Nobel Prize Organisation*. Text of speech reproduced courtesy of The Nobel Foundation.

chapter 17 – mckenna

1. National University of Ireland, Galway (NUIG), 'Thank you letter from Sally Swing Shelley', Chief NGO Section UN, Department of Public Information, T20/41/198.
2. 'Apartheid', *Encyclopaedia Britannica*, www.britannica.com/topic/apartheid, accessed 11 Jul. 2021.
3. Sahm Venter, *Exploring Our National Days: Human Rights Day 21 March* (Auckland, 2007), p. 22.
4. United Nations, 'Resolutions adopted and decisions taken by the Security Council in 1960', S/RES/134(1960), p. 2, *United Nations Digital Library*, https:// digitallibrary. un.org/record/112105?ln=en#record-files-collapse-header, accessed 26 Aug. 2021.
5. 'Key dates in the UN campaign against apartheid [2 December 1968]', *United Nations*, www.un.org/en/events/mandeladay/un_against_apartheid.shtml, accessed 11 Jul. 2021.
6. United Nations Centre against Apartheid, 'Register of entertainers, actors and others who have performed in apartheid South Africa', *Aluka*, http://psimg. jstor. org/fsi/img/pdf/t0/10.5555/al.sff.document.nuun1986_03_final.pdf, accessed 26 Aug. 2021.
7. Margaret MacCurtain, 'Mckenna, Siobhán', in *Dictionary of Irish Biography* (www.dib.ie).
8. David Coughlan, 'Remembering when an Irish rugby tour divided the nation', *RTÉ*, 8 July 2021, www.rte.ie/sport/rugby/2021/0708/1233879-remembering-when-an-irish-rugby-tour-divided-the-nation/, accessed 14 Jul. 2021.
9. Details from David Coughlan, 'Crossing the line', *RTÉ*, www.rte.ie/radio/doconone/ 1233770-crossing-the-line, accessed 14 Jul. 2021.
10. NUIG, 'Letter from Siobhán McKenna', Siobhán McKenna Papers, T20/41/200.
11. *Irish Press*, 17 Nov. 1986.
12. *Ulster Herald*, 22 Nov. 1986.
13. *Connacht Sentinel*, 18 Nov. 1986.
14. In October 1989 the IRFU ceased all contact with South Africa.
15. 'Address by Nelson Mandela to Dáil Éireann', *Irish Times*, 8 Jun. 2013.
16. Dame Peggy Ashcroft (1907–91) was an Academy Award-winning English actress. She was made a Dame of the British Empire in 1956.
17. NUIG, 'United Nations Speech', Anti-Apartheid Movement, T20/1/5/1/5, in Siobhán McKenna Papers, DS/UK/15. Text of speech reproduced courtesy of NUIG.

CHAPTER 18 – FENNELL

1. Sonja Tiernan, 'Fennell, Nuala', in *Dictionary of Irish Biography* (hereafter *DIB*) (www.dib.ie).
2. Nuala Fennell, *Irish Marriage: How Are You!* (Dublin, 1974).
3. Nuala Fennell, Deirdre McDevitt and Bernadette Quinn, *Can You Stay Married?* (Dublin, 1980).

4. Patrick Maume, 'FitzGerald, Garret', in *DIB*.

5. Aideen Quilty, Sinéad Kennedy and Catherine Conlon (eds), *The Abortion Papers:Volume 2* (Cork, 2015), p. 31.

6. Lindsey Earner-Byrne and Diane Urquhart, *The Irish Abortion Journey, 1920–2018* (Cham, 2019), p. 69.

7. Ibid.

8. The EC was replaced by the European Union (EU) in 1993 through the Maastricht Treaty. Ireland again voted through a referendum to maintain membership.

9. This was later inserted into the Irish Constitution as Article 40.3.3.

10. *Irish Times*, 16 Feb. 1983.

11. Ibid.

12. See Mary Robinson's speech in this volume.

13. Seanad Éireann debate,Vol. 79, No. 2, 4 Dec. 1974.

14. The Law Reform Commission, *Report on Illegitimacy* (Dublin, 1982).

15. Mary Fanning, 'New laws for non-marital children 1986', *RTÉ*, www.rte.ie/archives/2016/0511/787763-illegitimacy-bill/, accessed 26 Aug. 2021.

16. Mary Maher, 'Fennell defends stand on abortion poll', *Irish Times*, 22 Feb. 1983.

17. Rory P. Murray, 'Letter to the editor', *Irish Times*, 11 Mar. 1983.

18. *Irish Times*, 8 Apr. 1983.

19. Ibid., 18 Apr. 1983.

20. Working Party on Women's Affairs and Family Law Reform, *Irish Women:Agenda for Practical Action* (Dublin, 1985).

21. Pádraig Yeates, 'Sheila Hodgers: A case in question', *Irish Times*, 2 Sep. 1983, as cited in Earner-Byrne and Urquhart, *The Irish Abortion Journey*, pp 78–9.

22. Tiernan, 'Fennell, Nuala', in *DIB*.

23. Dáil Éireann debate,Vol. 415, No. 8, 18 Feb. 1992.

24. Ibid.

25. Ibid.

26. Dáil Éireann debate,Vol. 415, No. 9, 19 Feb. 1992.

27. *Irish Press*, 30 May 1992.

28. *Irish Independent*, 18 Sep. 1992.

29. Nuala Fennell, *Political Woman:A Memoir* (Dublin, 2009).

30. See Clare Daly's speech in this volume.

31. *Irish Times*, 28 May 2018.

32. Dáil Éireann debate,Vol. 340, No. 3, 17 Feb. 1983.

CHAPTER 19 – JOYCE

1. In 1997 the name of the university was changed to the National University of Ireland Galway, or NUI Galway for short.

2. *Irish Times*, 18 Jun. 1983.

3. *Irish Press*, 18 Jun. 1983.

4. Caroline Banton, 'Third World', *Investopedia*, updated 26 Oct. 2020, www.investopedia.com/terms/t/third-world.asp, accessed 12 May 2021.

5. *Irish Press*, 20 Jun. 1983.

6. Nan Joyce, *Traveller: An Autobiography by Nan Joyce*, Anna Farmar (ed.) (Dublin, 1985). Republished in 2000 under a new title, *My Life on the Road: An Autobiography by Nan Joyce*.

7. *Irish Times*, 28 Sep. 2021.

8. Patrick Nevin, 'Without reckoning with the state's treatment of Traveller Irish, we can't build a country safe for all minorities', *Dublin InQuirer*, 11 Mar. 2020, www.dublininquirer.com/2020/03/11/patrick-without-reckoning-with-the-state-s-treatment-of-traveller-irish-we-can-t-build-a-country-safe-for-all-minorities, accessed 12 May 2021.

9. Commission on Itinerancy, *Report on the Commission on Itinerancy* (Dublin, 1963), p. 11.

10. Ibid.

11. Nevin, 'Without reckoning with the state's treatment of Traveller Irish'.

12. Joyce, *Traveller*, p. 99.

13. Sharon B. Gmelch and George Gmelch, 'The itinerant settlement movement: Its policies and effects on Irish Travellers', in *Studies: An Irish Quarterly Review* 63 (Spring 1974), pp 1–16.

14. Patricia McCarthy, 'Travellers fighting back', in *Red & Black Revolution* 2 (Mar. 2001), p. 23.

15. Travelling People Review Body, *Report of the Travelling People Review Body* (Dublin, 1983), p. 1.

16. Equality Authority, *Traveller Ethnicity* (Dublin, 2006), p. 15.

17. Joyce, *Traveller*, pp 88–9.

18. Ibid.

19. Ibid., p. 100.

20. Members included Joyce's husband John, her brother Peter Donoghue, her sister Chrissie Ward and Chrissie's husband Paddy, and Michael McCann and his brothers. Members from the settled community in Tallaght included Tony and Marie Hackett, Seamus Leonard, Mervyn Ennis and Wille Power. Joyce, *Traveller*, p. 102.

21. Ann Joyce, 'Leaflet from Ann Joyce', *Irish Election Literature*, https://irishelection literature.com/2020/04/30/leaflet-from-ann-joyce-independent-dublin-south-west-november-1982-general-election/#more-41004, accessed 13 May 2021.

22. Ibid.

23. Joyce, *Traveller*, p. 107.

24. Ibid., p. 109.

25. 'Sinn Féin candidate resigns over anti-Traveller comments on Facebook', *The Journal*, 22 May 2014.

26. 'General Election: 24 November 1982: Dublin South West', *ElectionsIreland.org*, https://electionsireland.org/result.cfm?election=1982nov&cons=105, accessed 13 May 2021.

27. Joyce, *Traveller*, p. 113.

28. *Irish Times*, 18 Aug. 2018.

29. Joyce, *Traveller*, p. 115.

30. Due to his steadfast work on human rights, MacBride was awarded the Nobel Peace Prize and the Lenin Peace Prize in 1974. His many accomplishments include co-founding Amnesty International. He was president of the International Peace

Bureau (IPB) from 1974–85, during which time he met Nan Joyce. The IPB awards a Seán MacBride Peace Prize annually in his honour. 'Seán MacBride Peace Prize', *International Peace Bureau*, www.ipb.org/sean-macbride-peace-prize/, accessed 17 May 2021.
31. Catherine Conlon, *Women: The Picture of Health: A Review of Research on Women's Health in Ireland* (Dublin, 1999), p. 28.
32. Mary Daly, 'Ireland grants ethnic minority recognition for Irish Travellers', *European Social Policy Network Flash Report* (May 2017), p. 1.
33. *Irish Times*, 1 Mar. 2017.
34. T. P. O'Mahony, 'End plight of Travellers', *Irish Press*, 18 Jun. 1983.
35. Joseph Power, 'It's apartheid says itinerant', *Evening Herald*, 17 Jun. 1983.

CHAPTER 20 – MCDONALD

1. 'Women don't even have a dog's life', *Evening Herald*, 9 Nov. 1984; 'Greyhounds treated better than women', *Evening Echo*, 9 Nov. 1984; 'In Kerry you're better off to be a greyhound', *Irish Examiner*, 10 Nov. 1984.
2. *Kerryman*, 16 Nov. 1984.
3. Speech at the Annual Dinner of the Association of Advertisers in Ireland, 20 Apr. 1971, quoted in Michael Geary, *An Inconvenient Wait: Ireland's Quest for Membership of the EEC, 1957–73* (Dublin, 2010), p. 187.
4. The presidency rotates on a six-month basis around member states. This term of Ireland's presidency was from July to December in 1984. 'Previous Irish Presidencies', *Archive eu2013*, www.eu2013.ie/ireland-and-the-presidency/about-the-presidency/previousirishpresidencies/, accessed 26 Jul. 2021.
5. *Irish Times*, 24 Jun. 2021.
6. Sonja Tiernan, 'Sligo co-operative movements (1895–1905): The birth of an Irish political activist', in Shane Alcobia-Murphy, Lindsay Milligan and Dan Wall (eds), *Founder to Shore: Cross-Currents in Irish and Scottish Studies* (Aberdeen, 2009), pp 189–96.
7. Carla King and Liam Kennedy, 'Irish co-operatives: From creameries at the crossroads to multinationals', in *History Ireland* 2:4 (Winter 1994), www.historyireland.com/20th-century-contemporary-history/irish-co-operatives-from-creameries-at-the-crossroads-to-multinationals-by-carla-king-liam-kennedy/.
8. Ibid.
9. National President John Keane, North West Vice-President Luna Orofiamma, Munster Vice-President Elaine Houlihan, and Leinster Vice-President Claire Gough. This team will serve from 2021 to 2023.
10. 'Farm Family Committee', *IFA*, www.ifa.ie/cross-sector-committees/farm-family-committee/, accessed 26 Jul. 2021.
11. *Evening Echo*, 8 Nov. 1984.
12. *Irish Examiner*, 9 Nov. 1984.
13. *Irish Press*, 11 Nov. 1984.
14. Working Party on Women's Affairs and Family Law Reform, *Irish Women: Agenda for Practical Action* (Dublin, 1985).

15. 'Seanad Éireann debate, 'Report of Working Party on Women's Affairs and Family Law Reform: Motion,' Vol. 108, No. 12, 2 Jul. 1985.

16. Ibid.

17. Marie Christie and Aisling Molloy, 'International Day of Rural Women', in *Today's Farm*, Sep.-Oct. 2019, p. 12.

18. 'Why are just 12% of Irish farmers women?', *RTÉ*, 8 Mar. 2021, www.rte. ie/brainstorm/2021/0308/1201578-ireland-women-farmers/, accessed 25 Aug. 2021.

19. Mamo McDonald, *Circling* (Galway, 2015).

20. *Irish Times*, 24 Jun. 2021.

21. Speech first reported in *Irish Woman*, 21 Dec. 1984, reproduced in Angela Bourke et al. (eds), *The Field Day Anthology of Irish Writing: Volume 5* (Cork, 2002), pp 275–7. Text of speech reproduced here courtesy of Mamo McDonald with thanks to Jade Pepper of the ICA.

CHAPTER 21 – GLENN

1. *Irish Independent*, 17 Oct. 1985.

2. Diane Urquhart, *Irish Divorce: A History* (Cambridge, 2020), p. 215.

3. *Irish Times*, 24 Dec. 2011.

4. Terry Calvin, 'Glenn, Alice', in *Dictionary of Irish Biography* (www.dib.ie).

5. Ibid.

6. The other TDs expelled for voting against the Fine Gael bill were Oliver Flanagan and Tom O'Donnell.

7. Christy Moore, 'Delirium Tremens', on *Ordinary Man* (WEA, 1985).

8. *Irish Independent*, 17 Oct. 1985.

9. *Sunday Independent*, 27 Oct. 1985.

10. Joint Committee on Marriage Breakdown, *Report of the Joint Committee on Marriage Breakdown* (Dublin, 1985), p. viii.

11. 'Alice Glenn on divorce', *YouTube*, www.youtube.com/watch?v=ueuw9zbNOrw, accessed 2 Aug. 2021.

12. Ibid.

13. Joint Committee on Marriage Breakdown, *Report of the Joint Committee on Marriage Breakdown*, p. 89.

14. Article 41.3.2 of the Irish Constitution, 1986.

15. 'Alice Glenn v. Mary Robinson (1986 Divorce Referendum)', *YouTube*, www. youtube.com/watch?v=z8iFEROKwSk, accessed 2 Aug. 2021.

16. Ciara Meehan, *A Just Society for Ireland? 1964–1987* (Basingstoke, 2013), p. 3.

17. Ibid., pp 3–4.

18. Dáil Éireann debate, 'Tenth Amendment of the Constitution Bill, 1986: Second Stage', Vol. 366, No. 5, 14 May 1986.

19. Maxime Bercholz and John FitzGerald, 'Recent trends in female labour force participation in Ireland', in *ESRI Quarterly Economic Commentary: Special Articles* (Autumn 2016), pp 49–81.

20. *Alice Glenn Report* 1:3 (May 1986), p. 1.

21. Urquhart, *Irish Divorce*, p. 220.

22. National Library of Ireland, Dublin, 'Proposal from Labour Women's National Committee to the National Referendum Committee, 21 May 1986', Ms 94,494/925, as cited in Urquhart, *Irish Divorce*, p. 220.

23. *NewYork Times*, 28 Jun. 1986.

24. *Evening Herald*, 29 Nov. 1986.

25. Calvin, 'Glenn, Alice'.

26. Urquhart, *Irish Divorce*, p. 235.

27. Ibid., p. 238.

28. 'Crude divorce rate', *eurostat*, https://ec.europa.eu/eurostat, accessed 2 Sep. 2021.

29. 'Alice, tough in the Dail and fearless on streets', *Irish Independent*, 22 Dec. 2011.

30. *Irish Times*, 24 Dec. 2011.

31. Dáil Éireann debate,Vol. 366, No. 5, 14 May 1986.

CHAPTER 22 – MCCORMACK

1. The Women's Education Project is now the Women's Resource and Development Agency in Belfast. With thanks to Margaret Ward for her comments regarding the impetus for the symposium.

2. Margaret Ward, email to author, 23 Mar. 2021.

3. The hotel was renamed the Forum Hotel in 1983 when it changed ownership but reverted back to its original name in October 1986.

4. See Dehra Parker's speech in this volume for background on the suspension and later abolition of the Northern Ireland parliament.

5. Margaret Ward, 'A difficult, dangerous honesty', in *Trouble and Strife* 12 (Winter 1987), p. 37.

6. Margaret Ward, Myrtle Hill and Lynda Walker, 'A century of women – 1980s', *A Century of Women*, www.acenturyofwomen.com/1980s/, accessed 3 Sep. 2021.

7. Christina Loughran, 'Writing our own history: Organizing against the odds', in *Trouble and Strife* 11 (Summer 1987), p. 49.

8. Ward, 'A difficult, dangerous honesty', p. 36.

9. See Bernadette Devlin's speech in this volume.

10. *Independent*, 23 Jan. 2013.

11. Inez McCormack, 'The long, long march from '68', in *Fortnight* 257 (Dec. 1987), p. 16.

12. In May 2021, following the longest-running inquests in the history of Northern Ireland, Mrs Justice Siobhán Keegan found that all the victims were 'entirely innocent of any wrongdoing on the day in question'. *Irish Times*, 11 May 2021.

13. 'Inez McCormack: A challenging woman', *BBC*, 21 Jan. 2015, www.bbc.com/news/uk-northern-ireland-30914555, accessed 3 Sep. 2021.

14. *Irish Times*, 27 Nov. 2014.

15. The other sponsors were Seán MacBride, Catholic priest Fr. Brian Brady, and Protestant peace campaigner Dr John Robb.

16. Father Sean McManus, 'The MacBride principles', Dec. 1997, *Human Rights Library*, http://hrlibrary.umn.edu/links/macbride.html, accessed 3 Sep. 2021.

17. Ibid.

18. *An Phobhlact*, 26 Nov. 2009.

19. Margaret Ward (ed.), *A Difficult, Dangerous Honesty: 10 Years of Feminism in Northern Ireland* (Belfast, 1987).

20. Ward, 'A difficult, dangerous honesty', p. 36.

21. Ibid.

22. Ibid., p. 43.

23. An international organisation with a mission to 'search the world for women leaders with daring vision for change, and partner with [them] to make that vision a reality'. 'About us', *Vital Voices*, www.vitalvoices.org/who-we-are/, accessed 3 Sep. 2021.

24. The other six women featured in *Seven* are Marina Pisklakova-Parker, Russia; Mu Sochua, Cambodia; Anabella De Leon, Guatemala; Farida Azizi, Afghanistan; Hafsat Abiola, Nigeria; and Mukhtar Mai, Pakistan.

25. *Seven*, https://seventheplay.com, accessed 3 Sep. 2021.

26. *Daily Beast*, 1 Mar. 2010.

27. Susan McKay, 'Inez McCormack: Remembering one of our great social justice campaigners', *Irish Times*, 27 Nov. 2014.

28. *Inez: A Challenging Woman*, dir. Trevor Birney and Eimhear O'Neill, produced and narrated by Susan McKay, Fine Point Films, 2014.

29. Ibid.

30. *Belfast Telegraph*, 24 Jan. 2013.

31. Ibid.

32. 'Meryl Streep's tribute to Inez McCormack at the 2013 Women in the World Summit', *YouTube*, www.youtube.com/watch?v=o2JxEE3EzI8, accessed 3 Sep. 2021.

33. *Independent*, 23 Jan. 2013.

34. Ward, *A Difficult, Dangerous Honesty*. Text reproduced courtesy of Margaret Ward.

CHAPTER 23 – ROBINSON

1. John Cooney, *John Charles McQuaid: Ruler of Catholic Ireland* (Dublin, 1999), p. 162.

2. Mary Robinson, *Everybody Matters: A Memoir* (London, 2012), p. 46.

3. Ibid., p. 47.

4. *Irish Times*, 4 Feb. 1967.

5. Robinson, *Everybody Matters*, p. 54.

6. Out of a total of 60 seats in the upper house, six candidates were elected for university seats by alumni of that university. Robinson stood for election for one of three Trinity College seats.

7. 'Seanad Éireann debate, Vol. 67, No. 1, 5 Nov. 1969.

8. *Irish Times*, 6 Nov. 1969.

9. Ibid.

10. Robinson, *Everybody Matters*, p. 64.

11. Sandra McAvoy, "'A perpetual nightmare": Women, fertility control, the Irish state, and the 1935 ban on contraceptives', in Margaret Preston and Margaret Ó hÓgartaigh (eds), *Gender and Medicine in Ireland 1700–1950* (Syracuse, 2012), p. 202.

12. Robinson, *Everybody Matters*, p. 65.

13. Correspondence between John Horgan and Brian Girvin, 28 Aug. 2007 and Nov. 2009, cited in Brian Girvin, 'An Irish solution to an Irish problem: Catholicism, contraception and change, 1922–1979', in *Contemporary European History* 27:1 (2018), p. 22.

14. See Máire Geoghegan-Quinn's speech in this volume.

15. Robinson, *Everybody Matters*, p. 127.

16. Ibid., p. 136.

17. Austin Currie was eliminated after the first round of counts.

18. Robinson, *Everybody Matters*, p. 145.

19. Ibid., p. 147.

20. Ibid., p. 148.

21. Ibid., p. 149.

22. Ibid., p. 157.

23. Ibid., p. 149.

24. *Evening Herald*, 3 Dec. 1990.

25. *Irish Examiner*, 4 Dec. 1990.

26. *Irish Press*, 4 Dec. 1990.

27. *Evening Herald*, 4 Dec. 1990.

28. Robinson, *Everybody Matters*, p. 161.

29. 'Address by the President, Mary Robinson, on the occasion of her inauguration as President of Ireland, 3rd December, 1990', *President of Ireland*, https://president. ie/ en/media-library/speeches/address-by-the-president-mary-robinson-on-the-occasion- of-her-inauguration, accessed 2 Sep. 2021.

CHAPTER 24 – GEOGHEGAN-QUINN

1. Colm Tóibín, 'Foreword', in Richard Aldous, *Great Irish Speeches* (London, 2007), pp xvii–xviii.

2. Sonja Tiernan, *The History of Marriage Equality in Ireland: A Social Revolution Begins* (Manchester, 2020), p. 5.

3. Dáil Éireann debate, Vol. 432, No. 7, 23 Jun. 1993.

4. Mary Robinson, *Everybody Matters: A Memoir* (London, 2012), pp 120–1.

5. Case of Norris v. Ireland, Application no. 10581/83, Judgement, Strasbourg, 26 October 1988.

6. Tiernan, *The History of Marriage Equality in Ireland*, p. 7.

7. Robinson, *Everybody Matters*, p. 121.

8. Tiernan, *The History of Marriage Equality in Ireland*, p. 10.

9. Robinson, *Everybody Matters*, p. 122.

10. *Evening Herald*, 15 Dec. 1992.

11. Kieran Rose, *Diverse Communities: The Evolution of Lesbian and Gay Politics in Ireland* (Cork, 1994), p. 17.

12. David Norris, 'Gay rights and reform in Ireland: A personal history', Irish Research Council, 10 May 2017, https://research.ie/what-we-do/loveirishresearch/blog/loveirishresearch-blog-senator-david-norris-on-gay-rights-and-reform-in-ireland-a-personal-history/, accessed 30 Aug. 2021.
13. Dáil Éireann debate, 23 Jun. 1993.
14. Ibid. Daniel O'Connell (1775–1847) is known as the Liberator due to his campaigns on behalf of the poorest classes of Irish people, which helped secure Catholic emancipation.
15. Frances Gardiner and Mary O'Dowd, 'The women's movement and women politicians in the Republic of Ireland, 1980–2000', in Angela Bourke et al. (eds), *The Field Day Anthology of Irish Writing: Volume 5* (Cork, 2002), p. 236.
16. Dáil Éireann debate, Vol. 432, No. 8, 24 Jun. 1993.
17. Equal Status Act (2000) Section 3 (2).
18. Máire Geoghegan-Quinn, *The Green Diamond* (Dublin, 1996).
19. *Belfast Telegraph*, 27 Jan. 1997.
20. *Connacht Sentinel*, 28 Jan. 1997.
21. *Irish Times*, 28 Jan. 1997.
22. Seanad Éireann debate, Vol. 258, No. 11, 19 Jun. 2018.
23. Dáil Éireann debate, Vol. 432, No. 7, 23 Jun. 1993.

CHAPTER 25 – OWEN

1. Mary Coughlan went on to hold a number of Cabinet positions before becoming Tánaiste from 2008 to 2011.
2. Kitty met with Collins one hour before his assassination at Béal na mBláth. *Irish Independent*, 9 Sep. 2014.
3. Andrea Smith, 'I discovered I was pregnant after adopting my son and was asked if I wanted to give him back', *Independent.ie*, 9 Sep. 2014, www.independent.ie/life/family/family-features/i-discovered-i-was-pregnant-after-adopting-my-son-and-was-asked-if-i-wanted-to-give-him-back-30574191.html, accessed 8 Sep. 2021.
4. Fiona Buckley, 'Women and politics in Ireland: The road to sex quotas', in *Irish Political Studies* 28:3 (2013), p. 344.
5. Frances Gardiner, 'The women's movement and women politicians in the Republic of Ireland, 1980–2000', in Angela Bourke et al. (eds), *The Field Day Anthology of Irish Writing: Volume 5* (Cork, 2002), p. 235.
6. Frances Gardiner and Mary O'Dowd (eds), 'Second Commission on the Status of Women', in Angela Bourke et al. (eds), *The Field Day Anthology of Irish Writing: Volume 5* (Cork, 2002), p. 254.
7. Yvonne Galligan, 'The Report of the Second Commission on the Status of Women', in *Irish Political Studies* 8:1 (1993), p. 127.
8. Ibid.
9. Gardiner and O'Dowd, 'Second Commission on the Status of Women', p. 254.
10. Fine Gael, *Summary Report of the Commission on Renewal* (Dublin, 1993), p. 44, cited in Buckley, 'Women and politics in Ireland', p. 346.
11. Buckley, 'Women and politics in Ireland', p. 347.

12. *Irish Independent*, 16 Dec. 1994.
13. Dáil Éireann debate, Vol. 470, No. 1, 15 Oct. 1996.
14. 'Veronica Guerin: International Press Freedom Award Acceptance Address', *American Rhetoric*, www.americanrhetoric.com/speeches/veronicaguerinbraveryaward. htm, accessed 8 Sep. 2021.
15. Ibid.
16. An Post, the Irish postal service.
17. *Irish Independent*, 16 Dec. 1994.
18. Ivana Bacik, 'Sub-Committee on Women's Participation in Politics: Report', in Houses of the Oireachtas, Joint Committee on Justice, Equality Defence and Women's Rights, *Second Report: Women's Participation in Politics, October 2009*, PRN. A9/1468, p. 5.
19. Ibid.
20. Two Fine Gael TDs in Donegal at this time.
21. 'Nora Owen', in Angela Bourke et al. (eds), *The Field Day Anthology of Irish Writing: Volume 5* (Cork, 2002), pp 245–6. Text of speech reproduced courtesy of Nora Owen with thanks to Cliona Doyle of Fine Gael.

CHAPTER 26 – RODGERS

1. National Women's Council of Ireland, *National Women's Council of Ireland Annual Report 1998: 25 Years Working With and For Women* (Dublin: National Women's Council of Ireland, 1998).
2. Kimberly Cowell-Meyers, 'Social Democratic and Labour Party', *Encyclopaedia Britannica*, www.britannica.com/topic/Social-Democratic-and-Labour-Party, accessed 23 Sep. 2021.
3. Ibid.
4. 'Gníomhaí Polaiteoir Seanadóir 1986', *RTÉ*, 21 Jan. 1986, www.rte.ie/archives/category/politics/2021/0118/1190514-brid-rodgers/, accessed 19 Sep. 2021.
5. Seanad Éireann debate, Vol. 102, No. 4, 9 Nov. 1983.
6. *Irish Press*, 4 Apr. 1984.
7. Seanad Éireann debate, Vol. 103, No. 8, 4 Apr. 1984.
8. Ibid., Vol. 110, No. 3, 27 Nov. 1985.
9. Duncan Morrow, 'The Northern Ireland forum elections of 1996', in *Regional & Federal Studies* 7:2 (1997), p. 112.
10. 'Nineteenth Amendment of the Constitution Act, 1998', p. viii (Article 2), *Irish Statute Book*, www.irishstatutebook.ie/eli/1998/ca/19/enacted/en/pdf, accessed 23 Sep. 2021.
11. Ibid (Article 3).
12. *Sunday Independent*, 18 Oct. 1998.
13. Ibid.
14. *Irish Times*, 16 Aug. 2019.
15. Mary O'Dowd, 'Women and politics in Northern Ireland, 1993–2000', in Angela Bourke et al. (eds), *The Field Day Anthology of Irish Writing, Volume 5* (Cork, 2002), p. 412.

16. See Inez McCormack's speech in this volume.

17. *Irish Independent*, 18 Sep. 2002.

18. *CountryWide*, 2 Jul. 2016, *RTÉ*, www.rte.ie/radio/radio1/countrywide/programmes/2016/0702/799700-countrywide-saturday-2-july-2016/, accessed 23 Sep. 2021.

19. *Irish News*, 4 Dec. 2017.

20. *BBC News*, 21 July 2021, www.bbc.com/news/uk-politics-57911148, accessed 27 Sep. 2021.

21. Seanad Éireann debate, Vol. 276, No. 1, 10 May 2021.

22. See Monica McWilliams speech in this volume.

23. 'Bríd Rodgers', in Angela Bourke et al. (eds), *The Field Day Anthology of Irish Writing, Volume 5* (Cork, 2002), pp 452–3. Text reproduced courtesy of Bríd Rodgers with thanks to Ann McDonagh of the SDLP.

CHAPTER 27 – MCWILLIAMS

1. Monica McWilliams, 'From Peace Talks to Gender Justice', in Kaitlin Barker (ed.) *Joan B. Kroc Distinguished Lecture Series* (San Diego, 2010), p. 8.

2. George J. Mitchell, 'Negotiating in Business, Politics and Peace', in Emiko Noma (ed.) *Joan B. Kroc Distinguished Lecture Series* (San Diego, 2012).

3. 'From peace talks to gender justice: Monica McWilliams', *YouTube*, www.youtube.com/watch?v=ZozSwuKBOII, accessed 4 Oct. 2021.

4. McWilliams, 'From peace talks to gender justice'.

5. Margaret Ward, Myrtle Hill and Lynda Walker, 'Monica McWilliams', *A Century of Women*, www.acenturyofwomen.com/monica-mcwilliams/, accessed 27 Aug. 2021. Details about McWilliams' early life are also taken from this source.

6. George J. Mitchell, John de Chastelain and Harri Holkeri, 'Report of the International Body on Arms Decommissioning', 22 Jan. 1996, *CAIN*, https://cain.ulster.ac.uk/events/peace/docs/gm24196.htm, accessed 7 Oct. 2021.

7. 'Northern Ireland (Mitchell Report)', House of Commons Debate, vol 270 cc353-70, 24 Jan. 1996.

8. Announced at a summit in London on 28 February 1996.

9. Nell McCafferty, 'A women's party outwits the system in Northern Ireland', in *Canadian Woman Studies* 17:3 (1997), p. 64.

10. *Irish Independent*, 14 Sep. 1996.

11. Ibid.

12. McCafferty, 'A women's party', p. 64.

13. Interview with May Blood, *Northern Visions Archive*, http://archive.northernvisions.org/specialcollections/ogpersonal-stories/may-blood/, accessed 7 Oct. 2021.

14. *The Irish News*, 11 Dec. 2019.

15. Catherine O'Rourke, 'Northern Ireland Women's Coalition', in *Encyclopedia Britannica*, 20 May. 2016, www.britannica.com/topic/Northern-Ireland-Womens-Coalition, accessed 8 Oct. 2021.

16. Ibid.

17. McWilliams, 'From peace talks to gender justice', p. 39.

18. Ward et al, *A Century of Women*.

19. Ibid.

20. Ibid.

21. For example, Monica McWilliams and Joan McKiernan, *Bringing It Out in the Open: Domestic Violence in Northern Ireland* (Belfast, 1993); Monica McWilliams and Lynda Spence, *Taking Domestic Violence Seriously: Issues for the Civil and Criminal Justice System* (Belfast, 1996).

22. BBC, www.bbc.co.uk/programmes/b094mv30, accessed 7 Oct. 2021.

23. *Wave Goodbye to Dinosaurs*, dir. Eimhear O'Neill, produced by Trevor Birney, Brendan Byrne and Gini Reticker, Fine Point Films, 2017.

24. Monica McWilliams, 'Waving Goodbye to Dinosaurs', *Council on Foreign Relations*, www.cfr.org/blog/waving-goodbye-dinosaurs-strategic-advantage-women-peace-table, accessed 7 Oct. 2021.

25. Hillary Rodham Clinton, 'Chancellor Inauguration Address', Queen's University, 24 Sep. 2021, www.qub.ac.uk/home/chancellor-installation-ceremony/, accessed 27 Sep. 2021.

26. Monica McWilliams, *Stand Up, Speak Out: My Life Working for Women's Rights, Peace and Equality in Northern Ireland and Beyond* (Newtownards, 2021).

27. 'From peace talks to gender justice: Monica McWilliams', *YouTube*. Text of speech reproduced courtesy of Monica McWilliams with thanks to Margaret Ward.

CHAPTER 28 – ROCHE

1. Burton Bennett, Michael Repacholi and Zhanat Carr (eds), *Health Effects of the Chernobyl Accident and Special Health Care Programmes: Report of the UN Chernobyl Forum Expert Group "Health"* (Geneva, 2006), p. 2.

2. Holly Morris, 'Chernobyl's babushkas', in *The World Today* 72:2 (Apr. & May 2016), p. 44.

3. Sakharov International College on Radioecology, *The Consequences of the Chernobyl Accident in Belarus* (Minsk, 1992), cited in Svetlana Alexievich, *Voices From Chernobyl: The Oral History of a Nuclear Disaster* (New York, 2006), p. 18.

4. *Irish Times*, 20 Apr. 1996.

5. Chernobyl Children International has an Irish head office at 1A The Stables, Alfred Street, Cork, Ireland. Prior to 2010, CCI was known as the Chernobyl Children's Project International.

6. *Irish Times*, 15 Oct. 1997.

7. Adi Roche, *Chernobyl Heart: 20 Years On* (Dublin, 2006).

8. Ibid.

9. *New York Times*, 15 May 1986.

10. *Daily Express*, 6 Jun. 2019.

11. Interview with Ryan Tubridy on RTÉ Radio One, *RTÉ*, https://radio.rte.ie/radio1highlights/adi-roche-the-ryan-tubridy-show/, accessed 22 Sep. 2020.

12. Adam Higginbotham, *Midnight in Chernobyl: The Untold Story of the World's Greatest Nuclear Disaster* (New York, 2019), p. 240.

13. In 2006 the World Health Organisation confirmed that 600,000 people had by

then received certificates confirming their status as liquidators. Bennett, Repacholi and Carr, *Health Effects of the Chernobyl Accident and Special Health Care Programmes*, p. 2.

14. *Washington Post*, 25 Apr. 2006.

15. Bennett, Repacholi and Carr, *Health Effects of the Chernobyl Accident and Special Health Care Programmes*, p. 3.

16. '1986–2016: Chernobyl at 30: An update', *World Health Organisation*, 25 Apr. 2016, www.who.int/publications/m/item/1986-2016-chernobyl-at-30, accessed 22 Sep. 2020.

17. Rashid Alimov, *'Chernobyl still burns'*, *Greenpeace*, 23 Apr. 2020, www.greenpeace .org/international/story/30198/chernobyl-still-burns-forest-fires-ukraine-nuclear-radiation/, accessed 22 Sep. 2020.

18. The Ukrainian company that manages the Chernobyl plant is SSE Chernobyl NPP. The company signed a $78 million (US) contract with a construction company to take the sarcophagus apart by 2023. Aria Bendix, 'Chernobyl's sarcophagus is getting dismantled because it's teetering on collapse', *Business Insider Australia*, 20 Sep. 2019.

19. Adi Roche, email to author, 18 July 2020.

20. 'United Nations Chernobyl Disaster Remembrance Day message from President Michael D. Higgins', *Chernobyl Children International*, 25 Apr. 2017, www. chernobyl-international.com/president-ireland-michael-d-higgins-calls-country-remember-chernobyl-victims-ahead-inaugural-united-nations-chernobyl-disaster-remembrance-day/, accessed 22 Sep. 2020.

21. Her work on documentaries includes *Black Wind, White Land: Living with Chernobyl* (1993), which inspired over 7,000 volunteers to join the cause, and *Chernobyl Heart* (2003), which focused on children born with serious heart conditions after the disaster. An exhibition curated at the request of Kofi Annan, then General Secretary of the UN, was opened in New York on 26 April 2001.

22. On 11 March 2011 the Great East Japan Earthquake caused a critical nuclear accident at the Fukushima Daiichi Nuclear Power Plant in Japan. The accident was Level 7 – severe category – on the International Nuclear Event Scale. The official report of the Fukushima Nuclear Accident Independent Investigation Commission is available at https://warp.da.ndl.go.jp/info:ndljp/pid/3856371/naiic.go.jp/en/report/, accessed 20 Sep. 2020.

23. Video, *Facebook*, www.facebook.com/ChernobylChildrenInternational/videos/2189363861310828/, accessed 6 Sep. 2021. Text of speech reproduced courtesy of Adi Roche with thanks to Norrie McGregor of Chernobyl Children International.

CHAPTER 29 – MUSLEH

1. *Irish Examiner*, 10 Jun. 2016.
2. Sarah Webb (ed.), *Mum's the Word: The Truth About Being a Mother* (Dublin, 2007).
3. *The Sun*, 15 Sep. 2007.
4. Saffa Musleh, email to author, 28 Jun. 2021.

5. Timothy J. Hatton and Jeffrey G. Williamson, 'After the Famine: Emigration from Ireland, 1850–1913', in *Journal of Economic History* 53:3 (1993), p. 575.
6. For an insightful history of women who emigrated from Ireland to Britain in the twentieth century see, Jennifer Redmond, *Moving Histories: Irish Women's Emigration to Britain from Independence to Republic* (Liverpool, 2018).
7. Piaras Mac Éinrí and Allen White, 'Immigration into the Republic of Ireland: A bibliography of recent research', in *Irish Geography* 41:2 (2008), p. 151.
8. 'Population and migration estimates: April 2020', 20 Aug. 2020, *Central Statistics Office*, www.cso.ie/en/releasesandpublications/er/pme/populationandmigrationesti matesapril2020/, accessed 28 Jun. 2021.
9. Jon Burnett, *Racial Violence and the Brexit State* (London, 2016), p. 3.
10. Bryan Fanning, 'Rise of Ireland's far right relies on abandoned social conservatives', *Irish Times*, 15 May 2021.
11. Musleh, email to author.
12. Fanning, 'Rise of Ireland's far right relies on abandoned social conservatives'.
13. *The Journal*, 10 Feb. 2020, www.thejournal.ie/far-right-parties-ireland-election-2020-5001966-Feb2020/, accessed 8 Sep. 2021.
14. Musleh, email to author.
15. 'About the Lord Mayor', *Dublin City Council*, www.dublincity.ie/council/your-city-council/lord-mayor-dublin/about-lord-mayor, accessed 28 Jun. 2021.
16. Aoife Moore, 'Lord Mayor of Dublin harassed at her home by far-right protestors', *Irish Examiner*, 22 Jan. 2021.
17. *Irish Independent*, 20 Jun. 2021.
18. *NewsTalk*, 24 Dec. 2020.
19. The current population of the Republic of Ireland is 5,002,098, as of 2 Sep. 2021, based on Worldometer elaboration of United Nations data. The population of Northern Ireland is currently 1.89 million.
20. *New York Post*, 8 Sep. 2021.
21. *Irish Times*, 13 Jan. 2018.
22. 'The look of the Irish: Redefining the Irish person', *YouTube*, www.youtube. com/watch?v=OMmFRCWKreg, accessed 7 Sep. 2021. Text of speech reproduced courtesy of Saffa Musleh.

CHAPTER 30 – MCALEESE

1. Homepage, *Voices of Faith*, https://voicesoffaith.org, accessed 7 Sep. 2021.
2. *Irish Times*, 2 Feb. 2018.
3. Mary McAleese, *Here's the Story: A Memoir* (London, 2020), p. 368.
4. Ibid., p. 1.
5. *Irish Times*, 13 Oct. 1997.
6. McAleese, *Here's the Story*, p. 361.
7. Jeffrey Thomas VanderWilt, *Communion with Non-Catholic Christians: Risks, Challenges, and Opportunities* (Minnesota, 2003), p. 51.
8. Ibid.
9. *Irish Times*, 7 Feb. 2004.

10. *Irish Independent*, 25 May 2011.

11. McAleese, *Here's the Story*, p. 327.

12. Mary McAleese, 'The time is now for change in the Catholic Church', *YouTube*, www.youtube.com/watch?v=X9Q9VqkrfCw&t=1329s, accessed 10 Sep. 2021.

13. Sacred Congregation for the Doctrine of the Faith, *Declaration Inter Insigniores on the Question of the Admission of Women to the Ministerial Priesthood* (Washington, 1977), p. 15.

14. Survey conducted by Amarách Research.

15. *The Journal*, 12 Mar. 2018.

16. *The Nationalist*, 22 Mar. 2018.

17. Ibid.

18. *Western People*, 19 Mar. 2018.

19. Ibid.

20. 'Marian Finucane Sunday 11 March 2018', *RTÉ*, www.rte.ie/radio/radio1 / marian-finucane/programmes/2018/0311/946608-marian-finucane-sunday-11-march- 2018/, accessed 7 Sep. 2021.

21. Ibid.

22. *The Irish Catholic*, 8 Mar. 2018.

23. Ibid.

24. *Irish Times*, 30 Jan. 2018.

25. McAleese, *Here's the Story*, pp 368–9.

26. Ibid., p. 369.

27. Ibid.

28. RTÉ, 7 Aug. 2018, www.rte.ie/news/dublin/2018/0806/983471-mary-mcaleese-award/, accessed 15 Sep. 2021.

29. *Irish Independent*, 30 Sep. 2018.

30. *Irish Times*, 5 Nov. 2019.

31. *National Catholic Reporter*, 14 Sep. 2021.

32. Ibid.

33. Ban Ki-Moon, remarks at the opening of the United Nations General Assembly, Seventieth Session, 25 Sep. 2015, UN Doc A/70/PV.3, p. 2.

34. Pope Francis, *Apostolic Exhortation: Evangelii Gaudium* (Vatican, 2013), p. 82.

35. Text of speech reproduced courtesy of Mary McAleese.

CHAPTER 31 – DALY

1. *Thirty-Sixth Amendment of the Constitution Act 2018* (Dublin, 2018), p. 6, https://data.oireachtas.ie/ie/oireachtas/act/2018/C36/mul/enacted/36th-amdt-act-2018.pdf, accessed 11 Sep. 2021.

2. *Guardian*, 26 May 2018.

3. See Nuala Fennell's speech in this volume.

4. The meeting was themed 'From X to ABC: 20 years of inaction on reproductive rights'. National Women's Council of Ireland, *Working to Improve Women's Lives: Annual Report* (Dublin, 2012), p. 9.

5. *The Journal*, 17 Feb. 2012.

6. David Ralph, *Abortion and Ireland: How the 8th Was Overthrown* (London, 2020), p. 40.

7. Dáil Éireann debate, Vol. 761, No. 3, 18 Apr. 2012.

8. *Irish Times*, 17 Apr. 2012.

9. Ibid.

10. Dáil Éireann debate, Vol. 761, No. 3, 18 Apr. 2012.

11. Ibid., Vol. 762, No. 11, 9 Apr. 2012.

12. Health Service Executive, 'Final report: Investigation of incident 50278 from time of patient's self referral to hospital on the 21st of October 2012 to the patient's death on the 28th of October, 2012', June 2013, www.hse.ie/eng/services/news/nimtreport50278.pdf, accessed 9 Sep. 2021.

13. Vandita Agrawai, 'Ireland murders pregnant Indian dentist', *India Times*, 16 Nov. 2012, www.indiatimes.com/europe/ireland-murders-pregnant-indian-dentist-47214.html, accessed 9 Sep. 2021.

14. 'Woman dies after abortion request "refused" at Galway hospital', *BBC*, 14 Nov. 2012, www.bbc.com/news/uk-northern-ireland-20321741, accessed 9 Sep. 2021.

15. *Irish Times*, 14 Nov. 2012.

16. *Guardian*, 26 May 2018.

17. 'About us', *Together For Yes*, www.togetherforyes.ie/about-us/who-we-are/, accessed 9 Sep. 2021.

18. *Irish Examiner*, 2 Jun. 2018.

19. *The Journal*, 31 May 2018.

20. Ibid.

21. Ibid.

22. Health (Regulation of Termination of Pregnancy) Act 2018, p. 8, https://data.oireachtas.ie/ie/oireachtas/act/2018/31/eng/enacted/a3118.pdf, accessed 11 Sep. 2021.

23. *Guardian*, 3 Oct. 2019.

24. Dáil Éireann debate, Vol. 969, No. 7, 29 May 2018.

CHAPTER 32 – COPPIN

1. *Irish Times*, 17 Feb. 2020.

2. Ibid.

3. Committee against Torture (hereafter CAT), *Convention against Torture and Other Cruel, Inhuman or Degrading Treatment or Punishment: Advance Unedited Version*, 14 Jan. 2020, UN Doc CAT/C/68/D/879/2018, p. 2.

4. James M. Smith, *Ireland's Magdalene Laundries and the Nation's Architecture of Containment* (Notre Dame, 2007), p. 45.

5. For a compelling history, read Sarah-Anne Buckley, *The Cruelty Man: Child Welfare, the NSPCC and the State in Ireland, 1889–1956* (Manchester, 2013).

6. Seán Ryan, *The Commission to Inquire into Child Abuse: Volume Five* (Dublin, 2009), p. 1.

7. Ibid., p. 9.

8. Smith, *Ireland's Magdalene Laundries*, p. 47.

9. CAT, *Convention against Torture and Other Cruel, Inhuman or Degrading Treatment or Punishment* (2020), p. 3.

10. Ibid.

11. CAT, *Convention against Torture and Other Cruel, Inhuman or Degrading Treatment or Punishment*, 17 June 2011, UN Doc CAT/C/IRL/CO/1, p. 6.

12. Ibid.

13. James M. Smith et al., *State Involvement in the Magdalene Laundries* (Crocknahattina, 2013), p. 3.

14. Martin McAleese, *Report of the Inter-Departmental Committee to Establish the Facts of State Involvement with the Magdalene Laundries* (Dublin, 2013).

15. Ibid., p. i.

16. Dáil Éireann debate, Vol. 793, No. 11, 9 Feb. 2013.

17. Ibid.

18. CAT, *Convention against Torture and Other Cruel, Inhuman or Degrading Treatment or Punishment* (2020), p. 3.

19. Ibid., p. 4.

20. Coppin wrote to Minister Zappone in March 2017.

21. CAT, *Convention against Torture and Other Cruel, Inhuman or Degrading Treatment or Punishment* (2020), p. 4.

22. Organised by Norah Casey, with Katherine O'Donnell, Maeve O'Rourke and Claire McGettrick.

23. Michael D. Higgins, 'Speech to women who worked at the Magdalene Laundries', Áras an Uachtaráin, 5 Jun. 2018.

24. First aired on RTÉ television on 25 Jun. 2018.

25. *Coming Home: When Dublin Honoured the Magdalenes*, RTÉ, 2018.

26. Coppin's legal team included Wendy Lyon, Solicitor Abbey Law; and barristers Michael Lynn SC, Colin Smith BL, Lewis Mooney BL, Maeve O'Rourke (Irish Centre for Human Rights, NUI) and Jennifer MacLeod BL (Brick Court Chambers, London).

27. Information from *The Oxford Union*, www.oxford-union.org/node/1836, accessed 19 Aug. 2021.

28. CAT, *Convention against Torture and Other Cruel, Inhuman or Degrading Treatment or Punishment* (2020), p. 10.

29. See Catherine Connolly's speech in this volume.

30. *Irish Examiner*, 27 Feb. 2020.

31. Claire McGettrick, Katherine O'Donnell, Maeve O'Rourke, James M. Smith and Mari Steed, *Ireland and the Magdalene Laundries: A Campaign for Justice* (London, 2021).

32. *Irish Examiner*, 26 Feb. 2020.

33. Elizabeth Coppin, 'The Catholic Church can never pay for its sins (5/8), Oxford Union', *YouTube*, www.youtube.com/watch?v=5OJEzNeZ1nU, accessed 13 Sep. 2021. Text of speech reproduced courtesy of Elizabeth Coppin, with thanks to Maeve O'Rourke.

CHAPTER 33 – CONNOLLY

1. 'Mother and Baby Homes Commission of Investigation: Final report', 30 Oct. 2020, https://assets.gov.ie/118565/107bab7e-45aa-4124-95fd-1460893dbb43.pdf, accessed 18 Sep. 2021.

2. Dáil Éireann debate, Vol. 1003, No. 1, 13 Jan. 2021.

3. For further information on the remarkable work of Corless, see Catherine Corless, *Belonging: A Memoir by Catherine Corless* (Dublin, 2021).

4. Catherine Corless, 'The Home', in *Journal of the Old Tuam Society* 9 (2012), pp 75–82.

5. 'Mother and Baby Homes Commission of Investigation: Fifth interim report', 15 Mar. 2019, p. 9, https://assets.gov.ie/25783/a141b69a4a3c46fd8daef2010bf51268.pdf, accessed 18 Sep. 2021.

6. *Daily Mail*, 2 Jun. 2014.

7. *Irish Times*, 5 Jun. 2014.

8. 'Mother and Baby Homes Commission of Investigation: Final report', p. 2.

9. *Irish Times*, 12 Jun. 2020.

10. *Irish Times*, 11 Jan. 2021.

11. Ibid.

12. Martin Sixsmith, *The Lost Child of Philomena Lee: A Mother, Her Son and a Fifty-Year Search* (London, 2010).

13. *Irish Independent*, 17 Jan. 2021.

14. 'Transcript: Dr Deirdre Foley and Professor Ian McBride in conversation with Professor Mary Daly, 2nd June 2021', p. 22, *Clann Project*, http://clannproject.org/wp-content/uploads/Oxford-University-Seminar_Prof-Mary-Daly_02-06-2021.pdf, accessed 16 Sep. 2021.

15. Ailbhe Conneely and Paul Cunningham, 'Govt, Opposition call for clarification over mother-and-baby homes report', *RTÉ*, 3 Jun. 2021, www.rte.ie/news/ireland/2021/0603/1225774-mother-and-baby-homes-ireland/, accessed 16 Sep. 2021.

16. *Irish Examiner*, 4 Jun. 2021.

17. James M. Smith, *Ireland's Magdalen Laundries and the Nation's Architecture of Containment* (Notre Dame, 2007).

18. Justice Francis D. Murphy, Helen Buckley and Laraine Joyce, *The Ferns Report* (Dublin, 2005), www.lenus.ie/bitstream/handle/10147/560434/thefernsreportoctober2005.pdf;jsessionid=8FCBADC10C937FC1FC96207470438998?sequence=2, accessed 18 Sep. 2021.

19. Ibid., p. 253.

20. Eoin O'Sullivan and Ian O'Donnell, 'Mother and baby homes inquiry: Now reveal the secrets of Ireland's psychiatric hospitals', *The Conversation*, 27 Jan. 2021, https://theconversation.com/mother-and-baby-homes-inquiry-now-reveal-the-secrets-of-irelands-psychiatric-hospitals-153608, accessed 18 Sep. 2021.

21. Commission of Investigation, *Report of the Commission of Investigation into the Catholic Archdiocese of Dublin* (Dublin, 2009), p. 1, www.justice.ie/en/JELR/Pages/PB09000504, accessed 18 Sep. 2021.

22. 'Mother and Baby Homes Commission of Investigation: Final report', p. 70.

23. Ibid.

24. *Offaly Express*, 9 Aug. 2021.

25. *Irish Examiner*, 5 Jun. 2021.
26. Ibid.
27. Clann: Ireland's Unmarried Mothers and Their Children, http://clannproject.org, accessed 27 Sep. 2021.
28. *Adoption Rights Alliance*, http://adoption.ie/report/, accessed 27 Sep. 2021.
29. *The Journal*, 22 Oct. 2020.
30. *Irish Times*, 8 Oct. 2021.
31. Dáil Éireann debate, Vol. 1003, No. 1, 13 Jan. 2021.
32. Ibid.

BIBLIOGRAPHY

1916 Rebellion Handbook (Dublin: Irish Times, 1917).

Aldous, Richard, *Great Irish Speeches* (London: Quercus, 2007).

Alexievich, Svetlana, *Voices From Chernobyl: The Oral History of a Nuclear Disaster* (New York: Picador, 2006).

Arrington, Lauren, *Revolutionary Lives: Constance and Casimir Markievicz* (Princeton: Princeton University Press, 2016).

Ayres, Margaret, 'Equal pay for women: Words not deeds?', in *Saothar*, 36, 2011, pp 89–96.

Beaumont, Caitriona, 'Women, citizenship and Catholicism in the Irish Free State, 1922–1948', in *Women's History Review*, 6:4, 1997, pp 563–85.

Bennett, Burton, Michael Repacholi and Zhanat Carr, eds, *Health Effects of the Chernobyl Accident and Special Health Care Programmes: Report of the UN Chernobyl Forum Expert Group 'Health'* (Geneva: World Health Organisation, 2006).

Bercholz, Maxime and John FitzGerald, 'Recent trends in female labour force participation in Ireland', in *ESRI Quarterly Economic Commentary: Special Articles*, Autumn 2016, pp 49–81.

Bew, Paul, *Ireland: The Politics of Enmity, 1789–2006* (Oxford: Oxford University Press, 2007).

Bleakley, David, *Saidie Patterson: Irish Peacemaker* (Belfast: Blackstaff Press, 1980).

Blood, Baroness May, *Watch My Lips, I'm Speaking* (London: Gill & Macmillan, 2007).

Bourke, Angela, Siobhán Kilfeather, Maria Luddy, Margaret Mac Curtain, Gerardine Meaney, Máirín Ní Dhonnchadha, Mary O'Dowd and Clair Wills, eds, *The Field Day Anthology of Irish Writing, Volume 5: Irish Women's Writings and Traditions* (Cork: Cork University Press, 2002).

Brookes, Barbara, *A History of New Zealand Women* (Wellington: Bridget Williams Books, 2016).

Buckley, Fiona, 'Women and politics in Ireland: The road to sex quotas', in *Irish Political Studies*, 28:3, 2013, pp 341–59.

Buckley, Sarah-Anne, *The Cruelty Man: Child Welfare, the NSPCC and the State in Ireland, 1889–1956* (Manchester: Manchester University Press, 2013).

Burnett, Jon, *Racial Violence and the Brexit State* (London: Institute of Race Relations, 2016).

Buscher, Sarah and Bettina Ling, *Mairead Corrigan and Betty Williams: Making Peace in Northern Ireland* (New York: Feminist Press at the City University of New York, 1999).

Byrne, J. F., *Silent Years: An Autobiography* (New York: Farrar, Straus and Young, 1953).

Calvin, Terry, 'Glenn, Alice', in *Dictionary of Irish Biography* (www.dib.ie).

Christie, Marie and Aisling Molloy, 'International Day of Rural Women', in *Today's Farm*, Sept–Oct. 2019, pp 12–13.

Clarke, Frances, 'Chenevix, Helen Sophia', in *Dictionary of Irish Biography* (www.dib.ie).

Coming Home: When Dublin Honoured the Magdalenes, RTÉ, 2018.

Commission of Investigation, *Report of the Commission of Investigation into the Catholic Archdiocese of Dublin* (Dublin: Stationery Office, 2009).

Commission on Itinerancy, *Report on the Commission on Itinerancy* (Dublin: Stationery Office, 1963).

Conlon, Catherine, *Women: The Picture of Health: A Review of Research on Women's Health in Ireland* (Dublin: The Women's Health Council, 1999).

Connolly, James, *The Re-Conquest of Ireland* (Dublin: Maunsel, 1917).

Cooney, John, *John Charles McQuaid: Ruler of Catholic Ireland* (Dublin: The O'Brien Press, 1999).

Corless, Catherine, 'The Home', in *Journal of the Old Tuam Society*, 9, 2012, pp 75–82.

—— *Belonging: A Memoir by Catherine Corless* (Dublin: Hachette Ireland, 2021).

D'Arcy, Fergus A., 'Connolly, James', in *Dictionary of Irish Biography* (www.dib.ie).

Daly, Mary, 'Ireland grants ethnic minority recognition for Irish Travellers', *European Social Policy Network Flash Report*, May 2017, pp 1–2.

de Valera, Éamon, *Ireland's Case Against Conscription* (Dublin: Maunsel, 1918).

Devlin, Bernadette, *The Price of My Soul* (London: Pan Books, 1969).

Earner-Byrne, Lindsey and Diane Urquhart, *The Irish Abortion Journey, 1920–2018* (Cham: Palgrave Pivot, 2019).

Equality Authority, *Traveller Ethnicity* (Dublin: Equality Authority, 2006).

Fanning, Ronan, 'de Valera, Éamon', in *Dictionary of Irish Biography* (www.dib.ie).

Fennell, Nuala, *Irish Marriage: How Are You!* (Dublin: Mercier Press, 1974).

—— *Political Woman: A Memoir* (Dublin: Currach Press, 2009).

Fennell, Nuala, Deirdre McDevitt and Bernadette Quinn, *Can You Stay Married?* (Dublin: Kincora, 1980).

Ferguson, Trish, *Maud Gonne* (Dublin: University College Dublin Press, 2019).

Ferriter, Diarmaid, 'Larkin, Delia', in *Dictionary of Irish Biography* (www.dib.ie).

Finley-Bowman, Rachel E., 'An ideal unionist: The political career of Theresa, Marchioness of Londonderry, 1911–1919', in *Journal of International Women's Studies*, 4:3, 2003, pp 15–29.

Galligan, Yvonne, 'The Report of the Second Commission on the Status of Women', in *Irish Political Studies*, 8:1, 1993, pp 125–30.

—— 'Women MPs from Northern Ireland: Challenges and contributions, 1953–2020', in *Open Library of Humanities*, 6:2, 2020, pp 1–45, doi: http://doi.org/10.16995/olh.591.

Geary, Michael, *An Inconvenient Wait: Ireland's Quest for Membership of the EEC, 1957–73* (Dublin: Institute of Public Administration, 2010).

Geoghegan-Quinn, Máire, *The Green Diamond* (Dublin: Marino Books, 1996).

Girvin, Brian, 'An Irish solution to an Irish problem: Catholicism, contraception and change, 1922–1979', in *Contemporary European History*, 27:1, 2018, pp 1–22.

Gmelch, Sharon B. and George Gmelch, 'The itinerant settlement movement: Its policies and effects on Irish Travellers', in *Studies: An Irish Quarterly Review*, 63, Spring 1974, pp 1–16.

Gore-Booth, Eva, *Broken Glory* (Dublin: Maunsel, 1918).

Harper, Ida Husted, ed., *The History of Women Suffrage: Volume V 1900–1920* (New York: National American Woman Suffrage Association, 1922).

Hatton, Timothy J. and Jeffrey G. Williamson, 'After the Famine: Emigration from Ireland, 1850–1913', in *Journal of Economic History*, 53:3, 1993, pp 575–600.

Higginbotham, Adam, *Midnight in Chernobyl: The Untold Story of the World's Greatest Nuclear Disaster* (New York: Simon & Schuster, 2019).

Hoare, Paddy and Denis M. Leonard, *Limerick: An Appreciation* (Limerick: Limerick Civic Trust, 1992).

Hogan, Liam, 'Margaret Hinchey: Immigrant, labour leader, suffragette', in *Old Limerick Journal*, 53, Winter 2018, pp 16–20.

Hopkinson, M. A., 'Collins, Michael', in *Dictionary of Irish Biography* (www.dib.ie).

Hyde, H. Montgomery, *The Londonderrys: A Family Portrait* (London: H. Hamilton, 1979).

Inez: A Challenging Woman, dir. Trevor Birney and Eimhear O'Neill, produced and narrated by Susan McKay, Fine Point Films, 2014.

Joint Committee on Marriage Breakdown, *Report of the Joint Committee on Marriage Breakdown* (Dublin: Stationery Office, 1985).

Jones, Mary Harris, *The Autobiography of Mother Jones*, Mary Field Parton, ed. (Chicago: Charles H. Kerr & Company, 1925).

Joyce, Nan, *Traveller: An Autobiography by Nan Joyce*, Anna Farmar, ed. (Dublin: Gill and Macmillan, 1985).

Kilfeather, Siobhán Marie, *Dublin: A Cultural History* (Oxford: Oxford University Press, 2005).

Labour Party, *Report of the Thirty-Ninth National Conference of Labour Women, Spanish Hall, Winter Gardens, Blackpool, May 29, 30 and 31, 1962* (London: Labour Party, 1962).

Laffan, Michael, 'Griffith, Arthur Joseph', in *Dictionary of Irish Biography* (www. dib. ie).

Law Reform Commission, *Report on Illegitimacy* (Dublin: Law Reform Commission, 1982).

Loughran, Christina, 'Writing our own history: Organizing against the odds', in *Trouble and Strife*, 11, Summer 1987, pp 48–54.

Luddy, Maria, 'Skeffington, (Johanna) Hanna Sheehy-', in *Dictionary of Irish Biography* (www.dib.ie).

MacCurtain, Margaret, 'Mckenna, Siobhán', in *Dictionary of Irish Biography* (www. dib.ie).

Mac Éinrí, Piaras and Allen White, 'Immigration into the Republic of Ireland: A bibliography of recent research', in *Irish Geography*, 41:2, 2008, pp 151–79.

Markievicz, Constance de, *Women, Ideals and the Nation: A Lecture Delivered to the Students' National Literary Society* (Dublin: Inghinidhe na hÉireann, 1909).

Maume, Patrick, 'MacSwiney, Terence James', in *Dictionary of Irish Biography* (www. dib.ie).

—— 'Somers, Elizabeth', in *Dictionary of Irish Biography* (www.dib.ie).

—— 'O'Malley, Donogh', in *Dictionary of Irish Biography* (www.dib.ie).

—— 'FitzGerald, Garret', in *Dictionary of Irish Biography* (www.dib.ie).

McAleese, Martin, *Report of the Inter-Departmental Committee to Establish the Facts of State Involvement with the Magdalen Laundries* (Dublin: Department of Justice and Equality, 2013).

McAleese, Mary, *Here's the Story: A Memoir* (London: Penguin, 2020).

McAuliffe, Mary and Liz Gillis, *Richmond Barracks 1916: We Were There: 77 Women of the Easter Rising* (Dublin: Dublin City Council, 2016).

McAuliffe, Mary, *Margaret Skinnider* (Dublin: University College Dublin Press, 2020).

McAvoy, Sandra, '"A perpetual nightmare": Women, fertility control, the Irish state, and the 1935 ban on contraceptives', in Margaret Preston and Margaret Ó hÓgartaigh, eds, *Gender and Medicine in Ireland 1700–1950* (Syracuse: Syracuse University Press, 2012), pp 189–202.

McCabe, Ian, 'JFK in Ireland', in *History Ireland*, 1:4, 1993, pp 38–42.

McCafferty, Nell, 'A women's party outwits the system in northern Ireland [Northern Ireland Women's Coalition]', in *Canadian Woman Studies*, 17:3, 1997, pp 64–6.

McCarthy, Patricia, 'Racism in Ireland: Travellers fighting back', in *Red & Black Revolution*, 2, 1996, pp 22–5.

McCarthy, Tara M., 'Woman suffrage and Irish nationalism: Ethnic appeals and alliances in America', in *Women's History Review*, 23:2, 2014, pp 188–203.

McCormack, Inez, 'The long, long march from '68', in *Fortnight*, 257, Dec. 1987, pp 16–18.

McDonald, Mamo, *Circling* (Galway: Arlen House, 2015).

McGettrick, Claire, Katherine O'Donnell, Maeve O'Rourke, James M. Smith and Mari Steed, *Ireland and the Magdalene Laundries: A Campaign for Justice* (London: Bloomsbury, 2021).

McLachlan, Noel, 'Davitt, Michael', in *Dictionary of Irish Biography* (www.dib.ie).

McWilliams, Monica and Joan McKiernan, *Bringing It Out in the Open: Domestic Violence in Northern Ireland* (Belfast: HMSO, 1993).

McWilliams, Monica and Lynda Spence, *Taking Domestic Violence Seriously: Issues for the Civil and Criminal Justice System* (Belfast: HMSO, 1996).

McWilliams, Monica, 'From peace talks to gender justice,' in *Joan B. Kroc Distinguished Lecture Series*, Kaitlin Barker, ed., (San Diego: University of San Diego, 2010).

—— *Stand Up, Speak Out: My Life Working for Women's Rights, Peace and Equality in*

Northern Ireland and Beyond (Newtownards: Blackstaff Press, 2021).

Meehan, Ciara, *A Just Society for Ireland? 1964–1987* (Basingstoke: Palgrave Macmillan, 2013).

Mitchell, Arthur and Pádraig Ó Snodaigh, eds, *Irish Political Documents, 1916–1949* (Dublin: Irish Academic Press, 1985).

Mitchell, George J. 'Negotiating in business, politics and peace', in *Joan B. Kroc Distinguished Lecture Series*, Emiko Noma, ed., (San Diego: University of San Diego, 2012).

Morris, Holly, 'Chernobyl's babushkas', in *The World Today*, 72:2, 2016, pp 44–5.

Morrow, Duncan, 'The Northern Ireland forum elections of 1996', in *Regional & Federal Studies*, 7:2, 1997, pp 112–19.

Murphy, Justice Francis D., Helen Buckley and Laraine Joyce, *The Ferns Report* (Dublin: Stationery Office, 2005).

Murphy, William, 'Green, Alice Sophia Amelia Stopford', in *Dictionary of Irish Biography* (www.dib.ie).

Murphy, William and Lesa Ní Mhunghaile, 'Power, Jennie Wyse', in *Dictionary of Irish Biography* (www.dib.ie).

National Women's Council of Ireland, *Working to Improve Women's Lives: Annual Report* (Dublin: National Women's Council of Ireland, 2012).

Nevin, Donal, ed., *Trade Union Century* (Cork: Mercier Press, 1994).

O'Callaghan, Margaret and Caoimhe Nic Dháibhéid, 'MacBride, (Edith) Maud Gonne', in *Dictionary of Irish Biography* (www.dib.ie).

O'Neill, Marie, 'The Ladies' Land League', in *Dublin Historical Record*, 35:4, 1982, pp 122–33.

Orleck, Annelise, *Common Sense and a Little Fire: Women and Working-Class Politics in the United States, 1900–1965* (Chapel Hill: University of North Carolina Press, 2017).

Page, Dorothy, 'Women's suffrage: The Dunedin story', in *Otago Settler News*, 130, Spring 2016, pp 1–4.

Parnell, Anna, *The Tale of a Great Sham*, Dana Hearne, ed. (Dublin: University College Dublin Press, 2020).

Pašeta, Senia, 'Markievicz, Constance Georgine Countess Markievicz Gore-Booth', in *Dictionary of Irish Biography* (www.dib.ie).

Pearse, Patrick, *Collected Works of Pádraic H. Pearse: Political Writings and Speeches* (Dublin: Phoenix Publishing, 1916).

Philips, Charles, *Specimens of Irish Eloquence* (New York: William Grattan, 1820).

—— *Irish Eloquence: The Speeches of the Celebrated Irish Orators, Philips, Curran and Grattan* (Philadelphia: Key & Biddle, 1833).

Pope Francis, *Apostolic Exhortation: Evangelii Gaudium* (Vatican: Vatican Press, 2013).

Power, Bill, *Mitchelstown Through Seven Centuries* (Cork: Eigse Books, 1987).

Quilty, Aideen, Sinéad Kennedy and Catherine Conlon, eds, *The Abortion Papers: Volume 2* (Cork: Cork University Press, 2015).

Ralph, David, *Abortion and Ireland: How the 8th Was Overthrown* (London: Palgrave Pivot, 2020).

Redmond, Jennifer, *Moving Histories: Irish Women's Emigration to Britain from Independence to Republic* (Liverpool: Liverpool University Press, 2018).

Robinson, Mary, *Everybody Matters: A Memoir* (London: Hodder & Stoughton, 2012).

Roche, Adi, *Chernobyl Heart: 20 Years On* (Dublin: New Island, 2006).

Roper, Esther, ed., *The Prison Letters of Countess Markievicz* (London: Virago, 1987).

Rose, Kieran, *Diverse Communities: The Evolution of Lesbian and Gay Politics in Ireland* (Cork: Cork University Press, 1994).

Ryan, Seán, *The Commission to Inquire into Child Abuse: Volume Five* (Dublin: Stationery Office, 2009).

Sacred Congregation for the Doctrine of the Faith, *Declaration Inter Insigniores on the Question of the Admission of Women to the Ministerial Priesthood* (Washington: United States Catholic Conference, 1977).

Sheehy Skeffington, Hanna, *British Militarism As I Have Known It* (Tralee: Kerryman, 1946).

—— 'A pacifist dies' (Dublin, 1916), in Roger McHugh, ed., *Dublin 1916* (London: Arlington Books, 1966), pp 276–88.

Singer, Alan, 'Jones, Mary Harris ("Mother Jones")', in *Dictionary of Irish Biography* (www.dib.ie).

Sixsmith, Martin, *The Lost Child of Philomena Lee: A Mother, Her Son and a Fifty-Year Search* (London: Pan Macmillan, 2010).

Smith, James M., *Ireland's Magdalen Laundries and the Nation's Architecture of Containment* (Notre Dame: University of Notre Dame Press, 2007).

Smith, James M., Maeve O'Rourke, Raymond Hill and Claire McGettrick, *State Involvement in the Magdalene Laundries* (Crocknahattina: Justice for Magdalenes, 2013).

Spindler, Karl, *Gun Running for Casement*, trans. W. Montgomery (London: Collins, 1921).

'Statements concerning civilian deaths in the North King Street area of Dublin, between 6 p.m. April 28 and 10 a.m. April 29, 1916', in Roger McHugh, ed., *Dublin 1916* (New York: Hawthorn Books, 1966), pp 220–39.

Stiehm, Judith Hicks, 'Women and the Nobel Prize for Peace', in *International Feminist Journal of Politics*, 7:2, 2005, pp 258–79.

Sullivan, T. D., *Speeches From the Dock; or, Protests of Irish Patriotism* (New York: P. J. Kenedy, 1904).

Tax, Meredith, *The Rising of the Women: Feminist Solidarity and Class Conflict, 1880–1917* (New York: Monthly Review Press, 1980).

Thirty-Sixth Amendment of the Constitution Act 2018 (Dublin: Stationery Office, 2018).

Tiernan, Sonja, 'Sligo co-operative movements (1895–1905): The birth of an Irish political activist', in Shane Alcobia-Murphy, Lindsay Milligan and Dan Wall, eds, *Founder to Shore: Cross-Currents in Irish and Scottish Studies* (Aberdeen: AHRC Centre for Irish and Scottish Studies, 2009), pp 189–96.

—— *Eva Gore-Booth: An Image of Such Politics* (Manchester: Manchester University Press, 2012).

—— *The History of Marriage Equality in Ireland: A Social Revolution Begins* (Manchester: Manchester University Press, 2020).

—— '"No Conscription Now! Or after the harvest": Women and anti-conscription in Ireland and England', in Oona Frawley, ed., *Women and the Decade of*

Commemorations (Bloomington: Indiana University Press, 2021), pp 107–23.

—— 'Fennell, Nuala', in *Dictionary of Irish Biography* (www.dib.ie).

Tóibín, Colm, 'Foreword', in Richard Aldous, *Great Irish Speeches* (London: Quercus, 2007), pp ix–xix.

Travelling People Review Body, *Report of the Travelling People Review Body* (Dublin: Stationery Office, 1983).

Tubridy, Ryan, *JFK in Ireland: Four Days That Changed a President* (London: HarperCollins, 2010).

Urquhart, Diane, ed., *The Papers of the Ulster Women's Unionist Council and Executive Committee, 1911–1940* (Dublin: Irish Manuscripts Commission, 2001).

—— *Irish Divorce: A History* (Cambridge: Cambridge University Press, 2020).

VanderWilt, Jeffrey, *Communion with Non-Catholic Christians: Risks, Challenges, and Opportunities* (Collegeville: Liturgical Press, 2003).

Venter, Sahm, *Exploring Our National Days: Human Rights Day 21 March* (Auckland: Jacana Media, 2007).

Walby, Sylvia, *Globalization and Inequalities: Complexity and Contested Modernities* (London: Sage, 2009).

Ward, Margaret, 'A difficult, dangerous honesty', in *Trouble and Strife*, 12, Winter 1987, pp 36–43.

—— ed., *A Difficult, Dangerous Honesty: 10 Years of Feminism in Northern Ireland* (Belfast: Women's News, 1987).

—— *Unmanageable Revolutionaries: Women and Irish Nationalism* (London: Pluto Press, 1995).

—— *Hanna Sheehy Skeffington: Suffragette and Sinn Féiner: Her Memoirs and Political Writings* (Dublin: University College Dublin Press, 2017).

—— *Fearless Woman* (Dublin: University College Dublin Press, 2019).

—— 'Historical overview', in Anna Parnell, *The Tale of a Great Sham*, Dana Hearne, ed. (Dublin: University College Dublin Press, 2020), pp xi–xxx.

—— 'Parnell, Anna Mercer (Catherine Maria)', in *Dictionary of Irish Biography* (www.dib.ie).

—— 'Parnell, Fanny Isabel', in *Dictionary of Irish Biography* (www.dib.ie).

Wave Goodbye to Dinosaurs, dir. Eimhear O'Neill, produced by Trevor Birney, Brendan Byrne and Gini Reticker, Fine Point Films, 2017.

Webb, Sarah, ed., *Mum's the Word: The Truth About Being a Mother* (Dublin: New Island, 2007).

'Woman's work: In the national cause', in Margaret Ward, *In Their Own Voice: Women and Irish Nationalism* (Dublin: Attic Press, 2001), pp 38–41.

Working Party on Women's Affairs and Family Law Reform, *Irish Women: Agenda for Practical Action* (Dublin: Stationery Office, 1985).

Mandela, Nelson 143–4, 146
Mangakāhia, Meri Te Tai 21, *22*
Manning, Mary 145
Markievicz, Countess Constance 4–5, 25–6, *26*, 27–30, *31*, 31–3, 53, 56, 60–3, *66*, 67–8, 72, 78–9, 130, 208
marriage 151, 178–9, 188, 210, 227, 257, 262
marriage bar 171, 180
Martin, Diarmuid 266
Martin, Micheál 286–7, 292–5
Maudling, Reginald 128
Maxwell, John 62
Mayhew, Patrick 225
Medical Treatment (Termination of Pregnancy in Case of Risk to Life of Pregnant Woman) bill 269, 270
Meehan, Ciara 180
Mellet, Amanda 269–70, 274
Milholland, Inez 42
Military Service bill 72
Milroy, Sean 85, *92*
Minceir Misli 165
Mitchell, George J. 233–4, 240
Mitchell Report on Decommissioning 233–4
Mitchelstown evictions 10–11, 14–15
Mock, Desmond 137
Molony, Helena 109–10
Moore, Christy
    'Delirium Tremens' 178
Morison, Harriet 3–4, 16, *18*, 18–21, *22*, 22–4, 298 n. 3
Morrice, Jane 6, 227, 229, 234, 236–7
Mother and Baby Homes 273, 280, 287–9, 291, 293–5
    survivors of 286, 288–95
    the Tuam scandal 6, 287–8, 293–4
    vaccine trials in 291
Mother and Baby Homes report 2, 6, 282, 286–95
mother and child scheme 2, 110–12, 115
Mowlam, Mo 227, 229
Murphy, Yvonne 288, 290
    Murphy report 290, 293
Musleh, Saffa 4, 251–7

National American Women's Suffrage Association (NAWSA) 44
National Farm Family Committee 172, 175
National Party 253–5
National Union of Public Employees (NUPE) 188, 189
National Woman's Party (NWP) 47
National Women's Committee (Labour Party) 181
National Women's Council of Ireland (NWCI) 151, 223, 227, 269, 2701

Parker, Dehra 94–100
Parliament Act (1911) 37
Parliament of Northern Ireland 94–8, 296 n. 6
Parliament (Qualification of Women) Act (1918) 29, 77
Parnell, Anna 2–3, 7–12, *13*, 13–15, 27
    The Tale of a Great Sham 11–12
Parnell, Charles Stewart 8, 10–12, 26, 58
Parnell, Fanny 8, 11, 27
partition 39, 82, 144
pass laws 143
Patterson, Saidie 4, 101–7
peace 84, 170, 224
    women's roles in 2, 5, 56, 105–6, 112, 134–41, 189, 206, 225–6, 228–9, 232–41
    see also Good Friday Agreement
peace marches 134–6
Peace People, Movement of the 133–7, 140–1
peace process 138, 225–6, 228, 232, 236–7, 240, 267
peace talks 6, 225–7, 229, 233–7, 239–40
Pearse, Margaret 29, *31*, 79–80
Pearse, Patrick 28, 61–2, 67
People's Democracy 126–7, 187–8
Philbin, William 137
Phillips, Francis 53, 303 n. 11
Plunkett, Horace 171, 174
politics 4, 5, 7, 23, 35, 99, 194, 255
    in Northern Ireland 94–8, 124, 126–8, 223–6, 230–1, 235–7
    women in 2, 27–9, 34, 36, 73, 77, 88, 97, 130, 150, 177–8, 181–2, 193, 216–22, 227–9, 232, 234–7, 239–40, 254
Pope Francis 261–3, 266–7
Pope Paul VI 261, 264
Population Registration Act (1950) 142–3, 146
Power, Joseph 161
Pride festival (Dublin) 262–3
Proclamation of the Irish Republic 28, 61, 81, 91
prostitution 89, 210, 277
pregnancy 150, 152, 154, 157, 220, 274, 287, 294
    termination of 151–5, 268–70, 272, 274
    unwanted or unplanned 150, 152–3, 157–8
President of Ireland 195, 198–23, 206
Pro-Life Amendment Campaign (PLAC) 152
Provisional IRA 135

Quinlan, Maria 161
Quinn, Madeline Taylor 155

racism 4, 142–3, 148, 160–5, 167–8, 253–5
Rankin, Jeannette 45